Two Years before the Mast

TWO YEARS
BEFORE THE MAST

*A Personal Narrative of Life at
Sea* · RICHARD HENRY DANA, *Jr.*

Abridged for Modern Reading

Illustrated by ROBERT FRANKENBERG

JUNIOR DELUXE EDITIONS
Garden City, New York

Preface

I AM UNWILLING to present this narrative to the public without a few words in explanation of my reasons for publishing it. Since Mr. Cooper's *Pilot* and *Red Rover*, there have been so many stories of sea life written that I should really think it unjustifiable in me to add one to the number without being able to give reasons in some measure warranting me in so doing.

With the single exception, as I am quite confident, of Mr. Ames's entertaining, but hasty and desultory, work called *Mariner's Sketches*, all the books professing to give life at sea have been written by persons who have gained their experience as naval officers or passengers, and of these there are very few which are intended to be taken as narratives of facts.

Now in the first place, the whole course of life and daily duties, the discipline, habits, and customs, of a man-of-war are very different from those of the merchant service; and in the next place, however entertaining and well written these books may be, and however accurately they may give sea life as it appears to their authors, it must still be plain to everyone that a naval officer who goes to sea as a gentleman, "with his gloves on" (as the phrase is), and who associates only with his fellow officers, and hardly speaks to a sailor except through a boatswain's mate, must take a very different view of the whole matter from that which would be taken by a common sailor.

Besides the interest which everyone must feel in exhibitions of life in those forms in which he himself has never experienced it, there has been of late years a great deal of attention directed toward common seamen, and a strong sympathy awakened in their behalf. Yet I believe that, with the single exception which I have mentioned, there has not been a book written professing to give their life and experiences by one who has been of them, and can know what their life really is. *A voice from the forecastle* has hardly yet been heard.

In the following pages I design to give an accurate and authentic narrative of a little more than two years spent as a common sailor, before the mast, in the American merchant service. It is written out from a journal which I kept at the time, and from notes which I made of most of the events as they happened; and in it I have adhered closely to fact in every particular, and endeavored to give each thing its true character. In so doing, I have been obliged occasionally to use strong and coarse expressions, and in some instances to give scenes which may be painful to nice feelings; but I have very carefully avoided doing so whenever I have not felt them essential to giving the true character of a scene. My design is, and it is this which has induced me to publish the book, to present the life of a common sailor at sea as it really is—the light and the dark together.

There may be in some parts a good deal that is unintelligible to the general reader; but I have found from my own experience, and from what I have heard from others, that plain matters of fact in relation to customs and habits of life new to us, and descriptions of life under new aspects, act upon the inexperienced through the imagination, so that we are hardly aware of our want of technical knowledge. Thousands read the escape of the American frigate through the British Channel and the chase and wreck of the Bristol trader in *The Red Rover*, and follow the minute nautical maneuvers with breathless interest, who do not know the name of a rope in the ship—and perhaps with none the less admiration and enthusiasm for their want of acquaintance with the professional detail.

In preparing this narrative I have carefully avoided incorporating into it any impressions but those made upon me by the events as they occurred, leaving to my concluding chapter, to which I shall respectfully call the reader's attention, those views which have been suggested to me by subsequent reflection.

These reasons, and the advice of a few friends, have led me to give this narrative to the press. If it shall interest the general reader, and call more attention to the welfare of seamen, or give any information as to their real condition which may serve to raise them in the rank of beings, and to promote in any measure their religious and moral improvement and diminish the hardships of their daily life, the end of its publication will be answered.

R. H. D., Jr.

Boston, July, 1840

Contents

Two Years before the Mast

1 ~~~~~~~~~~~~~~~~~~~~

Departure

THE FOURTEENTH of August was the day fixed upon for the sailing of the brig *Pilgrim* on her voyage from Boston round Cape Horn to the western coast of North America. As she was to get under way early in the afternoon, I made my appearance on board at twelve o'clock, in full sea rig, and with my chest containing an outfit for a two or three years' voyage, which I had undertaken from a determination to cure, if possible, by an entire change of life and by a long absence from books and study, a weakness of the eyes which had obliged me to give up my pursuits, and which no medical aid seemed likely to cure.

The change from the tight dress coat, silk cap, and kid gloves of an undergraduate at Cambridge to the loose duck trousers, checked shirt, and tarpaulin hat of a sailor, though somewhat of a transformation, was soon made, and I supposed that I should pass very well for a jack tar. But it is impossible to deceive the practiced eye in these matters, and while I supposed myself to be looking as salt as Neptune himself, I was no doubt known for a landsman by everyone on board as soon as I hove in sight. A sailor has a peculiar cut to his clothes, and a way of wearing them which a green hand can never get. The trousers, tight round the hips and thence hanging long and loose round the feet, a superabundance of checked shirt, a low-crowned, well-varnished black hat worn on the back of the head, with half a fathom of black ribbon hanging over the left eye, and a peculiar tie to the black silk neckerchief, with sundry other minutiae, are signs the want of which betray the beginner at once. Besides the points in my dress which were out of the way, doubtless my complexion and hands were enough to distinguish me from the regular "salt" who with sunburnt cheek, wide step, and rolling gait, swings his bronzed and toughened hands athwartships half-open, as though just ready to grasp a rope.

"With all my imperfections on my head," I joined the crew, and we hauled out into the stream and came to anchor for the night. The next day we were employed in preparations for sea, reeving studding-sail gear, crossing royal yards, putting on chafing gear, and taking on board our powder. On the following night I stood my first watch. I remained awake nearly all the first part of the night from fear I might not hear when I was called; and when I went on deck, so great were my ideas of the importance of my trust that I walked regularly fore and aft the whole length of the vessel, looking out over the bows and taffrail at each turn, and was not a little surprised at the coolness of the old salt whom I called to take my place in stowing himself snugly away under the longboat for a nap. That was a sufficient lookout, he thought, for a fine night at anchor in a safe harbor.

The next morning was Saturday, and a breeze having sprung up from the southward, we took a pilot on board, hove up our anchor, and began beating down the bay. I took leave of those of my friends who came to see me off, and had barely opportunity to take a last look at the city and well-known objects, as no time is allowed on board ship for sentiment. As we drew down into the lower harbor, we found the wind ahead in the bay, and were obliged to come to anchor in the roads. We remained there through the day and a part of the night. My watch began at eleven o'clock at night, and I received orders to call the captain if the wind came out from the westward. About midnight the wind became fair, and having called the captain, I was ordered to call all hands. How I accomplished this I do not know, but I am quite sure that I did not give the true hoarse, boatswain call of "A-a-ll ha-a-a-nds! Up anchor a-ho-oy!" In a short time everyone was in motion, the sails loosed, the yards braced, and we began to heave up the anchor which was our last hold upon Yankeeland. I could take but little part in all these preparations. My little knowledge of a vessel was all at fault. Unintelligible orders were so rapidly given and so immediately executed, there was such a hurrying about and such an intermingling of strange cries and stranger actions, that I was completely bewildered. There is not so helpless and pitiable an object in the world as a landsman beginning a sailor's life. At length those peculiar, long-drawn sounds which denote that the crew are heaving at the windlass began, and in a few moments we were under way. The noise of the water thrown from the bows began to be heard, the vessel leaned over from the damp night breeze and rolled with the heavy ground swell, and we had actually begun our long, long journey. This was literally bidding "good night" to my native land.

First Impressions · *"Sail Ho!"*

THE FIRST DAY we passed at sea was the Sabbath. As we were just from port, and there was a great deal to be done on board, we were kept at work all day, and at night the watches were set, and everything put into sea order. When we were called aft to be divided into watches, I had a good specimen of the manner of a sea captain. After the division had been made, he gave a short characteristic speech, walking the quarter-deck with a cigar in his mouth, and dropping the words out between the puffs.

"Now, my men, we have begun a long voyage. If we get along well together, we shall have a comfortable time; if we don't, we shall have hell afloat.—All you've got to do is to obey your orders and do your duty like men—then you'll fare well enough; if you don't, you'll fare hard enough, I can tell you. If we pull together, you'll find me a clever fellow; if we don't, you'll find me a 'bloody' rascal.—That's all I've got to say.—Go below, the larboard watch!"

I, being in the starboard or second mate's watch, had the opportunity of keeping the first watch at sea. S—, a young man making, like myself, his first voyage, was in the same watch, and as he was the son of a professional man, and had been in a counting room in Boston, we found that we had many friends and topics in common. We talked these matters over—Boston, what our friends were probably doing, our voyage, etc.—until he went to take his turn at the lookout and left me to myself. I had now a fine time for reflection. I felt for the first time the perfect silence of the sea. The officer was walking the quarter-deck, where I had no right to go, one or two men were talking on the forecastle, whom I had little inclination to join, so that I was left open to the full impression of everything about me. However much I was affected by the beauty of the sea, the bright stars,

and the clouds driven swiftly over them, I could not but remember that I was separating myself from all the social and intellectual enjoyments of life. Yet, strange as it may seem, I did then and afterward take pleasure in these reflections, hoping by them to prevent my becoming insensible to the value of what I was leaving.

But all my dreams were soon put to flight by an order from the officer to trim the yards, as the wind was getting ahead; and I could plainly see by the looks the sailors occasionally cast to windward, and by the dark clouds that were fast coming up, that we had bad weather to prepare for, and had heard the captain say that he expected to be in the Gulf Stream by twelve o'clock. In a few minutes eight bells were struck, the watch called, and we went below. I now began to feel the first discomforts of a sailor's life. The steerage in which I lived was filled with coils of rigging, spare sails, old junk, and ship stores which had not been stowed away. Moreover, there had been no berths built for us to sleep in, and we were not allowed to drive nails to hang our clothes on. The sea, too, had risen, the vessel was rolling heavily, and everything was pitched about in grand confusion. There was a complete "hurrah's nest," as the sailors say, "everything on top and nothing at hand." A large hawser had been coiled away on my chest; my hats, boots, mattress, and blankets had all "fetched away" and gone over to leeward, and were jammed and broken under the boxes and coils of rigging. To crown all, we were allowed no light to find anything with, and I was just beginning to feel strong symptoms of seasickness, and that listlessness and inactivity which accompany it. Giving up all attempts to collect my things together, I lay down on the sails, expecting every moment to hear the cry of "All hands ahoy!" which the approaching storm would soon make necessary. I shortly heard the raindrops falling on deck, thick and fast, and the watch evidently had their hands full of work, for I could hear the loud and repeated orders of the mate, the trampling of feet, the creaking of blocks, and all the accompaniments of a coming storm. In a few minutes the slide of the hatch was thrown back, which let down the noise and tumult of the deck still louder, the loud cry of "All hands ahoy! Tumble up here and take in sail!" saluted our ears, and the hatch was quickly shut again. When I got on deck, a new scene and a new experience were before me. The little brig was close-hauled upon the wind, and lying over, as it then seemed to me, nearly upon her beam ends. The heavy head sea was beating against her bows with the noise and force almost of a sledge hammer, and flying over the deck, drenching us completely through. The topsail halyards had been let go, and the great sails were filling out and backing against the masts with a noise like thunder. The wind was whistling through the rigging, loose ropes were flying about; loud and, to me, unintelligible orders constantly given and rapidly executed; and the sailors "singing out" at the ropes in their hoarse and peculiar strains. In addition to all this, I had not got my "sea legs on," was dreadfully sick, with hardly strength enough to hold onto anything, and it was "pitch-dark." This was my state when I was ordered aloft for the first time, to reef topsails.

How I got along I cannot now remember. I "laid out" on the yards and held on with all my strength. I could not have been of much service, for I remember having been sick several times before I left the topsail yard. Soon all was snug aloft, and we were again allowed to go below. This I did not consider much of a favor, for the confusion of everything below, and that inexpressible sickening smell caused by the shaking up of the bilge water in the hold, made the steerage but an indifferent refuge from the cold, wet decks. I had often read of the nautical experiences of others, but I felt as though there could be none worse than mine; for in addition to every other evil, I could not but remember that this was only the first night of a two years' voyage. When we were on deck we were not much better off, for we were continually ordered about by the officer, who said that it was good for us to be in motion. Yet anything was better than the horrible state of things below. I remember very well going to the hatchway and putting my head down when I was oppressed by nausea, and always being relieved immediately. It was as good as an emetic.

This state of things continued for two days.

WEDNESDAY, AUG. 20. We had the watch on deck from four till eight this morning. When we came on deck at four o'clock, we found things much changed for the better. The sea and wind had gone down, and the stars were out bright. I experienced a

corresponding change in my feelings, yet continued extremely
weak from my sickness. I stood in the waist on the weather side,
watching the gradual breaking of the day and the first streaks
of the early light. Much has been said of the sunrise at sea, but
it will not compare with the sunrise on shore. It wants the accompaniments of the songs of birds, the awakening hum of men, and
the glancing of the first beams upon trees, hills, spires, and house-
tops, to give it life and spirit. But though the actual *rise of the
sun* at sea is not so beautiful, yet nothing will compare with the
early breaking of day upon the wide ocean.

There is something in the first gray streaks stretching along
the eastern horizon and throwing an indistinct light upon the
face of the deep which combines with the boundlessness and unknown depth of the sea around you, and gives you a feeling of
loneliness, of dread, and of melancholy foreboding which nothing
else in nature can give. This gradually passes away as the light
grows brighter, and when the sun comes up, the ordinary monotonous sea day begins.

From such reflections as these I was aroused by the order from
the officer: "Forward there! Rig the head pump!" I found that
no time was allowed for daydreaming, but that we must "turn
to" at the first light. Having called up the "idlers"—namely, carpenter, cook, steward, etc.—and rigged the pump, we commenced
washing down the decks. This operation, which is performed
every morning at sea, takes nearly two hours, and I had hardly
strength enough to get through it. After we had finished,
swabbed down, and coiled up the rigging, I sat down on the
spars, waiting for seven bells, which was the sign for breakfast.
The officer, seeing my lazy posture, ordered me to slush the
mainmast from the royal masthead down. The vessel was then
rolling a little, and I had taken no sustenance for three days,
so that I felt tempted to tell him that I had rather wait till
after breakfast; but I knew that I must "take the bull by the
horns," and that if I showed any sign of want of spirit or of
backwardness, I should be ruined at once. So I took my bucket
of grease and climbed up to the royal masthead. Here the rock-
ing of the vessel, which increases the higher you go from the
foot of the mast, which is the fulcrum of the lever, and the smell
of the grease, which offended my fastidious senses, upset my

stomach again, and I was not a little rejoiced when I got on the comparative terra firma of the deck. In a few minutes seven bells were struck, the log was hove, the watch called, and we went to breakfast. Here I cannot but remember the advice of the cook, a simple-hearted African. "Now," says he, "my lad, you are well cleaned out; you haven't got a drop of your longshore swash aboard of you. You must begin on a new tack—pitch all your sweetmeats overboard, and turn to upon good hearty salt beef and sea bread, and I'll promise you you'll have your ribs well sheathed, and be as hearty as any of 'em, afore you are up to the Horn." This would be good advice to give to passengers when they speak of the little niceties which they have laid in in case of seasickness.

I cannot describe the change which half a pound of cold salt beef and a biscuit or two produced in me. I was a new being. We had a watch below until noon, so that I had some time to myself; and getting a huge piece of strong cold salt beef from the cook, I kept gnawing on it until twelve o'clock. When we went on deck I felt somewhat like a man, and could begin to learn my sea duty with considerable spirit. At about two o'clock we heard the loud cry of "Sail ho!" from aloft, and soon saw two sails to windward, going directly athwart our hawse. This was the first time that I had seen a sail at sea. I thought then, and have always since, that it exceeds every other sight in interest and beauty. They passed to leeward of us, and out of hailing distance; but the captain could read the names on their sterns with the glass. They were the ship *Helen Mar,* of New York, and the brig *Mermaid,* of Boston. They were both steering westward, and were bound in for our "dear native land."

THURSDAY, AUG. 21. This day the sun rose clear, we had a fine wind, and everything was bright and cheerful. I had now got my sea legs on, and was beginning to enter upon the regular duties of a sea life. About six bells—that is, 3 P.M.—we saw a sail on our larboard bow. I was very anxious, like every new sailor, to speak her. She came down to us, backed her main-topsail, and the two vessels stood "head on," bowing and curveting at each other like a couple of war horses reined in by their riders. It was the first vessel that I had seen near, and I was surprised to find how much she rolled and pitched in so quiet a sea. She

plunged her head into the sea and then, her stern settling gradually down, her huge bows rose up, showing the bright copper,
and her stern and breasthooks dripping, like old Neptune's locks,
with the brine. Her decks were filled with passengers who had
come up at the cry of "Sail ho!" and who by their dress and
features appeared to be Swiss and French emigrants. She hailed
us at first in French, but receiving no answer, she tried us in
English. She was the ship *Carolina*, from Havre for New York.
We desired her to report the brig *Pilgrim*, from Boston for the
northwest coast of America, five days out. She then filled away
and left us to plow on through our waste of waters. This day
ended pleasantly; we had got into regular and comfortable
weather, and into that routine of sea life which is only broken
by a storm, a sail, or the sight of land.

Ship's Duties · Tropics

As WE HAD now a long "spell" of fine weather, without any incident to break the monotony of our lives, there can be no better place to describe the duties, regulations, and customs of an American merchantman, of which ours was a fair specimen.

The captain, in the first place, is lord paramount. He stands no watch, comes and goes when he pleases, and is accountable to no one, and must be obeyed in everything without a question, even from his chief officer. He has the power to turn his officers off duty, and even to break them and make them do duty as sailors in the forecastle. Where there are no passengers and no supercargo, as in our vessel, he has no companion but his own dignity, and no pleasures—unless he differs from most of his kind —but the consciousness of possessing supreme power and, occasionally, the exercise of it.

The prime minister, the official organ, and the active and superintending officer is the chief mate. He is first lieutenant, boatswain, sailing master, and quartermaster. The captain tells him what he wishes to have done, and leaves to him the care of overseeing, of allotting the work, and also the responsibility of its being well done. *The* mate (as he is always called, par excellence) also keeps the logbook, for which he is responsible to the owners and insurers, and has the charge of the stowage, safe-keeping, and delivery of the cargo. He is also, ex-officio, the wit of the crew; for the captain does not condescend to joke with the men, and the second mate no one cares for; so that when "the mate" thinks fit to entertain "the people" with a coarse joke or a little practical wit, everyone feels bound to laugh.

The second mate's is proverbially a dog's berth. He is neither officer nor man. The men do not respect him as an officer, and he is obliged to go aloft to reef and furl the topsails, and to put his hands into the tar and slush, with the rest. The crew call him the "sailors' waiter," as he has to furnish them with spun yarn, marline, and all other stuffs that they need in their work, and has charge of the boatswain's locker, which includes serving boards, marlinespikes, etc., etc. He is expected by the captain to maintain his dignity and to enforce obedience, and still is kept at a great distance from the mate, and obliged to work with the crew. He is one to whom little is given and of whom much is required. His wages are usually double those of a common sailor, and he eats and sleeps in the cabin; but he is obliged to be on deck nearly all his time, and eats at the second table—that is, makes a meal out of what the captain and chief mate leave.

The steward is the captain's servant, and has charge of the pantry, from which everyone, even the mate himself, is excluded. These distinctions usually find him an enemy in the mate, who does not like to have anyone on board who is not entirely under his control; the crew do not consider him as one of their number, so he is left to the mercy of the captain.

The cook is the patron of the crew, and those who are in his favor can get their wet mittens and stockings dried, or light their pipes at the galley on the night watch. These two worthies, together with the carpenter and sailmaker, if there be one, stand no watch but, being employed all day, are allowed to "sleep in" at night, unless all hands are called.

The crew are divided into two divisions, as equally as may be, called the watches. Of these the chief mate commands the larboard and the second mate the starboard. They divide the time between them, being on and off duty, or as it is called on deck and below, every other four hours. If, for instance, the chief mate with the larboard watch has the first night watch from eight to twelve, at the end of the four hours the starboard watch is called, and the second mate takes the deck, while the larboard watch and the first mate go below until four in the morning, when they come on deck again and remain until eight, having what is called the morning watch. As they will have been on deck eight hours out of twelve, while those who had the middle watch—from twelve to four—will only have been up four hours, they have what is called a "forenoon watch below"; that is, from 8 A.M., till 12 M. In a man-of-war, and in some merchantmen, this alternation of watches is kept up throughout the twenty-four hours; but our ship, like most merchantmen, had "all hands" from twelve o'clock till dark except in bad weather, when we had "watch and watch."

An explanation of the "dog watches" may perhaps be of use to one who has never been at sea. They are to shift the watches each night so that the same watch need not be on deck at the same hours. In order to effect this, the watch from 4 to 8 P.M. is divided into two half, or dog, watches, one from 4 to 6, and the other from 6 to 8. By this means they divide the twenty-four hours into *seven* watches instead of *six*, and thus shift the hours every night. As the dog watches come during twilight, after the day's work is done and before the night watch is set, they are the watches in which everybody is on deck. The captain is up, walking on the weather side of the quarter-deck, the chief mate on the leeside, and the second mate about the weather gangway. The steward has finished his work in the cabin and has come up to smoke his pipe with the cook in the galley. The crew are sitting on the windlass or lying on the forecastle, smoking, singing, or telling long yarns. At eight o'clock, eight bells are struck, the log is hove, the watch set, the wheel relieved, the galley shut up, and the other watch goes below.

The morning commences with the watch on deck's turning to at daybreak and washing down, scrubbing, and swabbing the decks. This, together with filling the "scuttle butt" with fresh water and coiling up the rigging, usually occupies the time until seven bells (half after seven), when all hands get breakfast. At eight the day's work begins, and lasts until sundown, with the exception of an hour for dinner.

Before I end my explanations, it may be well to define a *day's work*, and to correct a mistake prevalent among landsmen about a sailor's life. Nothing is more common than to hear people say: "Are not sailors very idle at sea?—What can they find to do?" This is a very natural mistake, and being very frequently made, it is one which every sailor feels interested in having corrected. In the first place, then, the discipline of the ship requires every man to be at work upon *something* when he is on deck, except at night and on Sundays. Except at these times, you will never see a man on board a well-ordered vessel standing idle on deck, sitting down, or leaning over the side. It is the officers' duty to keep everyone at work, even if there is nothing to be done but to scrape the rust from the chain cables. In no state prison are the convicts more regularly set to work, and more closely watched. No conversation is allowed among the crew at their duty, and though they frequently do talk when aloft, or when near one another, yet they always stop when an officer is nigh.

With regard to the work upon which the men are put, it is a matter which probably would not be understood by one who has not been at sea. When I first left port and found that we were kept regularly employed for a week or two, I supposed that we were getting the vessel into sea trim, and that it would soon be over and we should have nothing to do but to sail the ship; but I found that it continued so for two years, and at the end of the two years there was as much to be done as ever. As has often been said, a ship is like a lady's watch, always out of repair. When first leaving port, studding-sail gear is to be rove, all the running rigging to be examined, that which is unfit for use to be got down and new rigging rove in its place; then the standing rigging is to be overhauled, replaced, and repaired in a thousand different ways; and wherever any of the numberless ropes or the yards are chafing or wearing upon it, there "chafing gear," as it is called, must be put on. This chafing gear consists of worming, parceling, roundings, battens, and service of all kinds—both rope yarns, spun yarn, marline, and seizing stuffs. Taking off, putting on, and mending the chafing gear alone upon a vessel would find constant employment for two or three men, during working hours, for a whole voyage.

The next point to be considered is that all the "small stuffs" which are used on board a ship—such as spun yarn, marline, seizing stuff, etc., etc.—are made on board. The owners of a vessel buy up incredible quantities of "old junk," which the sailors unlay, after drawing out the yarns, knot them together, and roll them up in balls. These "rope yarns" are constantly used for various purposes, but the greater part is manufactured into spun yarn. For this purpose every vessel is furnished with a "spun-yarn winch," which is very simple, consisting of a wheel and a spindle. This may be heard constantly going on deck in pleasant weather; and we had employment during a great part of the time for three hands in drawing and knotting yarns and making spun yarn.

Another method of employing the crew is "setting up" rigging. Whenever any of the standing rigging becomes slack (which is continually happening), the seizings and coverings must be taken off, tackles got up, and after the rigging is bowsed well taut, the seizings and coverings replaced—which is a very nice piece of work. There is also such a connection between different parts of a vessel that one rope can seldom be touched without altering another. You cannot stay a mast aft by the backstays without slacking up the head stays, etc., etc. If we add to this all the tarring, greasing, oiling, varnishing, painting, scraping, and scrubbing which is required in the course of a long voyage, and also remember this is all to be done *in addition to* watching at night, steering, reefing, furling, bracing, making and setting sail, and pulling, hauling, and climbing in every direction, one will hardly ask, "What can a sailor find to do at sea?"

If, after all this labor—after exposing their lives and limbs in storms, wet and cold—

> *Wherein the cub-drawn bear would couch;*
> *The lion and the belly-pinched wolf*
> *Keep their furs dry—*

the merchants and captains think that they have not earned their twelve dollars a month (out of which they clothe themselves), and their salt beef and hard bread, they keep them picking oakum—ad infinitum. This is the usual resource on a rainy day, for then it will not do to work on rigging; and when it is pouring down in floods, instead of letting the sailors stand about in sheltered places and talk, and keep themselves comfortable, they are separated to different parts of the ship and kept at work picking oakum. I have seen oakum stuff placed about in different parts of the ship, so that the sailors might not be idle in the "snatches" between the frequent squalls upon crossing the equator. Some officers have been so driven to find work for the crew in a ship ready for sea that they have set them to pounding the anchors (often done) and scraping the chain cables. The "Philadelphia Catechism" is:

Six days shalt thou labor and do all thou art able,
And on the seventh—holystone the decks and scrape the cable.

This kind of work, of course, is not kept up off Cape Horn, Cape of Good Hope, and in extreme north and south latitudes; but I have seen the decks washed down and scrubbed when the water would have frozen if it had been fresh; and all hands kept at work upon the rigging when we had on our pea jackets, and our hands so numb that we could hardly hold our marlinespikes.

I have here gone out of my narrative course in order that any who read this may form as correct an idea of a sailor's life and duty as possible. I have done it in this place because for some time our life was nothing but the unvarying repetition of these duties, which can be better described together. Before leaving this description, however, I would state, in order to show landsmen how little they know of the nature of a ship, that a ship carpenter is kept in constant employ during good weather on board vessels which are in what is called perfect sea order.

A Rogue · Trouble on Board
"Land Ho!" · Pampero ·
Cape Horn

AFTER SPEAKING the *Carolina*, on the twenty-first of August,
nothing occurred to break the monotony of our life until
FRIDAY, SEPTEMBER 5, when we saw a sail on our weather
(starboard) beam. She proved to be a brig under English colors,
and passing under our stern, reported herself as forty-nine days
from Buenos Aires, bound to Liverpool. Before she had passed
us, "Sail ho!" was cried again, and we made another sail, far on
our weather bow and steering athwart our hawse. She passed out
of hail, but we made her out to be a hermaphrodite brig with
Brazilian colors in her main rigging. By her course, she must
have been bound from Brazil to the south of Europe, probably
Portugal.

SUNDAY, SEPT. 7. Fell in with the northeast trade winds. This
morning we caught our first dolphin, which I was very eager to
see. I was disappointed in the colors of this fish when dying.
They were certainly very beautiful, but not equal to what has
been said of them. They are too indistinct. To do the fish justice,
there is nothing more beautiful than the dolphin when swimming
a few feet below the surface on a bright day. It is the most elegantly formed, and also the quickest, fish in salt water; and the
rays of the sun striking upon it in its rapid and changing motions,
reflected from the water, make it look like a stray beam from a
rainbow.

This day was spent like all pleasant Sabbaths at sea. The decks
are washed down, the rigging coiled up, and everything put in
order; and throughout the day only one watch is kept on deck at

a time. The men are all dressed in their best white duck trousers
and red or checked shirts, and have nothing to do but to make
the necessary changes in the sails. They employ themselves in
reading, talking, smoking, and mending their clothes. If the
weather is pleasant, they bring their work and their books on
deck, and sit down on the forecastle and windlass. This is the
only day on which these privileges are allowed them. When
Monday comes, they put on their tarry trousers again, and prepare for six days of labor.

To enhance the value of the Sabbath to the crew, they are
allowed on that day a pudding or, as it is called, a duff. This is
nothing more than flour boiled with water, and eaten with molasses. It is very heavy, dark, and clammy, yet it is looked upon
as a luxury, and really forms an agreeable variety with salt beef
and pork. Many a rascally captain has made friends of his crew
by allowing them duff twice a week on the passage home.

On board some vessels this is made a day of instruction and of
religious exercises; but we had a crew of swearers, from the
captain to the smallest boy, and a day of rest and of something
like quiet, social enjoyment was all that we could expect.

We continued running large before the northeast trade winds
for several days, until Monday,

September 22, when upon coming on deck at seven bells in
the morning, we found the other watch aloft, throwing water
upon the sails; and looking astern, we saw a small clipper-built
brig with a black hull heading directly after us. We went to work
immediately, and put all the canvas on the brig which we could
get upon her, rigging out ours for studding-sail yards, and continued wetting down the sails by buckets of water whipped up
to the masthead until about nine o'clock, when there came on a
drizzling rain. The vessel continued in pursuit, changing her
course as we changed ours to keep before the wind. The captain,
who watched her with his glass, said that she was armed and
full of men, and showed no colors. We continued running dead
before the wind, knowing that we sailed better so, and that clip-
pers are fastest *on* the wind. We had also another advantage.
The wind was light, and we spread more canvas than she did,
having royals and skysails fore and aft, and ten studding sails,
while she, being a hermaphrodite brig, had only a gaff-topsail,

aft. Early in the morning she was overhauling us a little, but after the rain came on and the wind grew lighter, we began to leave her astern. All hands remained on deck throughout the day, and we got our arms in order; but we were too few to have done anything with her if she had proved to be what we feared. Fortunately there was no moon, and the night which followed was exceedingly dark, so that by putting out all the lights on board and altering our course four points, we hoped to get out of her reach. We had no light in the binnacle, but steered by the stars, and kept perfect silence through the night. At daybreak there was no sign of anything on the horizon, and we kept the vessel off to her course.

WEDNESDAY, OCTOBER 1. Crossed the equator in long. 24° 24′ W. I now for the first time felt at liberty, according to the old usage, to call myself a son of Neptune, and was very glad to be able to claim the title without the disagreeable initiation which so many have to go through. After once crossing the line you can never be subjected to the process, but are considered as a son of Neptune, with full powers to play tricks upon others. This ancient custom is now seldom allowed unless there are passengers on board, in which case there is always a good deal of sport.

It had been obvious to all hands for some time that the second mate, whose name was F—, was an idle, careless fellow, and not much of a sailor, and that the captain was exceedingly dissatisfied with him. The power of the captain in these cases was well known, and we all anticipated a difficulty. F— (called "Mr." by virtue of his office) was but half a sailor, having always been short voyages and remained at home a long time between them. His father was a man of some property, and intended to have given his son a liberal education; but he, being idle and worthless, was sent off to sea, and succeeded no better there, for, unlike many scamps, he had none of the qualities of a sailor—he was "not of the stuff that they make sailors of." He was one of that class of officers who are disliked by their captain and despised by the crew. He used to hold long yarns with the crew, and talk about the captain, and play with the boys, and relax discipline in every way. This kind of conduct always makes the captain suspicious, and is never pleasant, in the end, to the men, they preferring to have an officer active, vigilant, and distant as may be, with kindness. Among other bad practices, he frequently slept on his watch, and having been discovered asleep by the captain, he was told that he would be turned off duty if he did it again. To prevent it in every way possible, the hencoops were ordered to be knocked up, for the captain never sat down on deck himself, and never permitted an officer to do so.

The second night after crossing the equator, we had the watch from eight till twelve, and it was "my helm" for the last two hours. There had been light squalls through the night, and the captain told Mr. F—, who commanded our watch, to keep a bright lookout. Soon after I came to the helm I found that he was quite drowsy, and at last he stretched himself on the companion and went fast asleep. Soon afterward the captain came very quietly on deck, and stood by me for some time looking at the compass. The officer at length became aware of the captain's presence, but pretending not to know it, began humming and whistling to himself, to show that he was not asleep, and went forward, without looking behind him, and ordered the main royal to be loosed. On turning round to come aft, he pretended surprise at seeing the master on deck. This would not do. The captain was too "wide-awake" for him, and beginning upon him at once, gave him a grand blowup in true nautical style: "You're a lazy, good-for-nothing rascal; you're neither man, boy, soger, nor sailor! You're no more than a *thing* aboard a vessel! You don't earn your salt! You're worse than a Mahon soger!" and other still more choice extracts from the sailor's vocabulary. After the poor fellow had taken this harangue, he was sent into his state-room, and the captain stood the rest of the watch himself.

At seven bells in the morning all hands were called aft and told that F— was no longer an officer on board, and that we might choose one of our own number for second mate. It is usual for the captain to make this offer, and it is very good policy, for the crew think themselves the choosers and are flattered by it, but have to obey nevertheless. Our crew, as is usual, refused to take the responsibility of choosing a man of whom we would never be able to complain, and left it to the captain. He picked out an active and intelligent young sailor born near the Kennebec, who had been several Canton voyages, and proclaimed him in the following manner: "I choose Jim Hall—he's your second mate. All you've got to do is to obey him as you would me, and remember that he is *Mr.* Hall." F— went forward into the forecastle as a common sailor, and lost the "handle to his name," while young foremast Jim became Mr. Hall, and took up his quarters in the land of knives and forks and teacups.

SUNDAY, OCTOBER 5. It was our morning watch when, soon after the day began to break, a man on the forecastle called out, "Land ho!" I had never heard the cry before, and did not know what it meant (and few would suspect what the words were when hearing the strange sound for the first time), but I soon found, by the direction of all eyes, that there was land stretching along on our weather beam. We immediately took in studding sails and hauled our wind, running in for the land. This was done to determine our longitude; for by the captain's chronometer we were in 25° W., but by his observations we were much farther, and he had been for some time in doubt whether it was his chronometer or his sextant which was out of order. This landfall settled the matter, and the former instrument was condemned and, becoming still worse, was never afterward used.

As we ran in toward the coast we found that we were directly off the port of Pernambuco, and could see with the telescope the roofs of the houses and one large church, and the town of Olinda. We ran along by the mouth of the harbor, and saw a full-rigged brig going in. At 2 P.M. we again kept off before the wind, leaving the land on our quarter, and at sundown it was out of sight. It was here that I first saw one of those singular things called catamarans. They are composed of logs lashed together upon the water, have one large sail, are quite fast, and, strange as it may seem, are trusted as good sea boats. We saw several, with from one to three men in each, boldly putting out to sea after it had become almost dark. The Indians go out in them after fish, and as the weather is regular in certain seasons, they have no fear. After taking a new departure from Olinda, we kept off on our way to Cape Horn.

We met with nothing remarkable until we were in the latitude of the river La Plata. Here there are violent gales from the southwest called pamperos, which are very destructive to the shipping in the river, and are felt for many leagues at sea. They are usually preceded by lightning. The captain told the mates to keep a

bright lookout, and if they saw lightning at the southwest, to take
in sail at once. We got the first touch of one during my watch
on deck. I was walking in the lee gangway, and thought that I
saw lightning on the lee bow. I told the second mate, who came
over and looked out for some time. It was very black in the
southwest, and in about ten minutes we saw a distinct flash. The
wind, which had been southeast, had now left us, and it was
dead calm. We sprang aloft immediately and furled the royals
and topgallant sails, and took in the flying jib, hauled up the
mainsail and trysail, squared the after yards, and awaited the
attack. A huge mist capped with black clouds came driving toward us, extending over that quarter of the horizon and covering
the stars, which shone brightly in the other part of the heavens.
It came upon us at once with a blast, and a shower of hail and
rain, which almost took our breath from us. The hardiest was
obliged to turn his back. We let the halyards run, and fortunately
were not taken aback. The little vessel "paid off" from the wind,
and ran on for some time directly before it, tearing through the
water with everything flying. Having called all hands, we close-
reefed the topsails and trysail, furled the courses and jib, set the
fore-topmast staysail, and brought her up nearly to her course,
with the weather braces hauled in a little, to ease her.

This was the first blow that I had seen which could really be
called a gale. We had reefed our topsails in the Gulf Stream, and
I thought it something serious, but an older sailor would have
thought nothing of it. As I had now become used to the vessel
and to my duty, I was of some service on a yard, and could knot
my reef point as well as anybody. I obeyed the order to lay*
aloft with the rest, and found the reefing a very exciting scene;
for one watch reefed the fore-topsail, and the other the main,
and everyone did his utmost to get his topsail hoisted first. We
had a great advantage over the larboard watch, because the chief
mate never goes aloft, while our new second mate used to jump
into the rigging as soon as we began to haul out the reef tackle,

* This word "lay," which is in such general use on board ship, being used
in giving orders instead of "go"—as, "Lay forward!" "Lay aft!" "Lay aloft!"
etc.—I do not understand to be the neuter verb lie mispronounced, but to be
the active verb lay, with the objective case understood as, "Lay yourselves
forward!" "Lay yourselves aft!" etc.

and have the weather earing passed before there was a man on
the yard. In this way we were almost always able to raise the cry
of "Haul out to leeward!" before them, and having knotted our
points, would slide down the shrouds and backstays, and sing out
at the topsail halyards to let it be known that we were ahead of
them. Reefing is the most exciting part of a sailor's duty. All
hands are engaged upon it, and after the halyards are let go,
there is no time to be lost—no "sogering," or hanging back, then.
If one is not quick enough, another runs over him. The first on
the yard goes to the weather earing, the second to the lee, and
the next two to the "dog's-ears," while the others lay along
into the bunt, just giving each other elbow room. In reefing, the
yardarms (the extremes of the yards) are the posts of honor;
but in furling, the strongest and most experienced stand in the
slings (or middle of the yard) to make up the bunt. If the second
mate is a smart fellow, he will never let anyone take either of
these posts from him; but if he is wanting either in seamanship,
strength, or activity, some better man will get the bunt and
earings from him—which immediately brings him into disrepute.

We remained for the rest of the night, and throughout the next
day, under the same close sail, for it continued to blow very
fresh; and though we had no more hail, yet there was a soaking
rain and it was quite cold and uncomfortable, the more so because we were not prepared for cold weather, but had on our
thin clothes. We were glad to get a watch below and put on our
thick clothing, boots, and southwesters. Toward sundown the
gale moderated a little, and it began to clear off in the southwest.
We shook our reefs out, one by one, and before midnight had
topgallant sails on her.

We had now made up our minds for Cape Horn and cold
weather, and entered upon every necessary preparation.

TUESDAY, Nov. 4. At daybreak saw land on our larboard quarter. There were two islands, of different size but of the same
shape, rather high, beginning low at the water's edge and running
with a curved ascent to the middle. They were so far off as to be
of a deep-blue color, and in a few hours we "sank" them in the
northeast. These were the Falkland Islands. We had run between
them and the main land of Patagonia. At sunset the second mate,

who was at the masthead, said that he saw land on the starboard bow. This must have been the island of Staten Land, and we were now in the region of Cape Horn, with a fine breeze from the northward, topmast and topgallant studding sails set, and every prospect of a speedy and pleasant passage round.

5

Cape Horn · A Visit

WEDNESDAY, Nov. 5. The weather was fine during the previous night, and we had a clear view of the Magellan Clouds, and of the Southern Cross. The Magellan Clouds consist of three small nebulae in the southern part of the heavens —two bright, like the Milky Way, and one dark. These are first seen, just above the horizon, soon after crossing the southern tropic. When off Cape Horn, they are nearly overhead. The cross is composed of four stars in that form, and is said to be the brightest constellation in the heavens.

During the first part of this day (Wednesday) the wind was light, but after noon it came on fresh, and we furled the royals. We still kept the studding sails out, and the captain said he should go round with them, if he could. Just before eight o'clock (then about sundown in that latitude) the cry of "All hands ahoy!" was sounded down the fore scuttle and the after hatchway, and hurrying on deck, we found a large black cloud rolling on toward us from the southwest, and blackening the whole heavens. "Here comes Cape Horn!" said the chief mate, and we had hardly time to haul down and clew up before it was upon us. In a few moments, a heavier sea was raised than I had ever seen before, and as it was directly ahead, the little brig, which was no better than a bathing machine, plunged into it, and all the forward part of her was under water, the sea pouring in through the bow ports and hawsehole and over the knightheads, threatening to wash everything overboard. In the lee scuppers it was up to a man's waist. We sprang aloft and double-reefed the topsails and furled all the other sails, and made all snug. But this would not do; the brig was laboring and straining against the head sea, and the gale was growing worse and worse. At the same time sleet and hail were driving with all fury against us. We clewed down, and hauled out the reef tackles again, and close-reefed the fore-topsail and furled the main, and hove her to on the starboard tack. Here was an end to our fine prospects. We made up our minds to head winds and cold weather, sent down the royal yards, and unrove the gear; but all the rest of the top hamper remained aloft, even to the skysail masts and studding-sail booms.

Throughout the night it stormed violently—rain, hail, snow, and sleet beating upon the vessel—the wind continuing ahead, and the sea running high. At daybreak (about 3 A.M.) the deck was covered with snow. The captain sent up the steward with a glass of grog to each of the watch, and all the time that we were off the Cape, grog was given to the morning watch, and to all hands whenever we reefed topsails. The clouds cleared away at sunrise, and the wind becoming more fair, we again made sail and stood nearly up to our course.

THURSDAY, Nov. 6. It continued more pleasant through the first part of the day, but at night we had the same scene over again. This time we did not heave to, as on the night before, but endeavored to beat to windward under close-reefed topsails, balance-reefed trysail, and fore-topmast staysail. This night it was my turn to steer, or as the sailors say, my trick at the helm, for two hours. Inexperienced as I was, I made out to steer to the satisfaction of the officer, and neither S— nor myself gave up our tricks all the time that we were off the Cape. This was something to boast of, for it requires a good deal of skill and watchfulness to steer a vessel close-hauled in a gale of wind against a heavy head sea. "Ease her when she pitches" is the word; and a little carelessness in letting her ship a heavy sea might sweep the decks, or knock the masts out of her.

FRIDAY, Nov. 7. Toward morning the wind went down, and during the whole forenoon we lay tossing about in a dead calm, and in the midst of a thick fog. The calms here are unlike those in most parts of the world, for there is always such a high sea running, and the periods of calm are so short that it has no time to go down; and vessels, being under no command of sails or rudder, lie like logs on the water. We were obliged to steady the booms and yards by guys and braces, and to lash everything well below. We now found our top hamper of some use, for though it is liable to be carried away or sprung by the sudden "bringing-up" of a vessel when pitching in a chopping sea, yet it is a great help in steadying a vessel when rolling in a long swell, giving more slowness, ease, and regularity to the motion.

The calm of the morning reminds me of a scene which I forgot to describe at the time of its occurrence, but which I remember from its being the first time that I had heard the near breathing of whales. It was on the night that we passed between the Falkland Islands and Staten Land. We had the watch from twelve to four, and coming on deck, found the little brig lying perfectly still, surrounded by a thick fog, and the sea as smooth as though oil had been poured upon it, yet now and then a long, low swell rolling over its surface, slightly lifting the vessel but without breaking the glassy smoothness of the water. We were surrounded far and near by shoals of sluggish whales and grampuses —which the fog prevented our seeing—rising slowly to the surface or perhaps lying out at length, heaving out those peculiar lazy, deep, and long-drawn breathings which give such an impression of supineness and strength. Some of the watch were asleep, and the others were perfectly still, so that there was nothing to break the illusion, and I stood leaning over the bulwarks listening to the slow breathings of the mighty creatures—now one breaking the water just alongside, whose black body I almost fancied that I could see through the fog, and again another which I could just hear in the distance—until the low and regular swell seemed like the heaving of the ocean's mighty bosom to the sound of its heavy and long-drawn respirations.

Toward the evening of this day (Friday, seventh) the fog cleared off, and we had every appearance of a cold blow; and soon after sundown it came in. Again it was clew up and haul down, reef and furl, until we had got her down to close-reefed topsails, double-reefed trysail, and reefed fore spencer. Snow, hail, and sleet were driving upon us most of the night, and the sea breaking over the bows and covering the forward part of the little vessel; but as she would lay her course the captain refused to heave her to.

SATURDAY, Nov. 8. This day commenced with calm and thick fog, and ended with hail, snow, a violent wind, and close-reefed topsails.

SUNDAY, Nov. 9. Today the sun rose clear, and continued so

until twelve o'clock, when the captain got an observation. This
was very well for Cape Horn, and we thought it a little remarkable that as we had not had one unpleasant Sunday during the
whole voyage, the only tolerable day here should be a Sunday.
We got time to clear up the steerage and forecastle and set things
to rights, and to overhaul our wet clothes a little. But this did
not last very long. Between five and six—the sun was then nearly
three hours high—the cry of "All starbowlines ahoy!" summoned
our watch on deck, and immediately all hands were called. A true
specimen of Cape Horn was coming upon us. A great cloud of a
dark slate-color was driving on us from the southwest; and we
did our best to take in sail (for the light sails had been set during
the first part of the day) before we were in the midst of it. We
had got the light sails furled, the courses hauled up, and the
topsail reef tackles hauled out, and were just mounting the fore
rigging, when the storm struck us. In an instant the sea, which
had been comparatively quiet, was running higher and higher,
and it became almost as dark as night. The hail and sleet were
harder than I had yet felt them, seeming almost to "pin us down"
to the rigging. We were longer taking in sail than ever before;
for the sails were stiff and wet, the ropes and rigging covered
with snow and sleet, and we ourselves cold and nearly blinded
with the violence of the storm. By the time we had got down on
deck again, the little brig was plunging madly into a tremendous
head sea, which at every drive rushed in through the bow ports
and over the bows, and buried all the forward part of the vessel.
At this instant the chief mate, who was standing on the top of the
windlass at the foot of the spencer mast, called out, "Lay out
there and furl the jib!" This was no agreeable or safe duty, yet
it must be done. An old Swede (the best sailor on board) who
belonged on the forecastle sprang out on the bowsprit. Another
one must go. I was near the mate, and sprang forward, threw
the downhaul over the windlass, and jumped between the knightheads out on the bowsprit. The crew stood abaft the windlass
and hauled the jib down while we got out on the weather side
of the jib boom, our feet on the footropes, holding on by the
spar, the great jib flying off to leeward and "slatting" so as almost
to throw us off the boom. For some time we could do nothing
but hold on, and the vessel, diving into two huge seas one after

the other, plunged us twice into the water up to our chins. We hardly knew whether we were on or off; when coming up, dripping from the water, we were raised high into the air. John (that was the sailor's name) thought the boom would go every moment, and called out to the mate to keep the vessel off and haul down the staysail; but the fury of the wind and the breaking of the seas against the bows defied every attempt to make ourselves heard, and we were obliged to do the best we could in our situation. Fortunately, no other seas so heavy struck her, and we succeeded in furling the jib "after a fashion" and, coming in over the staysail nettings, were not a little pleased to find that all was snug, and the watch gone below; for we were soaked through, and it was very cold. The weather continued nearly the same through the night.

MONDAY, Nov. 10. During a part of this day we were hove to, but the rest of the time were driving on, under close-reefed sails, with a heavy sea, a strong gale, and frequent squalls of hail and snow.

TUESDAY, Nov. 11. The same.

WEDNESDAY. The same.

THURSDAY. The same.

We had now got hardened to Cape weather, the vessel was under reduced sail, and everything secured on deck and below, so that we had little to do but to steer and to stand our watch. Our clothes were all wet through, and the only change was from wet to more wet. It was in vain to think of reading or working below, for we were too tired, the hatchways were closed down, and everything was wet and uncomfortable, black and dirty, heaving and pitching. We had only to come below when the watch was out, wring out our wet clothes, hang them up, and turn in and sleep as soundly as we could until the watch was called again. A sailor can sleep anywhere—no sound of wind, water, wood, or iron can keep him awake—and we were always fast asleep when three blows on the hatchway, and the unwelcome cry of "All starbowlines ahoy! Eight bells there below! Do you hear the news?" (the usual formula of calling the watch) roused us up from our berths upon the cold, wet decks. The only time when we could be said to take any pleasure was at night and morning, when we were allowed a tin pot full of hot tea

(or as the sailors significantly call it, "water bewitched") sweet-
ened with molasses. This, bad as it was, was still warm and
comforting, and together with our sea biscuit and cold salt beef
made quite a meal. Yet even this meal was attended with some
uncertainty. We had to go ourselves to the galley and take our
kid of beef and tin pots of tea, and run the risk of losing them
before we could get below. Many a kid of beef have I seen rolling
in the scuppers, and the bearer lying at his length on the decks.
I remember an English lad who was always the life of the crew,
but whom we afterward lost overboard, standing for nearly ten
minutes at the galley with his pot of tea in his hand, waiting for
a chance to get down into the forecastle; and seeing what he
thought was a "smooth spell," he started to go forward. He had
just got to the end of the windlass when a great sea broke over
the bows, and for a moment I saw nothing of him but his head
and shoulders; and at the next instant, being taken off his legs,
he was carried aft with the sea, until her stern lifting up and
sending the water forward, he was left high and dry at the side
of the longboat, still holding on to his tin pot, which had now
nothing in it but salt water. But nothing could ever daunt him,
or overcome for a moment his habitual good humor. Regaining
his legs, and shaking his fist at the man at the wheel, he rolled
below, saying as he passed, "A man's no sailor if he can't take a
joke." The ducking was not the worst of such an affair, for as
there was an allowance of tea, you could get no more from the
galley; and though the sailors would never suffer a man to go
without, but would always turn in a little from their own pots to
fill up his, yet this was at best but dividing the loss among all
hands.

Something of the same kind befell me a few days after. The
cook had just made for us a mess of hot "scouse"—that is, biscuit
pounded fine, salt beef cut into small pieces, and a few potatoes
boiled up together and seasoned with pepper. This was a rare
treat, and I, being the last at the galley, had it put in my charge
to carry down for the mess. I got along very well as far as the
hatchway, and was just getting down the steps when a heavy sea,
lifting the stern out of water and passing forward, dropping it
down again, threw the steps from their place, and I came down
into the steerage a little faster than I meant to, with the kid on

top of me, and the whole precious mess scattered over the floor. Whatever your feelings may be, you must make a joke of everything at sea; and if you were to fall from aloft and be caught in the belly of a sail, and thus saved from instant death, it would not do to look at all disturbed, or to make a serious matter of it.

FRIDAY, Nov. 14. We were now well to the westward of the Cape, and were changing our course to the northward as much as we dared, since the strong southwest winds, which prevailed then, carried us in toward Patagonia. At 2 P.M. we saw a sail on our larboard beam, and at four we made it out to be a large ship steering our course, under single-reefed topsails. We at that time had shaken the reefs out of our topsails, as the wind was lighter, and set the main topgallant sail. As soon as our captain saw what sail she was under, he set the fore-topgallant sail and flying jib; and the old whaler—for such his boats and short sail showed him to be—felt a little ashamed, and shook the reefs out of his topsails, but could do no more, for he had sent down his topgallant

masts off the Cape. He ran down for us, and answered our hail
as the whaleship *New England*, of Poughkeepsie, one hundred
and twenty days from New York. Our captain gave our name,
and added "ninety-two days from Boston." They then had a little
conversation about longitude, in which they found that they
could not agree. The ship fell astern, and continued in sight during the night. Toward morning, the wind having become light,
we crossed our royal and skysail yards, and at daylight we were
seen under a cloud of sail, having royals and skysails fore and
aft. The "spouter," as the sailors call a whaleman, had sent up
his main topgallant mast and set the sail, and made signal for
us to heave to. About half-past seven their whaleboat came alongside, and Captain Job Terry sprang on board, a man known in
every port and by every vessel in the Pacific Ocean. "Don't you
know Job Terry? I thought everybody knew Job Terry," said a
green hand who came in the boat to me when I asked him about
his captain. He was indeed a singular man. He was six feet high,
wore thick cowhide boots and brown coat and trousers, and,
except a sunburnt complexion, had not the slightest appearance
of a sailor; yet he had been forty years in the whale trade and,
as he said himself, had owned ships, built ships, and sailed ships.
His boat's crew were a pretty raw set, just out of the bush, and
as the sailor's phrase is, "hadn't got the hayseed out of their hair."
Captain Terry convinced our captain that our reckoning was a
little out, and, having spent the day on board, put off in his boat
at sunset for his ship, which was now six or eight miles astern.
He began a "yarn" when he came aboard which lasted, with but
little intermission, for four hours. It was all about himself, and
the Peruvian Government, and the *Dublin* frigate, and Lord
James Townshend, and President Jackson, and the ship *Ann
M'Kim*, of Baltimore. It would probably never have come to an
end had not a good breeze sprung up, which sent him off to his
own vessel. One of the lads who came in his boat, a thoroughly
countrified-looking fellow, seemed to care very little about the
vessel, rigging, or anything else, but went round looking at the
livestock, and leaned over the pigsty and said he wished he was
back again tending his father's pigs.

At eight o'clock we altered our course to the northward, bound
for Juan Fernández.

This day we saw the last of the albatrosses which had been our companions a great part of the time off the Cape. I had been interested in the bird from descriptions which I had read of it, and was not at all disappointed. We caught one or two with a baited hook which we floated astern on a shingle. Their long, flapping wings, long legs, and large staring eyes give them a very peculiar appearance. They look well on the wing; but one of the finest sights that I have ever seen was an albatross asleep on the water during a calm off Cape Horn when a heavy sea was running. There being no breeze, the surface of the water was unbroken, but a long, heavy swell was rolling, and we saw the fellow, all white, directly ahead of us, asleep upon the waves with his head under his wing, now rising on the top of a huge billow and then falling slowly until he was lost in the hollow between. He was undisturbed for some time, until the noise of our bows, gradually approaching, roused him, when, lifting his head, he stared upon us for a moment and then spread his wide wings and took his flight.

6

Loss of a Man · Superstition

MONDAY, Nov. 19. This was a black day in our calendar. At seven o'clock in the morning, it being our watch below, we were aroused from a sound sleep by the cry of "All hands ahoy! A man overboard!" This unwonted cry sent a thrill through the heart of everyone, and hurrying on deck, we found the vessel hove flat aback, with all her studding sails set; for the boy who was at the helm left it to throw something overboard, and the carpenter, who was an old sailor, knowing that the wind was light, put the helm down and hove her aback. The watch on deck were lowering away the quarter-boat, and I got on deck just in time to heave myself into her as she was leaving the side; but it was not until out upon the wide Pacific in our little boat that I knew whom we had lost. It was George Ballmer, a young English sailor who was prized by the officers as an active and willing seaman, and by the crew as a lively, hearty fellow, and a good shipmate. He was going aloft to fit a strap round the main topmasthead, for ringtail halyards, and had the strap and block, a coil of halyards, and a marlinespike about his neck. He fell from the starboard futtock shrouds, and not knowing how to swim, and being heavily dressed, with all those things round his neck, he probably sank immediately. We pulled astern in the direction in which he fell, and though we knew that there was no hope of saving him, yet no one wished to speak of returning, and we rowed about for nearly an hour, without the hope of doing anything, but unwilling to acknowledge to ourselves that we must give him up. At length we turned the boat's head and made toward the vessel.

Death is at all times solemn, but never so much so as at sea. A man dies on shore—his body remains with his friends, and "the mourners go about the streets"; but when a man falls overboard at sea and is lost, there is a suddenness in the event, and a diffi-

culty in realizing it, which give to it an air of awful mystery. A
man dies on shore—you follow his body to the grave, and a stone
marks the spot. You are often prepared for the event. There is
always something which helps you to realize it when it happens,
and to recall it when it has passed. A man is shot down by your
side in battle, and the mangled body remains an *object,* and a
real evidence; but at sea, the man is near you—at your side—you
hear his voice, and in an instant he is gone, and nothing but a
vacancy shows his loss. Then too, at sea—to use a homely but
expressive phrase—you *miss* a man so much. A dozen men are
shut up together in a little bark on the wide, wide sea, and for
months and months see no forms and hear no voices but their
own, and one is taken suddenly from among them, and they miss
him at every turn. It is like losing a limb. There are no new faces
or new scenes to fill up the gap. There is always an empty berth
in the forecastle, and one man wanting when the small night
watch is mustered. There is one less to take the wheel, and one
less to lay out with you upon the yard. You miss his form, and
the sound of his voice, for habit had made them almost necessary
to you, and each of your senses feels the loss.

All these things make such a death peculiarly solemn, and the
effect of it remains upon the crew for some time. There is more
kindness shown by the officers to the crew, and by the crew to
one another. There is more quietness and seriousness. The oath
and the loud laugh are gone. The officers are more watchful, and
the crew go more carefully aloft. The lost man is seldom mentioned, or is dismissed with a sailor's rude eulogy: "Well, poor
George is gone! His cruise is up soon! He knew his work, and did
his duty, and was a good shipmate." Then usually follows some
allusion to another world, for sailors are almost all believers; but
their notions and opinions are unfixed and at loose ends. They
say, "God won't be hard on the poor fellow," and seldom get
beyond the common phrase which seems to imply that their
sufferings and hard treatment here will excuse them hereafter—
*"To work hard, live hard, die hard, and go to hell after all would
be hard indeed!"* Our cook, a simplehearted old African who had
been through a good deal in his day, and was rather seriously
inclined, always going to church twice a day when on shore and
reading his Bible on a Sunday in the galley, talked to the crew

about spending their Sabbaths badly, and told them that they might go as suddenly as George had, and be as little prepared.

Yet a sailor's life is at best but a mixture of a little good with much evil, and a little pleasure with much pain. The beautiful is linked with the revolting, the sublime with the commonplace, and the solemn with the ludicrous.

We had hardly returned on board with our sad report before an auction was held of the poor man's clothes. The captain had first, however, called all hands aft and asked them if they were satisfied that everything had been done to save the man, and if they thought there was any use in remaining there longer. The crew all said that it was in vain, for the man did not know how to swim, and was very heavily dressed. So we then filled away and kept her off to her course.

The laws regulating navigation make the captain answerable for the effects of a sailor who dies during the voyage, and it is either a law or a universal custom, established for convenience, that the captain should immediately hold an auction of his things, in which they are bid off by the sailors, and the sums which they give are deducted from their wages at the end of the voyage. In this way the trouble and risk of keeping his things through the voyage are avoided, and the clothes are usually sold for more than they would be worth on shore. Accordingly, we had no sooner got the ship before the wind than his chest was brought up on the forecastle, and the sale began. The jackets and trousers in which we had seen him dressed but a few days before were exposed and bid off while the life was hardly out of his body, and his chest was taken aft and used as a store chest, so that there was nothing left which could be called *his*. Sailors have an unwillingness to wear a dead man's clothes during the same voyage, and they seldom do so unless they are in absolute want.

As is usual after a death, many stories were told about George. Some had heard him say that he repented never having learned to swim, and that he knew that he should meet his death by drowning. Another said that he never knew any good to come of a voyage made against the will, and the deceased man shipped and spent his advance, and was afterward very unwilling to go, but not being able to refund, was obliged to sail with us. A boy, too, who had become quite attached to him said that George talked to him during most of the watch on the night before about his mother and family at home, and this was the first time that he had mentioned the subject during the voyage.

The night after this event, when I went to the galley to get a light I found the cook inclined to be talkative, so I sat down on the spars and gave him an opportunity to hold a yarn. I was the more inclined to do so as I found that he was full of the superstitions once more common among seamen, and which the recent death had waked up in his mind. He talked about George's having spoken of his friends, and said he believed few men died without having a warning of it, which he supported by a great many stories of dreams and the unusual behavior of men before death. From this he went on to other superstitions—the Flying Dutchman, etc.—and talked rather mysteriously, having something evidently on his mind. At length he put his head out of the galley and looked carefully about to see if anyone was within hearing, and being satisfied on that point, asked me in a low tone:

"I say! You know what countryman 'e carpenter be?"

"Yes," said I, "he's a German."

"What kind of a German?" said the cook.

"He belongs to Bremen," said I.

"Are you sure o' dat?" said he.

I satisfied him on that point by saying that he could speak no language but German and English.

"I'm plaguy glad o' dat," said the cook. "I was mighty 'fraid he was a Finn. I tell you what, I been plaguy civil to that man all the voyage."

I asked him the reason of this, and found that he was fully possessed with the notion that Finns are wizards, and especially have power over winds and storms. I tried to reason with him about it, but he had the best of all arguments, that from experience, at hand, and was not to be moved. He had been in a vessel at the Sandwich Islands in which the sailmaker was a Finn, and could do anything he was of a mind to. This sailmaker kept a junk bottle in his berth which was always just half full of rum, though he got drunk on it nearly every day. He had seen him sit for hours together talking to this bottle, which he stood up before him on the table. The same man cut his throat in his berth, and everybody said he was possessed.

He had heard of ships, too, beating up the Gulf of Finland against a head wind and having a ship heave in sight astern overhaul and pass them, with as fair a wind as could blow, and all studding sails out, and find she was from Finland.

"Oh ho!" said he. "I've seen too much of them men to want to see 'em 'board a ship. If they can't have their own way, they'll play the devil with you."

As I still doubted, he said he would leave it to John, who was the oldest seaman aboard and would know if anybody did. John, to be sure, was the oldest, and at the same time the most ignorant, man in the ship; but I consented to have him called. The cook stated the matter to him, and John, as I anticipated, sided with the cook, and said that he himself had been in a ship where they had a head wind for a fortnight, and the captain found out at last that one of the men, whom he had had some hard words with a short time before, was a Finn, and immediately told him if he didn't stop the head wind he would shut him down in the forepeak. The Finn would not give in, and the captain shut him down in the forepeak, and would not give him anything to eat. The Finn held out for a day and a half, when he could not stand it any longer, and did something or other which brought the wind round again, and they let him up.

"There," said the cook, "what do you think o' dat?"

I told him I had no doubt it was true, and that it would have been odd if the wind had not changed in fifteen days, Finn or no Finn.

"Oh," says he, "go way! You think 'cause you been to college, you know better than anybody. You know better than them as 'as seen it with their own eyes. You wait till you've been to sea as long as I have and you'll know."

7

Juan Fernández · The Pacific

WE CONTINUED sailing along with a fair wind and fine weather until

TUESDAY, Nov. 25, when at daylight we saw the island of Juan Fernández directly ahead, rising like a deep-blue cloud out of the sea. We were then probably nearly seventy miles from it, and so high and so blue did it appear that I mistook it for a cloud resting over the island, and looked for the island under it until it gradually turned to a deader and greener color and I could mark the inequalities upon its surface. At length we could distinguish trees and rocks; and by the afternoon this beautiful island lay fairly before us, and we directed our course to the only harbor. Arriving at the entrance soon after sundown, we found a Chilean man-of-war brig, the only vessel, coming out. She hailed us, and an officer on board, whom we supposed to be an American, advised us to run in before night, and said that they were bound to Valparaiso. We ran immediately for the anchorage, but owing to the winds which drew about the mountains and came to us in flaws from every point of the compass, we did not come to an anchor until nearly midnight. We had a boat ahead all the time that we were working in, and those aboard were continually bracing the yards about for every puff that struck us, until about twelve o'clock, when we came to in 40 fathoms water, and our anchor struck bottom for the first time since we left Boston—one hundred and three days. We were then divided into three watches, and thus stood out the remainder of the night.

I was called on deck to stand my watch at about three in the morning, and I shall never forget the peculiar sensation which I experienced on finding myself once more surrounded by land, feeling the night breeze coming from off shore, and hearing the frogs and crickets. The mountains seemed almost to hang over us, and apparently from the very heart of them there came out,

at regular intervals, a loud echoing sound which affected me as
hardly human. We saw no lights, and could hardly account for
the sound until the mate, who had been there before, told us that
it was the "*alerta*" of the Spanish soldiers who were stationed
over some convicts confined in caves nearly halfway up the
mountain. At the expiration of my watch I went below feeling
not a little anxious for the day, that I might see more nearly, and
perhaps tread upon, this romantic—I may almost say classic—
island.

When all hands were called it was nearly sunrise, and between
that time and breakfast, although quite busy on board in getting
up water casks, etc., I had a good view of the objects about
me. The harbor was nearly landlocked, and at the head of it was
a landing place protected by a small breakwater of stones, upon
which two large boats were hauled up, with a sentry standing
over them. Near this was a variety of huts or cottages, nearly a
hundred in number, the best of them built of mud and white-
washed, but the greater part only Robinson Crusoe-like—of posts
and branches of trees. The governor's house, as it is called, was
the most conspicuous, being large, with grated windows, plastered walls, and roof of red tiles, yet, like all the rest, only of one
story. Near it was a small chapel, distinguished by a cross, and a
long, low, brown-looking building surrounded by something like
a palisade, from which an old and dingy-looking Chilean flag was
flying. This, of course, was dignified by the title of presidio. A
sentinel was stationed at the chapel, another at the governor's
house, and a few soldiers armed with bayonets, looking rather
ragged, with shoes out at the toes, were strolling about among
the houses or waiting at the landing place for our boat to come
ashore.

• The mountains were high, but not so overhanging as they
appeared to be by starlight. They seemed to bear off toward the
center of the island, and were green and well wooded, with some
large and I am told exceedingly fertile valleys, with mule tracks
leading to different parts of the island.

I cannot here forget how my friend S— and myself got the
laugh of the crew upon us by our eagerness to get on shore. The
captain having ordered the quarter-boat to be lowered, we both
sprang down into the forecastle, filled our jacket pockets with

tobacco to barter with the people ashore, and when the officer
called for "four hands in the boat," nearly broke our necks in our
haste to be first over the side, and had the pleasure of pulling
ahead of the brig with a towline for a half an hour, and coming
on board again to be laughed at by the crew, who had seen our
maneuver.

After breakfast the second mate was ordered ashore with five
hands to fill the water casks, and to my joy I was among the
number. We pulled ashore with the empty casks, and here again
fortune favored me, for the water was too thick and muddy to be
put into the casks and the governor had sent men up to the head
of the stream to clear it out for us, which gave us nearly two
hours of leisure. This leisure we employed in wandering about
among the houses, and eating a little fruit which was offered to
us. Ground apples, melons, grapes, strawberries of an enormous
size, and cherries abound here. The latter are said to have been
planted by Lord Anson. The soldiers were miserably clad, and
asked with some interest whether we had shoes to sell on board.

I doubt very much if they had the means of buying them. They were very eager to get tobacco, for which they gave shells, fruits, etc. Knives also were in demand, but we were forbidden by the governor to let anyone have them, as he told us that all the people there except the soldiers and a few officers were convicts sent from Valparaiso, and that it was necessary to keep all weapons from their hands. The island, it seems, belongs to Chile, and had been used by the government as a sort of Botany Bay for nearly two years; and the governor—an Englishman who had entered the Chilean navy—with a priest, half a dozen taskmasters, and a body of soldiers, was stationed there to keep them in order. This was no easy task; and only a few months before our arrival a few of them had stolen a boat at night, boarded a brig lying in the harbor, sent the captain and crew ashore in their boat, and gone off to sea. We were informed of this, and loaded our arms and kept strict watch on board through the night, and were careful not to let the convicts get our knives from us when on shore. The worst part of the convicts, I found, were locked up under sentry in caves dug into the side of the mountain, nearly halfway up, with mule tracks leading to them, whence they were taken by day and set to work under taskmasters on building an aqueduct, a wharf, and other public works; the rest lived in the houses which they put up for themselves, had their families with them, and seemed to me to be the laziest people on the face of the earth. They did nothing but take a *paseo* into the woods, a *paseo* among the houses, a *paseo* at the landing place, looking at us and our vessel, and too lazy to speak fast; while the others were driving—or rather driven—about at a rapid trot in single file, with burdens on their shoulders, and followed up by their taskmasters, with long rods in their hands and broad-brimmed straw hats on their heads. Upon what precise grounds this great distinction was made I do not know, and I could not very well know, for the governor was the only man who spoke English on the island, and he was out of my walk.

Having filled our casks, we returned on board, and soon after the governor, dressed in a uniform like that of an American militia officer, the padre, in the dress of the Gray Friars, with hood and all complete, and the *capitán* with big whiskers and dirty regimentals, came on board to dine. While they were at

dinner, a large ship appeared in the offing, and soon afterward
we saw a light whaleboat pulling into the harbor. The ship lay
off and on, and a boat came alongside of us and put on board
the captain, a plain young Quaker dressed all in brown. The ship
was the *Cortes,* whaleman, of New Bedford, and had put in to
see if there were any vessels from round the Horn, and to hear
the latest news from America. They remained aboard a short
time, when they left us and pulled off to their ship, which, having
filled away, was soon out of sight.

A small boat which came from the shore to take away the
governor and suite—as they styled themselves—brought as a present to the crew a large pail of milk, a few shells, and a block of
sandalwood. The milk, which was the first we had tasted since
leaving Boston, we soon dispatched; a piece of the sandalwood I
obtained, and learned that it grew on the hills in the center of
the island. I have always regretted that I did not bring away other
specimens of the products of the island, having afterward lost all
that I had with me—the piece of sandalwood, and a small flower
which I plucked and brought on board in the crown of my tarpaulin and carefully pressed between the leaves of a book.

About an hour before sundown, having stowed our water casks,
we commenced getting under way, and were not a little while
about it; for we were in 30 fathoms water, and in one of the
gusts which came from off shore had let go our other bow anchor; and as the southerly wind draws round the mountains
and comes off in uncertain flaws, we were continually swinging
round, and had thus got a very foul hawse. We hove in upon our
chain, and after stoppering and unshackling it again and again,
and hoisting and hauling down sail, we at length tipped our
anchor and stood out to sea. It was bright starlight when we
were clear of the bay, and the lofty island lay behind us in its
still beauty, and I gave a parting look, and bid farewell, to the
most romantic spot of earth that my eyes had ever seen. I did
then, and have ever since, felt an attachment for that island altogether peculiar. It was partly, no doubt, from its having been
the first land that I had seen since leaving home, and still more
from the associations which everyone has connected with it in
their childhood from reading *Robinson Crusoe.* To this I may add
the height and romantic outline of its mountains, the beauty and

freshness of its verdure and the extreme fertility of its soil, and
its solitary position in the midst of the wide expanse of the South
Pacific, as all concurring to give it its peculiar charm.

When thoughts of this place have occurred to me at different
times, I have endeavored to recall more particulars with regard
to it. It is situated in about 33° 30′ S., and is distant a little more
than three hundred miles from Valparaiso on the coast of Chile,
which is in the same latitude. It is about fifteen miles in length
and five in breadth. The harbor in which we anchored (called by
Lord Anson Cumberland Bay) is the only one in the island, two
small "bights" of land on each side of the main bay (sometimes
dignified by the name of bays) being little more than landing
places for boats. The best anchorage is at the western side of the
bay, where we lay at about three cables' lengths from the shore,
in a little more than 30 fathoms water. This harbor is open to the
N.N.E., and in fact nearly from N. to E., but the only dangerous
winds being the southwest, on which side are the highest mountains, it is considered very safe. The most remarkable thing perhaps about it is the fish with which it abounds. Two of our crew
who remained on board caught in a few minutes enough to last
us for several days, and one of the men who was a Marblehead
man said that he never saw or heard of such an abundance. There
were cod, breams, silverfish, and other kinds whose names they
did not know, or which I have forgotten.

There is an abundance of the best of water on the island, small
streams running through every valley and leaping down from the
sides of the hills. One stream of considerable size flows through
the center of the lawn upon which the houses are built, and fur-
nishes an easy and abundant supply to the inhabitants. This, by
means of a short wooden aqueduct, was brought quite down to
our boats. The convicts had also built something in the way of a
breakwater, and were to build a landing place for boats and
goods, after which the Chilean Government intended to lay port
charges.

Of the wood I can only say that it appeared to be abundant;
the island in the month of November, when we were there, being
in all the freshness and beauty of spring, appeared covered with
trees. These were chiefly aromatic, and the largest was the
myrtle. The soil is very loose and rich, and wherever it is broken

up, there spring up immediately radishes, turnips, ground apples, and other garden fruits. Goats, we were told, were not abundant, and we saw none, though it was said we might if we had gone into the interior. We saw a few bullocks winding about in the narrow tracks on the sides of the mountains, and the settlement was completely overrun with dogs of every nation, kindred, and degree. Hens and chickens were also abundant, and seemed to be taken good care of by the women. The men appeared to be the laziest people on the face of the earth; and indeed, as far as my observation goes, there are no people to whom the newly invented Yankee word of "loafer" is more applicable than to the Spanish Americans. These men stood about doing nothing, with their cloaks, little better in texture than an Indian's blanket but of rich colors, thrown over their shoulders with an air which it is said that a Spanish beggar can always give to his rags; and with great politeness and courtesy in their address, though with holes in their shoes and without a sou in their pockets. The only interruption to the monotony of their day seemed to be when a gust of wind drew round between the mountains and blew off the boughs which they had placed for roofs to their houses, and gave them a few minutes' occupation in running about after them. One of these gusts occurred while we were ashore, and afforded us no little amusement at seeing the men look round, and if they found that their roofs had stood, conclude that they might stand too, while those who saw theirs blown off, after uttering a few Spanish oaths, gathered their cloaks over their shoulders and started off after them. However, they were not gone long, but soon returned to their habitual *occupation* of doing nothing.

It is perhaps needless to say that we saw nothing of the interior, but all who have seen it give very glowing accounts of it. Our captain went with the governor and a few servants upon mules over the mountains, and upon their return I heard the governor request him to stop at the island on his passage home and offer him a handsome sum to bring a few deer with him from California, for he said that there were none upon the island, and he was very desirous of having it stocked.

A steady though light southwesterly wind carried us well off from the island, and when I came on deck for the middle watch I could just distinguish it from its hiding a few low stars in the

southern horizon, though my unpracticed eyes would hardly have
known it for land. At the close of the watch a few trade-wind
clouds which had arisen, though we were hardly yet in their
latitude, shut it out from our view, and the next day,

THURSDAY, Nov. 27, upon coming on deck in the morning we
were again upon the wide Pacific, and saw no more land until
we arrived on the western coast of the great continent of
America.

"Tarring Down"·Daily Life· *"Going Aft"·California*

A̲s̲ ̲w̲e̲ ̲s̲a̲w̲ neither land nor sail from the time of leaving Juan
Fernández until our arrival in California, nothing of interest occurred except our own doings on board. We caught
the southeast trades, and ran before them for nearly three weeks
without so much as altering a sail or bracing a yard. The captain
took advantage of this fine weather to get the vessel in order for
coming on the coast. The carpenter was employed in fitting up
a part of the steerage into a trade room; for our cargo, we now
learned, was not to be landed, but to be sold by retail from on
board, and this trade room was built for the samples and the
lighter goods to be kept in, and as a place for the general business. In the meantime we were employed in working on the
rigging. Everything was set up taut, the lower rigging rattled
down, or rather rattled *up* (according to the modern fashion),
an abundance of spun yarn and seizing stuff made, and finally
the whole standing rigging, fore and aft, was tarred down. This
was my first essay at this latter business, and I had enough of it,
for nearly all of it came upon my friend S— and myself. The men
were needed at the other work, and M—, the other young man
who came out with us, was laid up with the rheumatism in his
feet. The boy was rather too young and small for the business,
and as the winds were light and regular, he was kept during
most of the daytime at the helm, so that nearly all the tarring
came upon us. We put on short duck frocks, and taking a small
bucket of tar and a bunch of oakum in our hands, went aloft, one
at the main royal masthead and the other at the fore, and began
tarring down. This is an important operation, and is usually done
about once in six months in vessels upon a long voyage. It was

done in our vessel several times afterward, but by the whole crew at once, and finished off in a day; but at this time, as most of it came upon two of us and we were new at the business, it took us several days. In this operation they always begin at the mast-head and work down, tarring the shrouds, backstays, standing parts of the lifts, the tyes, runners, etc., and go out to the yard-arms and come in, tarring as they come the lifts and footropes. Tarring the stays is more difficult, and is done by an operation which the sailors call "riding down." A long piece of rope—top-gallant-studding-sail halyards, or something of the kind—is taken up to the masthead from which the stay leads, and rove through a block for a girtline, or as the sailors usually call it, a *gant*line. With the end of this a bowline is taken round the stay, into which the man gets with his bucket of tar and a bunch of oakum, and the other end being fast on deck, with someone to tend it, he is lowered down gradually, and tars the stay carefully as he goes. There he "swings aloft 'twixt heaven and earth," and if the rope slips, breaks, or is let go, or if the bowline slips, he falls overboard or breaks his neck. This, however, is a thing which never enters into a sailor's calculation. He only thinks of leaving no "holidays" (places not tarred), for in case he should, he would have to go over the whole again; or of dropping no tar upon the deck, for then there would be a soft word in his ear from the mate. In this manner I tarred down all the headstays, but found the rigging about the jib booms, martingale, and spritsail yard, upon which I was afterward put, the hardest. Here you have to hang on with your eyelids and tar with your hands.

This dirty work could not last forever, and on Saturday night we finished it, scraped all the spots from the deck and rails and, what was of more importance to us, cleaned ourselves thoroughly, rolled up our tarry frocks and trousers and laid them away for the next occasion, and put on our clean duck clothes and had a good comfortable sailor's Saturday night.

On Monday we commenced painting and getting the vessel ready for port. This work, too, is done by the crew, and every sailor who has been long voyages is a little of a painter, in addition to his other accomplishments. We painted her, both inside and out, from the truck to the water's edge. The outside is painted by lowering stages over the side by ropes, and on those we sat, with our brushes and paintpots by us and our feet half the time in the water. This must be done, of course, on a smooth day when the vessel does not roll much. I remember very well being over the side painting in this way one fine afternoon, our vessel going quietly along at the rate of four or five knots, and a pilot fish, the sure precursor of a shark, swimming alongside of us. The captain was leaning over the rail watching him, and we went quietly on with our work. In the midst of our painting, on

FRIDAY, DEC. 19, we crossed the equator for the second time. I had the feeling which all have when for the first time they find themselves living under an entire change of seasons—as crossing the line under a burning sun in the midst of December, and, as I afterward was, beating about among ice and snow on the Fourth of July.

THURSDAY, DEC. 25. This day was Christmas, but it brought us no holiday. The only change was that we had a plum duff for dinner, and the crew quarreled with the steward because he did not give us our usual allowance of molasses to eat with it. He thought the plums would be a substitute for the molasses, but we were not to be cheated out of our rights.

Such are the trifles which produce quarrels on shipboard. In fact, we had been too long from port. We were getting tired of one another, and were in an irritable state, both forward and aft. Our fresh provisions were of course gone, and the captain had stopped our rice, so that we had nothing but salt beef and salt pork throughout the week, with the exception of a very small duff on Sunday. This added to the discontent, and a thousand little things, daily and almost hourly occurring, which no one who has not himself been on a long and tedious voyage can conceive of or properly appreciate—little wars and rumors of wars, reports of things said in the cabin, misunderstanding of words and looks, apparent abuses—brought us into a state in which everything seemed to go wrong. Every encroachment upon the time allowed for rest appeared unnecessary. Every shifting of the studding sails was only to "haze"* the crew.

* "Haze" is a word of frequent use on board ship, and never, I believe, used elsewhere. It is very expressive to a sailor, and means to punish by hard work. Let an officer once say, "I'll haze you," and your fate is fixed. You will be "worked up," if you are not a better man than he is.

In the midst of this state of things, my messmate S— and my-self petitioned the captain for leave to shift our berths from the steerage, where we had previously lived, into the forecastle. This, to our delight, was granted, and we turned in to "bunk" and mess with the crew forward. We now began to feel like sailors, which we never fully did when we were in the steerage. While there, however useful and active you may be, you are but a mongrel—and sort of afterguard and "ship's cousin." You are immediately under the eye of the officers, cannot dance, sing, play, smoke, make a noise, or *growl* (complain), or take any other sailor's pleasure; and you live with the steward, who is usually a go-between; and the crew never feel as though you were *one of them*. But if you live in the forecastle, you are "as independent as a wood-sawyer's clerk" (nauticé), and are a *sailor*. You hear sailors' talk, learn their ways, their peculiarities of feeling as well as speaking and acting, and moreover pick up a great deal of curious and useful information in seamanship, ship's customs, foreign countries, etc. from their long yarns and equally long disputes. No man can be a sailor, or know what sailors are, unless he has lived in the forecastle with them—turned in and out with them, eaten of their dish and drunk of their cup. After I had been a week there, nothing would have tempted me to go back to my old berth, and never afterward, even in the worst of weather when in a close and leaking forecastle off Cape Horn, did I for a moment wish myself in the steerage. Another thing which you learn better in the forecastle than you can any-where else is to make and mend clothes, and this is indispensable to sailors. A large part of their watches below they spend at this work, and here I learned that art which stood me in so good stead afterward.

But to return to the state of the crew. Upon our coming into the forecastle, there was some difficulty about the uniting of the allowances of bread, by which we thought we were to lose a few pounds. This set us into a ferment. The captain would not conde-scend to explain, and we went aft in a body, with a Swede, the oldest and best sailor of the crew, for spokesman. The recollection of the scene that followed always brings up a smile, especially the quarter-deck dignity and eloquence of the captain. He was walking the weather side of the quarter-deck, and seeing us coming aft, stopped short in his walk, and with a voice and look intended to annihilate us, called out, "Well, what the devil do you want now?" Whereupon we stated our grievances as respectfully as we could, but he broke in upon us, saying that we were getting fat and lazy, didn't have enough to do, and that made us find fault. This provoked us, and we began to give word for word. This would never answer. He clenched his fist, stamped and swore, and sent us all forward, saying, with oaths enough interspersed to send the words home: "Away with you! Go forward, every one of you! I'll haze you! I'll work you up! You don't have enough to do! If you ain't careful I'll make a hell of the ship! . . . You've mistaken your man! I'm F— T—, all the way from Down East. I've been through the mill, ground, and bolted, and come out a *regular-built Down East johnnycake,* good when it's hot, but when it's cold, sour and indigestible—and you'll find me so!" The latter part of this harangue I remember well, for it made a strong impression, and the "Down East johnnycake" became a byword for the rest of the voyage. So much for our petition for the redress of grievances. The matter was however set right, for the mate, after allowing the captain due time to cool off, explained it to him, and at night we were all called aft to hear another harangue, in which of course the whole blame of the misunderstanding was thrown upon us. We ventured to hint that he would not give us time to explain; but it wouldn't do. We were driven back discomfited. Thus the affair blew over, but the irritation caused by it remained, and we never had peace or a good understanding again so long as the captain and crew remained together.

We continued sailing along in the beautiful temperate climate of the Pacific. The Pacific well deserves its name, for except in the southern part, at Cape Horn, and in the western parts, near the China and Indian oceans, it has few storms, and is never either extremely hot or cold. Between the tropics there is a slight haziness, like a thin gauze, drawn over the sun, which, without obstructing or obscuring the light, tempers the heat which comes down with perpendicular fierceness in the Atlantic and Indian tropics. We sailed well to the westward to have the full advantage of the northeast trades, and when we had reached the latitude of Point Conception, where it is usual to make the land, we were several hundred miles to the westward of it. We immediately changed our course due east, and sailed in that direction for a number of days. At length we began to heave to after dark, for fear of making the land at night on a coast where there are no lighthouses and but indifferent charts, and at daybreak on the morning of

TUESDAY, JAN. 13, 1835, we made the land at Point Conception, lat. 34° 32′ N., long. 120° 06′ W. The port of Santa Barbara, to which we were bound, lying about sixty miles to the southward of this point, we continued sailing down the coast during the day and following night, and on the next morning,

JAN. 14, 1835, we came to anchor in the spacious bay of Santa Barbara, after a voyage of one hundred and fifty days from Boston.

California · A Southeaster

CALIFORNIA extends along nearly the whole of the western coast of Mexico, between the Gulf of California in the south and the bay of Sir Francis Drake on the north, or between the 22d and 38th degrees of north latitude. It is subdivided into two provinces—Lower or Old California, lying between the gulf and the 32d degree of latitude or near it (the division line running, I believe, between the bay of Todos Santos and the port of San Diego) and New or Upper California, the southernmost port of which is San Diego, in lat. 32° 39′, and the northernmost San Francisco, situated in the large bay discovered by Sir Francis Drake, in lat. 37° 58′, and called after him by the English, though the Mexicans call it Yerba Buena. Upper California has the seat of its government at Monterey, where is also the customhouse, the only one on the coast, and at which every vessel intending to trade on the coast must enter its cargo before it can commence its traffic. We were to trade upon this coast exclusively, and therefore expected to go to Monterey at first; but the captain's orders from home were to put in at Santa Barbara, which is the central port of the coast, and wait there for the agent who lives there and transacts all the business for the firm to which our vessel belonged.

The bay, or as it was commonly called the "canal," of Santa Barbara, is very large, being formed by the mainland on one side (between Point Conception on the north and Point San Buenaventura on the south), which here bends in like a crescent, and three large islands opposite to it and at the distance of twenty miles. This is just sufficient to give it the name of a bay, while at the same time it is so large and so much exposed to the southeast and northwest winds that it is little better than an open roadstead and the whole swell of the Pacific Ocean rolls in here before a southeaster and breaks with so heavy a surf in the shallow waters that it is highly dangerous to lie near in to the shore during the southeaster season; that is, between the months of November and April.

This wind (the southeaster) is the bane of the coast of California. Between the months of November and April (including a part of each), which is the rainy season in this latitude, you are never safe from it, and accordingly in the ports which are open to it vessels are obliged during these months to lie at anchor at a distance of three miles from the shore, with slip ropes on their cables, ready to slip and go to sea at a moment's warning. The only ports which are safe from this wind are San Francisco and Monterey in the north and San Diego in the south.

As it was January when we arrived, and the middle of the southeaster season, we accordingly came to anchor at the distance of three miles from the shore, in 11 fathoms water, and bent a slip rope and buoys to our cables, cast off the yardarm gaskets from the sails, and stopped them all with rope yarns. After we had done this, the boat went ashore with the captain, and returned with orders to the mate to send a boat ashore for him at sundown. I did not go in the first boat, and was glad to find that there was another going before night; for after so long a voyage as ours had been a few hours is long to pass in sight and out of reach of land. We spent the day on board in the usual avocations; but as this was the first time we had been without the captain, we felt a little more freedom, and looked about us to see what sort of a country we had got into and were to spend a year or two of our lives in.

In the first place, it was a beautiful day, and so warm that we had on straw hats, duck trousers, and all the summer gear, and as this was midwinter, it spoke well for the climate; and we afterward found that the thermometer never fell to the freezing point throughout the winter, and that there was very little difference between the seasons, except that during a long period of rainy and southeasterly weather thick clothes were not uncomfortable.

The large bay lay about us, nearly smooth, as there was hardly a breath of wind stirring, though the boat's crew who went ashore told us that the long ground swell broke into a heavy surf on the beach. There was only one vessel in the port—a long, sharp brig of about 300 tons, with raking masts and very square yards, and

English colors at her peak. We afterward learned that she was built at Guayaquil, and named the *Ayacucho*, after the place where the battle was fought that gave Peru her independence, and was now owned by a Scotchman named Wilson, who commanded her, and was engaged in the trade between Callao, the Sandwich Islands, and California. She was a fast sailer, as we frequently afterward perceived, and had a crew of Sandwich Islanders on board. Besides this vessel there was no object to break the surface of the bay. Two points ran out as the horns of the crescent, one of which—the one to the westward—was low and sandy, and is that to which vessels are obliged to give a wide berth when running out for a southeaster; the other is high, bold, and well wooded, and we were told has a mission on it called San Buenaventura, from which the point is named. In the middle of this crescent, directly opposite the anchoring ground, lie the mission and town of Santa Barbara, on a low, flat plain but little above the level of the sea, covered with grass though entirely without trees, and surrounded on three sides by an amphitheater of mountains, which slant off to the distance of fifteen or twenty miles. The mission stands a little back of the town, and is a large building, or rather collection of buildings, in the center of which is a high tower with a belfry of five bells; and the whole, being plastered, makes quite a show at a distance, and is the mark by which vessels come to anchor. The town lies a little nearer to the beach—about half a mile from it—and is composed of one-story houses built of brown clay, some of them plastered, with red tiles on the roofs. I should judge that there were about a hundred of them, and in the midst of them stands the presidio, or fort, built of the same materials, and apparently but little stronger. The town is certainly finely situated, with a bay in front and an amphitheater of hills behind. The only thing which diminishes its beauty is that the hills have no large trees upon them, they having been all burned by a great fire which swept them off about a dozen years before, and they had not yet grown up again. The fire was described to me by an inhabitant as having been a very terrible and magnificent sight. The air of the whole valley was so heated that the people were obliged to leave the town and take up their quarters for several days on the beach.

Just before sundown the mate ordered a boat's crew ashore,

and I went as one of the number. We passed under the stern of the English brig, and had a long pull ashore. I shall never forget the impression which our first landing on the beach of California made upon me. The sun had just gone down; it was getting dusky; the damp night wind was beginning to blow, and the heavy swell of the Pacific was setting in and breaking in loud and high "combers" upon the beach. We lay on our oars in the swell, just outside of the surf, waiting for a good chance to run in, when a boat which had put off from the *Ayacucho* just after us came alongside of us, with a crew of dusky Sandwich Islanders talking and hallooing in their outlandish tongue. They knew that we were novices in this kind of boating, and waited to see us go in. The second mate, however, who steered our boat, determined to have the advantage of their experience, and would not go in first. Finding at length how matters stood, they gave a shout, and taking advantage of a great comber which came swelling in, rearing its head and lifting up the stern of our boat nearly perpendicular, and again dropping it in the trough, they gave three or four long and strong pulls and went in on top of the great wave, throwing their oars overboard and as far from the boat as they could throw them, and jumping out the instant that the boat touched the beach, and then seizing hold of her and running her up high and dry on the sand. We saw at once how it was to be done, and also the necessity of keeping the boat "stern on" to the sea; for the instant the sea should strike upon her broadside or quarter, she would be driven up broadside on, and capsized. We pulled strongly in, and as soon as we felt that the sea had got hold of us and was carrying us in with the speed of a race horse, we threw the oars as far from the boat as we could and took hold of the gunwale, ready to spring out and seize her when she struck, the officer using his utmost strength to keep her stern on. We were shot up on the beach like an arrow from a bow, and seizing the boat, ran her up high and dry, and soon picked up our oars, and stood by her, ready for the captain to come down.

Finding that the captain did not come immediately, we put our oars in the boat, and leaving one to watch it, walked about the beach to see what we could of the place. The beach is nearly a mile in length between the two points, and of smooth sand. We had taken the only good landing place, which is in the middle, it being more stony toward the ends. It is about twenty yards in width from high-water mark to a slight bank at which the soil begins, and so hard that it is a favorite place for running horses. It was growing dark, so that we could just distinguish the dim outlines of the two vessels in the offing; and the great seas were rolling in in regular lines, growing larger and larger as they approached the shore, and hanging over the beach upon which they were to break, when their tops would curl over and turn white with foam and, beginning at one extreme of the line, break rapidly to the other, as a long card house falls when the children knock down the cards at one end. The Sandwich Islanders, in the meantime, had turned their boat round and run her down into the water, and were loading her with hides and tallow. As this was the work in which we were soon to be engaged, we looked on with some curiosity. They ran the boat into the water so far that every large sea might float her, and two of them, with their trousers rolled up, stood by the bows, one on each side, keeping her in her right position. This was hard work; for beside the force they had to use upon the boat, the large seas nearly took them off their legs. The others were running from the boat to the bank on which, out of the reach of the water, was a pile of dry bullocks' hides, doubled lengthwise in the middle, and nearly as stiff as boards. These they took on their heads, one or two at a time, and carried down to the boat, where one of their number stowed them away. They were obliged to carry them on their heads to keep them out of the water, and we observed that they had on thick woolen caps. "Look here, Bill, and see what you're coming to!" said one of our men to another who stood by the boat. "Well, D—," said the second mate to me, "this does not look much like Cambridge college, does it? This is what I call '*headwork.*'" To tell the truth, it did not look very encouraging.

After they had got through with the hides, they laid hold of the bags of tallow (the bags are made of hide, and are about the size of a common meal bag), and lifting each upon the shoulders of two men, one at each end, walked off with them to the boat, and prepared to go aboard. Here too was something for us to learn. The man who steered shipped his oar and stood up in the stern, and those that pulled the afteroars sat on their benches with their oars shipped, ready to strike out as soon as she was

afloat. The two men at the bows kept their places, and when at
length a large sea came in and floated her, seized hold of the
gunwale and ran out with her till they were up to their armpits,
and then tumbled over the gunwale into the bows, dripping with
water. The men at the oars struck out, but it wouldn't do—the
sea swept back and left them nearly high and dry. The two fellows jumped out again, and the next time they succeeded better,
and with the help of a deal of outlandish hallooing and bawling
got her well off. We watched them till they were out of the
breakers, and saw them steering for their vessel, which was now
hidden in the darkness.

The sand of the beach began to be cold to our bare feet; the
frogs set up their croaking in the marshes, and one solitary owl,
from the end of the distant point, gave out his melancholy note,
mellowed by the distance; and we began to think that it was
high time for the "old man," as the captain is generally called,
to come down. In a few minutes we heard something coming
toward us. It was a man on horseback. He came up on the full
gallop, reined up near us, addressed a few words to us, and receiving no answer, wheeled round and galloped off again. He
was nearly as dark as an Indian, with a large Spanish hat, blanket
cloak or serape, and leather leggings with a long knife stuck in
them. "This is the seventh city that ever I was in, and no Christian one neither," said Bill Brown. "Stand by!" said Tom. "You
haven't seen the worst of it yet." In the midst of this conversation the captain appeared, and we winded the boat round,
shoved her down, and prepared to go off. The captain, who had
been on the coast before and "knew the ropes," took the steering
oar, and we went off in the same way as the other boat. I, being
the youngest, had the pleasure of standing at the bow and getting
wet through. We went off well, though the seas were high. Some
of them lifted us up, and sliding from under us, seemed to let us
drop through the air like a flat plank on the body of the water.
In a few minutes we were in the low, regular swell, and pulled
for a light, which as we came up we found had been run up to
our trysail gaff.

Coming aboard, we hoisted up all the boats, and diving down
into the forecastle, changed our wet clothes, and got our supper.
After supper the sailors lighted their pipes (cigars, those of us

who had them) and we had to tell all we had seen ashore. Then
followed conjectures about the people ashore, the length of the
voyage, carrying hides, etc., etc., until eight bells, when all hands
were called aft, and the anchor watch set. We were to stand two
in a watch, and as the nights were pretty long, two hours were
to make a watch. The second mate was to keep the deck until
eight o'clock, and all hands were to be called at daybreak, and
the word was passed to keep a bright lookout, and to call the
mate if it should come on to blow from the southeast. We had
also orders to strike the bells every half-hour through the night,
as at sea. My watchmate was John, the Swedish sailor, and we
stood from twelve to two, he walking the larboard side and I the
starboard. At daylight all hands were called, and we went
through the usual process of washing down, swabbing, etc., and
got breakfast at eight o'clock. In the course of the forenoon, a
boat went aboard of the *Ayacucho* and brought off a quarter of
beef, which made us a fresh bite for dinner. This we were glad
enough to have, and the mate told us that we should live on fresh
beef while we were on the coast, as it was cheaper here than the
salt. While we were at dinner, the cook called, "Sail ho!" and
coming on deck, we saw two sails coming round the point. One
was a large ship under topgallant sails, and the other a small
hermaphrodite brig. They both backed their topsails and sent
boats aboard of us. The ship's colors had puzzled us, and we
found that she was from Genoa, with an assorted cargo, and was
trading on the coast. She filled away again, and stood out, being
bound up the coast to San Francisco. The crew of the brig's boat
were Sandwich Islanders, but one of them who spoke a little
English told us that she was the *Loriotte*, Captain Nye, from
Oahu, and was engaged in this trade. She was a lump of a thing
—what the sailors call a butterbox. This vessel, as well as the
Ayacucho, and others which we afterward saw engaged in the
same trade, have English or Americans for officers, and two or
three before the mast to do the work on the rigging, and to rely
upon for seamanship, while the rest of the crew are Sandwich
Islanders, who are active, and very useful in boating.

The three captains went ashore after dinner, and came off
again at night. When in port, everything is attended to by the
chief mate; the captain, unless he is also supercargo, has little to

do, and is usually ashore much of his time. This we thought
would be pleasanter for us, as the mate was a good-natured man
and not very strict. So it was for a time, but we were worse off
in the end; for wherever the captain is a severe, energetic man
and the mate is wanting in both these qualities, there will always
be trouble. And trouble we had already begun to anticipate. The
captain had several times found fault with the mate in presence
of the crew, and hints had been dropped that all was not right
between them. When this is the case, and the captain suspects
that his chief officer is too easy and familiar with the crew, then
he begins to interfere in all the duties, and to draw the reins
tauter, and the crew have to suffer.

A Southeaster ·
Passage up the Coast

THIS NIGHT after sundown it looked black at the southward and eastward, and we were told to keep a bright lookout. Expecting to be called up, we turned in early. Waking up about midnight, I found a man who had just come down from his watch striking a light. He said that it was beginning to puff up from the southeast, and that the sea was rolling in, and he had called the captain; and as he threw himself down on his chest with all his clothes on, I knew that he expected to be called. I felt the vessel pitching at her anchor, and the chain surging and snapping, and lay awake expecting an instant summons. In a few minutes it came—three knocks on the scuttle, and "All hands ahoy! Bear a hand up and make sail!" We sprang up for our clothes, and were about halfway dressed when the mate called out down the scuttle, "Tumble up here, men! Tumble up before she drags her anchor!" We were on deck in an instant. "Lay aloft and loose the topsails!" shouted the captain as soon as the first man showed himself. Springing into the rigging, I saw that the *Ayacucho's* topsails were loosed, and heard her crew singing out at the sheets as they were hauling them home. This had probably started our captain, as "Old Wilson" (the captain of the *Ayacucho*) had been many years on the coast, and knew the signs of the weather. We soon had the topsails loosed; and one hand remaining, as usual, in each top, to overhaul the rigging and light the sail out, the rest of us laid down to man the sheets. While sheeting home, we saw the *Ayacucho* standing athwart our bows, sharp upon the wind, cutting through the head sea like a knife, with her raking masts and sharp bows running up like the head of a greyhound. It was a beautiful sight. She was like a bird which had been frightened and had spread her wings in flight. After the topsails had been sheeted home, the head yards braced aback, the fore-topmast staysail hoisted and the buoys streamed, and all ready forward for slipping, we went aft and manned the slip rope which came through the stern port with a turn round the timberheads. "All ready forward?" asked the captain. "Aye, aye, sir, all ready," answered the mate. "Let go!" "All gone, sir." And the iron cable grated over the windlass and through the hawsehole, and the little vessel's head swinging off from the wind under the force of her backed headsails, brought the strain on the slip rope. "Let go aft!" Instantly all was gone, and we were under way. As soon as she was well off from the wind, we filled away the head yards, braced all up sharp, set the foresail and trysail, and left our anchorage well astern, giving the point a good berth. "Nye's off too," said the captain to the mate, and looking astern, we could just see the little hermaphrodite brig under sail standing after us.

It now began to blow fresh, the rain fell fast, and it grew very black; but the captain would not take in sail until we were well clear of the point. As soon as we left this on our quarter and were standing out to sea, the order was given, and we sprang aloft, double-reefed each topsail, furled the foresail, and double-reefed the trysail, and were soon under easy sail. In these cases of slipping for southeasters, there is nothing to be done after you have got clear of the coast but to lie to under easy sail and wait for the gale to be over, which seldom lasts more than two days, and is often over in twelve hours; but the wind never comes back to the southward until there has a good deal of rain fallen. "Go below, the watch," said the mate; but here was a dispute which watch it should be, which the mate soon however settled by sending his watch below, saying that we should have our turn the next time we got under way. We remained on deck till the expiration of the watch, the wind blowing very fresh and the rain coming down in torrents. When the watch came up, we wore ship and stood on the other tack, in toward land. When we came up again, which was at four in the morning, it was very dark, and there was not much wind, but it was raining as I thought I had never seen it rain before. We had on oilcloth suits and southwester caps, and had nothing to do but to stand bolt upright and let it pour down upon us. There are no umbrellas, and no sheds to go under, at sea.

While we were standing about on deck, we saw the little brig drifting by us, hove to under her fore-topsail double-reefed, and she glided by like a phantom. Not a word was spoken, and we saw no one on deck but the man at the wheel. Toward morning the captain put his head out of the companionway and told the second mate, who commanded our watch, to look out for a change of wind, which usually followed a calm and heavy rain; and it was well that he did, for in a few minutes it fell dead calm, the vessel lost her steerageway, and the rain ceased. We hauled up the trysail and courses, squared the after yards, and waited for the change, which came in a few minutes, with a vengeance, from the northwest, the opposite point of the compass. Owing to our precautions, we were not taken aback, but ran before the wind with square yards. The captain coming on deck, we braced up a little and stood back for our anchorage. With the change of wind came a change of weather, and in two hours the wind moderated into the light steady breeze which blows down the coast the greater part of the year, and, from its regularity, might be called a trade wind. The sun came up bright, and we set royals, skysails, and studding sails, and were under fair way for Santa Barbara. The little *Loriotte* was astern of us, nearly out of sight, but we saw nothing of the *Ayacucho*. In a short time she appeared, standing out from Santa Rosa Island, under the lee of which she had been hove to all night. Our captain was anxious to get in before her, for it would be a great credit to us on the coast to beat the *Ayacucho*, which had been called the best sailer in the North Pacific, in which she had been known as a trader for six years or more. We had an advantage over her in light winds, from our royals and skysails which we carried both at the fore and main, and also in our studding sails; for Captain Wilson carried nothing but topgallant sails, and always unbent his studding sails when on the coast. As the wind was light and fair, we held our own for some time, when we were both obliged to brace up and come on a taut bowline after rounding the point; and here he had us on fair ground, and walked away from us as you would haul in a line. He afterward said that we sailed well enough with the wind free, but that give him a taut bowline, and he would beat us if we had all the canvas of the *Royal George*.

The *Ayacucho* got to the anchoring ground about half an hour before us, and was furling her sails when we came up to it. This picking up your cables is a very nice piece of work. It requires some seamanship to do it and come to at your former moorings without letting go another anchor. Captain Wilson was remarkable among the sailors on the coast for his skill in doing this, and our captain never let go a second anchor during all the time that I was with him. Coming a little to windward of our buoy, we clewed up the light sails, backed our main-topsail, and lowered a boat, which pulled off and made fast a spare hawser to the buoy on the end of the slip rope. We brought the other end to the capstan, and hove in upon it until we came to the slip rope, which we took to the windlass and walked her up to her chain, the captain helping her by backing and filling the sails. The chain is then passed through the hawsehole and round the windlass and bitted, the slip rope taken round outside and brought into the stern port, and she is safe in her old berth. After we had got through, the mate told us that this was a small touch of California the like of which we must expect to have through the winter.

After we had furled the sails and got dinner, we saw the *Loriotte* nearing, and she had her anchor before night. At sundown we went ashore again, and found the *Loriotte's* boat waiting on the beach. The Sandwich Islander who could speak English told us that he had been up to the town; that our agent, Mr. R—, and some other passengers were going to Monterey with us, and that we were to sail the same night. In a few minutes Captain T—, with two gentlemen and one female, came down, and we got ready to go off. They had a good deal of baggage, which we put into the bows of the boat, and then two of us took the señora in our arms and waded with her through the water, and put her down safely in the stern. She appeared much amused with the transaction, and her husband was perfectly satisfied, thinking any arrangement good which saved his wetting his feet. I pulled the afteroar, so that I heard the conversation, and learned that one of the men, who, as well as I could see in the darkness, was a young-looking man in the European dress and covered up in a large cloak, was the agent of the firm to which our vessel belonged; and the other, who was dressed in the Spanish dress of

the country, was a brother of our captain who had been many years a trader on the coast and had married the lady who was in the boat. She was a delicate, dark-complexioned young woman, and of one of the best families in California. I also found that we were to sail the same night. As soon as we got on board the boats were hoisted up, the sails loosed, the windlass manned, the slip ropes and gear cast off, and after about twenty minutes of heaving at the windlass, making sail, and bracing yards, we were well under way, and going with a fair wind up the coast to Monterey. The *Loriotte* got under way at the same time, and was also bound up to Monterey, but as she took a different course from us, keeping the land aboard while we kept well out to sea, we soon lost sight of her. We had a fair wind, which is something unusual when going up, as the prevailing wind is the north, which blows directly down the coast; whence the northern are called the windward and the southern the leeward ports.

Passage up the Coast · Monterey

W<small>E GOT CLEAR</small> of the islands before sunrise the next morning, and by twelve o'clock were out of the canal and off Point Conception, the place where we first made the land upon our arrival. This is the largest point on the coast, and is an uninhabited headland stretching out into the Pacific, and has the reputation of being very windy. Any vessel does well which gets by it without a gale, especially in the winter season. We were going along with studding sails set on both sides when, as we came round the point, we had to haul our wind, and took in the lee studding sails. As the brig came more upon the wind she felt it more, and we doused the skysails, but kept the weather studding sails on her, bracing the yards forward so that the swinging boom nearly touched the spritsail yard. She now lay over to it, the wind was freshening, and the captain was evidently "dragging onto her." His brother and Mr. R—, looking a little squally, said something to him, but he only answered that he knew the vessel and what she would carry. He was evidently showing off his vessel, and letting them know how he could carry sail. He stood up to windward, holding on by the backstays, and looking up at the sticks to see how much they would bear, when a puff came which settled the matter. Then it was "haul down," and "clew up," royals, flying jib, and studding sails, all at once. There was what the sailors call a "mess"—everything let go, nothing hauled in, and everything flying. The poor Spanish woman came to the companionway looking as pale as a ghost, and nearly frightened to death. The mate and some men forward were trying to haul in the lower studding sail, which had blown over the spritsail yardarm and round the guys; while the topmast studding-sail boom, after buckling up and springing out again like a piece of whalebone, broke off at the boom iron. I sprang aloft to take in the main topgallant studding sail, but before I got into the top, the tack parted, and away went the sail, swinging forward of the topgallant sail, and tearing and slatting itself to pieces. The halyards were at this moment let go by the run and such a piece of work I never had before in taking in a sail. After great exertions I got it, or the remains of it, into the top, and was making it fast when the captain, looking up, called out to me, "Lay aloft there, D—, and furl that main royal." Leaving the studding sail, I went up to the crosstrees, and here it looked rather squally. The foot of the topgallant mast was working between the cross and trestle trees, and the royal mast lay over at a fearful angle with the mast below, while everything was working and cracking, strained to the utmost.

There's nothing for Jack to do but to obey orders, and I went up on the yard; and there was a worse "mess," if possible, than I had left below. The braces had been let go, and the yard was swinging about like a turnpike gate, and the whole sail having blown over to leeward, the lee leech was over the yardarm, and the skysail was all adrift and flying over my head. I looked down, but it was in vain to attempt to make myself heard, for everyone was busy below, and the wind roared and sails were flapping in every direction. Fortunately, it was noon and broad daylight, and the man at the wheel, who had his eyes aloft, soon saw my difficulty, and after numberless signs and gestures, got someone to haul the necessary ropes taut. During this interval I took a look below. Everything was in confusion on deck; the little vessel was tearing through the water as if she were mad, the seas flying over her, and the masts leaning over at an angle of forty-five degrees from the vertical. At the other royal masthead was S—, working away at the sail, which was blowing from him as fast as he could gather it in. The topgallant sail below me was soon clewed up, which relieved the mast, and in a short time I got my sail furled and went below; but I lost overboard a new tarpaulin hat, which troubled me more than anything else. We worked for about half an hour with might and main; and in an hour from the time the squall struck us, from having all our flying kites abroad, we came down to double-reefed topsails and the storm sails.

The wind had hauled ahead during the squall, and we were standing directly in for the point. So as soon as we had got all snug, we wore round and stood off again, and had the pleasant prospect of beating up to Monterey, a distance of a hundred miles, against a violent head wind. Before night it began to rain, and we had five days of rainy, stormy weather, under close sail all the time, and were blown several hundred miles off the coast. In the midst of this, we discovered that our fore-topmast was sprung (which no doubt happened in the squall) and were obliged to send down the fore-topgallant mast and carry as little sail as possible forward. Our four passengers were dreadfully sick, so that we saw little or nothing of them during the five days. On the sixth day it cleared off, and the sun came out bright, but the wind and sea were still very high. It was quite like being at sea again: no land for hundreds of miles, and the captain taking the sun every day at noon. Our passengers now made their appearance, and I had for the first time the opportunity of seeing what a miserable and forlorn creature a seasick passenger is. Since I had got over my own sickness the first two days from Boston, I had seen nothing but hale, hearty men with their sea legs on, and able to go anywhere (for we had no passengers), and I will own there was a pleasant feeling of superiority in being able to walk the deck, and eat, and go about, and comparing one's self with two poor, miserable, pale creatures staggering and shuffling about decks, or holding on and looking up with giddy heads to see us climbing to the mastheads or sitting quietly at work on the ends of the lofty yards. A well man at sea has little sympathy with one who is seasick; he is too apt to be conscious of a comparison favorable to his own manhood.

After a few days we made the land at Point Pinos (Pines), which is the headland at the entrance of the bay of Monterey. As we drew in and ran down the shore, we could distinguish well the face of the country, and found it better wooded than that to the southward of Point Conception. In fact, as I afterward discovered, Point Conception may be made the dividing line between two different faces of the country. As you go to the northward of the point, the country becomes more wooded, has a richer appearance, and is better supplied with water. This is the case with Monterey, and still more so with San Francisco; while to the southward of the point, as at Santa Barbara, San Pedro, and particularly San Diego, there is very little wood, and the country has a naked, level appearance, though it is still very fertile.

The bay of Monterey is very wide at the entrance, being about twenty-four miles between the two points. Año Nuevo at the north, and Pinos at the south, but narrows gradually as you approach the town, which is situated in a bend, or large cove, at the southeastern extremity, and about eighteen miles from the points, which makes the whole depth of the bay. The shores are extremely well wooded (the pine abounding upon them), and as it was now the rainy season, everything was as green as nature could make it—the grass, the leaves, and all; the birds were singing in the woods, and great numbers of wildfowl were flying over our heads. Here we could lie safe from the southeasters. We came to anchor within two cable lengths of the shore, and the town lay directly before us, making a very pretty appearance, its houses being plastered, which gives a much better effect than those of Santa Barbara, which are of a mud-color. The red tiles, too, on the roofs contrasted well with the white plastered sides and with the extreme greenness of the lawn on which the houses—about a hundred in number—were dotted about here and there, irregularly. There are in this place, and in every other town which I saw in California, no streets, or fences (except here and there a small patch was fenced in for a garden), so that the houses are placed at random on the green, which, as they are of one story and of the cottage form, gives them a pretty effect when seen from a little distance.

It was a fine Saturday afternoon when we came to anchor, the sun about an hour high, and everything looking pleasant. The Mexican flag was flying from the little square presidio, and the drums and trumpets of the soldiers, who were out on parade, sounded over the water and gave great life to the scene. Everyone was delighted with the appearance of things. We felt as though we had got into a Christian (which in the sailor's vocabulary means civilized) country. The first impression which California had made upon us was very disagreeable: the open roadstead of Santa Barbara; anchoring three miles from the shore; running out to sea before every southeaster; landing in a high surf, with a little dark-looking town a mile from the beach, and not a sound to be heard, or anything to be seen, but Sandwich Islanders, hides, and tallow bags. Add to this the gale off Point Conception, and no one can be at a loss to account for our agreeable disappointment in Monterey. Besides all this, we soon learned, which was of no small importance to us, that there was little or no surf here, and this afternoon the beach was as smooth as a duckpond.

We landed the agent and passengers, and found several persons waiting for them on the beach, among whom were some who, though dressed in the costume of the country, spoke English, and who we afterward learned were English and Americans who had married and settled in the country.

I also connected with our arrival here another circumstance which more nearly concerns myself; viz., my first act of what the sailors will allow to be seamanship—sending down a royal yard. I had seen it done once or twice at sea, and an old sailor whose favor I had taken some pains to gain had taught me carefully everything which was necessary to be done, and in its proper order, and advised me to take the first opportunity when we were in port and try it. I told the second mate, with whom I had been pretty "thick" when he was before the mast, that I would do it, and got him to ask the mate to send me up the first time they were struck. Accordingly I was called upon, and went up, repeating the operations over in my mind, taking care to get everything in its order, for the slightest mistake spoils the whole. Fortunately, I got through without any word from the officer, and heard the "Well done" of the mate when the yard reached the deck with as much satisfaction as I ever felt at Cambridge on seeing a "*Bene*" at the foot of a Latin exercise.

Life at Monterey

T HE NEXT DAY being Sunday, which is the liberty day among merchantmen, when it is usual to let a part of the crew go ashore, the sailors had depended upon a day on land, and were already disputing who should ask to go when, upon being called in the morning, we were turned to upon the rigging, and found that the topmast, which had been sprung, was to come down and a new one to go up, and topgallant and royal masts, and the rigging to be set up. This was too bad. If there is anything that irritates sailors and makes them feel hardly used, it is being deprived of their Sabbath. Not that they would always, or indeed generally, spend it religiously, but it is their only day of rest. Then too, they are so often necessarily deprived of it by storms, and unavoidable duties of all kinds, that to take it from them when lying quietly and safely in port, without any urgent reason, bears the more hardly. The only reason in this case was that the captain had determined to have the customhouse officers on board on Monday, and wished to have his brig in order. Jack is a slave aboard ship; but still he has many opportunities of thwarting and balking his master. When there is danger, or necessity, or when he is well used, no one can work faster than he; but the instant he feels that he is kept at work for nothing, no sloth could make less headway. He must not refuse his duty, or be in any way disobedient, but all the work that an officer gets out of him he may be welcome to. Every man who has been three months at sea knows how to "work Tom Cox's traverse"—"three turns round the longboat, and a pull at the scuttle butt." This morning everything went in this way. "Sogering" was the order of the day. Send a man below to get a block and he would capsize everything before finding it, then not bring it up till an officer had called him twice, and take as much time to put things in order again. Marlinespikes were not to be found; knives wanted a prodigious deal of sharpening, and generally three or four were waiting round the grindstone at a time. When a man got to the masthead, he would come slowly down again to get something he had forgotten; and after the tackles were got up, six men would pull less than one who pulled "with a will." When the mate was out of sight, nothing was done. It was all uphill work and at eight o'clock, when we went to breakfast, things were nearly where they were when we began.

During our short meal the matter was discussed. One proposed refusing to work; but that was mutiny, and of course was rejected at once. I remember, too, that one of the men quoted Father Taylor (as they call the seamen's preacher at Boston), who told them that if they were ordered to work on Sunday, they must not refuse their duty, and the blame would not come upon them. After breakfast it leaked out through the officers that if we would get through work soon, we might have a boat in the afternoon and go a-fishing. This bait was well thrown, and took with several who were fond of fishing; and all began to find that as we had one thing to do, and were not to be kept at work for the day, the sooner we did it, the better. Accordingly things took a new aspect, and before two o'clock this work, which was in a fair way to last two days, was done and five of us went a-fishing in the jolly boat, in the direction of Point Pinos; but leave to go ashore was refused. Here we saw the *Loriotte*, which sailed with us from Santa Barbara, coming slowly in with a light sea breeze which sets in toward afternoon, having been becalmed off the point all the first part of the day. We took several fish of various kinds, among which cod and perch abounded, and F— (the cidevant second mate), who was of our number, brought up with his hook a large and beautiful pearl-oyster shell. We afterward learned that this place was celebrated for shells, and that a small schooner had made a good voyage by carrying a cargo of them to the United States.

We returned by sundown, and found the *Loriotte* at anchor within a cable's length of the *Pilgrim*. The next day we were turned to early, and began taking off the hatches, overhauling the cargo, and getting everything ready for inspection. At eight, the officers of the customs, five in number, came on board and began overhauling the cargo, manifest, etc. The Mexican revenue laws are very strict, and require the whole cargo to be landed, examined, and taken on board again; but our agent, Mr. R—, had succeeded in compounding with them for the last two vessels, and saving the trouble of taking the cargo ashore. The officers were dressed in the costume which we found prevailed through the country. A broad-brimmed hat, usually of a black or dark-brown color, with a gilt or figured band round the crown and lined inside with silk; a short jacket of silk or figured calico (the European skirted body coat is never worn); the shirt open in the neck; rich waistcoat, if any; pantaloons wide, straight, and long, usually of velvet, velveteen, or broadcloth, or else short breeches and white stockings. They wear the deerskin shoe, which is of a dark-brown color, and (being made by Indians) usually a good deal ornamented. They have no suspenders, but always wear a sash round the waist, which is generally red, and varying in quality with the means of the wearer. Add to this the never-failing cloak and you have the dress of the Californian. This last garment, the cloak, is always a mark of the rank and wealth of the owner. The *gente de razón*, or aristocracy, wear cloaks of black or dark-blue broadcloth, with as much velvet and trimmings as may be; and from this they go down to the blanket of the Indian, the middle classes wearing something like a large tablecloth with a hole in the middle for the head to go through. This is often as coarse as a blanket, but being beautifully woven with various colors, is quite showy at a distance. Among the Spaniards there is no working class (the Indians being slaves and doing all the hard work), and every rich man looks like a grandee, and every poor scamp like a broken-down gentleman. I have often seen a man with a fine figure and courteous manners—dressed in broadcloth and velvet, with a noble horse completely covered with trappings—without a real in his pockets, and absolutely suffering for something to eat.

Trading · A British Sailor

THE NEXT DAY, the cargo having been entered in due form, we began trading. The trade room was fitted up in the steerage, and furnished out with the lighter goods and with specimens of the rest of the cargo; and M—, a young man who came out from Boston with us before the mast, was taken out of the forecastle and made supercargo's clerk. He was well qualified for the business, having been clerk in a countinghouse in Boston. He had been troubled for some time with the rheumatism, which unfitted him for the wet and exposed duty of a sailor on the coast. For a week or ten days all was life on board. The people came off to look and to buy—men, women, and children. And we were continually going in the boats, carrying goods and passengers—for they have no boats of their own. Everything must dress itself and come aboard and see the new vessel, if it were only to buy a paper of pins. The agent and his clerk managed the sales, while we were busy in the hold or in the boats. Our cargo was an assorted one; that is, it consisted of everything under the sun. We had spirits of all kinds (sold by the cask), teas, coffee, sugars, spices, raisins, molasses, hardware, crockeryware, tinware, cutlery, clothing of all kinds, boots and shoes from Lynn, calicoes and cottons from Lowell, crapes, silks; also shawls, scarfs, necklaces, jewelry, and combs for the ladies; furniture; and in fact, everything that can be imagined, from Chinese fireworks to English cartwheels—of which we had a dozen pairs with their iron rims on.

The Californians are an idle, thriftless people, and can make nothing for themselves. The country abounds in grapes, yet they buy bad wine made in Boston and brought round by us, at an immense price, and retail it among themselves at a real (12½ cents) by the small wineglass. Their hides, too, which they value at two dollars in money, they give for something which costs seventy-five cents in Boston—and buy shoes (as like as not made of their own hides, which have been carried twice round Cape Horn) at three and four dollars, and "chicken-skin" boots at fifteen dollars apiece. Things sell, on an average, at an advance of nearly 300 per cent upon the Boston prices. This is partly owing to the heavy duties which the government, in their wisdom

—with the intent, no doubt, of keeping the silver in the country— has laid upon imports. These duties, and the enormous expenses of so long a voyage, keep all merchants but those of heavy capital from engaging in the trade. Nearly two-thirds of all the articles imported into the country from round Cape Horn for the last six years have been by the single house of Bryant, Sturgis & Co., to whom our vessel belonged, and who have a permanent agent on the coast.

This kind of business was new to us, and we liked it very well for a few days, though we were hard at work every minute from daylight to dark, and sometimes even later.

By being thus continually engaged in transporting passengers

with their goods to and fro, we gained considerable knowledge
of the character, dress, and language of the people. The dress of
the men was as I have before described it. The women wore
gowns of various texture—silks, crepe, calicoes, etc.—made after
the European style, except that the sleeves were short, leaving
the arm bare, and that they were loose about the waist, having
no corsets. They wore shoes of kid or satin, sashes or belts of
bright colors, and almost always a necklace and earrings. Bonnets
they had none. I saw only one on the coast, and that belonged
to the wife of an American sea captain who had settled in San
Diego, and had imported the chaotic mass of straw and ribbon
as a choice present to his new wife. They wear their hair (which
is almost invariably black, or a very dark brown) long in their
necks, sometimes loose and sometimes in long braids, though the
married women often do it up on a high comb. Their only protection against the sun and weather is a large mantle which they
put over their heads, drawing it close round their faces when
they go out of doors, which is generally only in pleasant weather.
When in the house, or sitting out in front of it, which they often
do in fine weather, they usually wear a small scarf or neckerchief
of a rich pattern. A band, also, about the top of the head, with
a cross, star, or other ornament in front, is common. Their complexions are various, depending—as well as their dress and manner—upon their rank; or in other words, upon the amount of
Spanish blood they can lay claim to. Those who are of pure
Spanish blood, having never intermarried with the aborigines,
have clear brunet complexions, and sometimes even as fair as
those of English women. There are but few of these families in
California, being mostly those in official stations, or who on the
expiration of their offices have settled here upon property which
they have acquired; and others who have been banished for state
offenses. These form the aristocracy, intermarrying, and keeping
up an exclusive system in every respect. They can be told by their
complexions, dress, manner, and also by their speech; for, calling
themselves Castilians, they are very ambitious of speaking the
pure Castilian language, which is spoken in a somewhat cor-
rupted dialect by the lower classes. From this upper class, they
go down by regular shades, growing more and more dark and
muddy until you come to the pure Indian, who runs about with

nothing on him but a small piece of cloth kept up by a wide leather strap drawn round his waist. Generally speaking, each person's caste is decided by the quality of the blood, which shows itself, too plainly to be concealed, at first sight. Yet the least drop of Spanish blood, if it be only of quadroon or octoroon, is sufficient to raise them from the rank of slaves, and entitle them to a suit of clothes—boots, hat, cloak, spurs, long knife, and all complete, though coarse and dirty as may be—and to call themselves Españoles, and to hold property, if they get any.

The fondness for dress among the women is excessive and is often the ruin of many of them. A present of a fine mantle, or of a necklace or pair of earrings, gains the favor of the greater part of them. Nothing is more common than to see a woman living in a house of only two rooms, and the ground for a floor, dressed in spangled satin shoes, silk gown, high comb, and gilt, if not gold, earrings and necklace. If their husbands do not dress them well enough, they will soon receive presents from others. They used to spend whole days on board our vessel examining the fine clothes and ornaments, and frequently made purchases at a rate which would have made a seamstress or waiting maid in Boston open her eyes.

Next to the love of dress, I was most struck with the fineness of the voices and beauty of the intonations of both sexes. Every common ruffian-looking fellow with a slouched hat, blanket cloak, dirty underdress, and soiled leather leggings appeared to me to be speaking elegant Spanish. It was a pleasure simply to listen to the sound of the language before I could attach any meaning to it. They have a good deal of the Creole drawl, but it is varied with an occasional extreme rapidity of utterance, in which they seem to skip from consonant to consonant until, lighting upon a broad, open vowel, they rest upon that to restore the balance of sound. The women carry this peculiarity of speaking to a much greater extreme than the men, who have more evenness and stateliness of utterance. A common bullock-driver on horseback, delivering a message, seemed to speak like an ambassador at an audience. In fact, they sometimes appeared to me to be a people on whom a curse had fallen and stripped them of everything but their pride, their manners, and their voices.

Another thing that surprised me was the quantity of silver that was in circulation. I certainly never saw so much silver at one time in my life as during the week that we were at Monterey. The truth is they have no credit system, no banks, and no way of investing money but in cattle. They have no circulating medium but silver and hides—which the sailors call "California banknotes." Everything that they buy they must pay for in one or the other of these things. The hides they bring down, dried and doubled, in clumsy oxcarts or on mules' backs, and the money they carry tied up in a handkerchief—fifty, eighty, or a hundred dollars and half-dollars.

I had never studied Spanish while at college, and could not speak a word when at Juan Fernández; but during the latter part of the passage out I borrowed a grammar and dictionary from the cabin, and by a continual use of these and a careful attention to every word that I heard spoken, I soon got a vocabulary together, and began talking for myself. As I soon knew more Spanish than any of the crew (who indeed knew none at all) and had been at college and knew Latin, I got the name of a great linguist, and was always sent by the captain and officers to get provisions, or to carry letters and messages to different parts of the town. I was often sent to get something which I could not tell the name of to save my life; but I liked the business, and accordingly never pleaded ignorance. Sometimes I managed to jump below and take a look at my dictionary before going ashore; or else I overhauled some English resident on my way and got the word from him, and then, by signs and the help of my Latin and French, contrived to get along. This was a good exercise for me, and no doubt taught me more than I should have learned by months of study and reading. It also gave me opportunities of seeing the customs, characters, and domestic arrangements of the people, besides being a great relief from the monotony of a day spent on board ship.

Monterey, as far as my observation goes, is decidedly the pleasantest and most civilized-looking place in California. In the center of it is an open square surrounded by four lines of one-story plastered buildings, with half a dozen cannon in the center, some mounted and others not. This is the presidio, or fort. Every town has a presidio in its center; or rather, every presidio has a town built around it, for the forts were first built by the Mexican

Government, and then the people built near them for protection. The presidio here was entirely open and unfortified. There were several officers with long titles, and about eighty soldiers, but they were poorly paid, fed, clothed, and disciplined. The governor general, or as he is commonly called, the "general," lives here, which makes it the seat of government. He is appointed by the central Government at Mexico, and is the chief civil and military officer. In addition to him, each town has a commandant—who is the chief military officer and has charge of the fort, and of all transactions with foreigners and foreign vessels—and two or three alcaldes and corregidors, elected by the inhabitants, who are the civil officers. Courts and jurisprudence they have no knowledge of. Small municipal matters are regulated by the alcaldes and corregidors, and everything relating to the general government, to the military, and to foreigners, by the commandants, acting under the governor general. Capital cases are decided by him, upon personal inspection if he is near, or upon minutes sent by the proper officers if the offender is at a distant place. No Protestant has any civil rights, nor can he hold any property, or indeed remain more than a few weeks on shore, unless he belong to some vessel. Consequently, the Americans and English who intend to reside here become Catholics, to a man, the current phrase among them being "A man must leave his conscience at Cape Horn."

But to return to Monterey. The houses here, as everywhere else in California, are of one story, built of clay made into large bricks about a foot and a half square and three or four inches thick, and hardened in the sun. These are cemented together by mortar of the same material, and the whole is of a common dirt-color. The floors are generally of earth, the windows grated and without glass; and the doors, which are seldom shut, open directly into the common room, there being no entries. Some of the more wealthy inhabitants have glass to their windows and board floors, and in Monterey nearly all the houses are plastered on the outside. The better houses, too, have red tiles on the roofs. The common ones have two or three rooms which open into each other, and are furnished with a bed or two, a few chairs and tables, a looking-glass, a crucifix of some material or other, and small daubs of paintings enclosed in glass and representing some miracle or martyrdom. They have no chimneys or fireplaces in the houses, the climate being such as to make a fire unnecessary, and all their cooking is done in a small cookhouse separated from the house. The Indians, as I have said before, do all the hard work, two or three being attached to each house; and the poorest persons are able to keep one at least, for they have only to feed them and give them a small piece of coarse cloth and a belt for the males, and a coarse gown, without shoes or stockings, for the females.

In Monterey there are a number of English and Americans (English or *Ingles* all are called who speak the English language) who have married Californians, become united to the Catholic Church, and acquired considerable property. Having more industry, frugality, and enterprise than the natives, they soon get nearly all the trade into their hands. They usually keep shops in which they retail the goods purchased in larger quantities from our vessels, and also send a good deal into the interior, taking hides in pay, which they again barter with our vessels. In every town on the coast there are foreigners engaged in this kind of trade, while I recollect but two shops kept by natives. The people are naturally suspicious of foreigners, and they would not be allowed to remain were it not that they become good Catholics and by marrying natives, and bringing up their children as Catholics and Spaniards, and not teaching them the English language, they quiet suspicion, and even become popular and leading men. The chief alcaldes in Monterey and Santa Barbara were both Yankees by birth.

The men in Monterey appeared to me to be always on horseback. Horses are as abundant here as dogs and chickens were in Juan Fernández. There are no stables to keep them in, but they are allowed to run wild and graze wherever they please, being branded, and having long leather ropes called "lassos" attached to their necks and dragging along behind them, by which they can be easily taken. The men usually catch one in the morning, throw a saddle and bridle on him, and use him for the day and let him go at night, catching another the next day. When they go on long journeys, they ride one horse down and catch another, throw the saddle and bridle on him, and after riding him down, take a third, and so on to the end of the journey. There are

probably no better riders in the world. They get on a horse when
only four or five years old, their little legs not long enough to
come halfway over his sides, and may almost be said to keep on
him until they have grown to him. The stirrups are covered or
boxed up in front, to prevent their catching when riding through
the woods; and the saddles are large and heavy, strapped very

tight upon the horse, and have large pommels, or loggerheads,
in front, round which the lasso is coiled when not in use. They
can hardly go from one house to another without getting on a
horse, there being generally several standing tied to the doorposts
of the little cottages. When they wish to show their activity, they
make no use of their stirrups in mounting, but striking the horse,
spring into the saddle as he starts, and sticking their long spurs
into him, go off on the full run. Their spurs are cruel things, having four or five rowels, each an inch in length, dull and rusty.
The flanks of the horses are often sore from them, and I have
seen men come in from chasing bullock with their horses' hind
legs and quarters covered with blood. They frequently give exhibitions of their horsemanship, in races, bullbaitings, etc.; but as

we were not ashore during any holiday, we saw nothing of it.
Monterey is also a great place for cockfighting, gambling of all
sorts, fandangos, and every kind of amusement and knavery.
Trappers and hunters, who occasionally arrive here from over the
Rocky Mountains with their valuable skins and furs, are often
entertained with every sort of amusement and dissipation until
they have wasted their time and their money, and go back
stripped of everything.

Nothing but the character of the people prevents Monterey
from becoming a great town. The soil is as rich as man could
wish, climate as good as any in the world, water abundant, and
situation extremely beautiful. The harbor, too, is a good one, being subject only to one bad wind, the north; and though the
holding ground is not the best, yet I heard of but one vessel's
being driven ashore here. That was a Mexican brig, which went
ashore a few months before our arrival and was a total wreck,
all the crew but one being drowned. Yet this was from the carelessness or ignorance of the captain, who paid out all his small
cable before he let go his other anchor. The ship *Lagoda*, of Boston, was there at the time, and rode out the gale in safety without
dragging at all, or finding it necessary to strike her topgallant
masts.

The only vessel in port with us was the little *Loriotte*. I frequently went on board her, and became very well acquainted
with her Sandwich Island crew. One of them could speak a little
English, and from him I learned a good deal about them. They
were well formed and active, with black eyes, intelligent counte-
nances, dark-olive—or I should rather say copper—complexions,
and coarse black hair, but not woolly like the Negroes. They appeared to be talking continually. In the forecastle there was a
complete Babel. Their language is extremely guttural, and not
pleasant at first, but improves as you hear it more, and is said to
have great capacity. They use a good deal of gesticulation, and
are exceedingly animated, saying with their might what their
tongues find to say. They are complete water dogs, and therefore
very good in boating. It is for this reason that there are so many
of them on the coast of California, they being very good hands
in the surf. They are also quick and active in the rigging, and
good hands in warm weather; but those who have been with

them round Cape Horn, and in high latitudes, say that they are useless in cold weather. In their dress they are precisely like our sailors. In addition to these Islanders, the vessel had two English sailors, who acted as boatswains over the Islanders and took care of the rigging. One of them I shall always remember as the best specimen of the thoroughbred English sailor that I ever saw. He had been to sea from a boy, having served a regular apprenticeship of seven years, as all English sailors are obliged to do, and was then about four or five and twenty. He was tall, but you only perceived it when he was standing by the side of others, for the great breadth of his shoulders and chest made him appear but little above the middle height. His chest was as deep as it was wide, his arm like that of Hercules, and his hand "the fist of a tar—every hair a rope yarn." With all this he had one of the pleasantest smiles I ever saw. His cheeks were of a handsome brown, his teeth brilliantly white; his hair, of a raven black, waved in loose curls all over his head and fine, open forehead; and his eyes he might have sold to a duchess at the price of diamonds, for their brilliancy. As for their color, they were like the Irishman's pig, which would not stay to be counted; every change of position and light seemed to give them a new hue, but their prevailing color was black, or nearly so. Take him with his well-varnished black tarpaulin stuck on the back of his head, his long locks coming down almost into his eyes, his white duck trousers and shirt, blue jacket, and black kerchief tied loosely round his neck, and he was a fine specimen of manly beauty. On his broad chest he had stamped with India ink "Parting moments;"—a ship ready to sail, a boat on the beach, and a girl and her sailor lover taking their farewell. Underneath were printed the initials of his own name and two other letters standing for some name which he knew better than I did. This was very well done, having been executed by a man who made it his business to print with India ink for sailors, at Le Havre. On one of his broad arms he had the crucifixion, and on the other the sign of the "foul anchor."

He was very fond of reading, and we lent him most of the books we had in the forecastle, which he read and returned to us the next time we fell in with him. He had a good deal of information, and his captain said he was a perfect seaman, and worth his weight in gold on board a vessel in fair weather and in

foul. His strength must have been immense, and he had the sight of a vulture. It is strange that one should be so minute in the description of an unknown, outcast sailor whom one may never see again, and whom no one may care to hear about; but so it is. Some people we see under no remarkable circumstances, but whom, for some reason or other, we never forget. He called himself Bill Jackson; and I know no one of all my accidental acquaintances to whom I would more gladly give a shake of the hand than to him. Whoever falls in with him will find a handsome, hearty fellow, and a good shipmate.

Sunday came again while we were at Monterey, but as before it brought us no holiday. The people on shore dressed themselves and came off in greater numbers than ever, and we were employed all day in boating and breaking out cargo, so that we had hardly time to eat. Our cidevant second mate, who was determined to get liberty if it was to be had, dressed himself in a long coat and black hat and polished his shoes, and went aft and asked to go ashore. He could not have done a more imprudent thing, for he knew that no liberty would be given; and besides, sailors, however sure they may be of having liberty granted them, always go aft in their working clothes, to appear as though they had no reason to expect anything, and then wash, dress, and shave after they have got their liberty. But this poor fellow was always getting into hot water, and if there was a wrong way of doing a thing, was sure to hit upon it. We looked to see him go aft, knowing pretty well what his reception would be. The captain was walking the quarter-deck smoking his morning cigar, and F— went as far as the break of the deck, and there waited for him to notice him. The captain took two or three turns, and then walking directly up to him, surveyed him from head to foot, and lifting up his forefinger, said a word or two in a tone too low for us to hear, but which had a magical effect upon poor F—. He walked forward, sprang into the forecastle, and in a moment more made his appearance in his common clothes, and went quietly to work again. What the captain said to him we never could get him to tell, but it certainly changed him outwardly and inwardly in a most surprising manner.

Santa Barbara · Hide-Droghing · Harbor Duties · Discontent · San Pedro

AFTER A FEW DAYS, finding the trade beginning to slacken, we hove our anchor up, set our topsails, ran the Stars and Stripes up to the peak, fired a gun—which was returned from the presidio—and left the little town astern, running out of the bay and bearing down the coast again, for Santa Barbara. As we were now going to leeward, we had a fair wind and a plenty of it. After doubling Point Pinos, we bore up, set studding sails alow and aloft, and were walking off at the rate of eight or nine knots, promising to traverse in twenty-four hours the distance which we were nearly three weeks in traversing on the passage up. We passed Point Conception at a flying rate, the wind blowing so that it would have seemed half a gale to us if we had been going the other way and close-hauled. As we drew near the islands off Santa Barbara, it died away a little, but we came to at our old anchoring ground in less than thirty hours from the time of leaving Monterey.

Here everything was pretty much as we left it—the large bay without a vessel in it; the surf roaring and rolling in upon the beach; the white mission; the dark town and the high, treeless mountains. Here, too, we had our southeaster tacks aboard again —slip ropes, buoy ropes, sails furled with reefs in them, and rope yarns for gaskets. We lay here about a fortnight, employed in landing goods and taking off hides, occasionally, when the surf was not high; but there did not appear to be one-half the business doing here that there was in Monterey. In fact, so far as we were concerned, the town might almost as well have been in the middle of the Cordilleras. We lay at a distance of three miles from the beach and the town was nearly a mile farther, so that we saw little or nothing of it. Occasionally we landed a few goods, which were taken away by Indians in large, clumsy oxcarts, with the yoke on the ox's neck instead of under it, and with small solid wheels. A few hides were brought down, which we carried off in the California style. This we had now got pretty well accustomed to—and hardened to also, for it does require a little hardening even to the toughest.

The hides are always brought down dry, or they would not be received. When they are taken from the animal, they have holes cut in the ends and are staked out, and thus dried in the sun without shrinking. They are then doubled once, lengthwise, with the hair side usually in, and sent down on mules or in carts and piled above high-water mark. And then we take them upon our heads, one at a time, or two if they are small, and wade out with them and throw them into the boat, which, as there are no wharves, we usually kept anchored by a small kedge, or killick, just outside of the surf. We all provided ourselves with thick Scotch caps, which would be soft to the head and at the same time protect it; for we soon found that however it might look or feel at first, the "head-work" was the only system for California. For besides that the seas, breaking high, often obliged us to carry the hides so in order to keep them dry, we found that as they were very large and heavy and nearly as stiff as boards, it was the only way that we could carry them with any convenience to ourselves. Some of the crew tried other expedients, saying that that looked too much like West India Negroes; but they all came to it at last. The great art is in getting them on the head. We had to take them from the ground, and as they were often very heavy, and as wide as the arms could stretch, and easily taken by the wind, we used to have some trouble with them. I have often been laughed at myself, and joined in laughing at others, pitching themselves down in the sand trying to swing a large hide up on their heads, or nearly blown over with one in a little gust of wind. The captain made it harder for us by telling us that it was "California-fashion" to carry two on the head at a time; and as he insisted upon it, and we did not wish to be outdone by other vessels, we carried two for the first few months; but after falling in with a few other "hide-droghers," and finding that they carried only one at a time, we "knocked off" the extra one, and thus made our duty somewhat easier.

After we had got our heads used to the weight, and had learned the true California style of "tossing a hide," we could carry off two or three hundred in a short time without much trouble; but it was always wet work, and if the beach was stony, bad for our feet—for we of course always went barefooted on this duty, as no shoes could stand such constant wetting with salt water. Then too, we had a long pull of three miles with a loaded boat, which often took a couple of hours.

We had now got well settled down into our harbor duties, which, as they are a good deal different from those at sea, it may be well enough to describe. In the first place, all hands are called at daylight, or rather—especially if the days are short—before day-light, as soon as the first gray of the morning. The cook makes his fire in the galley, the steward goes about his work in the cabin, and the crew rig the head pump and wash down the decks. The chief mate is always on deck, but takes no active part, all the duty coming upon the second mate, who has to roll up his trousers and paddle about decks barefooted, like the rest of the crew. The washing, swabbing, squilgeeing, etc. lasts, or is made to last, until eight o'clock, when breakfast is ordered, fore and aft. After breakfast, for which half an hour is allowed, the boats are lowered down and made fast astern, or out to the swinging booms, by guess-warps, and the crew are turned to upon their day's work. This is various, and its character depends upon circumstances. There is always more or less of boating in small boats; and if heavy goods are to be taken ashore, or hides are brought down to the beach for us, then all hands are sent ashore with an officer in the longboat. Then there is always a good deal to be done in the hold: goods to be broken out and cargo to be shifted to make room for hides, or to keep the trim of the vessel. In addition to this, the usual work upon the rigging must be going on. There is a good deal of the latter kind of work which can only be done when the vessel is in port—and then everything must be kept taut and in good order, spun yarn made, chafing gear repaired, and all the other ordinary work. The great difference between sea and harbor duty is in the division of time. Instead of having a watch on deck and a watch below, as at sea, all hands are at work together, except at mealtimes, from daylight till dark; and at night an anchor watch is kept, which consists of only two at a time, the whole crew taking turns. An hour is allowed for dinner, and at dark the decks are cleared up, the boats hoisted, supper ordered; and at eight, the lights put out, except in the binnacle, where the glass stands, and the anchor watch is set. Thus when at anchor the crew have more time at night (standing watch only about two hours) but have no time to themselves in the day, so that reading, mending clothes, etc., have to be put off until Sunday, which is usually given. Some religious captains give their crews Saturday afternoons to do their washing and mending in, so that they may have their Sundays free. This is a good arrangement, and does much toward creating the preference sailors usually show for religious vessels. We were well satisfied if we got Sunday to ourselves, for if any hides came down on that day, as was often the case when they were brought from a distance, we were obliged to bring them off, which usually took half a day,

and as we now lived on fresh beef, and ate one bullock a week,
the animal was almost always brought down on Sunday, and we
had to go ashore, kill it, dress it, and bring it aboard, which was
another interruption. Then too, our common day's work was protracted and made more fatiguing by hides coming down late in
the afternoon, which sometimes kept us at work in the surf by
starlight, with the prospect of pulling on board and stowing them
all away before supper.

But all these little vexations and labors would have been nothing—they would have been passed by as the common evils of a
sea life, which every sailor who is a man will go through without
complaint—were it not for the uncertainty, or worse than uncertainty, which hung over the nature and length of our voyage.
Here we were, in a little vessel with a small crew, on a half-
civilized coast at the ends of the earth, and with a prospect of
remaining an indefinite period, two or three years at the least.
When we left Boston we supposed that it was to be a voyage of
eighteen months, or two years at most; but upon arriving on the
coast, we learned something more of the trade, and found that
in the scarcity of hides, which was yearly greater and greater, it
would take us a year at least to collect our own cargo, besides
the passage out and home; and that we were also to collect a
cargo for a large ship belonging to the same firm which was soon
to come on the coast, and to which we were to act as tender. We
had heard rumors of such a ship to follow us, which had leaked
out from the captain and mate, but we passed them by as mere
"yarns" till our arrival, when they were confirmed by the letters
which we brought from the owners to their agent. The ship *California,* belonging to the same firm, had been nearly two years on
the coast, had collected a full cargo, and was now at San Diego,
from which port she was expected to sail in a few weeks for Boston; and we were to collect all the hides we could and deposit
them at San Diego, when the new ship, which would carry forty
thousand, was to be filled and sent home; and then we were to
begin anew and collect our own cargo. Here was a gloomy prospect before us indeed. The *California* had been twenty months
on the coast, and the *Lagoda,* a smaller ship, carrying only thirty-
one or thirty-two thousand, had been two years getting her cargo;
and we were to collect a cargo of forty thousand besides our

own, which would be twelve or fifteen thousand, and hides were said to be growing scarcer. Then too, this ship, which had been to us a worse phantom than any Flying Dutchman, was no phantom, or ideal thing, but had been reduced to a certainty—so much so that a name was given her, and it was said that she was to be the *Alert,* a well-known Indiaman which was expected in Boston in a few months when we sailed. There could be no doubt, and all looked black enough. Hints were thrown out about three years and four years—the older sailors said they never should see Boston again, but lay their bones in California—and a cloud seemed to hang over the whole voyage. Besides, we were not provided for so long a voyage, and clothes, and all sailors' necessaries, were excessively dear—300 or 400 per cent advance upon the Boston prices. This was bad enough for them, but still worse was it for me, who did not mean to be a sailor for life, having intended only to be gone eighteen months or two years. Three or four years would make me a sailor in every respect, mind and habits as well as body—nolens volens—and would put all my companions so far ahead of me that college and a profession would be in vain to think of; and I made up my mind that, feel as I might, a sailor I must be, and to be master of a vessel must be the height of my ambition.

Besides the length of the voyage and the hard and exposed life, we were at the ends of the earth, on a coast almost solitary, in a country where there is neither law nor gospel and where sailors are at their captain's mercy, there being no American consul, or anyone to whom a complaint could be made. We lost all interest in the voyage, cared nothing about the cargo, which we were only collecting for others, began to patch our clothes, and felt as though we were fixed beyond all hope of change.

In addition to, and perhaps partly as a consequence of, this state of things, there was trouble brewing on board the vessel. Our "mate" (as the first mate is always called, par excellence) was a worthy man—a more honest, upright, and kindhearted man I never saw—but he was too good for the mate of a merchantman. He was not the man to call a sailor a "son of a bitch," and knock him down with a handspike. He wanted the energy and spirit for such a voyage as ours, and for such a captain. Captain T— was a vigorous, energetic fellow. As sailors say, "he hadn't a lazy bone

in him." He was made of steel and whalebone. He was a man to
"toe the mark," and to make everyone else step up to it. During
all the time that I was with him I never saw him sit down on
deck. He was always active and driving, severe in his discipline,
and expected the same of his officers. The mate not being enough
of a "driver" for him, and being perhaps too easy with the crew,
he was dissatisfied with him, became suspicious that discipline
was getting relaxed, and began to interfere in everything. He
drew the reins taut, and as in all quarrels between officers the
sailors side with the one who treats them best, he became suspicious of the crew. He saw that everything went wrong—that nothing was done "with a will"—and in his attempt to remedy the
difficulty by severity he made everything worse. We were in
every respect unfortunately situated—captain, officers, and crew
entirely unfitted for one another—and every circumstance and
event was like a two-edged sword, and cut both ways. The length
of the voyage, which made us dissatisfied, made the captain at
the same time feel the necessity of order and strict discipline; and
the nature of the country, which caused us to feel that we had
nowhere to go for redress, but were entirely at the mercy of a
hard master, made the captain feel, on the other hand, that he
must depend entirely upon his own resources. Severity created
discontent, and signs of discontent provoked severity. Then too,
ill-treatment and dissatisfaction are no *"linimenta laborum,"* and
many a time have I heard the sailors say that they should not
mind the length of the voyage, and the hardships, if they were
only kindly treated, and if they could feel that something was
done to make things lighter and easier. We felt as though our
situation was a call upon our superiors to give us occasional re-
laxations, and to make our yoke easier. But the contrary policy
was pursued. We were kept at work all day when in port—which,
together with a watch at night, made us glad to turn in as soon
as we got below. Thus we got no time for reading, or—of more
importance to us—for washing and mending our clothes. And
then when we were at sea, sailing from port to port, instead of
giving us "watch and watch," as was the custom on board every
other vessel on the coast, we were all kept on deck and at work,
rain or shine, making spun yarn and rope and at other work in
good weather, and picking oakum when it was too wet for any-

thing else. All hands were called to "come up and see it rain," and kept on deck hour after hour in a drenching rain, standing round the deck so far apart as to prevent our talking with one another, with our tarpaulins and oilcloth jackets on, picking old rope to pieces, or laying up gaskets and robands. This was often done, too, when we were lying in port with two anchors down, and no necessity for more than one man on deck as a lookout. This is what is called "hazing" a crew, and "working their old iron up."

While lying at Santa Barbara, we encountered another southeaster; and like the first, it came on in the night, the great black clouds coming round from the southward, covering the mountain and hanging down over the town, appearing almost to rest on the roofs of the houses. We made sail, slipped our cable, cleared the point, and beat about for four days in the offing, under close sail, with continual rain and high seas and winds. No wonder, thought we, they have no rain in the other seasons, for enough seemed to have fallen in those four days to last through a common summer. On the fifth day it cleared up—after a few hours, as is usual, of rain coming down like a four hours' shower bath—and we found ourselves drifted nearly ten leagues from the anchorage; and having light head winds, we did not return until the sixth day. Having recovered our anchor, we made preparations for getting under way to go down to leeward. We had hoped to go directly to San Diego, and thus fall in with the *California* before she sailed for Boston; but our orders were to stop at an intermediate port called San Pedro, and as we were to lie there a week or two, and the *California* was to sail in a few days, we lost the opportunity. Just before sailing, the captain took on board a short, red-haired, round-shouldered, vulgar-looking fellow who had lost one eye and squinted with the other, and introducing him as "Mr." Russell, told us that he was an officer on board. This was too bad. We had lost overboard on the passage one of the best of our number, another had been taken from us and appointed clerk, and thus weakened and reduced, instead of shipping some hands to make our work easier, he had put another officer over us, to watch and drive us. We had now four officers, and only six in the forecastle. This was bringing her too much down by the stern for our comfort.

Leaving Santa Barbara, we coasted along down, the country appearing level or moderately uneven, and for the most part sandy and treeless, until, doubling a high, sandy point, we let go our anchor at a distance of three or three and a half miles from shore. It was like a vessel bound to Halifax coming to anchor on the Grand Banks; for the shore, being low, appeared to be at a greater distance than it actually was, and we thought we might as well have stayed at Santa Barbara and sent our boat down for the hides. The land was of a clayey consistency, and as far as the eye could reach entirely bare of trees and even shrubs; and there was no sign of a town—not even a house to be seen. What brought us into such a place we could not conceive. No sooner had we come to anchor than the slip rope, and the other preparations for southeasters, were got ready; and there was reason enough for it, for we lay exposed to every wind that could blow except the northwest, and that came over a flat country with a range of more than a league of water. As soon as everything was snug on board, the boat was lowered and we pulled ashore, our new officer, who had been several times in the port before, taking the place of steersman. As we drew in we found the tide low and the rocks and stones, covered with kelp and seaweed, lying bare for the distance of nearly an eighth of a mile. Picking our way barefooted over these, we came to what is called the landing place, at high-water mark. The soil was as it appeared at first, loose and clayey, and except the stalks of the mustard plant, there was no vegetation. Just in front of the landing, and immediately over it, was a small hill, which, from its being not more than thirty or forty feet high, we had not perceived from our anchorage. Over this hill we saw three men coming down, dressed partly like sailors and partly like Californians, one of them having on a pair of untanned leather trousers and a red-baize shirt. When they came down to us, we found that they were Englishmen, and they told us that they had belonged to a small Mexican brig which had been driven ashore here in a southeaster, and now lived in a small house just over the hill. Going up this hill with them, we saw, just behind it, a small, low building with one room containing a fireplace, cooking apparatus, etc., and the rest of it unfinished, and used as a place to store hides and goods. This, they told us, was built by some traders in the Pueblo (a town about thirty miles in the interior, to which this was the port), and used by them as a storehouse, and also as a lodging place when they came down to trade with the vessels. These three men were employed by them to keep the house in order, and to look out for the things stored in it. They said that they had been there nearly a year, had nothing to do most of the time, living on beef, hard bread, and frijoles (a peculiar kind of bean very abundant in California). The nearest house, they told us, was a rancho, or cattle farm, about three miles off; and one of them went up, at the request of our officer, to order a horse to be sent down, with which the agent, who was on board, might go up to the Pueblo. From one of them, who was an intelligent English sailor, I learned a good deal in a few minutes' conversation about the place, its trade, and the news from the southern ports. San Diego, he said, was about eighty miles to the leeward of San Pedro; that they had heard from there, by a Spaniard who came up on horseback, that the *California* had sailed for Boston, and that the *Lagoda*, which had been in San Pedro only a few weeks before, was taking in her cargo for Boston. The *Ayacucho* was also there, loading for Callao, and the little *Loriotte*, which had run directly down from Monterey, where we left her. San Diego, he told me, was a small, snug place, having very little trade but decidedly the best harbor on the coast, being completely landlocked, and the water as smooth as a duckpond. This was the depot for all the vessels engaged in the trade, each one having a large house there, built of rough boards, in which they stowed their hides as fast as they collected them in their trips up and down the coast, and when they had procured a full cargo, spent a few weeks there taking it in, smoking ship, supplying wood and water, and making other preparations for the voyage home. The *Lagoda* was now about this business. When we should be about it was more than I could tell—two years at least, I thought to myself.

I also learned, to my surprise, that the desolate-looking place we were in was the best place on the whole coast for hides. It was the only port for a distance of eighty miles, and about thirty miles in the interior was a fine plane country filled with herds of cattle, in the center of which was the Pueblo de los Angeles—the largest town in California—and several of the wealthiest missions, to all of which San Pedro was the seaport.

Having made our arrangements for a horse to take the agent to the Pueblo the next day, we picked our way again over the green, slippery rocks, and pulled aboard. By the time we reached the vessel, which was so far off that we could hardly see her in the increasing darkness, the boats were hoisted up, and the crew at supper. Going down into the forecastle, eating our supper, and lighting our cigars and pipes, we had, as usual, to tell all we had seen or heard ashore. We all agreed that it was the worst place we had seen yet, especially for getting off hides, and our lying-off at so great a distance looked as though it was bad for southeasters. After a few disputes as to whether we should have to carry our goods up the hill or not, we talked of San Diego, the probability of seeing the *Lagoda* before she sailed, etc., etc.

The next day we pulled the agent ashore, and he went up to visit the Pueblo and the neighboring missions; and in a few days, as the result of his labors, large oxcarts and droves of mules loaded with hides were seen coming over the flat country. We loaded our longboat with goods of all kinds, light and heavy, and pulled ashore. After landing and rolling them over the stones on the beach, we stopped, waiting for the carts to come down the hill and take them; but the captain soon settled the matter by ordering us to carry them all up to the top, saying that that was "California-fashion." So what the oxen would not do we were obliged to do. The hill was low, but steep, and the earth, being clayey and wet with the recent rains, was but bad holding ground for our feet. The heavy barrels and casks we rolled up with some difficulty, getting behind and putting our shoulders to them; now and then our feet, slipping, added to the danger of the casks rolling back upon us. But the greatest trouble was with the large boxes of sugar. These we had to place on oars, and lifting them up, rest the oars on our shoulders and creep slowly up the hill with the gait of a funeral procession. After an hour or two of hard work we got them all up, and found the carts standing full of hides, which we had to unload, and also to load again with our own goods, the lazy Indians, who came down with them, squatting down on their hams looking on, doing nothing, and when we asked them to help us, only shaking their heads, or drawling out "*No quiero.*"

Having loaded the carts, we started up the Indians, who went off, one on each side of the oxen, with long sticks sharpened at the end to punch them with. This is one of the means of saving labor in California—two Indians to two oxen. Now the hides were to be got down; and for this purpose we brought the boat round to a place where the hill was steeper, and threw them down, letting them slide over the slope. Many of them lodged, and we had to let ourselves down and set them a-going again, and in this way got covered with dust, and our clothes torn. After we had got them all down, we were obliged to take them on our heads and walk over the stones, and through the water to the boat. The water and the stones together would wear out a pair of shoes a day, and as shoes were very scarce and very dear, we were compelled to go barefooted. At night we went on board having had the hardest and most disagreeable day's work that we had yet experienced. For several days we were employed in this manner, until we had landed forty or fifty tons of goods and brought on board about two thousand hides, when the trade began to slacken, and we were kept at work on board during the latter part of the week, either in the hold or on the rigging. On Thursday night there was a violent blow from the northward, but as this was offshore, we had only to let go our other anchor and hold on. We were called up at night to send down the royal yards. It was as dark as a pocket, and the vessel pitching at her anchors. I went up to the fore, and my friend S— to the main, and we soon had them down "shipshape and Bristol-fashion"; for as we had now got used to our duty aloft, everything above the crosstrees was left to us, who were the youngest of the crew except one boy.

A Flogging · A Night on Shore · The State of Things on Board · San Diego

FOR SEVERAL DAYS the captain seemed very much out of humor. Nothing went right, or fast enough, for him. He quarreled with the cook and threatened to flog him for throwing wood on deck, and had a dispute with the mate about reeving a Spanish burton, the mate saying that he was right and had been taught how to do it by a man *who was a sailor!* This the captain took in dudgeon, and they were at swords' points at once. But his displeasure was chiefly turned against a large, heavy-molded fellow from the Middle States who was called Sam. This man hesitated in his speech, and was rather slow in his motions, but was a pretty good sailor, and always seemed to do his best; but the captain took a dislike to him, thought he was surly, and lazy—and "if you once give a dog a bad name," as the sailor phrase is, "he may as well jump overboard." The captain found fault with everything this man did, and hazed him for dropping a marlinespike from the main yard, where he was at work. This of course was an accident, but it was set down against him. The captain was on board all day Friday, and everything went on hard and disagreeably. "The more you drive a man, the less he will do" was as true with us as with any other people. We worked late Friday night, and were turned to early Saturday morning. About ten o'clock the captain ordered our new officer, Russell, who by this time had become thoroughly disliked by all the crew, to get the gig ready to take him ashore. John the Swede was sitting in the boat alongside, and Russell and myself were standing by the main hatchway waiting for the captain, who was

down in the hold, where the crew were at work, when we heard
his voice raised in violent dispute with somebody—whether it
was with the mate or one of the crew I could not tell—and then
came blows and scuffling. I ran to the side and beckoned to John,
who came up, and we leaned down the hatchway; and though
we could see no one, yet we knew that the captain had the advantage, for his voice was loud and clear:

"You see your condition! You see your condition! Will you ever
give me any more of your jaw?" No answer, and then came wres-
tling and heaving, as though the man was trying to turn him.
"You may as well keep still, for I have got you," said the captain.
Then came the question, "Will you ever give me any more of
your jaw?"

"I never gave you any, sir," said Sam, for it was his voice that
we heard, though low and half-choked.

"That's not what I ask you. Will you ever be impudent to me
again?"

"I never have been, sir," said Sam.

"Answer my question, or I'll make a spread eagle of you! I'll
flog you, by God."

"I'm no Negro slave," said Sam.

"Then I'll make you one," said the captain, and he came to the
hatchway and sprang on deck, threw off his coat, and rolling up
his sleeves, called out to the mate: "Seize that man up, Mr. A—!
Seize him up! Make a spread eagle of him! I'll teach you all who
is master aboard!"

The crew and officers followed the captain up the hatchway,
and after repeated orders the mate laid hold of Sam, who made
no resistance, and carried him to the gangway.

"What are you going to flog that man for, sir?" said John the
Swede to the captain.

Upon hearing this, the captain turned upon him, but knowing
him to be quick and resolute, he ordered the steward to bring the
irons, and calling upon Russell to help him, went up to John.

"Let me alone," said John. "I'm willing to be put in irons. You
need not use any force." He put out his hands, the captain slipped
the irons on, and sent him after to the quarter-deck. Sam by this
time was "seized up," as it is called; that is, placed against the
shrouds, with his wrists made fast to the shrouds, his jacket off,

and his back exposed. The captain stood on the break of the deck a few feet from him and a little raised, so as to have a good swing at him, and held in his hand the bight of a thick, strong rope. The officers stood round, and the crew grouped together in the waist. All these preparations made me feel sick and almost faint, angry and excited as I was. A man—a human being made in God's likeness—fastened up and flogged like a beast! A man too whom I had lived with and eaten with for months, and knew almost as well as a brother. The first and almost uncontrollable impulse was resistance. But what was to be done? The time for it had gone by. The two best men were fast, and there were only two beside myself and a small boy of ten or twelve years of age. And then there were (beside the captain) three officers, steward, agent, and clerk. But beside the numbers, what is there for sailors to do? If they resist, it is mutiny; and if they succeed and take the vessel, it is piracy. If they ever yield again, their punishment must come; and if they do not yield, they are pirates for life. If a sailor resist his commander, he resists the law, and piracy or submission are his only alternatives. Bad as it was, it must be borne. It is what a sailor ships for. Swinging the rope over his head, and bending his body so as to give it full force, the captain brought it down on the poor fellow's back. Once, twice—six times. "Will you ever give me any more of your jaw?" The man writhed with pain, but said not a word. Three times more. This was too much, and he muttered something which I could not hear. This brought as many more as the man could stand, when the captain ordered him to be cut down, and to go forward.

"Now for you," said the captain, making up to John and taking his irons off. As soon as he was loose, he ran forward to the forecastle. "Bring that man aft!" shouted the captain. The second mate, who had been a shipmate of John's, stood still in the waist, and the mate walked slowly forward; but our third officer, anxious to show his zeal, sprang forward over the windlass and laid hold of John; but he soon threw him from him. At this moment I would have given worlds for the power to help the poor fellow but it was all in vain. The captain stood on the quarter-deck, bareheaded, his eyes flashing with rage and his face as red as blood, swinging the rope and calling out to his officers: "Drag him aft!—Lay hold of him! I'll sweeten him!" etc., etc. The mate now

went forward and told John quietly to go aft and he, seeing resistance in vain, threw the blackguard third mate from him, said
he would go aft of himself, that they should not drag him, and
went up to the gangway and held out his hands. But as soon as
the captain began to make him fast, the indignity was too much,
and he began to resist; but the mate and Russell holding him, he
was soon seized up. When he was made fast, he turned to the
captain, who stood turning up his sleeves and getting ready for
the blow, and asked him what he was to be flogged for. "Have
I ever refused my duty, sir? Have you ever known me to hang
back, or to be insolent, or not to know my work?"

"No," said the captain, "it is not that that I flog you for. I flog
you for your interference—for asking questions."

"Can't a man ask a question here without being flogged?"

"No!" shouted the captain. "Nobody shall open his mouth
aboard this vessel but myself," and began laying the blows on
his back, swinging half-round between each blow, to give it full
effect. As he went on his passion increased, and he danced about
the deck, calling out as he swung the rope: "If you want to know
what I flog you for, I'll tell you. It's because I like to do it—because I like to do it!—It suits me! That's what I do it for!"

The man writhed under the pain until he could endure it no
longer, when he called out, with an exclamation more common
among foreigners than with us, "Oh, Jesus Christ! Oh, Jesus
Christ!"

"Don't call on Jesus Christ," shouted the captain. *"He can't
help you. Call on Captain T—.* He's the man! He can help you!
Jesus Christ can't help you now!"

At these words, which I never shall forget, my blood ran cold.
I could look on no longer. Disgusted, sick, and horror-struck, I
turned away and leaned over the rail and looked down into the
water. A few rapid thoughts of my own situation, and of the
prospect of future revenge, crossed my mind; but the falling of
the blows and the cries of the man called me back at once. At
length they ceased, and turning round, I found that the mate, at
a signal from the captain, had cut him down. Almost doubled up
with pain, the man walked slowly forward, and went down into
the forecastle. Everyone else stood still at his post, while the captain, swelling with rage and with the importance of his achieve-

ment, walked the quarter-deck, and at each turn as he came forward calling out to us: "You see your condition! You see where I've got you all, and you know what to expect!—You've been mistaken in me—you didn't know what I was! Now you know what I am! —I'll make you toe the mark, every soul of you, or I'll flog you all, fore and aft, from the boy up!—You've got a driver over you! Yes, a *slave-driver—a Negro-driver!* I'll see who'll tell me he isn't a Negro slave!" With this and the like matter, equally calculated to quiet us and to allay any apprehensions of future trouble, he entertained us for about ten minutes, when he went below. Soon after, John came aft, with his bare back covered with stripes and wales in every direction and dreadfully swollen, and asked the steward to ask the captain to let him have some salve, or balsam, to put on it. "No," said the captain, who heard him from below. "Tell him to put his shirt on—that's the best thing for him—and pull me ashore in the boat. Nobody is going to lay up on board this vessel." He then called to Mr. Russell to take those two men and two others in the boat and pull him ashore. I went for one. The two men could hardly bend their backs, and the captain called to them to "give way, give way!" but finding they did their best, he let them alone. The agent was in the stern sheets, but during the whole pull—a league or more—not a word was spoken. We landed; the captain, agent, and officer went up to the house, and left us with the boat. I, and the man with me, stayed near the boat, while John and Sam walked slowly away and sat down on the rocks. They talked sometime together, but at length separated, each sitting alone. I had some fears of John. He was a foreigner, and violently tempered, and under suffering; and he had his knife with him and the captain was to come down alone to the boat. But nothing happened, and we went quietly on board. The captain was probably armed, and if either of them had lifted a hand against him, they would have had nothing before them but flight, and starvation in the woods of California or capture by the soldiers and Indian bloodhounds, whom the offer of twenty dollars would have set upon them.

After the day's work was done, we went down into the forecastle and ate our plain supper, but not a word was spoken. It was Saturday night, but there was no song—no "sweethearts and wives." A gloom was over everything. The two men lay in their

berths groaning with pain, and we all turned in, but for myself, not to sleep. A sound coming now and then from the berths of the two men showed that they were awake, as awake they must have been, for they could hardly lie in one posture a moment. The dim, swinging lamp of the forecastle shed its light over the dark hole in which we lived, and many and various reflections and purposes coursed through my mind. I thought of our situation, living under a tyranny; of the character of the country we were in; of the length of the voyage, and of the uncertainty attending our return to America; and then, if we should return, of the prospect of obtaining justice and satisfaction for these poor men; and vowed that if God should ever give me the means, I would do something to redress the grievances and relieve the sufferings of that poor class of beings of whom I then was one.

The next day was Sunday. We worked as usual, washing decks, etc., until breakfasttime. After breakfast we pulled the captain ashore, and finding some hides there which had been brought down the night before, he ordered me to stay ashore and watch them, saying that the boat would come again before night. They left me, and I spent a quiet day on the hill, eating dinner with the three men at the little house. Unfortunately they had no books, and after talking with them and walking about, I began to grow tired of doing nothing. The little brig, the home of so much hardship and suffering, lay in the offing, almost as far as one could see; and the only other thing which broke the surface of the great bay was a small, desolate-looking island, steep and conical, of a clayey soil and without the sign of vegetable life upon it, yet which had a peculiar and melancholy interest to me, for on the top of it were buried the remains of an Englishman, the commander of a small merchant brig, who died while lying in this port. It was always a solemn and interesting spot to me. There it stood, desolate and in the midst of desolation, and there were the remains of one who died and was buried alone and friendless. Had it been a common burying place, it would have been nothing. The single body corresponded well with the solitary character of everything around. It was the only thing in California from which I could ever extract anything like poetry. Then too, the man died far from home, without a friend near him—by poison, it was suspected, and no one to inquire into it—

and without proper funeral rites, the mate (as I was told) glad
to have him out of the way, hurrying him up the hill and into the
ground without a word or a prayer.

I looked anxiously for a boat during the latter part of the afternoon, but none came until toward sundown, when I saw a speck
on the water, and as it drew near I found it was the gig, with the
captain. The hides, then, were not to go off. The captain came
up the hill with a man bringing my monkey jacket and a blanket.
He looked pretty black, but inquired whether I had enough to
eat, told me to make a house out of the hides and keep myself
warm, as I should have to sleep there among them and to keep
good watch over them. I got a moment to speak to the man who
brought my jacket.

"How do things go aboard?" said I.

"Bad enough," said he. "Hard work and not a kind word
spoken."

"What," said I, "have you been at work all day?"

"Yes! No more Sunday for us. Everything has been moved in
the hold, from stem to stern and from the waterways to the keelson."

I went up to the house to supper. We had frijoles (the perpetual food of the Californians, but which when well cooked are
the best beans in the world), coffee made of burnt wheat, and
hard bread. After our meal the three men sat down by the light
of a tallow candle, with a pack of greasy Spanish cards, to the
favorite game of *"treinte-uno,"* a sort of Spanish "everlasting." I
left them and went out to take up my bivouac among the hides.
It was now dark, the vessel was hidden from sight, and except the
three men in the house, there was not a living soul within a
league. The coatis (a wild animal of a nature and appearance
between that of the fox and the wolf) set up their sharp, quick
bark, and two owls, at the end of two distant points running out
into the bay on different sides of the hill where I lay, kept up
their alternate dismal notes. I had heard the sound before at
night, but did not know what it was until one of the men who
came down to look at my quarters told me it was the owl. Mellowed by the distance, and heard alone at night, I thought it was
the most melancholy, boding sound I had ever heard. Through
nearly all the night they kept it up, answering one another slowly

at regular intervals. This was relieved by the noisy coatis, some of which came quite near to my quarters, and were not very pleasant neighbors. The next morning before sunrise the longboat came ashore, and the hides were taken off.

We lay at San Pedro about a week, engaged in taking off hides and in other labors which had now become our regular duties. I spent one more day on the hill watching a quantity of hides and goods, and this time succeeded in finding a part of a volume of Scott's *Pirate* in a corner of the house; but it failed me at a most interesting moment, and I betook myself to my acquaintances on shore, and from them learned a good deal about the customs of the country, the harbors, etc. This, they told me, was a worse harbor than Santa Barbara for southeasters, the bearing of the headland being a point and a half more to windward, and it being so shallow that the sea broke often as far out as where we lay at anchor. The gale from which we slipped at Santa Barbara had been so bad a one here that the whole bay for a league out was filled with the foam of the breakers, and seas actually broke over the dead man's island.

On board the *Pilgrim* everything went on regularly, each one trying to get along as smoothly as possible; but the comfort of the voyage was evidently at an end. "That is a long lane which has no turning"—"Every dog must have his day, and mine will come by and by"—and the like proverbs were occasionally quoted; but no one spoke of any probable end to the voyage, or of Boston, or anything of the kind. Or if he did, it was only to draw out the perpetual surly reply from his shipmate: "Boston, is it? You may thank your stars if you ever see that place. You had better have your back sheathed, and your head coppered, and your feet shod, and make out your log for California for life!" Or else something of this kind: "Before you get to Boston the hides will wear all the hair off your head, and you'll take up all your wages in clothes, and won't have enough left to buy a wig with!"

The flogging was seldom if ever alluded to by us in the forecastle. If anyone was inclined to talk about it, the others, with a delicacy which I hardly expected to find among them, always stopped him, or turned the subject. But the behavior of the two men who were flogged toward one another showed a delicacy and a sense of honor which would have been worthy of admiration in the highest walks of life. Sam knew that the other had suffered solely on his account, and in all his complaints he said that if he alone had been flogged, it would have been nothing; but that he never could see that man without thinking what had been the means of bringing that disgrace upon him. And John never, by word or deed, let anything escape him to remind the other that it was by interfering to save his shipmate that he had suffered.

Having got all our spare room filled with hides, we hove up our anchor and made sail for San Diego. In no operation can the disposition of a crew be discovered better than in getting under way. Where things are done "with a will," everyone is like a cat aloft: sails are loosed in an instant, each one lays out his strength on his handspike and the windlass goes briskly round with the loud cry of "Yo heave ho! Heave and pawl! Heave hearty ho!" But with us at this time it was all dragging work. No one went aloft beyond his ordinary gait, and the chain came slowly in over the windlass. The mate, between the knightheads, exhausted all his official rhetoric in calls of "Heave with a will!"—"Heave hearty, men!—Heave hearty!"—"Heave and raise the dead!"—"Heave, and away!" etc., etc.; but it would not do. Nobody broke his back or his handspike by his efforts. And when the cat-tackle fall was strung along, and all hands—cook, steward, and all—laid hold to cat the anchor, instead of the lively song of "Cheerily, men!" in which all hands join in the chorus, we pulled a long, heavy, silent pull, and—as sailors say a song is as good as ten men—the anchor came to the cathead pretty slowly. "Give us 'Cheerily!'" said the mate, but there was no "cheerily" for us, and we did without it. The captain walked the quarter-deck and said not a word. He must have seen the change, but there was nothing which he could notice officially.

We sailed leisurely down the coast before a light fair wind, keeping the land well aboard, and saw two other missions looking like blocks of white plaster shining in the distance, one of which, situated on the top of a high hill, was San Juan Campestrano, under which vessels sometimes come to anchor in the summer season, and take off hides. The most distant one was San Luis Rey, which the third mate said was only fifteen miles from

San Diego. At sunset on the second day we had a large and well-wooded headland directly before us, behind which lay the little harbor of San Diego. We were becalmed off this point all night, but the next morning, which was Saturday, the fourteenth of March, having a good breeze, we stood round the point and hauling our wind, brought the little harbor, which is rather the outlet of a small river, right before us. Everyone was anxious to get a view of the new place. A chain of high hills, beginning at the point (which was on our larboard hand, coming in), protected the harbor on the north and west, and ran off into the interior as far as the eye could reach. On the other sides, the land was low, and green, but without trees. The entrance is so narrow as to admit but one vessel at a time, the current swift, and the channel runs so near to a low stony point that the ship's sides appeared almost to touch it. There was no town in sight, but on the smooth sand beach abreast, and within a cable's length of which three vessels lay moored, were four large houses—built of rough boards and looking like the great barns in which ice is stored on the borders of the large ponds near Boston—with piles of hides standing round them, and men in red shirts and large straw hats walking in and out of the doors. These were the hide houses. Of the vessels, one, a short, clumsy little hermaphrodite brig, we recognized as our old acquaintance the *Loriotte;* another, with sharp bows and raking masts, newly painted and tarred and glittering in the morning sun, with the blood-red banner and cross of St. George at her peak, was the handsome *Ayacucho.* The third was a large ship with topgallant masts housed and sails unbent, and looking as rusty and worn as two years' hide-droghing could make her. This was the *Lagoda.* As we drew near, carried rapidly along by the current, we overhauled our chain and clewed up the topsails. "Let go the anchor!" said the captain; but either there was not chain enough forward of the windlass, or the anchor went down foul, or we had too much headway on, for it did not bring us up. "Pay out chain!" shouted the captain, and we gave it to her; but it would not do. Before the other anchor could be let go, we drifted down, broadside on, and went smash into the *Lagoda.* Her crew were at breakfast in the forecastle, and the cook, seeing us coming, rushed out of his galley and called up the officers and men.

Fortunately, no great harm was done. Her jib boom ran between our fore and main masts, carrying away some of our rigging and breaking down the rail. She lost her martingale. This brought us up, and as they paid out chain, we swung clear of them and let go the other anchor; but this had as bad luck as the first, for before anyone perceived it, we were drifting onto the *Loriotte.* The captain now gave out his orders rapidly and fiercely, sheeting home the topsails and backing and filling the sails, in hope of starting or clearing the anchors; but it was all in vain, and he sat down on the rail taking it very leisurely and calling out to Captain Nye that he was coming to pay him a visit. We drifted fairly into the *Loriotte,* her larboard bow into our starboard quarter, carrying away a part of our starboard-quarter railing, and breaking off her larboard bumpkin and one or two stanchions above the deck. We saw our handsome sailor Jackson on the forecastle with the Sandwich Islanders, working away to get us clear. After paying out chain, we swung clear, but our anchors were no doubt afoul of hers. We manned the windlass, and hove and hove away, but to no purpose. Sometimes we got a little on the cable, but a good surge would take it all back again. We now began to drift down toward the *Ayacucho,* when her boat put off and brought her commander, Captain Wilson, on board. He was a short, active, well-built man between fifty and sixty years of age, and being nearly thirty years older than our captain, and a thorough seaman, he did not hesitate to give his advice; and from giving advice he gradually came to taking the command, ordering us when to heave and when to pawl, and backing and filling the topsails, setting and taking in jib and trysail whenever he thought best. Our captain gave a few orders, but as Wilson generally countermanded them, saying in an easy, fatherly kind of way, "Oh no, Captain T—, you don't want the jib on her!" or, "It isn't time yet to heave!" he soon gave it up. We had no objections to this state of things, for Wilson was a kind old man, and had an encouraging and pleasant way of speaking to us which made everything go easily. After two or three hours of constant labor at the windlass, heaving and "Yoho"-ing with all our might, we brought up an anchor with the *Loriotte's* small bower fast to it. Having cleared this and let it go, and cleared our hawse, we soon got our other anchor, which had dragged half over the harbor. "Now," said Wilson, "I'll find you a good berth," and setting both the topsails, he carried us down and brought us to anchor in handsome style directly abreast of the hide house which we were to use. Having done this, he took his leave, while we furled the sails, and got our breakfast, which was welcome to us, for we had worked hard and it was nearly twelve o'clock. After breakfast, and until night, we were employed in getting out the boats and mooring ship.

After supper, two of us took the captain on board the *Lagoda*. As he came alongside he gave his name, and the mate, in the gangway, called out to the captain down the companionway, "Captain T— has come aboard, sir!" "Has he brought his brig with him?" said the rough old fellow, in a tone which made itself heard fore and aft. This mortified our captain a little, and it became a standing joke among us for the rest of the voyage. The captain went down into the cabin, and we walked forward and put our heads down the forecastle, where we found the men at supper. "Come down, shipmates! Come down!" said they as soon as they saw us; and we went down, and found a large, high forecastle, well lighted; and a crew of twelve or fourteen men eating out of their kids and pans, and drinking their tea, and talking and laughing, all as independent and easy as so many "wood-sawyer's clerks." This looked like comfort and enjoyment, compared with the dark little forecastle and scanty, discontented crew of the brig. It was Saturday night; they had got through their work for the week, and being snugly moored, had nothing to do until Monday again. After two years' hard service, they had seen the worst, and all, of California—had got their cargo nearly stowed, and expected to sail in a week or two for Boston. We spent an hour or more with them, talking over California matters, until the word was passed, "Pilgrims, away!" and we went back with our captain. They were a hardy but intelligent crew, a little roughened, and their clothes patched and old from California wear—all able seamen, and between the ages of twenty and thirty-five. They inquired about our vessel, the usage, etc., and were not a little surprised at the story of the flogging. They said there were often difficulties in vessels on the coast, and sometimes knockdowns and fightings, but they had never heard before of a regular seizing-up and flogging. "Spread eagles" were a new kind of bird in California.

Sunday, they said, was always given in San Diego, both at the hide houses and on board the vessels, a large number usually going up to the town on liberty. We learned a good deal from them about curing and stowing of hides, etc., and they were anxious to have the latest news (seven months old) from Boston. One of their first inquiries was for Father Taylor, the seamen's preacher in Boston. Then followed the usual strain of conversation, inquiries, stories, and jokes which one must always hear in a ship's forecastle, but which are perhaps, after all, no worse, nor indeed more gross, than that of many well-dressed gentlemen at their clubs.

Liberty Day on Shore

T HE NEXT DAY being Sunday, after washing and clearing decks and getting breakfast, the mate came forward with leave for one watch to go ashore on liberty. We drew lots, and it fell to the larboard, which I was in. Instantly all was preparation. Buckets of fresh water (which we were allowed in port) and soap were put in use; go-ashore jackets and trousers got out and brushed; pumps, neckerchiefs, and hats overhauled; one lending to another, so that among the whole each one got a good fit-out. A boat was called to pull the "liberty men" ashore, and we sat down in the stern sheets "as big as pay passengers," and jumping ashore, set out on our walk for the town, which was nearly three miles off.

It is a pity that some other arrangement is not made in merchant vessels with regard to the liberty day. When in port, the crews are kept at work all the week, and the only day they are allowed for rest or pleasure is the Sabbath; and unless they go ashore on that day they cannot go at all. I have heard of a religious captain who gave his crew liberty on Saturdays after twelve o'clock. This would be a good plan, if shipmasters would bring themselves to give their crews so much time. For young sailors especially, many of whom have been brought up with a regard for the sacredness of the day, this strong temptation to break it is exceedingly injurious. As it is, it can hardly be expected that a crew on a long and hard voyage will refuse a few hours of freedom from toil and the restraints of a vessel, and an opportunity to tread the ground and see the sights of society and humanity, because it is on a Sunday. It is too much like escaping from prison, or being drawn out of a pit, on the Sabbath day.

I shall never forget the delightful sensation of being in the open air, with the birds singing around me, and escaped from the confinement, labor, and strict rule of a vessel—of being once

more in my life, though only for a day, my own master. A sailor's
liberty is but for a day, yet while it lasts it is perfect. He is under no one's eye, and can do whatever, and go wherever, he
pleases. This day, for the first time, I may truly say, in my whole
life, I felt the meaning of a term which I had often heard—the
sweets of liberty. My friend S— was with me, and turning our
backs on the vessels, we walked slowly along, talking of the
pleasure of being our own masters, of the times past, when we
were free and in the midst of friends in America, and of the prospect of our return; and planning where we would go, and what
we would do, when we reached home. It was wonderful how the
prospect brightened, and how short and tolerable the voyage
appeared, when viewed in this new light. Things looked differ-
ently from what they did when we talked them over in the little
dark forecastle the night after the flogging at San Pedro. It is not
the least of the advantages of allowing sailors occasionally a day
of liberty that it gives them a spring, and makes them feel cheerful and independent, and leads them insensibly to look on the
bright side of everything for some time after.

S— and myself determined to keep as much together as possible, though we knew that it would not do to "cut" our shipmates;
for, knowing our birth and education, they were a little suspicious
that we would try to put on the gentleman when we got ashore
and would be ashamed of their company, and this won't do with
Jack. When the voyage is at an end, you may do as you please,
but so long as you belong to the same vessel, you must be a shipmate to him on shore or he will not be a shipmate to you on
board. Being forewarned of this before I went to sea, I took no
"long togs" with me, and being dressed like the rest in white duck
trousers, blue jacket, and straw hat, which would prevent my going in better company, and showing no disposition to avoid them,
I set all suspicion at rest. Our crew fell in with some who belonged to the other vessels and, sailorlike, steered for the first
grogshop. This was a small mud building of only one room in
which were liquors, dry and West India goods, shoes, bread,
fruits, and everything which is vendible in California. It was kept
by a Yankee, a one-eyed man who belonged formerly to Fall
River, came out to the Pacific in a whale ship, left her at the
Sandwich Islands, and came to California and set up a *"pulperia."*

S— and I followed in our shipmates' wake, knowing that to refuse
to drink with them would be the highest affront, but determining
to slip away at the first opportunity. It is the universal custom
with sailors for each one, in his turn, to treat the whole, calling
for a glass all round and obliging everyone who is present, even
to the keeper of the shop, to take a glass with him. When we first
came in, there was some dispute between our crew and the others
whether the newcomers or the old California rangers should treat
first; but it being settled in favor of the latter, each of the crews
of the other vessels treated all round in their turn, and as there
were a good many present (including some "loafers" who had
dropped in, knowing what was going on, to take advantage of
Jack's hospitality) and the liquor was a real (12½ cents) a glass,
it made somewhat of a hole in their lockers. It was now our ship's
turn, and S— and I, anxious to get away, stepped up to call for
glasses; but we soon found that we must go in order—the oldest
first, for the old sailors did not choose to be preceded by a couple
of youngsters, and bon gré, mal gré, we had to wait our turn,
with the twofold apprehension of being too late for our horses
and of getting "corned"; for drink you must, every time, and if
you drink with one and not with another, it is always taken as
an insult.

Having at length gone through our turns and acquitted ourselves of all obligations, we slipped out and went about among
the houses endeavoring to get horses for the day, so that we
might ride round and see the country. At first we had but little
success, all that we could get out of the lazy fellows in reply to
our questions being the eternal drawling "*Quien sabe?*" ("Who
knows?"), which is an answer to all questions. After several efforts, we at length fell in with a little Sandwich Island boy who
belonged to Captain Wilson of the *Ayacucho,* and was well acquainted in the place; and he, knowing where to go, soon procured us two horses, ready saddled and bridled, each with a
lasso coiled over the pommel. These we were to have all day,
with the privilege of riding them down to the beach at night, for
a dollar, which we had to pay in advance. Horses are the cheapest
thing in California, the very best not being worth more than ten
dollars apiece, and very good ones being often sold for three and
four. In taking a day's ride, you pay for the use of the saddle,

and for the labor and trouble of catching the horses. If you bring
the saddle back safe, they care but little what becomes of the
horse. Mounted on our horses, which were spirited beasts—and
which, by the way, in this country are always steered by pressing
the contrary rein against the neck, and not by pulling on the bit—
we started off on a fine run over the country. The first place we
went to was the old ruinous presidio, which stands on a rising
ground near the village, which it overlooks. It is built in the form
of an open square, like all the other presidios, and was in a most
ruinous state with the exception of one side, in which the commandant lived with his family. There were only two guns, one of
which was spiked and the other had no carriage. Twelve half-
clothed and half-starved-looking fellows composed the garrison,
and they, it was said, had not a musket apiece. The small settlement lay directly below the fort, composed of about forty dark-
brown-looking huts, or houses, and two larger ones, plastered,
which belonged to two of the *gente de razón*. This town is not
more than half as large as Monterey or Santa Barbara, and has
little or no business. From the presidio, we rode off in the direction of the mission, which we were told was three miles distant.
The country was rather sandy, and there was nothing for miles
which could be called a tree, but the grass grew green and rank
and there were many bushes and thickets, and the soil is said to
be good. After a pleasant ride of a couple of miles, we saw the
white walls of the mission, and fording a small river, we came
directly before it. The mission is built of mud, or rather of the
unburned bricks of the country, and plastered. There was something decidedly striking in its appearance: a number of irregular
buildings, connected with one another and disposed in the form
of a hollow square, with a church at one end rising above the
rest, with a tower containing five belfries, in each of which hung
a large bell, and with an immense rusty iron cross at the top. Just
outside of the buildings, and under the walls, stood twenty or
thirty small huts built of straw and of the branches of trees,
grouped together, in which a few Indians lived under the protection and in the service of the mission.

Entering a gateway, we rode into the open square, in which
the stillness of death reigned. On one side was the church; on another, a range of high buildings with grated windows; a third

was a range of smaller buildings, or offices; and the fourth seemed to be little more than a high connecting wall. Not a living creature could we see. We rode twice round the square, in the hope of waking up someone, and in one circuit saw a tall monk with shaven head, sandals, and the dress of the Gray Friars pass rapidly through a gallery, but he disappeared without noticing us. After two circuits, we stopped our horses, and saw at last a man show himself in front of one of the small buildings. We rode up to him, and found him dressed in the common dress of the country, with a silver chain round his neck, supporting a large bunch of keys. From this we took him to be the steward of the mission, and addressing him as "*Mayordomo,*" received a low bow and an invitation to walk into his room. Making our horses fast, we went in. It was a plain room, containing a table, three or four chairs, a small picture or two of some saint, or miracle, or martyrdom, and a few dishes and glasses. "*Hay algunas cosas a comer?*" said I. "*Si, señor!*" said he. "*Que gusta usted?*" I mentioned frijoles, which I knew they must have if they had nothing else, and beef and bread, and a hint for wine, if they had any. He went off to another building, across the court, and returned in a few moments with a couple of Indian boys bearing dishes and a decanter of wine. The dishes contained baked meats, frijoles stewed with peppers and onions, boiled eggs, and California flour baked into a kind of macaroni. These, together with the wine, made the most sumptuous meal we had eaten since we left Boston, and compared with the fare we had lived on for seven months, it was a regal banquet. After dispatching our meal, we took out some money and asked him how much we were to pay. He shook his head and crossed himself, saying that it was charity—that the Lord gave it to us. Knowing the amount of this to be that he did not sell, but was willing to receive a present, we gave him ten or twelve reals, which he pocketed with admirable nonchalance, saying, "*Dios se lo pague.*" Taking leave of him, we rode out to the Indians' huts. The little children were running about among the huts stark-naked, and the men were not much better; but the women had generally coarse gowns of a sort of tow cloth. The men are employed most of the time in tending the cattle of the mission, and in working in the garden, which is a very large one, including several acres and filled, it is said, with the best fruits

of the climate. The language of these people, which is spoken by all the Indians of California, is the most brutish and inhuman language, without any exception, that I ever heard, or that could well be conceived of. It is a complete "slabber." The words fall off the ends of their tongues, and a continual "slabbering" sound is made in the cheeks, outside of the teeth. It cannot have been the language of Montezuma and the independent Mexicans.

Here among the huts we saw the oldest man that I had ever seen, and indeed I never supposed that a person could retain life and exhibit such marks of age. He was sitting out in the sun, leaning against the side of a hut; and his legs and arms, which were bare, were of a dark-red color, the skin withered and shrunk up like burnt leather, and the limbs not larger round than those of a boy of five years. He had a few gray hairs, which were tied together at the back of his head; and he was so feeble that when we came up to him, he raised his hands slowly to his face, and taking hold of his lids with his fingers, lifted them up to look at us, and being satisfied, let them drop again. All command over the lid seemed to have gone. I asked his age, but could get no answer but *"Quien sabe?"* and they probably did not know the age.

Leaving the mission, we returned to the village, going nearly all the way on a full run. The California horses have no medium gait which is pleasant between walking and running; for as there are no streets and parades, they have no need of the genteel trot, and their riders usually keep them at the top of their speed until they are tired, and then let them rest themselves by walking. The fine air of the afternoon; the rapid rate of the animals, who seemed almost to fly over the ground, and the excitement and novelty of the motion to us, who had been so long confined on shipboard, were exhilarating beyond expression, and we felt willing to ride all day long. Coming into the village, we found things looking very lively. The Indians, who always have a holiday on Sunday, were engaged at playing a kind of running game of ball on a level piece of ground near the houses. The old ones sat down in a ring, looking on, while the young ones—men, boys, and girls —were chasing the ball, and throwing it with all their might. Some of the girls ran like greyhounds. At every accident, or remarkable feat, the old people set up a deafening screaming and clapping of hands. Several bluejackets were reeling about among the houses, which showed that the *pulperias* had been well patronized. One or two of the sailors had got on horseback, but being rather indifferent horsemen, and the Spaniards having given them vicious horses, they were soon thrown, much to the amusement of the people. A half-dozen Sandwich Islanders from the hide houses and the two brigs, who are bold riders, were dashing about on the full gallop, hallooing and laughing like so many wild men.

It was now nearly sundown, and S— and myself went into a house and sat quietly down to rest ourselves before going down to the beach. Several people soon collected to see *"los Ingles marineros,"* and one of them—a young woman—took a great fancy to my pocket handkerchief, which was a large silk one that I had before going to sea, and a handsomer one than they had been in the habit of seeing. Of course I gave it to her, which brought us into high favor, and we had a present of some pears and other fruits, which we took down to the beach with us. When we came to leave the house, we found that our horses, which we left tied at the door, were both gone. We had paid for them to ride down to the beach, but they were not to be found. We went to the man of whom we hired them, but he only shrugged his shoulders, and to our question, "Where are the horses?" only answered, *"Quien sabe?"* But as he was very easy, and made no inquiries for the saddles, we saw that he knew very well where they were. After a little trouble, determined not to walk down—a distance of three miles—we procured two, at four reals apiece, with an Indian boy to run on behind and bring them back. Determined to have "the go" out of the horses for our trouble, we went down at full speed, and were on the beach in fifteen minutes. Wishing to make our liberty last as long as possible, we rode up and down among the hide houses, amusing ourselves with seeing the men as they came down (it was now dusk), some on horseback and others on foot. The Sandwich Islanders rode down, and were in "high snuff." We inquired for our shipmates, and were told that two of them had started on horseback and been thrown or had fallen off, and were seen heading for the beach but steering pretty wild, and by the looks of things, would not be down much before midnight.

The Indian boys having arrived, we gave them our horses, and having seen them safely off, hailed for a boat and went aboard. Thus ended our first liberty day on shore. We were well tired, but had had a good time, and were more willing to go back to our old duties. About midnight we were waked up by our two watchmates, who had come aboard in high dispute. It seems they had started to come down on the same horse, double-backed, and each was accusing the other of being the cause of his fall. They soon, however, turned in and fell asleep, and probably forgot all about it, for the next morning the dispute was not renewed.

San Diego · A Desertion · San Pedro Again · Beating Upcoast

THE NEXT SOUND that we heard was "All hands ahoy!" and looking up the scuttle, saw that it was just daylight. Our liberty had now truly taken flight, and with it we laid away our pumps, stockings, blue jackets, neckerchiefs, and other go-ashore paraphernalia, and putting on old duck trousers, red shirts, and Scotch caps, began taking out and landing our hides. For three days we were hard at work from the gray of the morning until starlight, with the exception of a short time allowed for meals. For landing and taking on board hides, San Diego is decidedly the best place in California. The harbor is small and landlocked; there is no surf; the vessels lie within a cable's length of the beach; and the beach itself is smooth, hard sand, without rocks or stones. For these reasons, it is used by all the vessels in the trade as a depot; and indeed it would be impossible, when loading with the cured hides for the passage home, to take them on board at any of the open ports without getting them wet in the surf, which would spoil them. We took possession of one of the hide houses, which belonged to our firm and had been used by the *California*. It was built to hold forty thousand hides, and we had the pleasing prospect of filling it before we could leave the coast; and toward this our thirty-five hundred which we brought down with us would do but little. There was not a man on board who did not go a dozen times into the house and make some calculation of the time it would require.

The hides as they come rough and uncured from the vessels are piled up outside of the houses, whence they are taken and carried through a regular process of pickling, drying, cleaning, etc., and stowed away in the house, ready to be put on board. This process is necessary in order that they may keep during a long voyage and in warm latitudes. For the purpose of curing and taking care of these hides, an officer and a part of the crew of each vessel are usually left ashore; and it was for this business, we found, that our new officer had joined us. As soon as the hides were landed, he took charge of the house, and the captain intended to leave two or three of us with him, hiring Sandwich Islanders to take our places on board. But he could not get any Sandwich Islanders to go, though he offered them fifteen dollars a month; for the report of the flogging had got among them, and he was called *"aole maikai"* ("no good"), and that was an end of the business. They were, however, willing to work on shore, and four of them were hired and put with "Mr." Russell to cure the hides.

After landing our hides, we next sent ashore all our spare spars and rigging, all the stores which we did not want to use in the course of one trip to windward, and in fact everything which we could spare, so as to make room for hides—among other things, the pigsty, and with it "Old Bess." This was an old sow that we had brought from Boston, and which lived to get round Cape Horn, where all the other pigs died from cold and wet. Report said that she had been a Canton voyage before. She had been the pet of the cook during the whole passage, and he had fed her with the best of everything, and taught her to know his voice, and to do a number of strange tricks for his amusement. Tom Cringle says that no one can fathom a Negro's affection for a pig, and I believe he is right, for it almost broke our poor darky's heart when he heard that Bess was to be taken ashore, and that he was to have the care of her no more during the whole voyage. He had depended upon her as a solace during the long trips up and down the coast. "Obey orders, if you break owners!" said he. "Break *hearts*," he meant to have said, and lent a hand to get her over the side, trying to make it as easy for her as possible. We got a whip up on the main yard, and hooking it to a strap round her body, swayed away, and giving a wink to one another, ran her chock up to the yard. " 'Vast there! 'Vast!" said the mate —"none of your skylarking! Lower away!" But he evidently en-

joyed the joke. The pig squealed like the "crack of doom," and
tears stood in the poor darky's eyes, and he muttered something
about having no pity on a dumb beast. "*Dumb* beast!" said Jack.
"If she's what you call a dumb beast, then my eyes ain't mates."
This produced a laugh from all but the cook. He was too intent
upon seeing her safe in the boat. He watched her all the way
ashore, where upon her landing she was received by a whole
troop of her kind, who had been set ashore from the other vessels
and had multiplied and formed a large commonwealth. From the
door of his galley, the cook used to watch them in their maneuvers, setting up a shout and clapping his hands whenever Bess
came off victorious in the struggles for pieces of rawhide and
half-picked bones which were lying about the beach. During the
day, he saved all the nice things and made a bucket of swill, and
asked us to take it ashore in the gig, and looked quite discon-
certed when the mate told him that he would pitch the swill
overboard, and him after it, if he saw any of it go into the boats.
We told him that he thought more about the pig than he did
about his wife, who lived down in Robinson's Alley; and indeed
he could hardly have been more attentive, for he actually on
several nights after dark, when he thought he would not be seen,
sculled himself ashore in a boat with a bucket of nice swill, and
returned like Leander from crossing the Hellespont.

The next Sunday the other half of our crew went ashore on
liberty, and left us on board to enjoy the first quiet Sunday which
we had had upon the coast. We washed and mended our clothes
in the morning, and spent the rest of the day in reading and
writing. Several of us wrote letters to send home by the *Lagoda*.
At twelve o'clock the *Ayacucho* dropped her fore-topsail, which
was a signal for her sailing. She unmoored and warped down
into the bight, from which she got under way. During this operation her crew were a long time heaving at the windlass, and I
listened for nearly an hour to the musical notes of a Sandwich
Islander called Mahannah who "sang out" for them. Sailors, when
heaving at a windlass, in order that they may heave together always have one to sing out, which is done in a peculiar high and
long-drawn note, varying with the motion of the windlass. This
requires a high voice, strong lungs, and much practice, to be
done well. This fellow had a very peculiar, wild sort of note,

breaking occasionally into a falsetto. The sailors thought that it was too high, and not enough of the boatswain hoarseness about it; but to me it had a great charm. The harbor was perfectly still, and his voice rang among the hills. Toward sundown, a good breeze having sprung up, she got under way, and with her long, sharp head cutting elegantly through the water on a taut bowline, she stood directly out of the harbor, and bore away to the southward.

At the close of the week we were ready to sail, but were delayed a day or two by the running away of F—, the man who had been our second mate and was turned forward. From the time that he was "broken" he had had a dog's berth on board the vessel, and determined to run away at the first opportunity. Having shipped for an officer when he was not half a seaman, he found little pity with the crew, and was not man enough to hold his ground among them. The captain called him a soger,* and promised to "ride him down as he would the main tack"; and when officers are once determined to "ride a man down," it is a gone case with him. He had had several difficulties with the captain, and asked leave to go home in the *Lagoda*, but this was refused him. One night he was insolent to an officer on the beach, and refused to come aboard in the boat. He was reported to the captain and as he came aboard—it being past the proper hour—he was called aft, and told that he was to have a flogging. Immediately he fell down on deck, calling out, "Don't flog me, Captain T—, don't flog me!" and the captain, angry with him and disgusted with his cowardice, gave him a few blows over the back with a rope's end, and sent him forward. He was not much hurt, but a good deal frightened, and made up his mind to run away that very night. This was managed better than anything else he ever did in his life, and seemed really to show some spirit

* "Soger" (soldier) is the worst term of reproach that can be applied to a sailor. It signifies a *skulk*, a *shirk*—one who is always trying to get clear of work, and is out of the way, or hanging back, when duty is to be done. "Marine" is the term applied more particularly to a man who is ignorant and clumsy about seaman's work—a greenhorn, a landlubber. To make a sailor shoulder a handspike and walk fore and aft the deck like a sentry is the most ignominious punishment that could be put upon him. Such a punishment inflicted upon an able seaman in a vessel of war would break his spirit down more than a flogging.

and forethought. He gave his bedding and mattress to one of the *Lagoda's* crew, who took it aboard his vessel and promised to keep it for him. He then unpacked his chest, putting all his valuable clothes into a large canvas bag, and told one of us who had the watch to call him at midnight. Coming on deck at midnight, and finding no officer on deck and all still aft, he lowered his bag into a boat, got softly down into it, cast off the painter, and let it drop down silently with the tide until he was out of hearing, when he sculled ashore.

The next morning when all hands were mustered, there was a great stir to find F—. Of course we would tell nothing, and all they could discover was that he had left an empty chest behind him, and that he went off in a boat; for they saw it lying up high and dry on the beach. After breakfast the captain went up to the town and offered a reward of twenty dollars for him; and for a couple of days the soldiers, Indians, and all others who had nothing to do were scouring the country for him on horseback, but without effect; for he was safely concealed all the time within fifty rods of the hide houses. As soon as he had landed, he went directly to the *Lagoda's* hide house, and a part of her crew, who were living there on shore, promised to conceal him and his "traps" until the *Pilgrim* should sail, and then to intercede with Captain Bradshaw to take him on board the ship. Just behind the hide houses, among the thickets and underwood, was a small cave, the entrance to which was known only to two men on the beach, and which was so well concealed that though when I afterward came to live on shore it was shown to me two or three times, I was never able to find it alone. To this cave he was carried before daybreak in the morning, and supplied with bread and water, and there remained until he saw us under way and well round the point.

FRIDAY, MARCH 27. The captain, having given up all hope of finding F— and being unwilling to delay any longer, gave orders for unmooring ship, and we made sail, dropping slowly down with the tide and light wind. We left letters with Captain Bradshaw to take to Boston, and had the satisfaction of hearing him say that he should be back again before we left the coast. The wind, which was very light, died away soon after we doubled the point, and we lay becalmed for two days, not moving three miles the whole time. On the third day about noon a cool sea breeze came rippling and darkening the surface of the water, and by sundown we were off San Juan's, which is about forty miles from San Diego, and is called halfway to San Pedro, where we were now bound. Our crew was now considerably weakened. One man we had lost overboard; another had been taken aft as clerk; and a third had run away; so that, besides S— and myself, there were only three able seamen and one boy of twelve years of age. With this diminished and discontented crew, and in a small vessel, we were now to battle the watch through a couple of years of hard service, yet there was not one who was not glad that F— had escaped; for, shiftless and good-for-nothing as he was, no one could wish to see him dragging on a miserable life, cowed down and disheartened. And we were all rejoiced to hear, upon our return to San Diego about two months afterward, that he had been immediately taken aboard the *Lagoda,* and went home in her on regular seaman's wages.

After a slow passage of five days, we arrived on Wednesday, the first of April, at our old anchoring ground at San Pedro. The bay was as deserted, and looked as dreary, as before, and formed no pleasing contrast with the security and snugness of San Diego and the activity and interest which the loading and unloading of four vessels gave to that scene. In a few days the hides began to come slowly down, and we got into the old business of rolling goods up the hill, pitching hides down, and pulling our long league off and on. Nothing of note occurred while we were lying here, except that an attempt was made to repair the small Mexican brig which had been cast away in a southeaster, and which now lay up, high and dry, over one reef of rocks and two sandbanks. Our carpenter surveyed her, and pronounced her capable of refitting, and in a few days the owners came down from the Pueblo and, waiting for the high spring tides, with the help of our cables, kedges, and crew got her off and afloat, after several trials. The three men at the house on shore, who had formerly been a part of her crew, now joined her, and seemed glad enough at the prospect of getting off the coast.

On board our own vessel things went on in the common monotonous way. The excitement which immediately followed the flogging scene had passed off, but the effect of it upon the crew, and especially upon the two men themselves, remained. The different manner in which these men were affected, corresponding to their different characters, was not a little remarkable. John was a foreigner and high-tempered, and though mortified, as anyone would be at having had the worst of an encounter, yet his chief feeling seemed to be anger; and he talked much of satisfaction and revenge, if he ever got back to Boston. But with the other it was very different. He was an American, and had had some education, and this thing coming upon him seemed completely to break him down. He had a feeling of the degradation that had been inflicted upon him which the other man was incapable of. Before that, he had a good deal of fun, and amused us often with queer Negro stories (he was from a slave state); but afterward he seldom smiled, seemed to lose all life and elasticity, and appeared to have but one wish, and that was for the voyage to be at an end.

After a stay of about a fortnight we got under way for Santa Barbara. It was now the middle of April, and the southeaster season was nearly over; the light, regular trade winds which blow down the coast began to set steadily in during the latter part of each day. Against these, we beat slowly up to Santa Barbara—a distance of about ninety miles—in three days. There we found, lying at anchor, the large Genoese ship which we saw in the same place on the first day of our coming upon the coast. She had been up to San Francisco, or as it is called, "chock up to windward," had stopped at Monterey on her way down, and was shortly to proceed to San Pedro and San Diego, and thence, taking in her cargo, to sail for Valparaiso and Cádiz. She was a large, clumsy ship, and with her topmasts stayed forward, and high poop deck, looked like an old woman with a crippled back. It was now the close of Lent, and on Good Friday she had all her yards acockbill, which is customary among Catholic vessels. Some also have an effigy of Judas, which the crew amuse themselves with keelhauling and hanging by the neck from the yardarms.

Easter Sunday · "Sail Ho!" · Whales · San Juan · Romance of Hide-Droghing · San Diego Again

THE NEXT SUNDAY was Easter Sunday, and as there had been no liberty at San Pedro, it was our turn to go ashore and misspend another Sabbath. Soon after breakfast a large boat filled with men in blue jackets, scarlet caps, and various-colored underclothes, bound ashore on liberty, left the Italian ship and passed under our stern, the men singing beautiful Italian boat songs all the way in fine, full chorus. Among the songs I recognized the favorite *"O pescator dell' onda."* It brought back to my mind pianofortes, drawing-rooms, young ladies singing, and a thousand other things which as little befitted me, in my situation, to be thinking upon. Supposing that the whole day would be too long a time to spend ashore, as there was no place to which we could take a ride, we remained quietly on board until after dinner. We were then pulled ashore in the stern of the boat and, with orders to be on the beach at sundown, we took our way for the town. There, everything wore the appearance of a holiday. The people were all dressed in their best, the men riding about on horseback among the houses and the women sitting on carpets before the doors. Under the piazza of a *pulperia,* two men were seated, decked out with knots of ribbons and bouquets and playing the violin and the Spanish guitar. These are the only instruments, with the exception of the drums and trumpets at Monterey, that I ever heard in California; and I suspect they play upon no others, for at a great fandango at which I was afterward present, and where they mustered all the music they could find, there were three violins and two guitars, and no other instru-

ments. As it was now too near the middle of the day to see any
dancing, and hearing that a bull was expected down from the
country to be baited in the presidio square, in the course of an
hour or two we took a stroll among the houses. Inquiring for an
American who we had been told had married in the place, and
kept a shop, we were directed to a long, low building at the end
of which was a door with a sign over it in Spanish. Entering the
shop, we found no one in it, and the whole had an empty, deserted appearance. In a few minutes the man made his appearance, and apologized for having nothing to entertain us with,
saying that he had had a fandango at his house the night before,
and the people had eaten and drunk up everything.

"Oh yes," said I, "Easter holidays!"

"No!" said he, with a singular expression to his face. "I had a
little daughter die the other day, and that's the custom of the
country."

Here I felt a little strangely, not knowing what to say, or
whether to offer consolation or no, and was beginning to retire
when he opened a side door and told us to walk in. Here I was
no less astonished; for I found a large room filled with young girls
from three or four years of age up to fifteen and sixteen, dressed
all in white, with wreaths of flowers on their heads and bouquets
in their hands. Following our conductor through all these girls,
who were playing about in high spirits, we came to a table at the
end of the room covered with a white cloth, on which lay a coffin
about three feet long, with the body of his child. The coffin was
lined on the outside with white cloth, and on the inside with
white satin, and was strewed with flowers. Through an open door
we saw in another room a few elderly people in common dresses,
while the benches and tables thrown up in a corner, and the
stained walls, gave evident signs of the last night's "high-go."
Feeling, like Garrick, between tragedy and comedy, an uncertainty of purpose and a little awkwardness, I asked the man when
the funeral would take place, and being told that it would move
toward the mission in about an hour, took my leave.

To pass away the time, we took horses and rode down to the
beach, and there found three or four Italian sailors mounted and
riding up and down on the hard sand at a furious rate. We joined
them, and found it fine sport. The beach gave us a stretch of a

mile or more, and the horses flew over the smooth, hard sand, apparently invigorated and excited by the salt sea breeze and by the continual roar and dashing of the breakers. From the beach we returned to the town, and finding that the funeral procession had moved, rode on and overtook it about halfway to the mission. Here was as peculiar a sight as we had seen before in the house, the one looking as much like a funeral procession as the other did like a house of mourning. The little coffin was borne by eight girls, who were continually relieved by others running forward from the procession and taking their places. Behind it came a straggling company of girls, dressed as before in white and flowers, and including, I should suppose by their numbers, nearly all the girls between five and fifteen in the place. They played along on the way, frequently stopping and running all together to talk to someone, or to pick up a flower, and then running on again to overtake the coffin. There were a few elderly women in common colors; and a herd of young men and boys, some on foot and others mounted, followed them, or walked or rode by their side, frequently interrupting them by jokes and questions. But the most singular thing of all was that two men walked, one on each side of the coffin, carrying muskets in their hands, which they continually loaded and fired into the air. Whether this was to keep off the evil spirits or not I do not know. It was the only interpretation that I could put upon it.

As we drew near the mission we saw the great gate thrown open, and the padre standing on the steps with a crucifix in his hand. The mission is a large and deserted-looking place, the outbuildings going to ruin, and everything giving one the impression of decayed grandeur. A large stone fountain threw out pure water, from four mouths, into a basin before the church door, and we were on the point of riding up to let our horses drink when it occurred to us that it might be consecrated, and we forbore. Just at this moment, the bells set up their harsh, discordant clang, and the procession moved into the court. I was anxious to follow and see the ceremony, but the horse of one of my companions had become frightened, and was tearing off toward the town; and having thrown his rider and got one of his feet caught in the saddle, which had slipped, was fast dragging and ripping it to pieces. Knowing that my shipmate could not speak a word of Spanish, and fearing that he would get into difficulty, I was obliged to leave the ceremony and ride after him. I soon overtook him trudging along swearing at the horse, and carrying the remains of the saddle, which he had picked up on the road. Going to the owner of the horse, we made a settlement with him, and found him surprisingly liberal. All parts of the saddle were brought back, and being capable of repair, he was satisfied with six reals. We thought it would have been a few dollars. We pointed to the horse, which was now halfway up one of the mountains; but he shook his head, saying, "*No importe!*" and giving us to understand that he had plenty more.

Having returned to the town, we saw a great crowd collected in the square before the principal *pulperia*, and riding up, found that all these people—men, women, and children—had been drawn together by a couple of bantam cocks. The cocks were in full tilt, springing into one another, and the people were as eager, laughing and shouting, as though the combatants had been men. There had been a disappointment about the bull; he had broken his bail and taken himself off, and it was too late to get another, so the people were obliged to put up with a cockfight. One of the bantams having been knocked in the head and had an eye put out, he gave in, and two monstrous prize cocks were brought on. These were the object of the whole affair, the two bantams having been merely served up as a first course, to collect the people together. Two fellows came into the ring holding the cocks in their arms and stroking them, and running about on all fours, encouraging and setting them on. Bets ran high, and, like most other contests, this one remained for some time undecided. They both showed great pluck, and fought probably better and longer than their masters would. Whether, in the end, it was the white or the red that beat I do not recollect; but whichever it was, he strutted off with the true veni-vidi-vici look, leaving the other lying panting on his beam ends.

This matter having been settled, we heard some talk about "*caballos*" and "*carrera*," and seeing the people all streaming off in one direction, we followed, and came upon a level piece of ground just out of the town which was used as a racecourse. Here the crowd soon became thick again; the ground was marked off, the judges stationed, and the horses led up to one end. Two fine-looking old gentlemen—Don Cárlos and Don Domingo, so called—held the stakes, and all was now ready. We waited some time, during which we could just see the horses twisting round and turning, until at length there was a shout along the lines, and on they came, heads stretched out and eyes starting—working all over, both man and beast. The steeds came by us like a couple of chain shot—neck and neck; and now we could see nothing but their backs and their hind hoofs flying in the air. As fast as the horses passed, the crowd broke up behind them and ran to the goal. When we got there, we found the horses returning on a slow walk, having run far beyond the mark, and heard that the long bony one had come in head and shoulders before the other. The riders were light-built men, had handkerchiefs tied round their heads, and were bare-armed and barelegged. The horses were noble-looking beasts, not so sleek and combed as our Boston stable horses, but with fine limbs, and spirited eyes. After this had been settled, and fully talked over, the crowd scattered again and flocked back to the town.

Returning to the large *pulperia*, we found the violin and guitar screaming and twanging away under the piazza, where they had been all day. As it was now sundown, there began to be some dancing. The Italian sailors danced, and one of our crew exhibited himself in a sort of West India shuffle, much to the amusement of the bystanders, who cried out, *"Bravo!" "Otra vez!"* and *"Vicán los marineros!"* but the dancing did not become general, as the women and the *gente de razón* had not yet made their appearance. We wished very much to stay and see the style of dancing; but although we had had our own way during the day, yet we were, after all, but foremast Jacks, and having been ordered to be on the beach by sundown, did not venture to be more than an hour behind the time; so we took our way down. We found the boat just pulling ashore through the breakers, which were running high, there having been a heavy fog outside, which, from some cause or other, always brings on or precedes a heavy sea. Liberty men are privileged from the time they leave the vessel until they step on board again, so we took our places in the stern sheets, and were congratulating ourselves upon getting off dry when a great comber broke fore and aft the boat and wet us through and through, filling the boat half-full of water. Having lost her buoyancy by the weight of the water, she dropped heavily into every sea that struck her, and by the time we had pulled out of the surf into deep water, she was but just afloat, and we were up to our knees. By the help of a small bucket and our hats, we bailed her out, got on board, hoisted the boats, ate our supper, changed our clothes, gave (as is usual) the whole history of our day's adventures to those who had stayed on board, and having taken a night smoke, turned in. Thus ended our second day's liberty on shore.

On Monday morning, as an offset to our day's sport, we were all set to work "tarring down" the rigging. Some got girtlines up for riding down the stays and backstays, and others tarred the shrouds, lifts, etc., laying out on the yards, and coming down the rigging. We overhauled our bags and took out our old tarry trousers and frocks which we had used when we tarred down before, and were all at work in the rigging by sunrise. After breakfast, we had the satisfaction of seeing the Italian ship's boat go ashore filled with men, gaily dressed as on the day before, and singing their *barcarollas*. The Easter holidays are kept up on shore during three days, and being a Catholic vessel, the crew had the advantage of them. For two successive days, while perched up in the rigging covered with tar and engaged in our disagreeable work, we saw these fellows going ashore in the morning and coming off again at night in high spirits. So much for being Protestants. There's no danger of Catholicism's spreading in New England; Yankees can't afford the time to be Catholics. American shipmasters get nearly three weeks more labor out of their crews in the course of a year than the masters of vessels from Catholic countries. Yankees don't keep Christmas, and shipmasters at sea never know when Thanksgiving comes, so Jack has no festival at all.

About noon, a man aloft called out "Sail ho!" and we saw the headsails of a vessel coming round the point. As she drew round, she showed the broadside of a full-rigged brig, with the Yankee ensign at her peak. We ran up our Stars and Stripes and, knowing that there was no American brig on the coast but ourselves, expected to have news from home. She rounded to and let go her anchor, but the dark faces on her yards when they furled the sails, and the Babel on deck, soon made known that she was from the Islands. Immediately afterward a boat's crew came aboard, bringing her skipper, and from them we learned that she was from Oahu, and was engaged in the same trade with the *Ayacucho, Loriotte,* etc., between the coast, the Sandwich Islands, and the leeward coast of Peru and Chile. Her captain and officers were Americans, and also a part of her crew; the rest were Islanders. She was called the *Catalina,* and like all the other vessels in that trade except the *Ayacucho,* her papers and colors were from Uncle Sam. They of course brought us no news, and we were doubly disappointed, for we had thought at first it might be the ship we were expecting from Boston.

After lying here about a fortnight, and collecting all the hides the place afforded, we set sail again for San Pedro. There we found the brig which we had assisted in getting off lying at anchor, with a mixed crew of Americans, English, Sandwich Islanders, Spaniards, and Spanish Indians; and though much smaller than we, yet she had three times the number of men—and she needed them, for her officers were Californians. No vessels in the world go so poorly manned as American and English, and none do so well. A Yankee brig of that size would have had a crew of four men, and would have worked round and round her. The Italian ship had a crew of thirty men—nearly three times as many as the *Alert,* which was afterward on the coast, and was of the same size; yet the *Alert* would get under way and come to in half the time, and get two anchors while they were all talking at once, jabbering like a parcel of "Yahoos," and running about decks to find their cat block.

There was only one point in which they had the advantage over us, and that was in lightening their labors in the boats by their songs. The Americans are a time- and money-saving people, but have not yet, as a nation, learned that music may be "turned to account." We pulled the long distances to and from the shore with our loaded boats without a word spoken, and with discontented looks, while they not only lightened the labor of rowing, but actually made it pleasant and cheerful, by their music. So true is it that:

> *For the tired slave, song lifts the languid oar,*
> *And bids it aptly fall, with chime*
> *That beautifies the fairest shore,*
> *And mitigates the harshest clime.*

We lay about a week in San Pedro, and got under way for San Diego, intending to stop at San Juan, as the southeaster season was nearly over, and there was little or no danger.

This being the spring season, San Pedro, as well as all the other open ports on the coast, was filled with whales that had come in to make their annual visit upon soundings. For the first few days that we were here and at Santa Barbara, we watched them with great interest—calling out "There she blows!" every time we saw the spout of one breaking the surface of the water; but they soon became so common that we took little notice of them. They often "broke" very near us, and one thick, foggy night during a dead calm, while I was standing anchor watch, one of them rose so near that he struck our cable, and made all surge again. He did not seem to like the encounter much himself, for he sheered off, and spouted at a good distance. We once came very near running one down in the gig, and should probably have been knocked to pieces and blown sky-high. We had been on board the little Spanish brig, and were returning, stretching out well at our oars, the little boat going like a swallow. Our backs were forward (as is always the case in pulling) and the captain, who was steering, was not looking ahead, when all at once we heard the spout of a whale directly ahead. "Back water! Back water, for your lives!" shouted the captain and we backed our blades in the water and brought the boat to in a smother of foam. Turning our heads, we saw a great rough hump-backed whale slowly crossing our fore-foot, within three or four yards of the boat's stem. Had we not backed water just as we did, we should inevitably have gone smash upon him, striking him with our stem just about amidships. He took no notice of us, but passed slowly on and dived a few yards beyond us, throwing his tail high in the air. He was so near that we had a perfect view of him and, as may be supposed, had no desire to see him nearer. He was a disgusting creature with a skin rough, hairy, and of an iron-gray color. This kind differs much from the sperm in color and skin, and is said to be fiercer. We saw a few sperm whales; but most of the whales that come upon the coast are finbacks, humpbacks, and right whales, which are more difficult to take, and are said not to give oil enough to pay for the trouble. For this reason whaleships do not come on the coast after them.

During the months of March, April, and May these whales appear in great numbers in the open ports of Santa Barbara, San Pedro, etc., and hover off the coast, while a few find their way into the close harbors of San Diego and Monterey. They are all off again before midsummer, and make their appearance on the "offshore ground." We saw some fine "schools" of sperm whales, which are easily distinguished by their spout, blowing away a few miles to windward.

Coasting along on the quiet shore of the Pacific, we came to anchor, in 20 fathoms' water, almost out at sea, as it were, and directly abreast of a steep hill which overhung the water, and was twice as high as our royal masthead. We had heard much of this place from the *Lagoda's* crew, who said it was the worst place in California. The shore is rocky, and directly exposed to the southeast, so that vessels are obliged to slip and run for their lives on the first sign of a gale; and late as it was in the season, we got up our slip ropes and gear, though we meant to stay only twenty-four hours. We pulled the agent ashore, and were ordered to wait for him while he took a circuitous way round the hill to the mission. We were glad of the opportunity to examine this singular place, and hauling the boat up and making her well fast, took different directions up and down the beach, to explore it.

San Juan is the only romantic spot in California. The country here for several miles is high tableland, running boldly to the shore and breaking off in a steep hill, at the foot of which the waters of the Pacific are constantly dashing. For several miles the water washes the very base of the hill, or breaks on ledges and fragments of rocks which run out into the sea. Just where we landed was a small cove, or "bight," which gave us at high tide a few square feet of sand beach between the sea and the bottom of the hill. This was the only landing place. Directly before us rose the perpendicular height of four or five hundred feet. How we were to get hides down, or goods up, on the tableland on which the mission was situated was more than we could tell. The agent had taken a long circuit, and yet had frequently to jump over breaks, and climb up steep places, in the ascent. No animal but a man or a monkey could get up it. However, that was not our lookout; and knowing that the agent would be gone an hour or more, we strolled about picking up shells, and following the sea where it tumbled in, roaring and spouting, among the crevices of the great rocks. What a sight, thought I, must this be in a south-easter! The rocks were as large as those of Nahant or Newport, but, to my eye, more grand and broken. Besides, there was a grandeur in everything around which gave almost a solemnity to the scene: a silence and solitariness which affected everything! Not a human being but ourselves for miles, and no sound heard but the pulsations of the great Pacific! And the great steep hill rising like a wall, and cutting us off from all the world but the "world of waters!" I separated myself from the rest and sat down on a rock just where the sea ran in and formed a fine spouting horn. Compared with the plain, dull sand beach of the rest of the coast, this grandeur was as refreshing as a great rock in a weary land. It was almost the first time that I had been positively alone —free from the sense that human beings were at my elbow, if not talking with me—since I had left home. My better nature returned strong upon me. Everything was in accordance with my state of feeling, and I experienced a glow of pleasure at finding that what of poetry and romance I ever had in me had not been entirely deadened by the laborious and frittering life I had led. Nearly an hour did I sit, almost lost in the luxury of this entire new scene of the play in which I had been so long acting, when I was aroused by the distant shouts of my companions, and saw that they were collecting, as the agent had made his appearance on his way back to our boat.

We pulled aboard, and found the longboat hoisted out and nearly laden with goods; and after dinner we all went on shore in the quarter-boat, with the longboat in tow. As we drew in, we found an oxcart and a couple of men standing directly on the brow of the hill; and having landed, the captain took his way round the hill, ordering me and one other to follow him. We followed, picking our way out, and jumping and scrambling up, walking over briers and prickly pears, until we came to the top. Here the country stretched out for miles, as far as the eye could reach, on a level, table surface; and the only habitation in sight was the small white mission of San Juan Campestrano, with a few Indian huts about it, standing in a small hollow about a mile from where we were. Reaching the brow of the hill where the cart stood, we found several piles of hides, and Indians sitting round them. One or two other carts were coming slowly on from the mission, and the captain told us to begin and throw the hides down. This, then, was the way they were to be got down—thrown down, one at a time, a distance of four hundred feet! This was doing the business on a great scale. Standing on the edge of the hill and looking down the perpendicular height, the sailors

> *That walk upon the beach,*
> *Appeared like mice; and* OUR *tall anchoring bark*
> *Diminished to her cock; her cock a buoy*
> *Almost too small for sight.*

Down this height we pitched the hides, throwing them as far out into the air as we could; and as they were all large, stiff, and doubled like the cover of a book, the wind took them, and they swayed and eddied about, plunging and rising in the air like a kite when it has broken its string. As it was now low tide, there was no danger of their falling into the water, and as fast as they came to ground, the men below picked them up, and taking them on their heads, walked off with them to the boat. It was really a picturesque sight: the great height; the scaling of the hides; and the continual walking to and fro of the men, who looked like mites, on the beach! This was the romance of hide-droghing!

Some of the hides lodged in cavities which were under the bank and out of our sight, being directly under us; but by sending others down in the same direction, we succeeded in dislodging them. Had they remained there the captain said he should have sent on board for a couple of pair of long halyards and got someone to have gone down for them. It was said that one of the crew of an English brig went down in the same way a few years before. We looked over, and thought it would not be a welcome task, especially for a few paltry hides. But no one knows what he can do until he is called upon; for six months afterward I went down the same place by a pair of topgallant-studding-sail halyards, to save half a dozen hides which had lodged there.

Having thrown them all down, we took our way back again, and found the boat loaded and ready to start. We pulled off, took the hides aboard, hoisted in the boats, hove up our anchor, made sail, and before sundown were on our way to San Diego.

FRIDAY, MAY 8, 1835. Arrived at San Diego. Here we found the little harbor deserted. The *Lagoda, Ayacucho, Loriotte,* and all had left the coast, and we were nearly alone. All the hide houses on the beach but ours were shut up, and the Sandwich Islanders, a dozen or twenty in number, who had worked for the other vessels and been paid off when they sailed, were living on the beach, keeping up a grand carnival. A Russian discovery ship which had been in this port a few years before had built a large oven for baking bread, and went away leaving it standing. This the Sandwich Islanders took possession of, and had kept, ever since, undisturbed. It was big enough to hold six or eight men— that is, it was as large as a ship's forecastle—had a door at the side, and a venthole at top. They covered it with Oahu mats for a carpet, stopped up the venthole in bad weather, and made it their headquarters. It was now inhabited by as many as a dozen or twenty men, who lived there in complete idleness—drinking, playing cards, and carousing in every way. They bought a bullock once a week, which kept them in meat, and one of them went up to the town every day to get fruit, liquor, and provisions. Besides this, they had bought a cask of ship bread and a barrel of flour from the *Lagoda,* before she sailed. There they lived, having a grand time, and caring for nobody. Captain T— was anxious to get three or four of them to come on board the *Pilgrim,* as we were so much diminished in numbers, and went up to the oven and spent an hour or two trying to negotiate with them. One of them—a finely built, active, strong, and intelligent fellow who was a sort of king among them—acted as spokesman. He was called Mannini—or rather, out of compliment to his known importance and influence, *Mr.* Mannini—and was known all over California. Through him, the captain offered them fifteen dollars a month and one month's pay in advance; but it was like throwing pearls before swine, or rather, carrying coals to Newcastle. So long as they had money, they would not work for fifty dollars a month, and when their money was gone, they would work for ten.

"What do you do here, Mr. Mannini?"* said the captain.

"Oh, we play cards, get drunk, smoke—do anything we're a mind to."

* The letter *i* in the Sandwich Island language is sounded like *e* in the English.

"Don't you want to come aboard and work?"

"*Aole! Aole make make makou i ka hana.* Now, got plenty money; no good, work. *Mamule,* money *pau*—all gone. Ah! very good, work!—*Maikai, hana hana nui!*"

"But you'll spend all your money in this way," said the captain.

"Aye! Me know that. By 'em by money *pau*—all gone. Then Kanaka work plenty."

This was a hopeless case, and the captain left them, to wait patiently until their money was gone.

We discharged our hides and tallow, and in about a week were ready to set sail again for the windward. We unmoored and got everything ready, when the captain made another attempt upon the oven. This time he had more regard to the *"mollia tempora fandi,"* and succeeded very well. He got Mr. Mannini in his interest, and as the shot was getting low in the locker, prevailed upon him and three others to come on board with their chests and baggage, and sent a hasty summons to me and the boy to come ashore with our things and join the gang at the hide house. This was unexpected to me, but anything in the way of variety I liked, so we got ready and were pulled ashore. I stood on the beach while the brig got under way, and watched her until she rounded the point, and then went up to the hide house to take up my quarters for a few months.

The Sandwich Islanders.
Hide-Curing · Wool-Cutting.
Rattlesnakes · Newcomers

HERE WAS a change in my life as complete as it had been sudden. In the twinkling of an eye I was transformed from a sailor into a "beachcomber" and a hide-curer; yet the novelty and the comparative independence of the life were not unpleasant. Our hide house was a large building made of rough boards, and intended to hold forty thousand hides. In one corner of it a small room was parted off, in which four berths were made, where we were to live, with Mother Earth for our floor. It contained a table, a small locker for pots, spoons, plates, etc., and a small hole cut to let in the light. Here we put our chests, threw our bedding into the berths, and took up our quarters. Over our head was another small room in which "Mr." Russell lived, who had charge of the hide house. There he lived in solitary grandeur, eating and sleeping alone (and these were his principal occupations), and communing with his own dignity. The boy was to act as cook, while myself, a giant of a Frenchman named Nicholas, and four Sandwich Islanders were to cure the hides. Sam the Frenchman and myself lived together in the room, and the four Sandwich Islanders worked and ate with us, but generally slept at the oven. My new messmate, Nicholas, was the most immense man that I had ever seen in my life. He came on the coast in a vessel which was afterward wrecked, and now let himself out to the different houses to cure hides. He was considerably over six feet, and of a frame so large that he might have been shown for a curiosity. But the most remarkable thing about him was his feet. They were so large that he could not find a pair of shoes in California to fit him, and was obliged to send to Oahu for a pair; and when he got them, he was compelled to wear them down at the heel. He told me once himself that he was wrecked in an American brig on the Goodwin Sands, and was sent up to London to the charge of the American consul without clothing to his back or shoes to his feet, and was obliged to go about London streets in his stocking feet three or four days, in the month of January, until the consul could have a pair of shoes *made for him*. His strength was in proportion to his size, and his ignorance to his strength—"strong as an ox, and ignorant as strong." He neither knew how to read nor how to write. He had been to sea from a boy, and had seen all kinds of service, and been in every kind of vessels: merchantmen, men-of-war, privateers, and slavers; and from what I could gather from his accounts of himself, and from what he once told me in confidence after we had become better acquainted, he had even been in worse business than slave-trading. He was once tried for his life in Charleston, South Carolina, and though acquitted, yet he was so frightened that he never would show himself in the United States again, and I could not persuade him that he could never be tried a second time for the same offense. He said he had got safe off from the breakers, and was too good a sailor to risk his timbers again.

Though I knew what his life had been, yet I never had the slightest fear of him. We always got along very well together, and though so much stronger and larger than I, he showed a respect for my education, and for what he had heard of my situation before coming to sea. "I'll be good friends with you," he used to say, "for by and by you'll come out here captain, and then you'll haze me well!" By holding well together, we kept the officer in good order, for he was evidently afraid of Nicholas, and never ordered us, except when employed upon the hides. My other companions, the Sandwich Islanders, deserve particular notice.

A considerable trade has been carried on for several years between California and the Sandwich Islands, and most of the vessels are manned with Islanders, who as they for the most part sign no articles, leave whenever they choose, and let themselves out to cure hides at San Diego, and to supply the places of the men of the American vessels while on the coast. In this way, quite a colony of them had become settled at San Diego as their headquarters. Some of these had recently gone off in the *Ayacucho* and *Loriotte,* and the *Pilgrim* had taken Mr. Mannini and three others, so that there were not more than twenty left. Of these, four were on pay at the *Ayacucho's* house, four more working with us, and the rest were living at the oven in a quiet way; for their money was nearly gone, and they must make it last until some other vessel came down to employ them.

During the four months that I lived here I got well acquainted with all of them, and took the greatest pains to become familiar with their language, habits, and characters. Their language I could only learn orally, for they had not any books among them, though many of them had been taught to read and write by the missionaries at home. They spoke a little English, and by a sort of compromise, a mixed language was used on the beach, which could be understood by all. The long name of Sandwich Islanders is dropped, and they are called by the whites, all over the Pacific Ocean, Kanakas, from a word in their own language which they apply to themselves, and to all South Sea Islanders, in distinction from whites, whom they call *Haole.* This name "Kanaka" they answer to, both collectively and individually. Their proper names, in their own language, being difficult to pronounce and remember, they are called by any names the captains or crews may choose to give them. Some are called after the vessel they are in; others by common names, as Jack, Tom, Bill; and some have fancy names, as Banyan, Foretop, Ropeyarn, Pelican, etc., etc. Of the four who worked at our house, one was named Mr. Bingham, after the missionary at Oahu; another, Hope, after a vessel that he had been in; a third, Tom Davis, the name of his first captain; and the fourth, Pelican, from his fancied resemblance to that bird. Then there was Lagoda Jack, California Bill, etc., etc. But by whatever names they might be called, they were the most interesting, intelligent, and kindhearted people that I ever fell in with. I felt a positive attachment for almost all of them; and many of them I have to this time a feeling for which would lead me to go a great way for the mere pleasure of seeing them, and which will always make me feel a strong interest in the mere name of a Sandwich Islander.

Tom Davis knew how to read, write, and cipher in common arithmetic, had been to the United States, and spoke English quite well. His education was as good as that of three-quarters of the Yankees in California, and his manners and principles a good deal better, and he was so quick of apprehension that he might have been taught navigation, and the elements of many of the sciences, with the most perfect ease. Old Mr. Bingham spoke very little English—almost none, and neither knew how to read nor to write; but he was the besthearted old fellow in the world. He must have been over fifty years of age, and had two of his front teeth knocked out, which was done by his parents as a sign of grief at the death of Kamehameha, the great king of the Sandwich Islands. We used to tell him that he ate Captain Cook, and lost his teeth in that way. That was the only thing that ever made him angry. He would always be quite excited at that and say: "*Aole!*" ("No!") "Me no eat Captain Cook! Me pikinini—small—so high—no more! My father see Captain Cook! Me—no!" None of them liked to have anything said about Captain Cook, for the sailors all believe that he was eaten, and that they cannot endure to be taunted with.—"New Zealand Kanaka eat white man—Sandwich Island Kanaka—no. Sandwich Island Kanaka *ua like pu na haole*—all 'e same a' you!"

Mr. Bingham was a sort of patriarch among them, and was always treated with great respect, though he had not the education and energy which gave Mr. Mannini his power over them. I have spent hours in talking with this old fellow about Kamehameha, the Charlemagne of the Sandwich Islands; his son and successor Lilohilo, who died in England, and was brought to Oahu in the frigate *Blonde,* Captain Lord Byron, and whose funeral he remembered perfectly; and also about the customs of his country in his boyhood, and the changes which had been made by the missionaries. He never would allow that human beings had been eaten there; and indeed it always seemed like an insult to tell so affectionate, intelligent, and civilized a class of men that such barbarities had been practiced in their own country within the recollection of many of them. Certainly, the history of no people on the globe can show anything like so rapid an advance. I would have trusted my life and my fortune in the hands of any one of these people; and certainly had I wished for a favor or act of sacrifice, I would have gone to them all, in turn, before I should have applied to one of my own countrymen on the coast, and should have expected to have seen it done before my own countrymen had got half through counting the cost. Their customs, and manner of treating one another, show a simple, primitive generosity which is truly delightful, and which is often a reproach to our own people. Whatever one has they all have. Money, food, clothes, they share with one another, even to the last piece of tobacco to put in their pipes. I once heard old Mr. Bingham say, with the highest indignation, to a Yankee trader who was trying to persuade him to keep his money to himself: "No! We no all 'e same a' you!—Suppose one got money, all got money. You—suppose one got money—lock him up in chest.—No good!—Kanaka all 'e same a' one!" This principle they carry so far that none of them will eat anything in sight of others without offering it all round. I have seen one of them break a biscuit which had been given him into five parts at a time when I knew he was on a very short allowance, as there was but little to eat on the beach.

My favorite among all of them, and one who was liked by both officers and men, and by whomever he had anything to do with, was Hope. He was an intelligent, kindhearted little fellow, and I never saw him angry, though I knew him for more than a year, and have seen him imposed upon by white people and abused by insolent officers of vessels. He was always civil, and always ready, and never forgot a benefit. Every Kanaka has one particular friend whom he considers himself bound to do everything for, and with whom he has a sort of contract—an alliance offensive and defensive—and for whom he will often make the greatest sacrifices. This friend they call *aikane;* and for such did Hope adopt me. I do not believe I could have wanted anything which he had that he would not have given me. In return for this, I was always his friend among the Americans, and used to teach him letters and numbers; for he left home before he had learned how to read. He was very curious about Boston (as they call the United States), asking many questions about the houses, the people, etc., and always wished to have the pictures in books explained to him. They were all astonishingly quick in catching at explanations, and many things which I had thought it utterly impossible to make them understand they often seized in an in-

stant, and asked questions which showed that they knew enough
to make them wish to go farther. The pictures of steamboats and
railroad cars in the columns of some newspapers which I had
gave me great difficulty to explain. The grading of the road, the
rails, the construction of the carriages, they could easily understand, but the motion produced by steam was a little too refined
for them. I attempted to show it to them once by an experiment
upon the cook's coppers, but failed—probably as much from my
own ignorance as from their want of apprehension—and I have
no doubt left them with about as clear an idea of the principle
as I had myself. This difficulty, of course, existed in the same
force with the steamboats, and all I could do was to give them
some account of the results in the shape of speed; for, failing in
the reason, I had to fall back upon the fact. In my account of the
speed I was supported by Tom, who had been to Nantucket and
seen a little steamboat which ran over to New Bedford.

A map of the world which I once showed them kept their attention for hours, those who knew how to read pointing out the
places and referring to me for the distances. I remember being
much amused with a question Hope asked me. Pointing to the
large irregular place which is always left blank round the poles,
to denote that it is undiscovered, he looked up and asked, *"Pau?"*
("Done? Ended?")

The system of naming the streets and numbering the houses
they easily understood, and the utility of it. They had a great
desire to see America, but were afraid of doubling Cape Horn,
for they suffer much in cold weather, and had heard dreadful
accounts of the Cape from those of their number who had been
round it.

They smoke a great deal, though not much at a time, using
pipes with large bowls and very short stems, or no stems at all.
These they light, and putting them to their mouths, take a long
draught, getting their mouths as full as they can hold, and their
cheeks distended, and then let it slowly out through their mouths
and nostrils. The pipe is then passed to others, who draw in the
same manner, one pipeful serving for half a dozen. They never
take short, continuous draughts, like Europeans, but one of these
"Oahu puffs," as the sailors call them, serves for an hour or two,
until someone else lights his pipe and it is passed round in the

same manner. Each Kanaka on the beach had a pipe, flint, steel, tinder, a hand of tobacco, and a jackknife which he always carried about with him.

That which strikes a stranger most peculiarly is their style of singing. They run on in a low, guttural, monotonous sort of chant, their lips and tongues seeming hardly to move, and the sounds apparently modulated solely in the throat. There is very little tune to it, and the words, so far as I could learn, are extempore. They sing about persons and things which are around them, and adopt this method when they do not wish to be understood by any but themselves; and it is very effectual, for with the most careful attention I never could detect a word that I knew. I have often heard Mr. Mannini, who was the most noted improvisatore among them, sing for an hour together when at work in the midst of Americans and Englishmen, and by the occasional shouts and laughter of the Kanakas who were at a distance, it was evident that he was singing about the different men that he was at work with. They have great powers of ridicule, and are excellent mimics, many of them discovering and imitating the peculiarities of our own people before we had seen them ourselves.

These were the people with whom I was to spend a few months, and who, with the exception of the officer, Nicholas the Frenchman, and the boy, made the whole population of the beach. I ought perhaps to except the dogs, for they were an important part of our settlement. Some of the first vessels brought dogs out with them, who, for convenience, were left ashore, and there multiplied until they came to be a great people. While I was on the beach, the average number was about forty, and probably an equal or greater number are drowned, or killed in some other way, every year. They are very useful in guarding the beach, the Indians being afraid to come down at night; for it was impossible for anyone to get within half a mile of the hide houses without a general alarm. The father of the colony, old Sachem, so called from the ship in which he was brought out, died while I was there, full of years, and was honorably buried. Hogs, and a few chickens, were the rest of the animal tribe, and formed, like the dogs, a common company, though they were all known and marked, and usually fed at the houses to which they belonged.

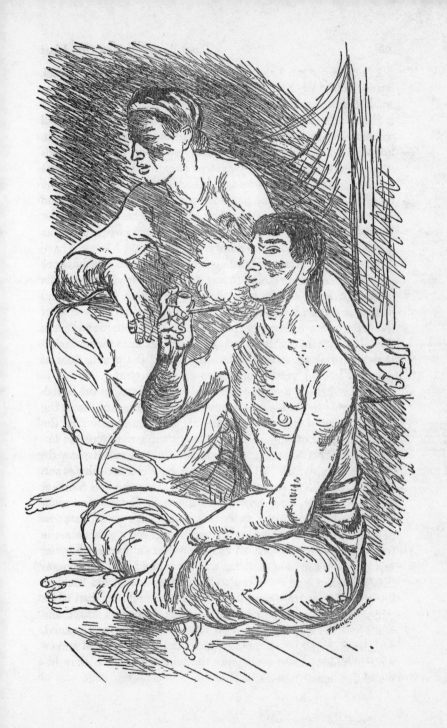

I had been but a few hours on the beach, and the *Pilgrim* was hardly out of sight, when the cry of "Sail ho!" was raised, and a small hermaphrodite brig rounded the point, bore up into the harbor, and came to anchor. It was the Mexican brig *Fazio*, which we had left at San Pedro, and which had come down to land her tallow, try it all over and make new bags, and then take it in and leave the coast. They moored ship, erected their tryworks on shore, put up a small tent, in which they all lived, and commenced operations. They made an addition to our "society," and we spent many evenings in their tent, where amid the Babel of English, Spanish, French, Indian, and Kanaka we found some words that we could understand in common.

The morning after my landing I began the duties of hide-curing. In order to understand these, it will be necessary to give the whole history of a hide, from the time it is taken from a bullock until it is put on board the vessel to be carried to Boston. When the hide is taken from the bullock, holes are cut round it near the edge, by which it is staked out to dry. In this manner it dries without shrinking. After they are thus dried in the sun, they are received by the vessels, and brought down to the depot. The vessels land them, and leave them in large piles near the houses. Then begins the hide-curer's duty. The first thing is to put them in soak. This is done by carrying them down at low tide and making them fast, in small piles, by ropes, and letting the tide come up and cover them. Every day we put in soak twenty-five for each man, which, with us, made a hundred and fifty. There they lie forty-eight hours, when they are taken out and rolled up in wheelbarrows, and thrown into the vats. These vats contain brine, made very strong, being sea water with great quantities of salt thrown in. This pickles the hides, and in this they lie forty-eight hours, the use of the sea water into which they are first put being merely to soften and clean them. From these vats they are taken, and lie on a platform twenty-four hours, and then are spread upon the ground and carefully stretched and staked out, so that they may dry smooth. After they were staked, and while yet wet and soft, we used to go on them with our knives and carefully cut off all the bad parts—the pieces of meat and fat, which would corrupt and infect the whole if stowed away in a vessel for many months, the large "flippers," the ears, and all other parts which would prevent close stowage. This was the most difficult part of our duty, as it required much skill to take everything necessary off and not to cut or injure the hide. It was also a long process, as six of us had to clean a hundred and fifty, most of which required a great deal to be done to them, as the Spaniards are very careless in skinning their cattle. Then too, as we cleaned them while they were staked out, we were obliged to kneel down upon them, which always gives beginners the backache. The first day I was so slow and awkward that I cleaned only eight; at the end of a few days I doubled my number, and in a fortnight or three weeks could keep up with the others and clean my proportion—twenty-five.

This cleaning must be got through with before noon, for by that time they get too dry. After the sun has been on them a few hours, they are carefully gone over with scrapers, to get off all the grease which the sun brings out. This being done, the stakes are pulled up, and the hides carefully doubled, with the hair side out, and left to dry. About the middle of the afternoon they are turned on the other side, and at sundown piled up and covered over. The next day they are spread out and opened again, and at night, if fully dry, are thrown upon a long, horizontal pole, five at a time, and beaten with flails. This takes all the dust from them. Then, being salted, scraped, cleaned, dried, and beaten, they are stowed away in the house.

By putting a hundred and fifty in soak every day we had the same number at each stage of curing on each day, so that we had every day the same work to do on the same number: a hundred and fifty to put in soak, a hundred and fifty to wash out and put in the vat, the same number to haul from the vat and put on the platform to drain, the same number to spread and stake out and clean, and the same number to beat and stow away in the house. I ought to except Sunday, for, by a prescription which no captain or agent has yet ventured to break in upon, Sunday has been a day of leisure on the beach for years. On Saturday night, the hides in every stage of progress are carefully covered up, and not uncovered until Monday morning. On Sundays we had absolutely no work to do, unless it was to kill a bullock, which was sent down for our use about once a week and sometimes came on Sunday. Another good arrangement was that we had just so much work to do, and when that was through, the time was our own. Knowing this, we worked hard, and needed no driving. We turned out every morning at the first signs of daylight, and allowing a short time about eight o'clock for breakfast, generally got through our labor between one and two o'clock, when we dined, and had the rest of the time to ourselves until just before sundown, when we beat the dry hides and put them in the house, and covered over all the others. By this means we had about three hours to ourselves every afternoon; and at sundown we had our supper, and our work was done for the day. There was no watch to stand, and no topsails to reef. The evenings we generally spent at one another's houses, and I often went up and spent an hour or so at the oven, which was called the "Kanaka Hotel," and the "Oahu Coffeehouse." Immediately after dinner we usually took a short siesta to make up for our early rising, and spent the rest of the afternoon according to our own fancies. I generally read, wrote, and made or mended clothes. The Kanakas went up to the oven and spent the time in sleeping, talking, and smoking; and my messmate Nicholas, who neither knew how to read or to write, passed away the time by a long siesta, two or three smokes with his pipe, and a *paseo* to the other houses. This leisure time is never interfered with, for the captains know that the men earn it by working hard and fast, and that if they interfered with it, the men could easily make their twenty-five hides apiece last through the day. We were pretty independent, too, for the master of the house—*"capitán de la casa"*—had nothing to say to us except when we were at work on the hides, and although we could not go up to the town without his permission, this was seldom or never refused.

The great weight of the wet hides, which we were obliged to roll about in wheelbarrows; the continual stooping upon those which were pegged out to be cleaned; and the smell of the vats, into which we were often obliged to get knee-deep to press down the hides—all made the work disagreeable and fatiguing. But we soon got hardened to it, and the comparative independence of our life reconciled us to it; for there was nobody to haze us and find fault, and when we got through, we had only to wash and change our clothes and our time was our own. There was, however, one exception to the time's being our own, which was that on two afternoons of every week we were obliged to go off and get wood for the cook to use in the galley. Wood is very scarce in the vicinity of San Diego, there being no trees of any size for miles. In the town, the inhabitants burn the small wood which grows in thickets, and for which they send out Indians in large numbers every few days. Fortunately, the climate is so fine that they have no need of a fire in their houses, and only use it for cooking. With us, the getting of wood was a great trouble, for all that in the vicinity of the houses had been cut down, and we were obliged to go off a mile or two, and to carry it some distance on our backs, as we could not get the handcart up the hills and over the uneven places. Two afternoons in the week we started off for the bush, each of us furnished with a hatchet and a long piece of rope, and dragging the handcart behind us, and followed by the whole colony of dogs, who were always ready for the bush and were half-mad whenever they saw our preparations. We went with the handcart as far as we could conveniently drag it, and leaving it in an open, conspicuous place, separated ourselves, each taking his own course and looking about for some good place to begin. Frequently we had to go nearly a mile from the handcart before we could find any fit place. Having lighted upon a good thicket, the next thing was to clear away the underbrush, and have fair play at the trees. These trees are seldom more than five or six feet high, and the highest that I ever saw in these expeditions could not have been more than twelve; so that, with lopping off the branches and clearing away the underwood, we had a good deal of cutting to do for a very little wood. Having cut enough for a "backload," the next thing was to make it well fast with the rope, and heaving the bundles on our backs, and taking the hatchet in hand, to walk off, up hill and down dale, to the handcart. Two good backloads apiece filled the handcart, and that was each one's proportion. When each had brought down his second load, we filled the handcart, and took our way again slowly back to the beach. It was generally sundown when we got back, and unloading, covering the hides for the night, and getting our supper finished the day's work.

These wooding excursions had always a mixture of something rather pleasant in them. Roaming about in the woods with hatchet in hand, like a backwoodsman, followed by a troop of dogs

—starting up of birds, snakes, hares, and foxes, and examining the various kinds of trees, flowers, and birds' nests—was at least a change from the monotonous drag and pull on shipboard. Frequently, too, we had some amusement and adventure. The coatis, of which I have before spoken—a sort of mixture of the fox and wolf breeds—fierce little animals with bushy tails and large heads, and a quick, sharp bark abound here, as in all other parts of California. These the dogs were very watchful for, and whenever they saw them, started off in full run after them. We had many fine chases, yet although our dogs ran finely, the rascals generally escaped. They are a match for the dog, one to one, but as the dogs generally went in squads, there was seldom a fair fight. A smaller dog belonging to us once attacked a coati single, and got a good deal worsted, and might perhaps have been killed had we not come to his assistance.

We had, however, one dog which gave them a good deal of trouble and many hard runs. He was a fine, tall fellow, and united strength and agility better than any dog that I have ever seen. He was born at the Islands, his father being an English mastiff and his mother a greyhound. He had the high head, long legs, narrow body, and springing gait of the latter, and the heavy jaw, thick jowls, and strong forequarters of the mastiff. When he was brought to San Diego, an English sailor said that he looked about the face precisely like the Duke of Wellington, whom he had once seen at the Tower; and indeed there was something about him which resembled the portraits of the Duke. From this time he was christened "Welly," and became the favorite and bully of the beach. He always led the dogs by several yards in the chase, and had killed two coatis at different times in single combats. We often had fine sport with these fellows. A quick, sharp bark from a coati and in an instant every dog was at the height of his speed. A few moments made up for an unfair start, and gave each dog his relative place. Welly, at the head, seemed almost to skim over the bushes—and after him came Fanny, Bravo, Childers, and the other fleet ones—the spaniels and terriers; and then, behind, followed the heavy corps—bulldogs, etc.— for we had every breed. Pursuit by us was in vain, and in about half an hour a few of them would come panting and straggling back.

Besides the coatis, the dogs sometimes made prizes of rabbits and hares, which are very plentiful here and great numbers of which we often shot for our dinners. There was another animal that I was not so much disposed to find amusement from, and that was the rattlesnake. These are very abundant here, especially during the spring of the year. The latter part of the time that I was on shore I did not meet with so many, but for the first two months we seldom went into "the bush" without one of our number starting some of them. The first that I ever saw I remember perfectly well. I had left my companions, and was beginning to clear away a fine clump of trees, when just in the midst of the thicket, not more than eight yards from me, one of these fellows set up his hiss. It is a sharp, continuous sound, and resembles very much the letting off of the steam from the small pipe of a steamboat, except that it is on a smaller scale. I knew by the sound of an ax that one of my companions was near, and called out to him to let him know what I had fallen on. He took it very lightly, and as he seemed inclined to laugh at me for being afraid, I determined to keep my place. I knew that so long as I could hear the rattle I was safe, for these snakes never make a noise when they are in motion. Accordingly I kept at my work, and the noise which I made with cutting and breaking the trees kept him in alarm, so that I had the rattle to show me his where-abouts. Once or twice the noise stopped for a short time, which gave me a little uneasiness, and retreating a few steps, I threw something into the bush, at which he would set his rattle a-going, and finding that he had not moved from his first place, I was easy again. In this way I continued at my work until I had cut a full load, never suffering him to be quiet for a moment. Having cut my load, I strapped it together and got everything ready for starting. I felt that I could now call the others without the impu-tation of being afraid, and went in search of them. In a few min-utes we were all collected, and began an attack upon the bush. The big Frenchman, who was the one that I had called to at first, I found as little inclined to approach the snake as I had been. The dogs, too, seemed afraid of the rattle, and kept up a barking at a safe distance; but the Kanakas showed no fear, and getting long sticks, went into the bush, and keeping a bright lookout, stood within a few feet of him. One or two blows struck near him, and a few stones thrown, started him, and we lost his track, and had the pleasant consciousness that he might be directly under our feet. By throwing stones and chips in different directions, we made him spring his rattle again, and began another attack. This time we drove him into the clear ground, and saw him gliding off, with head and tail erect, when a stone, well aimed, knocked him over the bank, down a declivity of fifteen or twenty feet, and stretched him at his length. Having made sure of him by a few more stones, we went down, and one of the Kanakas cut off his rattle. These rattles vary in number, it is said, according to the age of the snake, though the Indians think they indicate the number of creatures they have killed. We always preserved them as trophies, and at the end of the summer had quite a number.

Hares and rabbits, as I said before, were abundant, and during the winter months the waters are covered with wild ducks and geese. Crows, too, were very numerous, and frequently alighted in great numbers on our hides, picking at the pieces of dried meat and fat. Bears and wolves are numerous in the upper parts and in the interior (and indeed a man was killed by a bear within a few miles of San Pedro while we were there), but there were none in our immediate neighborhood. The only other animals were horses. Over a dozen of these were owned by different people on the beach, and were allowed to run loose among the hills, with a long lasso attached to them, and pick up feed wherever they could find it. We were sure of seeing them once a day, for there was no water among the hills, and they were obliged to come down to the well which had been dug on the beach. These horses were bought at from two to six and eight dollars apiece, and were held very much as common property. We generally kept one fast to one of the houses every day, so that we could mount him and catch any of the others. Some of them were really fine animals, and gave us many good runs up to the presidio and over the country.

Leisure · News from Home · "Burning the Water"

AFTER WE HAD been a few weeks on shore, and had begun to feel broken in to the regularity of our life, its monotony was interrupted by the arrival of two vessels from the windward. We were sitting at dinner in our little room when we heard the cry of "Sail ho!" This, we had learned, did not always signify a vessel, but was raised whenever a woman was seen coming down from the town or a squaw, or an oxcart, or anything unusual, hove in sight upon the road; so we took no notice of it. But it soon became so loud and general from all parts of the beach that we were led to go to the door, and there, sure enough, were two sails coming round the point, and leaning over from the strong northwest wind which blows down the coast every afternoon. The headmost was a ship, and the other a brig. Everybody was alive on the beach, and all manner of conjectures were abroad. Some said it was the *Pilgrim*, with the Boston ship which we were expecting; but we soon saw that the brig was not the *Pilgrim*, and the ship with her stump topgallant masts and rusty sides could not be a dandy Boston Indiaman. As they drew nearer, we soon discovered the high poop and topgallant forecastle and other marks of the Italian ship *Rosa*, and the brig proved to be the *Catalina*, which we saw at Santa Barbara, just arrived from Valparaiso. They came to anchor, moored ship, and commenced discharging hides and tallow. The *Rosa* had purchased the house occupied by the *Lagoda*, and the *Catalina* took the other spare one between ours and the *Ayacucho's*, so that now each one was occupied, and the beach for several days was all alive. The *Catalina* had several Kanakas on board, who were immediately besieged by the others and carried up to the oven,

where they had a long powwow, and a smoke. Two Frenchmen
who belonged to the *Rosa's* crew came in every evening to see
Nicholas, and from them we learned that the *Pilgrim* was at San
Pedro, and was the only other vessel now on the coast. Several
of the Italians slept on shore at their hide house, and there, and
at the tent in which the *Fazio's* crew lived, we had some very
good singing almost every evening. The Italians sang a variety
of songs—*barcarollas,* provincial airs, etc., in several of which I
recognized parts of our favorite operas and sentimental songs.
They often joined in a song, taking all the different parts; which
produced a fine effect, as many of them had good voices and all
seemed to sing with spirit and feeling. One young man in particular had a falsetto as clear as a clarionet.

The greater part of the crews of the vessels came ashore every
evening, and we passed the time in going about from one house
to another, and listening to all manner of languages. Spanish was
the common ground upon which we all met, for everyone knew
more or less of that. We had now, out of forty or fifty, representatives from almost every nation under the sun: two Englishmen, three Yankees, two Scotchmen, two Welshmen, one Irishman, three Frenchmen (two of whom were Normans, and the
third from Gascony), one Dutchman, one Austrian, two or three
Spaniards (from old Spain), half a dozen Spanish Americans
and half-breeds, two native Indians from Chile and the Island of
Chiloé, one Negro, one mulatto, about twenty Italians, from all
parts of Italy, as many more Sandwich Islanders, one Otaheitan,
and one Kanaka from the Marquesas Islands.

The night before the vessels were ready to sail, all the Europeans united and had an entertainment at the *Rosa's* hide
house, and we had songs of every nation and tongue. A German
gave us *"Ach, mein lieber Augustin!"* the three Frenchmen roared
through the Marseilles hymn, the English and Scotchmen gave
us "Rule Britannia," and "Wha'll Be King but Charlie?" the Italians and Spaniards screamed through some national affairs, for
which I was none the wiser; and we three Yankees made an attempt at the "Star-spangled Banner." After these national tributes
had been paid, the Austrian gave us a very pretty little love song
and the Frenchmen sang a spirited thing called *"Sentinelle! O
prenez garde á vous!"* and then followed the mélange which

might have been expected. When I left them, the aguardiente and *anisado* was pretty well in their heads, and they were all singing and talking at once, and their peculiar national oaths were getting as plenty as pronouns.

The next day the two vessels got under way for the windward, and left us in quiet possession of the beach. Our numbers were somewhat enlarged by the opening of the new houses, and the "society" of the beach a little changed. In charge of the *Catalina's* house was an old Scotchman who, like most of his countrymen, had a pretty good education and, like many of them, was rather pragmatical, and had a ludicrously solemn conceit. He employed his time in taking care of his pigs, chickens, turkeys, dogs, etc., and in smoking his long pipe. Everything was as neat as a pin in the house, and he was as regular in his hours as a chronometer, but as he kept very much by himself, was not a great addition to our society. He hardly spent a cent all the time he was on the beach, and the others said he was no shipmate. He had been a petty officer on board the British frigate *Dublin*, Captain Lord James Townshend, and had great ideas of his own importance. The man in charge of the *Rosa's* house was an Austrian by birth, but spoke, read, and wrote four languages with ease and correctness. German was his native tongue, but being born near the borders of Italy, and having sailed out of Genoa, the Italian was almost as familiar to him as his own language. He was six years on board of an English man-of-war, where he learned to speak our language with ease, and also to read and write it. He had been several years in Spanish vessels, and had acquired that language so well that he could read any books in it. He was between forty and fifty years of age, and was a singular mixture of the man-of-war's-man and Puritan. He talked a great deal about propriety and steadiness, and gave good advice to the youngsters and Kanakas, but seldom went up to the town without coming down "three sheets in the wind." One holiday, he and old Robert (the Scotchman from the *Catalina*) went up to the town, and got so "cozy" talking over old stories and giving one another good advice that they came down double-backed on a horse, and both rolled off into the sand as soon as the horse stopped. This put an end to their pretensions, and they never heard the last of it from the rest of the men. On the night of the entertainment at the

Rosa's house, I saw old Schmidt (that was the Austrian's name) standing up by a hogshead holding on by both hands, and calling out to himself: "Hold on, Schmidt! Hold on, my good fellow, or you'll be on your back!" Still, he was an intelligent, good-natured old fellow, and had a chestful of books, which he willingly lent me to read. In the same house with him were a Frenchman and an Englishman, the latter a regular-built "man-of-war Jack," a thorough seaman, a hearty, generous fellow and at the same time a drunken, dissolute dog. He made it a point to get drunk once a fortnight (when he always managed to sleep on the road, and have his money stolen from him) and to battle the Frenchman once a week. These, with a Chilean and a half a dozen Kanakas, formed the addition to our company.

In about six weeks from the time when the *Pilgrim* sailed we had got all the hides which she left us cured and stowed away; and having cleared up the ground, emptied the vats, and set everything in order, had nothing more to do until she should come down again but to supply ourselves with wood. Instead of going twice a week for this purpose, we determined to give one whole week to getting wood, and then we should have enough to last us half through the summer. Accordingly we started off every morning, after an early breakfast, with our hatchets in hand, and cut wood until the sun was over the point—which was our only mark of time, as there was not a watch on the beach— and then came back to dinner, and after dinner started off again with our handcart and ropes, and carted and "backed" it down until sunset. This we kept up for a week, until we had collected several cords—enough to last us for six or eight weeks—when we knocked off altogether, much to my joy; for though I liked straying in the woods, and cutting, very well, yet the backing the wood for so great a distance over an uneven country was, without exception, the hardest work I had ever done. I usually had to kneel down and contrive to heave the load, which was well strapped together, on my back, and then rise up and start off with it up the hills and down the vales, sometimes through thickets—the rough points sticking into the skin, and tearing the clothes so that at the end of the week I had hardly a whole shirt to my back.

We were now through all our work, and had nothing more to do until the *Pilgrim* should come down again. We had nearly got

through our provisions too, as well as our work; for our officer
had been very wasteful of them, and the tea, flour, sugar, and
molasses were all gone. We suspected him of sending them up
to the town, and he always treated the squaws with molasses
when they came down to the beach. Finding wheat coffee and
dry bread rather poor living, we clubbed together, and I went
up to the town on horseback with a great salt bag behind the
saddle and a few reals in my pocket, and brought back the bag
full of onions, pears, beans, watermelons, and other fruits; for
the young woman who tended the garden, finding that I belonged
to the American ship, and that we were short of provisions, put
in a double portion. With these we lived like fighting cocks for
a week or two, and had, besides, what the sailors call "a blowout
on sleep," not turning out in the morning until breakfast was
ready. I employed several days in overhauling my chest and
mending up all my old clothes until I had got everything in order—patch upon patch, like a sand barge's mainsail. Then I took
hold of Bowditch's *Navigator,* which I had always with me. I had
been through the greater part of it, and now went carefully
through it from beginning to end, working out most of the examples. That done, and there being no signs of the *Pilgrim,* I
made a descent upon old Schmidt, and borrowed and read all
the books there were on the beach. Such a dearth was there of
these latter articles that anything, even a little child's storybook
or the half of a shipping calendar, appeared like a treasure. I
actually read a jestbook through from beginning to end in one
day, as I should a novel, and enjoyed it very much. At last, when
I thought that there were no more to be got, I found at the bottom of old Schmidt's chest *Mandeville: A Romance,* by Godwin,
in five volumes. This I had never read, but Godwin's name was
enough, and after the wretched trash I had devoured, anything
bearing the name of a distinguished intellectual man was a prize
indeed. I bore it off, and for two days I was up early and late,
reading with all my might, and actually drinking in delight. It is
no extravagance to say that it was like a spring in a desert land.

From the sublime to the ridiculous—so with me, from Mandeville to hide-curing was but a step, for

WEDNESDAY, JULY 8, brought us the brig *Pilgrim* from the windward. As she came in, we found that she was a good deal altered

in her appearance. Her short topgallant masts were up; her bow-lines all unrove (except to the courses); the quarter boom irons off her lower yards; her jack crosstrees sent down; several blocks got rid of; running rigging rove in new places; and numberless other changes of the same character. Then too, there was a new voice giving orders, and a new face on the quarter-deck—a short, dark-complexioned man in a green jacket and a high leather cap. These changes of course set the whole beach on the *qui vive*, and we were all waiting for the boat to come ashore, that we might have things explained. At length, after the sails were furled and the anchor carried out, the boat pulled ashore, and the news soon flew that the expected ship had arrived at Santa Barbara, and that Captain T— had taken command of her, and her captain, Faucon, had taken the *Pilgrim* and was the green-jacketed man on the quarter-deck. The boat put directly off again, without giving us time to ask any more questions, and we were obliged to wait till night, when we took a little skiff that lay on the beach and paddled off. When I stepped aboard, the second mate called me aft and gave me a large bundle directed to me and marked "Ship *Alert*." This was what I had longed for, yet I refrained from opening it until I went ashore. Diving down into the fore-castle, I found the same old crew, and was really glad to see them again. Numerous inquiries passed as to the new ship, the latest news from Boston, etc., etc. S— had received letters from home, and nothing remarkable had happened.

The *Alert* was agreed on all hands to be a fine ship, and a large one: "Larger than the *Rosa*."—"Big enough to carry off all the hides in California."— "Rail as high as a man's head."—"A crack ship."—"A regular dandy," etc., etc. Captain T— took command of her, and she went directly up to Monterey; from thence she was to go to San Francisco, and probably would not be in San Diego under two or three months. Some of the *Pilgrim's* crew found old shipmates aboard of her, and spent an hour or two in her forecastle the evening before she sailed. They said her decks were as white as snow—holystoned every morning, like a man-of-war's; everything on board "shipshape and Bristol-fashion"; a fine crew, three mates, a sailmaker and carpenter, and all complete. "They've got a *man* for mate of that ship, and not a bloody *sheep* about decks!"—"A mate that knows his duty, and makes everybody do theirs, and won't be imposed upon either by captain or crew." After collecting all the information we could get on this point, we asked something about their new captain. He had hardly been on board long enough for them to know much about him, but he had taken hold strong as soon as he took command—sending down the topgallant masts, and unreeving half the rigging, the very first day.

Having got all the news we could, we pulled ashore; and as soon as we reached the house I, as might be supposed, proceeded directly to opening my bundle, and found a reasonable supply of duck, flannel shirts, shoes, etc., and, what was still more valuable, a packet of eleven letters. These I sat up nearly all night to read, and put them carefully away, to be read and reread again and again at my leisure. Then came a half a dozen newspapers, the last of which gave notice of Thanksgiving, and of the clearance of "ship *Alert,* Edward H. Faucon, master, for Callao and California, by Bryant, Sturgis & Co." No one has ever been on distant voyages and after a long absence received a newspaper from home who cannot understand the delight that they give one. I read every part of them—the houses to let, things lost or stolen, auction sales; and all. Nothing carries you so entirely to a place, and makes you feel so perfectly at home, as a newspaper. The very name of *Boston Daily Advertiser* sounded hospitably upon the ear.

The *Pilgrim* discharged her hides, which set us at work again, and in a few days we were in the old routine of dry hides—wet hides—cleaning—beating, etc. Captain Faucon came quietly up to me as I was at work with my knife cutting the meat from a dirty hide, asked me how I liked California, and repeated, "*Tityre, tu patulae recubans sub tegmine fagi.*" Very apropos, thought I, and, at the same time, serves to show that you understand Latin. However, a kind word from a captain is a thing not to be slighted, so I answered him civilly, and made the most of it.

SATURDAY, JULY 11. The *Pilgrim* set sail for the windward, and left us to go on in our old way. Having laid in such a supply of wood, and the days being now long and invariably pleasant, we had a good deal of time to ourselves. All the duck I received from home I soon made up into trousers and frocks, and displayed every Sunday a complete suit of my own make, from head to foot, having formed the remnants of the duck into a cap. Reading, mending, sleeping, with occasional excursions into the bush with the dogs in search of coatis, hares, and rabbits, or to encounter a rattlesnake, and now and then a visit to the presidio, filled up our spare time after hide-curing was over for the day. Another amusement which we sometimes indulged in was "burning the water" for crawfish. For this purpose, we procured a pair of "grains," with a long staff like a harpoon, and making torches with tarred rope twisted round a long pine stick, took the only boat on the beach, a small skiff, and with a torchbearer in the bow, a steersman in the stern, and one man on each side with the grains, went off on dark nights to burn the water. This is fine sport. Keeping within a few rods of the shore, where the water is not more than three or four feet deep, with a clear sandy bottom, the torches light everything up so that one could almost have seen a pin among the grains of sand. The crawfish are an easy prey, and we used soon to get a load of them. The other fish were more difficult to catch, yet we frequently speared a number of them, of various kinds and sizes. The *Pilgrim* brought us down a supply of fishhooks, which we had never had before on the beach, and for several days we went down to the point and caught a quantity of cod and mackerel. On one of these expeditions we saw a battle between two Sandwich Islanders and a shark. "Johnny" had been playing about our boat for some time, driving away the fish and showing his teeth at our bait, when we missed him, and in a few moments heard a great shouting between two Kanakas who were fishing on the rock opposite to us— "*E hana hana make i ka ia nui!*" "*E pii mai aikane!*" etc., etc.— and saw them pulling away on a stout line, and "Johnny Shark" floundering at the other end. The line soon broke, but the Kanakas would not let him off so easily, and sprang directly into the water after him. Now came the tug of war. Before he could get into deep water, one of them seized him by the tail and ran up with him upon the beach; but Johnny twisted round, turning his head under his body, and showing his teeth in the vicinity of the Kanaka's hand, made him let go and spring out of the way. The shark now turned tail and made the best of his way, by flapping and floundering, toward deep water; but here again, before he was fairly off the other Kanaka seized him by the tail and made a spring toward the beach, his companion at the same time paying away upon him with stones and a large stick. As soon, however, as the shark could turn, he was obliged to let go his hold; but the instant he made toward deep water, they were both behind him, watching their chance to seize him. In this way the battle went on for some time, the shark, in a rage, splashing and twisting about, and the Kanakas, in high excitement, yelling at the top of their voices; but the shark at last got off, carrying away a hook and line, and not a few severe bruises.

California and Its Inhabitants

W E KEPT UP a constant connection with the presidio, and
by the close of the summer I had added much to my
vocabulary, besides having made the acquaintance of
nearly everybody in the place and acquired some knowledge of
the character and habits of the people, as well as of the institu-
tions under which they live.

California was first discovered in 1536, by Cortès, and was
subsequently visited by numerous other adventurers, as well as
by commissioned voyagers of the Crown. It was found to be inhabited by numerous tribes of Indians, and to be in many parts
extremely fertile; to which, of course, were added rumors of gold
mines, pearl fishery, etc. No sooner was the importance of the
country known than the Jesuits obtained leave to establish themselves in it, to Christianize and enlighten the Indians. They established missions in various parts of the country toward the close
of the seventeenth century, and collected the natives about them,
baptizing them into the Church, and teaching them the arts of
civilized life. To protect the Jesuits in their missions, and at the
same time to support the power of the Crown over the civilized
Indians, two forts were erected and garrisoned, one at San Diego
and the other at Monterey. These were called presidios, and divided the command of the whole country between them. Presidios
have since been established at Santa Barbara and San Francisco,
thus dividing the country into four large districts, each with its
presidio, and governed by the commandant. The soldiers, for the
most part, married civilized Indians, and thus in the vicinity of
each presidio sprang up, gradually, small towns. In the course
of time, vessels began to come into the ports to trade with the
missions, and received hides in return; and thus began the great
trade of California. Nearly all the cattle in the country belonged
to the missions, and they employed their Indians, who became

in fact their slaves, in tending their vast herds. In the year 1793, when Vancouver visited San Diego, the missions had obtained great wealth and power, and are accused of having depreciated the country with the sovereign, that they might be allowed to retain their possessions. On the expulsion of the Jesuits from the Spanish dominions, the missions passed into the hands of the Franciscans, though without any essential change in their management. Ever since the independence of Mexico, the missions have been going down, until at last a law was passed stripping them of all their possessions, and confining the priests to their spiritual duties, and at the same time declaring all the Indians free and independent rancheros. The change in the condition of the Indians was, as may be supposed, only nominal: they are virtually slaves as much as they ever were. But in the missions the change was complete. The priests have now no power except in their religious character, and the great possessions of the missions are given over to be preyed upon by the harpies of the civil power, who are sent there in the capacity of *administradores,* to settle up the concerns—and who usually end in a few years by making themselves fortunes, and leaving their stewardships worse than they found them. The dynasty of the priests was much more acceptable to the people of the country, and indeed to everyone concerned with the country, by trade or otherwise, than that of the *administradores.* The priests were attached perpetually to one mission, and felt the necessity of keeping up its credit. Accordingly, their debts were regularly paid, and the people were, in the main, well treated, and attached to those who had spent their whole lives among them. But the *administradores* are strangers sent from Mexico, having no interest in the country, not identified in any way with their charge, and for the most part men of desperate fortunes—broken-down politicians and soldiers—whose only object is to retrieve their condition in as short a time as possible. The change had been made but a few years before our arrival on the coast, yet in that short time the trade was much diminished, credit impaired, and the venerable missions going rapidly to decay. The external arrangements remain the same. There are four presidios, having under their protection the various missions, and pueblos, which are towns formed by the civil power and containing no mission or presidio. The most northerly presidio is San Francisco; the next Monterey; the next Santa Barbara, including the mission of the same, San Luis Obispo, and San Buenaventura, which is the finest mission in the whole country, having very fertile soil and rich vineyards. The last, and most southerly, is San Diego, including the mission of the same, San Juan Campestrano, the Pueblo de los Angeles, the largest town in California, with the neighboring mission of San Gabriel. The priests in spiritual matters are subject to the Archbishop of Mexico, and in temporal matters to the governor general, who is the great civil and military head of the country.

The government of the country is an arbitrary democracy, having no common law, and no judiciary. Their only laws are made and unmade at the caprice of the legislature, and are as variable as the legislature itself. They pass through the form of sending representatives to the congress at Mexico, but as it takes several months to go and return, and there is very little communication between the capital and this distant province, a member usually stays there as permanent member, knowing very well that there will be revolutions at home before he can write and receive an answer; and if another member should be sent, he has only to challenge him, and decide the contested election in that way.

Revolutions are matters of constant occurrence in California. They are got up by men who are at the foot of the ladder and in desperate circumstances, just as a new political party is started by such men in our own country. The only object, of course, is the loaves and fishes; and instead of caucusing, paragraphing, libeling, feasting, promising, and lying, as with us, they take muskets and bayonets, and seizing upon the presidio and customhouse, divide the spoils, and declare a new dynasty. As for justice, they know no law but will and fear. A Yankee who had been naturalized and become a Catholic, and had married in the country, was sitting in his house at the Pueblo de los Angeles with his wife and children when a Spaniard with whom he had had a dif-culty entered the house and stabbed him to the heart before them all. The murderer was seized by some Yankees who had settled there, and kept in confinement until a statement of the whole affair could be sent to the governor general. He refused to do anything about it, and the countrymen of the murdered man, seeing no prospect of justice being administered, made known that if nothing was done, they should try the man themselves. It chanced that at this time there was a company of forty trappers and hunters from Kentucky, with their rifles, who had made their headquarters at the Pueblo; and these, together with the Americans and Englishmen in the place, who were between twenty and thirty in number, took possession of the town, and waiting a reasonable time, proceeded to try the man according to the forms in their own country. A judge and jury were appointed, and he was tried, convicted, sentenced to be shot, and carried out before the town with his eyes blindfolded. The names of all the men were then put into a hat, and each one pledging himself to perform his duty, twelve names were drawn out, and the men took their stations with their rifles and, firing at the word, laid him dead. He was decently buried, and the place was restored quietly to the proper authorities. A general with titles enough for a hidalgo was at San Gabriel, and issued a proclamation as long as the foretop bowline, threatening destruction to the rebels, but never stirred from his fort; for forty Kentucky hunters, with their rifles, were a match for a whole regiment of hungry, drawling, lazy half-breeds. This affair happened while we were at San Pedro (the port of the Pueblo), and we had all the particulars directly from those who were on the spot. A few months afterward another man, whom we had often seen in San Diego, murdered a man and his wife on the highroad between the Pueblo and San Luis Rey, and the foreigners not feeling themselves called upon to act in this case, the parties being all natives, nothing was done about it; and I frequently afterward saw the murderer in San Diego, where he was living with his wife and family.

When a crime has been committed by Indians, justice, or rather vengeance, is not so tardy. One Sunday afternoon while I was at San Diego an Indian was sitting on his horse when another with whom he had had some difficulty came up to him, drew a long knife, and plunged it directly into the horse's heart. The Indian sprang from his falling horse, drew out the knife, and plunged it into the other Indian's breast, over his shoulder, and laid him dead. The poor fellow was seized at once, clapped into the calabozo, and kept there until an answer could be received from Monterey. A few weeks afterward, I saw the poor wretch sitting on the bare ground in front of the calabozo, with his feet chained to a stake and handcuffs about his wrists. I knew there was very little hope for him. Although the deed was done in hot blood, the horse on which he was sitting being his own, and a great favorite, yet he was an Indian, and that was enough. In about a week after I saw him, I heard that he had been shot. These few instances will serve to give one a notion of the distribution of justice in California.

In their domestic relations, these people are no better than in their public. The men are thriftless, proud, and extravagant, and very much given to gaming; and the women have but little education and a good deal of beauty, and their morality, of course, is none of the best; yet the instances of infidelity are much less frequent than one would at first suppose. In fact, one vice is set over against another, and thus something like a balance is obtained. The women have but little virtue, but then the jealousy of their husbands is extreme, and their revenge deadly and almost certain. A few inches of cold steel has been the punishment of many an unwary man who has been guilty, perhaps, of nothing more than indiscretion of manner. The difficulties of the attempt are numerous, and the consequences of discovery fatal. With the unmarried women, too, great watchfulness is used. The main object of the parents is to marry their daughters well, and to this the slightest slip would be fatal. The sharp eyes of a dueña, and the cold steel of a father or brother, are a protection which the characters of most of them—men and women—render by no means useless; for the very men who would lay down their lives to avenge the dishonor of their own family would risk the same lives to complete the dishonor of another.

Of the poor Indians very little care is taken. The priests, indeed, at the missions are said to keep them very strictly, and some rules are usually made by the alcaldes to punish their misconduct; but it all amounts to but little. Indeed, to show the entire want of any sense of morality or domestic duty among them, I have frequently known an Indian to bring his wife, to whom he was lawfully married in the church, down to the beach and carry her back again dividing with her the money which she had got from the sailors. If any of the girls were discovered by the alcalde to be open evil-livers, they were whipped, and kept at work sweeping the square of the presidio, and carrying mud and bricks for the buildings; yet a few reals would generally buy them off. Intemperance, too, is a common vice among the Indians. The Spaniards, on the contrary, are very abstemious, and I do not remember ever having seen a Spaniard intoxicated.

Such are the people who inhabit a country embracing four or five hundred miles of seacoast, with several good harbors; with fine forests in the north; the waters filled with fish, and the plains covered with thousands of herds of cattle; blessed with a climate than which there can be no better in the world; free from all manner of diseases, whether epidemic or endemic; and with a soil in which corn yields from seventy- to eighty-fold. In the hands of an enterprising people, what a country this might be! we are ready to say. Yet how long would a people remain so, in such a country? The Americans (as those from the United States are called) and Englishmen who are fast filling up the principal towns, and getting the trade into their hands, are indeed more industrious and effective than the Spaniards; yet their children are brought up Spaniards in every respect, and if the "California fever" (laziness) spares the first generation, it always attacks the second.

22

Life on Shore · The "Alert"

SATURDAY, JULY 18. This day sailed the Mexican hermaphrodite brig, *Fazio*, for San Blas and Mazatlán. This was the brig which was driven ashore at San Pedro in a southeaster, and had been lying at San Diego to repair and take in her cargo. The owner of her had had a good deal of difficulty with the government about the duties, etc., and her sailing had been delayed for several weeks; but everything having been arranged, she got under way with a light breeze, and was floating out of the harbor when two horsemen came dashing down to the beach at full speed, and tried to find a boat to put off after her; but there being none on the beach, they offered a handful of silver to any Kanaka who would swim off and take a letter on board. One of the Kanakas, a fine, active, well-made young fellow, instantly threw off everything but his duck trousers, and putting the letter into his hat, swam off after the vessel. Fortunately, the wind was very light and the vessel was going slowly, so that although she was nearly a mile off when he started, he gained on her rapidly. He went through the water leaving a wake like a small steamboat. I certainly never saw such swimming before. They saw him coming from the deck, but did not heave to, suspecting the nature of his errand; yet, the wind continuing light, he swam alongside and got on board, and delivered his letter. The captain read the letter, told the Kanaka there was no answer, and giving him a glass of brandy, left him to jump overboard and find the best of his way to the shore. The Kanaka swam in for the nearest point of land, and in about an hour made his appearance at the hide house. He did not seem at all fatigued, had made three or four dollars, got a glass of brandy, and was in fine spirits. The brig kept on her course, and the government officers, who had come down to forbid her sailing, went back, each with something like a flea in his ear, having depended upon extorting a little more money from the owner.

It was now nearly three months since the *Alert* arrived at Santa Barbara, and we began to expect her daily. About a half a mile behind the hide house was a high hill; and every afternoon, as soon as we had done our work, some one of us walked up to see if there were any sail in sight coming down before the regular trades, which blow every afternoon. Each day after the latter part of July we went up the hill and came back disappointed. I was anxious for her arrival, for I had been told by letter that the owners in Boston, at the request of my friends, had written to Captain T— to take me on board the *Alert*, in case she returned to the United States before the *Pilgrim;* and I of course wished to know whether the order had been received, and what was the destination of the ship. One year more or less might be of small consequence to others, but it was everything to me. It was now just a year since we sailed from Boston, and at the shortest, no vessel could expect to get away under eight or nine months, which would make our absence two years in all. This would be pretty long, but would not be fatal. It would not necessarily be decisive of my future life. But one year more would settle the matter. I should be a sailor for life; and although I had made up my mind to it before I had my letters from home, and was, as I thought, quite satisfied, yet as soon as an opportunity was held out to me of returning, and the prospect of another kind of life was opened to me, my anxiety to return, and at least to have the chance of deciding upon my course for myself, was beyond measure. Besides that, I wished to be "equal to either fortune," and to qualify myself for an officer's berth, and a hide house was no place to learn seamanship in. I had become experienced in hide-curing, and everything went on smoothly, and I had many opportunities of becoming acquainted with the people and much leisure for reading and studying navigation; yet practical seamanship could only be got on board ship. Therefore I determined to ask to be taken on board the ship when she arrived. By the first of August we finished curing all our hides, stored them away, cleaned out our vats (in which latter work we spent two days, up to our knees in mud and the sediments of six months' hide-curing, in a stench which would drive an Irishman from his breakfast), and got in readiness for the arrival of the ship, and had another leisure interval of three of four weeks—which I spent, as usual, in reading, writing, studying, making and mending my clothes, and getting my wardrobe in complete readiness in case I should go on board the ship; and in fishing, ranging the woods with the dogs, and in occasional visits to the presidio and mission. A good deal of my time was spent in taking care of a little puppy which I had selected from thirty-six that were born within three days of one another at our house. He was a fine, promising pup, with four white paws and all the rest of his body of a dark brown. I built a little kennel for him, and kept him fastened there, away from the other dogs, feeding and disciplining him myself. In a few weeks I got him in complete subjection, and he grew finely, was very much attached to me, and bid fair to be one of the leading dogs on the beach. I called him "Bravo," and the only thing I regretted at the thought of leaving the beach was parting with him.

Day after day we went up the hill, but no ship was to be seen, and we began to form all sorts of conjectures as to her whereabouts; and the theme of every evening's conversation at the different houses, and in our afternoon's *paseo* on the beach, was the ship—where she could be, had she been to San Francisco? how many hides she would bring, etc., etc.

TUESDAY, AUGUST 25. This morning the officer in charge of our house went off beyond the point a-fishing in a small canoe, with two Kanakas; and we were sitting quietly in our room at the hide house when, just before noon, we heard a complete yell of "Sail ho!" breaking out from all parts of the beach at once—from the Kanakas' oven to the *Rosa's* house. In an instant everyone was out of his house, and there was a fine, tall ship, with royals and skysails set, bending over before the strong afternoon breeze and coming rapidly round the point. Her yards were braced sharp up; every sail was set, and drew well; the Yankee ensign was flying from her mizzenpeak; and having the tide in her favor, she came up like a race horse. It was nearly six months since a new vessel had entered San Diego, and of course everyone was on the qui vive. She certainly made a fine appearance. Her light sails were taken in as she passed the low, sandy tongue of land, and clewing up her headsails, she rounded handsomely to under her

mizzen topsail, and let go the anchor at about a cable's length
from the shore. In a few minutes the topsail yards were manned,
and all three of the topsails furled at once. From the fore-topgallant yard the men slid down the stay to furl the jib, and from
the mizzen-topgallant yard, by the stay, into the maintop, and
thence to the yard; and the men on the topsail yards came down
the lifts to the yardarms of the courses. The sails were furled with
great care, the bunts triced up by jiggers, and the jibs stowed
in cloth. The royal yards were then struck, tackles got on the
yardarms and the stay, the longboat hoisted out, a large anchor
carried astern, and the ship moored. Then the captain's gig was
lowered away from the quarter, and a boat's crew of fine lads
between the ages of fourteen and eighteen pulled the captain
ashore. The gig was a light whaleboat, handsomely painted, and
fitted up with cushions, etc., in the stern sheets. We immediately
attacked the boat's crew, and got very thick with them in a few
minutes. We had much to ask about Boston, their passage out,
etc., and they were very curious to know about the life we were
leading on the beach. One of them offered to exchange with me,
which was just what I wanted; we had only to get the permission
of the captain.

After dinner the crew began discharging their hides, and as
we had nothing to do at the hide houses, we were ordered aboard
to help them. I had now my first opportunity of seeing the ship
which I hoped was to be my home for the next year. She looked
as well on board as she did from without. Her decks were wide
and roomy (there being no poop, or house on deck, which dis-
figures the after part of most of our vessels), flush fore and aft,
and as white as snow, which the crew told us was from constant
use of holystones. There was no foolish gilding and gingerbread
work to take the eye of landsmen and passengers, but everything
was "shipshape and Bristol-fashion." There was no rust, no dirt,
no rigging hanging slack, no fag ends of ropes and "Irish pend-
ants" aloft, and the yards were squared "to a *t*" by lifts and
braces. The mate was a fine, hearty, noisy fellow with a voice
like a lion, and always wide-awake. He was "a man, every inch
of him," as the sailors said, and though "a bit of a horse," and
"a hard customer," yet he was generally liked by the crew. There
were also a second and third mate, a carpenter, sailmaker, stew-

ard, cook, etc., and twelve, including boys, before the mast. She had on board seven thousand hides which she had collected at the windward, and also horns and tallow. All these we began discharging, from both gangways at once, into the two boats, the second mate having charge of the launch and the third mate of the pinnace. For several days we were employed in this way, until all the hides were taken out, when the crew began taking in ballast and we returned to our old work, hide-curing.

SATURDAY, AUG. 29. Arrived, brig *Catalina*, from the windward.

SUNDAY, 30. This was the first Sunday that the crew had been in San Diego, and of course they were all for going up to see the town. The Indians came down early, with horses to let for the day, and all the crew who could obtain liberty went off to the presidio and mission, and did not return until night. I had seen enough of San Diego, and went on board and spent the day with some of the crew, whom I found quietly at work in the forecastle, mending and washing their clothes, and reading and writing. They told me that the ship stopped at Callao in the passage out, and there lay three weeks. She had a passage of little over eighty days from Boston to Callao, which is one of the shortest on record. There they left the *Brandywine* frigate, and other smaller American ships of war, and the English frigate *Blonde*, and a French seventy-four. From Callao they came directly to California, and had visited every port on the coast, including San Francisco. The forecastle in which they lived was large, tolerably well lighted by bull's-eyes, and being kept perfectly clean, had quite a comfortable appearance; at least, it was far better than the little, black, dirty hole in which I had lived so many months on board the *Pilgrim*. By the regulations of the ship, the forecastle was cleaned out every morning, and the crew, being very neat, kept it clean by some regulations of their own, such as having a large spit box always under the steps and between the bitts, and obliging every man to hang up his wet clothes. In addition to this, it was holystoned every Saturday morning. In the afterpart of the ship was a handsome cabin, a dining-room, and a trade room fitted out with shelves and furnished with all sorts of goods. Between these and the forecastle was the between-decks, as high as the gun deck of a frigate, being six feet and a half under the beams. These between-decks were holystoned regularly, and kept in the most perfect order, the carpenter's bench and tools being in one part, the sailmaker's in another, and the boatswain's locker, with the spare rigging, in a third. A part of the crew slept here, in hammocks swung fore and aft from the beams, and triced up every morning. The sides of the between-decks were clapboarded, the knees and stanchions of iron, and the latter made to unship. The crew said she was as tight as a drum, and a fine sea boat, her only fault being that of most fast ships—that she was wet forward. When she was going, as she sometimes would, eight or nine knots on a wind, there would not be a dry spot forward of the gangway. The men told great stories of her sailing, and had great confidence in her as a "lucky ship." She was seven years old, and had always been in the Canton trade, and never had met with an accident of any consequence, and had never made a passage that was not shorter than the average. The third mate, a young man of about eighteen, nephew of one of the owners, had been in the ship from a small boy, and "believed in the ship," and the chief mate thought more of her than he would of a wife and family.

The ship lay about a week longer in port, when, having discharged her cargo and taken in ballast, she prepared to get under way. I now made my application to the captain to go on board. He told me that I could go home in the ship when she sailed (which I knew before), and finding that I wished to be on board while she was on the coast, said he had no objection, if I could find one of my own age to exchange with me for the time. This I easily accomplished, for they were glad to change the scene by a few months on shore, and, moreover, escape the winter and the southeasters; and I went on board the next day, with my chest and hammock, and found myself once more afloat.

23

New Ship and Shipmates ·
My Watchmate

T UESDAY, SEPT. 8. This was my first day's duty on board the
ship, and though a sailor's life is a sailor's life wherever
it may be, yet I found everything very different here from
the customs of the brig *Pilgrim*. After all hands were called, at
daybreak, three minutes and a half were allowed for every man
to dress and come on deck, and if any were longer than that,
they were sure to be overhauled by the mate, who was always
on deck, and making himself heard all over the ship. The head
pump was then rigged, and the decks washed down by the second and third mates, the chief mate walking the quarter-deck
and keeping a general supervision, but not deigning to touch a
bucket or a brush. Inside and out, fore and aft, upper deck and
between-decks, steerage and forecastle, rail, bulwarks, and waterways, were washed, scrubbed, and scraped with brooms and
canvas, and the decks were wet and sanded all over and then
holystoned. The holystone is a large, soft stone, smooth on the
bottom, with long ropes attached to each end, by which the crew
keep it sliding fore and aft over the wet, sanded decks. Smaller
hand stones, which the sailors call "prayer books," are used to
scrub in among the crevices and narrow places where the large
holystone will not go. An hour or two we were kept at this work,
when the head pump was manned, and all the sand washed off
the decks and sides. Then came swabs and squilgees; and after
the decks were dry, each one went to his particular morning job.
There were five boats belonging to the ship—launch, pinnace,
jolly boat, larboard quarter-boat, and gig—each of which had a
coxswain, who had charge of it, and was answerable for the order
and cleanness of it. The rest of the cleaning was divided among

the crew, one having the brass and composition work about the capstan; another the bell, which was of brass, and kept as bright as a gilt button; a third, the harness cask; another, the manrope stanchions; others, the steps of the forecastle and hatchways, which were hauled up and holystoned. Each of these jobs must be finished before breakfast; and in the meantime the rest of the crew filled the scuttle butt, and the cook scraped his kids (wooden tubs out of which the sailors eat) and polished the hoops, and placed them before the galley to await inspection. When the decks were dry, the lord paramount made his appearance on the quarter-deck and took a few turns, when eight bells were struck, and all hands went to breakfast. Half an hour was allowed for breakfast, when all hands were called again, the kids, pots, bread bags, etc., stowed away; and, this morning, preparations were made for getting under way. We paid out on the chain by which we swung, hove in on the other, catted the anchor, and hove short on the first. This work was done in shorter time than was usual on board the brig; for though everything was more than twice as large and heavy, the cat block being as much as a man could lift and the chain as large as three of the *Pilgrim's*, yet there was a plenty of room to move about in, more discipline and system, more men, and more goodwill. Everyone seemed ambitious to do his best, officers and men knew their duty, and all went well. As soon as she was hove short, the mate, on the forecastle, gave the order to loose the sails, and in an instant everyone sprang into the rigging, up the shrouds, and out on the yards, scrambling by one another—the first up the best fellow—cast off the yardarm gaskets and bunt gaskets, and one man remained on each yard, holding the bunt jigger with a turn round the tye, all ready to let go, while the rest laid down to man the sheets and halyards. The mate then hailed the yards: "All ready forward?—All ready the crossjack yards?" etc., etc., and "Aye, aye, sir!" being returned from each, the word was given to let go; and in the twinkling of an eye the ship, which had shown nothing but her bare yards, was covered with her loose canvas from the royal mastheads to the decks. Everyone then laid down, except one man in each top, to overhaul the rigging, and the topsails were hoisted and sheeted home, all three yards going to the masthead at once, the larboard watch hoisting the fore, the starboard watch the main, and five light hands (of whom I was one) picked from the two watches, the mizzen. The yards were then trimmed, the anchor weighed, the cat block hooked on, the fall stretched out, manned by "all hands and the cook," and the anchor brought to the head with "Cheerily, men!" in full chorus. The ship being now under way, the light sails were set, one after another, and she was under full sail before she had passed the sandy point. The fore royal, which fell to my lot (being in the mate's watch), was more than twice as large as that of the *Pilgrim*, and though I could handle the brig's easily, I found my hands full with this, especially as there were no jacks to the ship, everything being for neatness, and nothing left for Jack to hold on by but his eyelids.

As soon as we were beyond the point, and all sail out, the order was given, "Go below, the watch!" and the crew said that ever since they had been on the coast they had had watch and watch while going from port to port; and in fact everything showed that, though strict discipline was kept, and the utmost was required of every man in the way of his duty, yet on the whole there was very good usage on board. Each one knew that he must be a man, and show himself smart when at his duty, yet everyone was satisfied with the usage; and a contented crew, agreeing with one another, and finding no fault, was a contrast indeed with the small, hard-used, dissatisfied, grumbling, desponding crew of the *Pilgrim*.

It being the turn of our watch to go below, the men went to work mending their clothes and doing other little things for themselves, and I, having got my wardrobe in complete order at San Diego, had nothing to do but to read. I accordingly overhauled the chests of the crew, but found nothing that suited me exactly until one of the men said he had a book which "told all about a great highwayman" at the bottom of his chest, and he producing it, I found, to my surprise and joy, that it was nothing else than Bulwer's *Paul Clifford*. This I seized immediately, and going to my hammock, lay there swinging and reading until the watch was out. The between-decks were clear, the hatchways open, and a cool breeze blowing through them, the ship under easy way, and everything comfortable. I had just got well into the story when eight bells were struck and we were all ordered to dinner. After dinner came our watch on deck for four hours, and at four o'clock I went below again, turned into my hammock, and read until the dog watch. As no lights were allowed after eight o'clock, there was no reading in the night watch. Having light winds and calms, we were three days on the passage, and each watch below during the daytime I spent in the same manner until I had finished my book. I shall never forget the enjoyment I derived from it. To come across anything with the slightest claims to literary merit was so unusual that this was a perfect feast to me. The brilliancy of the book, the succession of capital hits, lively and characteristic sketches, kept me in a constant state of pleasing sensations. It was far too good for a sailor. I could not expect such fine times to last long.

While on deck, the regular work of the ship went on. The sailmaker and carpenter worked between-decks, and the crew had their work to do on the rigging, drawing yarns, making spun yarn, etc., as usual in merchantmen. The night watches were much more pleasant than on board the *Pilgrim*. There, there were so few in a watch that, one being at the wheel and another on the lookout, there was no one left to talk with; but here we had seven in a watch, so that we had long yarns in abundance. After two or three night watches, I became quite well acquainted with all the larboard watch. The sailmaker was the head man of the watch, and was generally considered the most experienced seaman on board. He was a thoroughbred old man-of-war'sman, had been to sea twenty-two years, in all kinds of vessels, men-of-war, privateers, slavers, and merchantmen—everything except whalers, which a thorough sailor despises, and will always steer clear of if he can. He had, of course, been in all parts of the world, and was remarkable for drawing a long bow. His yarns frequently stretched through a watch, and kept all hands awake. They were always amusing from their improbability, and indeed he never expected to be believed, but spun them merely for amusement; and as he had some humor and a good supply of man-of-war slang and sailor's salt phrases, he always made fun. Next to him in age and experience, and of course in standing in the watch, was an Englishman named Harris, of whom I shall have more to say hereafter. Then came two or three Americans who had been the common run of European and South American voyages, and one who had been in a "spouter," and of course had all the whaling stories to himself. Last of all was a broad-backed, thick-headed boy from Cape Cod who had been in mackerel schooners, and was making his first voyage in a square-rigged vessel. He was born in Hingham, and of course was called "Bucketmaker." The other watch was composed of about the same number. A tall, fine-looking Frenchman with coal-black whiskers and curly hair, a first-rate seaman, and named John (one name is enough for a sailor), was the head man of the watch. Then came two Americans (one of whom had been a dissipated young man of property and family, and was reduced to duck trousers and monthly wages), a German, an English lad named Ben, who belonged on the mizzen-topsail yard with me, and was a good sailor for his years, and two Boston boys just from the public schools. The carpenter sometimes mustered in the starboard watch, and was an old sea dog, a Swede by birth, and accounted the best helmsman in the ship. This was our ship's company, beside cook and steward, who were blacks, three mates, and the captain.

The second day out, the wind drew ahead, and we had to beat up the coast, so that in tacking ship I could see the regulations of the vessel. Instead of going wherever was most convenient, and running from place to place wherever work was to be done, each man had his station. A regular tacking-and-wearing bill was made out. The chief mate commanded on the forecastle, and had charge of the headsails and the forward part of the ship. Two of the best men in the ship—the sailmaker from our watch and John the Frenchman from the other—worked the forecastle. The third mate commanded in the waist and, with the carpenter and one man, worked the main tack and bowline; the cook, ex-officio, the foresheet, and the steward the main. The second mate had charge of the afteryards, and let go the lee fore and main braces. I was stationed at the weather crossjack braces, three other light hands at the lee; one boy at the spanker sheet and guy; a man and a boy at the main topsail, topgallant, and royal braces; and all the rest of the crew—men and boys—tallied onto the main brace. Everyone here knew his station, must be there when all hands were called to put the ship about, and was answerable for every rope committed to him. Each man's rope must be let go and hauled in at the order, properly made fast, and neatly coiled away when the ship was about. As soon as all hands are at their stations, the captain, who stands on the weather side of the quarter-deck, makes a sign to the man at the wheel to put it down, and calls out "Helm's alee!" "Helm's alee!" answers the mate on the forecastle, and the head sheets are let go. "Raise tacks and sheets!" says the captain. "Tacks and sheets!" is passed forward, and the fore tack and main sheet are let go. The next thing is to haul taut for a swing. The weather crossjack braces and the lee main braces are each belayed together on two pins, and ready to be let go, and the opposite braces hauled taut. "Main-topsail haul!" shouts the captain. The braces are let go, and if he has taken his time well, the yards swing round like a top; but if he is too late, or too soon, it is like drawing teeth. The after yards are then braced up and belayed, the mainsheet hauled aft, the spanker eased over to leeward, and the men from the braces stand by the head yards. "Let go and haul!" says the captain. The second mate lets go the weather forebraces, and the men haul in to leeward. The mate, on the forecastle, looks out for the head yards. "Well the fore-topsail yard!" "Topgallant yard's well!" "Royal yard too much! Haul into windward! So! Well *that!*" "Well *all!*" Then the starboard watch board the main tack, and the larboard watch lay forward and board the fore tack and haul down the jib sheet, clapping a tackle on it if it blows very fresh. The after yards are then trimmed, the captain generally looking out for them himself. "Well, the crossjack yard!" "Small pull the main topgallant yard!" "Well *that!*" "Well the mizzen-topsail yard!" "Crossjack yards all *well!*" "Well all aft!" "Haul taut to windward!" Everything being now trimmed and in order, each man coils up the rigging at his own station, and the order is given, "Go below, the watch!"

During the last twenty-four hours of the passage we beat off and on the land, making a tack about once in four hours, so that I had a sufficient opportunity to observe the working of the ship; and certainly it took no more men to brace about this ship's lower yards, which were more than fifty feet square, than it did those of the *Pilgrim*, which were not much more than half the size. So much depends upon the manner in which the braces run, and the state of the blocks, and Captain Wilson, of the *Aya-cucho*, who was afterward a passenger with us upon a trip to windward, said he had no doubt that our ship worked two men lighter than his brig.

FRIDAY, SEPT. 11. This morning at four o'clock, went below, San Pedro point being about two leagues ahead, and the ship going on under studding sails. In about an hour we were waked up by the hauling of the chain about decks, and in a few minutes "All hands ahoy!" was called, and we were all at work hauling in and making up the studding sails, overhauling the chain forward, and getting the anchors ready. "The *Pilgrim* is there at anchor," said someone as we were running about decks, and taking a moment's look over the rail, I saw my old friend, deeply laden, lying at anchor inside of the kelp. In coming to anchor, as well as in tacking, each one had his station and duty. The light sails were clewed up and furled, the courses hauled up, and the jibs down; then came the topsails in the buntlines, and the anchor let go. As soon as she was well at anchor, all hands lay aloft to furl the topsails; and this I soon found was a great matter on board this ship, for every sailor knows that a vessel is judged a good deal by the furl of her sails. The third mate, sailmaker, and the larboard watch went upon the fore-topsail yard; the second mate, carpenter, and the starboard watch upon the main; and myself and the English lad, the two Boston boys, and the young Cape Cod man furled the mizzen topsail. This sail belonged to us altogether, to reef and to furl, and not a man was allowed to come on our yard. The mate took us under his special care, frequently making us furl the sail over three or four times, until we got the bunt up to a perfect cone and the whole sail without a wrinkle. As soon as each sail was hauled up and the bunt made, the jigger was bent onto the slack of the buntlines, and the bunt triced up on deck. The mate then took his place between the knightheads to "twig" the fore, on the windlass to twig the main, and at the foot of the mainmast for the mizzen; and if anything was wrong—too much bunt on one side, clews too taut or too slack, or any sail abaft the yard—the whole must be dropped again. When all was right, the bunts were triced well up, the yardarm gaskets passed so as not to leave a wrinkle forward of the yard—short gaskets with turns close together.

From the moment of letting go the anchor, when the captain ceases his care of things, the chief mate is the great man. With

a voice like a young lion, he was hallooing and bawling in all
directions, making everything fly, and at the same time doing
everything well. He was quite a contrast to the worthy, quiet
unobtrusive mate of the *Pilgrim*—not so estimable a man, perhaps, but a far better mate of a vessel—and the entire change in
Captain T—'s conduct since he took command of the ship was
owing, no doubt, in a great measure to this fact. If the chief officer wants force, discipline slackens, everything gets out of joint,
the captain interferes continually; that makes a difficulty between
them, which encourages the crew, and the whole ends in a three-
sided quarrel. But Mr. Brown (the mate of the *Alert*) wanted
no help from anybody, took everything into his own hands, and
was more likely to encroach upon the authority of the master
than to need any spurring. Captain T— gave his directions to
the mate in private and except in coming to anchor, getting under
way, tacking, reefing topsails, and other "all-hands work," seldom
appeared in person. This is the proper state of things, and while
this lasts, and there is a good understanding aft, everything will
go on well.

Having furled all the sails, the royal yards were next to be
sent down. The English lad and myself sent down the main,
which was larger than the *Pilgrim's* main top-gallant yard; two
more light hands, the fore; and one boy, the mizzen. This order
we always kept while on the coast, sending them up and down
every time we came in and went out of port. They were all
tripped and lowered together, the main on the starboard side,
and the fore and mizzen to port. No sooner was she all snug than
tackles were got up on the yards and stays, and the longboat
and pinnace hove out. The swinging booms were then guyed out,
and the boats made fast by guess-warps, and everything in harbor style. After breakfast, the hatches were taken off, and all got
ready to receive hides from the *Pilgrim*. All day boats were passing and repassing, until we had taken her hides from her and
left her in ballast trim. These hides made but little show in our
hold, though they had loaded the *Pilgrim* down to the water's
edge. This changing of the hides settled the question of the destination of the two vessels, which had been one of some speculation
to us. We were to remain in the leeward ports, while the *Pilgrim*
was to sail the next morning for San Francisco. After we had

knocked off work, and cleared up decks for the night, my friend
S— came on board and spent an hour with me in our berth between-decks. The *Pilgrim's* crew envied me my place on board
the ship, and seemed to think that I had got a little to windward
of them, especially in the matter of going home first. S— was determined to go home in the *Alert*, by begging or buying; if Captain T— would not let him come on other terms, he would purchase an exchange with some one of the crew. The prospect of
another year after the *Alert* should sail was rather "too much of
the monkey." About seven o'clock the mate came down into the
steerage in fine trim for fun, roused the boys out of the berth,
turned up the carpenter with his fiddle, sent the steward with
lights to put in the between-decks, and set all hands to dancing.
The between-decks were high enough to allow of jumping, and
being clear, and white from holystoning, made a fine dancing
hall. Some of the *Pilgrim's* crew were in the forecastle, and we
all turned to and had a regular sailor's shuffle, till eight bells.
The Cape Cod boy could dance the true fisherman's jig barefooted, knocking with his heels and slapping the decks with his
bare feet in time with the music. This was a favorite amusement
of the mate's, who always stood at the steerage door looking on,
and if the boys would not dance, he hazed them round with a
rope's end, much to the amusement of the men.

The next morning, according to the orders of the agent, the
Pilgrim set sail for the windward, to be gone three or four months.
She got under way with very little fuss, and came so near us as
to throw a letter on board, Captain Faucon standing at the tiller
himself and steering her as he would a mackerel smack. When
Captain T— was in command of the *Pilgrim*, there was as much
preparation and ceremony as there would be in getting a seventy-
four under way. Captain Faucon was a sailor, every inch of him;
he knew what a ship was, and was as much at home in one as
a cobbler in his stall. I wanted no better proof of this than the
opinion of the ship's crew, for they had been six months under
his command, and knew what he was; and if sailors allow their
captain to be a good seaman, you may be sure he is one, for that
is a thing they are not always ready to say.

After the *Pilgrim* left us, we lay three weeks at San Pedro,
from the eleventh of September until the second of October, en-

gaged in the usual port duties of landing cargo, taking off hides, etc., etc. These duties were much easier, and went on much more agreeably, than on board the *Pilgrim.* "The more the merrier" is the sailor's maxim; and a boat's crew of a dozen could take off all the hides brought down in a day without much trouble, by division of labor; and on shore, as well as on board, a goodwill, and no discontent or grumbling, make everything go well. The

officer, too, who usually went with us, the third mate, was a fine young fellow, and made no unnecessary trouble; so that we generally had quite a sociable time, and were glad to be relieved from the restraint of the ship. While here, I often thought of the miserable, gloomy weeks we had spent in this dull place in the brig—discontent and hard usage on board, and four hands to do all the work on shore. Give me a big ship. There is more room, more hands, better outfit, better regulation, more life, and more company. Another thing was better arranged here: we had a regular gig's crew. A light whaleboat, handsomely painted, and fitted out with stern seats, yoke, tiller ropes, etc., hung on the starboard quarter, and was used as the gig. The youngest lad in the ship, a Boston boy about thirteen years old, was coxswain of this boat, and had the entire charge of her, to keep her clean, and have her in readiness to go and come at any hour. Four light hands of about the same size and age, of whom I was one, formed the crew. Each had his oar and seat numbered, and we were obliged to be in our places, have our oars scraped white, our tholepins in, and the fenders over the side. The bowman had charge of the boathook and painter, and the coxswain of the rudder, yoke, and stern sheets. Our duty was to carry the captain and agent about, and passengers off and on—which last was no trifling duty, as the people on shore have no boats, and every purchaser, from the boy who buys his pair of shoes to the trader who buys his casks and bales, was to be taken off and on in our boat. Some days, when people were coming and going fast, we were in the boat, pulling off and on, all day long, with hardly time for our meals, making, as we lay nearly three miles from shore, from forty to fifty miles' rowing in a day. Still, we thought it the best berth in the ship; for when the gig was employed, we had nothing to do with the cargo, except small bundles which the passengers carried, and no hides to carry, besides the opportunity of seeing everybody, making acquaintances, hearing the news, etc. Unless the captain or the agent was in the boat, we had no officer with us, and often had fine times with the passengers, who were always willing to talk and joke with us. Frequently, too, we were obliged to wait several hours on shore, when we would haul the boat up on the beach, and leaving one to watch her, go up to the nearest house, or spend the time in strolling about the beach picking up shells, or playing hopscotch and other games on the hard sand. The rest of the crew never left the ship, except for bringing heavy goods and taking off hides; and though we were always in the water, the surf hardly leaving us a dry thread from morning till night, yet we were young, and the climate was good, and we thought it much better than the quiet, humdrum drag and pull on board ship. We made the acquaintance of nearly half of California; for besides carrying everybody in our boat—men, women, and children—all the messages, letters, and light packages went by us, and being known by our dress, we found a ready reception everywhere.

At San Pedro we had none of this amusement, for, there being but one house in the place, we of course had but little company. All the variety that I had was riding once a week to the nearest rancho, to order a bullock down for the ship.

The brig *Catalina* came in from San Diego, and being bound up to windward, we both got under way at the same time, for a trial of speed up to Santa Barbara, a distance of about eighty miles. We hove up and got under sail about eleven o'clock at night with a light land breeze, which died away toward morning, leaving us becalmed only a few miles from our anchoring place. The *Catalina*, being a small vessel of less than half our size, put out sweeps and got a boat ahead and pulled out to sea during the night, so that she had the sea breeze earlier and stronger than we did, and we had the mortification of seeing her standing up the coast with a fine breeze, the sea all ruffled about her, while we were becalmed inshore. When the sea breeze died away, she was nearly out of sight; and toward the latter part of the afternoon, the regular northwest wind set in fresh, we braced sharp upon it, took a pull at every sheet, tack, and halyard, and stood after her in fine style, our ship being very good on a tautened bowline. We had nearly five hours of fine sailing, beating up to windward by long stretches in and off shore, and evidently gaining on the *Catalina* at every tack. When this breeze left us, we were so near as to count the painted ports on her side. Fortunately, the wind died away when we were on our inward tack and she on her outward, so we were inshore, and caught the land breeze first, which came off upon our quarter about the middle of the first watch. All hands were turned up, and we set all sail, to the skysails and the royal studding sails; and with these we glided quietly through the water, leaving the *Catalina*, which could not spread so much canvas as we, gradually astern, and by daylight were off San Buenaventura, and our antagonist nearly out of sight. The sea breeze, however, favored her again while we were becalmed under the headland and laboring slowly along, she was abreast of us by noon. Thus we continued, ahead, astern, and abreast of one another alternately now far out at sea, and again close in under the shore. On the third morning we came into the great bay of Santa Barbara two hours behind the brig, and thus lost the bet, though if the race had been to the point, we should have beaten her by five or six hours. This, however, settled the relative sailing of the vessels, for it was admitted that although she, being small and light, could gain on us in very light winds, yet whenever there was breeze enough to set us a-going we walked away from her like hauling in a line; and in beating to windward, which is the best trial of a vessel, we had much the advantage of her.

SUNDAY, OCT. 4. This was the day of our arrival, and somehow or other, our captain always managed not only to sail, but to come into port, on a Sunday. The main reason for sailing on the Sabbath is not, as many people suppose, because Sunday is thought a lucky day, but because it is a leisure day. During the six days the crew are employed upon the cargo and other ship's works, and the Sabbath being their only day of rest, whatever additional work can be thrown into Sunday is so much gain to the owners. This is the reason of our coasters, packets, etc. sailing on the Sabbath. They get six good days' work out of the crew, and then throw all the labor of sailing into the Sabbath. Thus it was with us nearly all the time we were on the coast, and many of our Sabbaths were lost entirely to us. The Catholics on shore have no trading and make no journeys on Sunday, but the American has no national religion, and likes to show his independence of priestcraft by doing as he chooses on the Lord's Day.

Santa Barbara looked very much as it did when I left it five months before: the long sand beach with the heavy rollers breaking on it in a continual roar, and the little town imbedded on the plain, girt by its amphitheater of mountains. Day after day the sun shone clear and bright on the wide bay and the red roofs of the houses, everything being as still as death, the people really hardly seeming to earn their sunlight. Daylight actually seemed thrown away upon them. We had a few visitors, and collected about a hundred hides, and every night at sundown the gig was sent ashore to wait for the captain, who spent his evenings in the town. We always took our monkey jackets with us, and flint and steel, and made a fire on the beach with the driftwood and the bushes we pulled from the neighboring thickets, and lay down by it on the sand. Sometimes we would stray up to the town, if the captain was likely to stay late, and pass the time at some of the houses, in which we were almost always well received by the inhabitants. Sometimes earlier and sometimes later, the captain came down, when, after a good drenching in the surf, we went aboard, changed our clothes, and turned in for the night—yet not for all the night, for there was the anchor watch to stand.

This leads me to speak of my watchmate for nine months— and, taking him all in all, the most remarkable man I have ever seen—Tom Harris. An hour every night, while lying in port, Harris and myself had the deck to ourselves, and walking fore and aft night after night for months, I learned his whole character and history, and more about foreign nations, the habits of different peoples, and especially the secrets of sailors' lives and hardships, and also of practical seamanship (in which he was abundantly capable of instructing me) than I could ever have learned elsewhere. But the most remarkable thing about him was the power of his mind. His memory was perfect, seeming to form a regular chain reaching from his earliest childhood up to the time I knew him, without one link wanting. His power of calculation, too, was remarkable. I called myself pretty quick at figures, and had been through a course of mathematical studies; but, working by my head, I was unable to keep within sight of this man, who had never been beyond his arithmetic, so rapid was his calculation. He carried in his head not only a logbook of the whole voyage, in which everything was complete and accurate, and from which no one ever thought of appealing, but also an accurate registry of all the cargo, knowing precisely where each thing was, and how many hides we took in at every port.

One night he made a rough calculation of the number of hides that could be stowed in the lower hold between the fore and main masts, taking the depth of hold and breadth of beam (for he always knew the dimension of every part of the ship before he had been a month on board), and the average area and thickness of a hide; he came surprisingly near the number, as it afterward turned out. The mate frequently came to him to know the capacity of different parts of the vessel, and he could tell the sailmaker very nearly the amount of canvas he would want for each sail in the ship; for he knew the hoist of every mast and spread of every sail on the head and foot, in feet and inches. When we were at sea, he kept a running account in his head of the ship's way—the number of knots and the courses; and if the courses did not vary much during the twenty-four hours, by taking the whole progress, and allowing so many eighths southing or northing to so many easting or westing, he would make up his reckoning just before the captain took the sun at noon, and often came wonderfully near the mark. Calculation of all kinds was his delight. He had in his chest several volumes giving accounts of inventions in mechanics, which he read with great pleasure, and made himself master of. I doubt if he ever forgot anything that he read. The only thing in the way of poetry that he ever read was Falconer's *Shipwreck*, which he was delighted with, and whole pages of which he could repeat. He knew the name of every sailor that had ever been his shipmate, and also of every vessel, captain, and officer, and the principal dates of each voyage; and a sailor whom we afterward fell in with who had been in a ship with Harris nearly twelve years before was very much surprised at having Harris tell him things about himself which he had entirely forgotten. His facts, whether dates or events, no one thought of disputing; and his opinions few of the sailors dared to oppose, for, right or wrong, he always had the best of the argument with them. His reasoning powers were remarkable. I have had harder work maintaining an argument with him in a watch, even when I knew myself to be right and he was only doubting, than I ever had before—not from his obstinacy, but from his acuteness. Give him only a little knowledge of his subject and certainly among all the young men of my acquaintance and standing at college there was not one whom I had not rather meet than this man. I never answered a question from him, or advanced an opinion to him, without thinking more than once. With an iron memory, he seemed to have your whole past conversation at command, and if you said a thing now which ill agreed with something said months before, he was sure to have you on the hip. In fact, I always felt when with him that I was with no common man. I had a positive respect for his powers of mind, and felt often that if half the pains had been spent upon his education which are thrown away yearly in our colleges, he would have been a man of great weight in society. Like most self-taught men, he overestimated the value of an education, and this I often told him, though I profited by it myself; for he always treated me with respect, and often unnecessarily gave way

to me, from an overestimate of my knowledge. For the capacities
of all the rest of the crew, captain and all, he had the most sovereign contempt. He was a far better sailor, and probably a better navigator, than the captain, and had more brains than all the
afterpart of the ship put together. The sailors said, "Tom's got a
head as long as the bowsprit," and if anyone got into an argument with him, they would call out, "Ah, Jack, you'd better drop
that as you would a hot potato, for Tom will turn you inside out
before you know it."

I recollect his posing me once on the subject of the Corn Laws.
I was called to stand my watch and coming on deck, found him
there before me, and we began, as usual, to walk fore and aft in
the waist. He talked about the Corn Laws, asked me my opinion
about them, which I gave him; and my reasons, my small stock
of which I set forth to the best advantage, supposing his knowledge on the subject must be less than mine, if indeed he had
any at all. When I had got through, he took the liberty of differing from me and, to my surprise, brought arguments and facts
connected with the subject which were new to me, and to which
I was entirely unable to reply. I confessed that I knew almost
nothing of the subject, and expressed my surprise at the extent
of his information. He said that a number of years before, while
at a boardinghouse in Liverpool, he had fallen in with a pam-
phlet on the subject, and as it contained calculations, had read it
very carefully, and had ever since wished to find someone who
could add to his stock of knowledge on the question. Although it
was many years since he had seen the book, and it was a subject
with which he had no previous acquaintance, yet he had the
chain of reasoning, founded upon principles of political economy,
perfect in his memory; and his facts, so far as I could judge, were
correct—at least he stated them with great precision. The principles of the steam engine, too, he was very familiar with, having
been several months on board a steamboat, and made himself
master of its secrets. He knew every lunar star in both hemi-
spheres, and was a perfect master of his quadrant and sextant.
Such was the man who at forty was still a dog before the mast
at twelve dollars a month. The reason of this was to be found in
his whole past life as I had it, at different times, from himself.

He was an Englishman by birth, a native of Ilfracomb, in Cornwall. His father was skipper of a small coaster from Bristol, and dying, left him when quite young to the care of his mother, by whose exertions he received a common-school education, passing his winters at school and his summers in the coasting trade until his seventeenth year, when he left home to go on foreign voyages. Of this mother he often spoke with the greatest respect, and said that she was a strong-minded woman, and had the best system of education he had ever known, a system which had made respectable men of his three brothers and failed only in him, from his own indomitable obstinacy. One thing he often mentioned in which he said his mother differed from all other mothers that he had ever seen disciplining their children; that was that when he was out of humor and refused to eat, instead of putting his plate away, as most mothers would, and saying that his hunger would bring him to it in time, she would stand over him and oblige him to eat it—every mouthful of it. It was no fault of hers that he was what I saw him; and so great was his sense of gratitude for her efforts, though unsuccessful, that he determined at the close of the voyage to embark for home with all the wages he should get, to spend with and for his mother, if perchance he should find her alive.

After leaving home, he had spent nearly twenty years sailing on all sorts of voyages, generally out of the ports of New York and Boston. Twenty years of vice! Every sin that a sailor knows he had gone to the bottom of. Several times he had been hauled up in the hospitals, and as often the great strength of his constitution had brought him out again in health. Several times, too, from his known capacity, he had been promoted to the office of chief mate, and as often his conduct when in port, especially his drunkenness, which neither fear nor ambition could induce him to abandon, put him back into the forecastle. One night, when giving me an account of his life and lamenting the years of manhood he had thrown away, he said that there in the forecastle at the foot of the steps—a chest of old clothes—was the result of twenty-two years of hard labor and exposure, worked like a horse, and treated like a dog. As he grew older, he began to feel the necessity of some provision for his later years, and came gradually to the conviction that rum had been his worst enemy. One night in Havana a young shipmate of his was brought aboard drunk with a dangerous gash in his head, and his money and new clothes stripped from him. Harris had seen and been in hundreds of such scenes as these, but in his then state of mind it fixed his determination, and he resolved never to taste another drop of strong drink of any kind. He signed no pledge, and made no vow, but relied on his own strength of purpose. The first thing with him was a reason, and then a resolution, and the thing was done. The date of his resolution he knew, of course, to the very hour. It was three years before I knew him, and during all that time nothing stronger than cider or coffee had passed his lips. The sailors never thought of enticing Tom to take a glass, any more than they would of talking to the ship's compass. He was now a temperate man for life, and capable of filling any berth in a ship, and many a high station there is on shore which is held by a meaner man.

He understood the management of a ship upon scientific principles, and could give the reason for hauling every rope. And a long experience, added to careful observation at the time and a perfect memory, gave him a knowledge of the expedients and resorts in times of hazard which was remarkable, and for which I became much indebted to him, as he took the greatest pleasure in opening his stores of information to me in return for what I was enabled to do for him. Stories of tyranny and hardship which had driven men to piracy, of the incredible ignorance of masters and mates, and of horrid brutality to the sick, dead, and dying, as well as of the secret knavery and impositions practiced upon seamen by connivance of the owners, landlords, and officers—all these he had, and I could not but believe them, for men who had known him for fifteen years had never taken him even in an exaggeration, and as I have said, his statements were never disputed. I remember, among other things, his speaking of a captain whom I had known by report who never handed a thing to a sailor, but put it on deck and kicked it to him; and of another who was of the best connections in Boston who absolutely murdered a lad from Boston that went out with him before the mast to Sumatra, by keeping him hard at work while ill of the coast fever, and obliging him to sleep in the close steerage. (The same captain has since died of the same fever on the same coast.)

In fact, taking together all that I learned from him of seamanship, of the history of sailors' lives, of practical wisdom, and of human nature under new circumstances—a great history from which many are shut out—I would not part with the hours I spent in the watch with that man for any given hours of my life passed in study and social intercourse.

San Diego Again · A Descent · Hurried Departure · A New Shipmate

SUNDAY, OCT. 11. Set sail this morning for the leeward, passed within sight of San Pedro, and to our great joy, did not come to anchor, but kept directly on to San Diego, where we arrived and moored ship on

THURSDAY, OCT. 15. Found here the Italian ship *Rosa*, from the windward, which reported the brig *Pilgrim* at San Francisco, all well. Everything was as quiet here as usual. We discharged our hides, horns, and tallow, and were ready to sail again on the following Sunday. I went ashore to my old quarters, and found the gang at the hide house going on in the even tenor of their way, and spent an hour or two after dark at the oven taking a whiff with my old Kanaka friends, who really seemed glad to see me again, and saluted me as the "Aikane of the Kanakas." I was grieved to find that my poor dog Bravo was dead. He had sickened and died suddenly, the very day after I sailed in the *Alert*.

Sunday was again, as usual, our sailing day, and we got under way with a stiff breeze, which reminded us that it was the latter part of the autumn, and time to expect southeasters once more. We beat up against a strong head wind, under reefed topsails, as far as San Juan, where we came to anchor nearly three miles from the shore, with slip ropes on our cables in the old southeaster style of last winter.

TUESDAY, OCT. 20. Having got everything ready, we set the agent ashore, who went up to the mission to hasten down the hides for the next morning. This night we had the strictest orders to look out for southeasters, and the long, low clouds seemed rather threatening. But the night passed without any trouble, and early the next morning we hove out the longboat and pinnace, lowered away the quarter-boats, and went ashore to bring off our hides. Here we were again in this romantic spot—a perpendicular hill, twice the height of the ship's masthead, with a single circuitous path to the top and long sand beach at its base with the swell of the whole Pacific breaking high on it, and our hides ranged in piles on the overhanging summit. The captain sent me, who was the only one of the crew that had ever been there before, to the top, to count the hides and pitch them down. There I stood again, as six months before, throwing off the hides and watching them pitching and scaling to the bottom, while the men, dwarfed by the distance, were walking to and fro on the beach carrying the hides as they picked them up to the distant boats on the tops of their heads. Two or three boatloads were sent off, until at last all were thrown down, and the boats nearly loaded again, when we were delayed by a dozen or twenty hides which had lodged in the recesses of the hill, and which we could not reach by any missiles, as the general line of the side was exactly perpendicular, and these places were caved in and could not be seen or reached from the top. As hides are worth in Boston twelve and a half cents a pound, and the captain's commission was 2 per cent, he determined not to give them up, and sent on board for a pair of topgallant-studding-sail halyards, and requested someone of the crew to go to the top and come down by the halyards. The older sailors said the boys, who were light and active, ought to go, while the boys thought that strength and experience were necessary. Seeing the dilemma, and feeling myself to be near the medium of these requisites, I offered my services and went up, with one man to tend the rope, and prepared for the descent.

We found a stake fastened strongly into the ground and apparently capable of holding my weight, to which we made one end of the halyards well fast, and taking the coil, threw it over the brink. The end, we saw, just reached to a landing place from which the descent to the beach was easy. Having nothing on but shirt, trousers, and hat, the common sea rig of warm weather, I had no stripping to do, and began my descent by taking hold of the rope in each hand and slipping down, sometimes with hands and feet round the rope and sometimes breasting off with one hand and foot against the precipice and holding onto the rope with the other. In this way I descended until I came to a place which shelved in, and in which the hides were lodged. Keeping hold of the rope with one hand, I scrambled in, and by the other hand and my feet succeeded in dislodging all the hides, and continued on my way. Just below this place, the precipice projected again, and going over the projection, I could see nothing below me but the sea and the rocks on which it broke, and a few gulls flying in mid-air. I got down in safety, pretty well covered with dirt, and for my pains was told, "What a damned fool you were to risk your life for a half a dozen hides!"

While we were carrying the hides to the boat, I perceived what I had been too busy to observe before—that heavy black clouds were rolling up from seaward, a strong swell heaving in, and every sign of a southeaster. The captain hurried everything. The hides were pitched into the boats and, with some difficulty and by wading nearly up to our armpits, we got the boats through the surf, and began pulling aboard. Our gig's crew towed the pinnace astern of the gig, and the launch was towed by six men in the jolly boat. The ship was lying three miles off, pitching at her anchor, and the farther we pulled, the heavier grew the swell. Our boat stood nearly up and down several times, the pinnace parted her towline, and we expected every moment to see the launch swamped. We at length got alongside, our boats half-full of water. And now came the greatest difficulty of all—unloading the boats in a heavy sea which pitched them about so that it was almost impossible to stand in them, raising them sometimes even with the rail and again dropping them below the bends. With great difficulty, we got all the hides aboard and stowed under hatches, the yard and stay tackles hooked on, and the launch and pinnace hoisted, chocked, and gripped. The quarter-boats were then hoisted up, and we began heaving in on the chain. Getting the anchor was no easy work in such a sea, but as we were not coming back to this port, the captain determined not to slip. The ship's head pitched into the sea, and the water rushed through the hawseholes, and the chain surged so as almost to unship the barrel of the windlass. "Hove short, sir!" said the mate. "Aye, aye! Weather-bitt your chain and loose the topsails! Make sail

on her, men—with a will!" A few moments served to loose the topsails, which were furled with reefs, to sheet them home, and hoist them up. "Bear a hand!" was the order of the day, and everyone saw the necessity of it, for the gale was already upon us. The ship broke out her own anchor, which we catted and fished, after a fashion, and stood off from the lee shore against a heavy head sea, under reefed topsails, fore-topmast staysail, and spanker. The forecourse was given to her, which helped her a little; but as she hardly held her own against the sea, which was setting her to leeward, "Board the main tack!" shouted the captain, when the tack was carried forward and taken to the windlass, and all hands called to the handspikes. The great sail bellied out horizontally as though it would lift up the mainstay, the blocks rattled and flew about; but the force of machinery was too much for her. "Heave ho! Heave and pawl! Yo heave hearty ho!" and in time with the song, by the force of twenty strong arms, the windlass came slowly round, pawl after pawl, and the weather clew of the sail was brought down to the waterways. The starboard watch hauled aft the sheet, and the ship tore through the water like a mad horse, quivering and shaking at every joint, and dashing from her head the foam, which flew off at every blow yards and yards to leeward. A half-hour of such sailing served our turn, when the clews of the sail were hauled up, the sail furled, and the ship, eased of her press, went more quietly on her way. Soon after, the foresail was reefed, and we mizzentopmen were sent up to take another reef in the mizzen topsail. This was the first time I had taken a weather earing, and I felt not a little proud to sit astride of the weather yardarm, pass the earing, and sing out "Haul out to leeward!" From this time until we got to Boston, the mate never suffered anyone but our own gang to go on the mizzen-topsail yard, either for reefing or furling, and the young English lad and myself generally took the earings between us.

Having cleared the point and got well out to sea, we squared away the yards, made more sail, and stood on, nearly before the wind, for San Pedro. It blew strong, with some rain, nearly all night, but fell calm toward morning, and the gale having gone over, we came to,

THURSDAY, OCT. 22, at San Pedro, in the old southeaster berth, a league from shore, with a slip rope on the cable, reefs in the topsails, and rope yarns for gaskets. Here we lay ten days, with the usual boating, hide-carrying, rolling of cargo up the steep hill, walking barefooted over stones, and getting drenched in salt water.

The third day after our arrival, the *Rosa* came in from San Juan, where she went the day after the southeaster. Her crew said it was as smooth as a millpond after the gale, and she took off nearly a thousand hides, which had been brought down for us, and which we lost in consequence of the southeaster. This mortified us, not only that an Italian ship should have got to windward of us in the trade, but because every thousand hides went toward completing the forty thousand which we were to collect before we could say good-by to California.

Rumors of War · A Spouter ·
Shipping for a Southeaster ·
A Gale

SUNDAY, NOVEMBER 1. Sailed this day (Sunday again) for Santa Barbara, where we arrived on the fifth. Coming round San Buenaventura and nearing the anchorage, we saw two vessels in port, a large full-rigged and a small hermaphrodite brig. The former the crew said must be the *Pilgrim;* but I had been too long in the *Pilgrim* to be mistaken in her, and I was right in differing from them, for upon nearer approach her long, low shear, sharp bows and raking masts told quite another story. "Man-of-war brig," said some of them. "Baltimore clipper," said others. The *Ayacucho,* thought I, and soon the broad folds of the beautiful banner of St. George—white field with blood-red border and cross—were displayed from her peak. A few minutes put it beyond a doubt, and we were lying by the side of the *Ayacucho,* which had sailed from San Diego about nine months before while we were lying there in the *Pilgrim.* She had since been to Valparaiso, Callao, and the Sandwich Islands, and had just come on the coast. Her boat came on board, bringing Captain Wilson, and in half an hour the news was all over the ship that there was a war between the United States and France. Exaggerated accounts reached the forecastle. Battles had been fought, a large French fleet was in the Pacific, etc., etc.; and one of the boat's crew of the *Ayacucho* said that when they left Callao, a large French frigate and the American frigate *Brandywine,* which were lying there, were going outside to have a battle, and that the English frigate *Blonde* was to be umpire, and see fair play. Here was important news for us. Alone on an unprotected coast, with-

out an American man-of-war within some thousands of miles,
and the prospect of a voyage home through the whole length of
the Pacific and Atlantic oceans! A French prison seemed a much
more probable place of destination than the good port of Boston.
However, we were too salt to believe every yarn that comes into
the forecastle, and waited to hear the truth of the matter from
higher authority. By means of the supercargo's clerk, I got the
amount of the matter, which was that the governments had had
a difficulty about the payment of a debt; that war had been
threatened and prepared for, but not actually declared, although
it was pretty generally anticipated. This was not quite so bad, yet
was no small cause of anxiety. But we cared very little about the
matter ourselves. "Happy-go-lucky" with Jack! We did not believe that a French prison would be much worse than hide-
droghing on the coast of California; and no one who has not been
a long, dull voyage shut up in one ship can conceive of the effect
of monotony upon one's thoughts and wishes. The prospect of a
change is like a green spot in a desert, and the remotest probability of great events and exciting scenes gives a feeling of delight, and sets life in motion, so as to give a pleasure which anyone not in the same state would be entirely unable to account
for. In fact, a more jovial night we had not passed in the forecastle for months. Everyone seemed in unaccountably high spirits.
An undefined anticipation of radical changes, of new scenes, and
great doings, seemed to have possessed everyone, and the common drudgery of the vessel appeared contemptible. Here was a
new vein opened: a grand theme of conversation, and a topic
for all sorts of discussions. National feeling was wrought up. Jokes
were cracked on the only Frenchman in the ship, and comparisons made between "old horse" and "soup meager," etc., etc.

We remained in uncertainty as to this war for more than two
months, when an arrival from the Sandwich Islands brought us
the news of an amicable arrangement of the difficulties.

The other vessel which we found in port was the hermaphrodite brig *Avon,* from the Sandwich Islands. She was fitted up in
handsome style; fired a gun and ran her ensign up and down at
sunrise and sunset; had a band of four or five pieces of music
on board, and appeared rather like a pleasure yacht than a trader;
yet, in connection with the *Loriotte, Clementine, Bolivar, Con-*

voy, and other small vessels belonging to sundry Americans at Oahu, she carried on a great trade—legal and illegal—in otter skins, silks, teas, specie, etc.

The second day after our arrival, a full-rigged brig came round the point from the northward, sailed leisurely through the bay, and stood off again for the southeast, in the direction of the large island of Catalina. The next day the *Avon* got under way and stood in the same direction, bound for San Pedro. This might do for marines and Californians, but we knew the ropes too well. The brig was never again seen on the coast, and the *Avon* arrived at San Pedro in about a week with a full cargo of Canton and American goods.

This was one of the means of escaping the heavy duties the Mexicans lay upon all imports. A vessel comes on the coast, enters a moderate cargo at Monterey, which is the only customhouse, and commences trading. In a month or more, having sold a large part of her cargo, she stretches over to Catalina, or other of the large uninhabited islands which lie off the coast in a trip from port to port, and supplies herself with choice goods from a vessel from Oahu, which has been lying off and on the islands waiting for her. Two days after the sailing of the *Avon*, the *Loriotte* came in from the leeward, and without doubt had also a snatch at the brig's cargo.

TUESDAY, Nov. 10. Going ashore as usual in the gig just before sundown to bring off the captain, we found, upon taking in the captain and pulling off again, that our ship, which lay the farthest out, had run up her ensign. This meant "Sail ho!" of course, but as we were within the point we could see nothing. "Give way, boys! Give way! Lay out on your oars, and long stroke!" said the captain, and stretching to the whole length of our arms, bending back again so that our backs touched the thwarts, we sent her through the water like a rocket. A few minutes of such pulling opened the islands, one after another, in range of the point, and gave us a view of the canal, where was a ship under topgallant sails standing in, with a light breeze, for the anchorage. Putting the boat's head in the direction of the ship, the captain told us to lay out again; and we needed no spurring, for the prospect of boarding a new ship, perhaps from home, hearing the news and having something to tell of when we got back, was excitement enough for us, and we gave way with a will. In the meantime, it fell flat calm, and being within a couple of miles of the ship, we expected to board her in a few moments, when a sudden breeze sprang up, dead ahead for the ship, and she braced up and stood off toward the islands, sharp on the larboard tack, making good way through the water. This of course brought us up, and we had only to "ease larboard oars, pull round starboard!" and go aboard the *Alert*, with something very like a flea in the ear. There was a light land breeze all night, and the ship did not come to anchor until the next morning. As soon as her anchor was down we went aboard, and found her to be the whaleship *Wilmington and Liverpool Packet*, of New Bedford, last from the "offshore ground," with nineteen hundred barrels of oil. A "spouter" we knew her to be as soon as we saw her, by her cranes and boats, and by her stump topgallant masts and a certain slovenly look to the sails, rigging, spars, and hull; and when we got on board, we found everything to correspond—spouter-fashion. She had a false deck, which was rough and oily, and cut up in every direction by the chimes of oil casks; her rigging was slack and turning white; no paint on the spars or blocks; clumsy seizings and straps without covers, and homeward-bound splices in every direction. Her crew, too, were not in much better order. Her captain was a slab-sided, shamble-legged Quaker in a suit of brown, with a broad-brimmed hat, and sneaking about decks like a sheep with his head down; and the men looked more like fishermen and farmers than they did like sailors.

Though it was by no means cold weather (we having on only our red shirts and duck trousers), they all had on woolen trousers —not blue and shipshape, but of all colors—brown, drab, gray, aye, and *green*, with suspenders over their shoulders and pockets to put their hands in. This, added to guernsey frocks, striped comforters about the neck, thick cowhide boots, woolen caps, and a strong, oily smell and a decidedly green look, will complete the description. Eight or ten were on the fore-topsail yard, and as many more in the main, furling the topsails, while eight or ten were hanging about the forecastle doing nothing. This was a strange sight for a vessel coming to anchor, so we went up to them to see what was the matter. One of them, a stout, hearty-looking fellow, held out his leg and said he had the scurvy; another had cut his hand; and others had got nearly well, but said that there were plenty aloft to furl the sails, so they were sogering on the forecastle. There was only one "splicer" on board, a fine-looking old tar who was in the bunt of the fore-topsail. He was probably the only sailor in the ship, before the mast. The mates, of course, and the boat-steerers, and also two or three of the crew had been to sea before, but only whaling voyages; and the greater part of the crew were raw hands just from the bush, as green as cabbages, and had not yet got the hayseed out of their heads. A crew of thirty men were half an hour in doing what would have been done in the *Alert*, with eighteen hands to go aloft, in fifteen or twenty minutes.

We found they had been at sea six or eight months, and had no news to tell us, so we left them, and promised to get liberty to come on board in the evening, for some curiosities, etc. Accordingly, as soon as we were knocked off in the evening and had got supper, we obtained leave, took a boat, and went aboard and spent an hour or two. They gave us pieces of whalebone, and the teeth and other parts of curious sea animals, and we exchanged books with them—a practice very common among ships in foreign ports, by which you get rid of the books you have read and reread and a supply of new ones in their stead, and Jack is not very nice as to their comparative value.

THURSDAY, Nov. 12. This day was quite cool in the early part, and there were black clouds about; but as it was often so in the morning, nothing was apprehended and all the captains went ashore together to spend the day. Toward noon the clouds hung heavily over the mountains, coming halfway down the hills that encircle the town of Santa Barbara, and a heavy swell rolled in from the southeast. The mate immediately ordered the gig's crew away, and, at the same time we saw boats pulling ashore from the other vessels. Here was a grand chance for a rowing match, and everyone did his best. We passed the boats of the *Ayacucho* and *Loriotte*, but could gain nothing upon, and indeed hardly hold our own with, the long, six-oared boat of the whaleship.

In a few minutes the captains came hurrying down on the run, and there was no time to be lost, for the gale promised to be a severe one and the surf was breaking on the beach three deep, higher and higher every instant. The *Ayacucho's* boat, pulled by four Kanakas, put off first, and as they had no rudder or steering oar, would probably never have got off had we not waded out with them as far as the surf would permit. The next that made the attempt was the whaleboat, for we, being the most experienced "beachcombers," needed no help, and stayed till the last. Whalemen make the best boats' crews in the world for a long pull, but this landing was new to them, and notwithstanding the examples they had had, they slued round and were hove up—boat, oars, and men all together—high and dry upon the sand. The second time, they filled, and had to turn their boat over and set her off again. We could be of no help to them, for they were so many as to be in one another's way, without the addition of our numbers. The third time, they got off, though not without shipping a sea which drenched them all and half-filled their boat, keeping them bailing until they reached their ship. We now got ready to go off, putting the boat's head out, English Ben and I, who were the largest, standing on each side of the bows, to keep her "head on" to the sea, two more shipping and manning the two afteroars, and the captain taking the steering oar. Two or three Spaniards who stood upon the beach looking at us wrapped their cloaks about them, shook their heads, and muttered *"Caramba!"* They had no taste for such doings; in fact, the hydrophobia is a national malady, and shows itself in their persons as well as their actions.

Watching for a "smooth chance," we determined to show the other boats the way it should be done, and as soon as ours floated, ran out with her, keeping her head on with all our strength and the help of the captain's oar, and the two afteroarsmen giving way regularly and strongly until our feet were off the ground, we tumbled into the bows, keeping perfectly still, from fear of hindering the others. For some time it was doubtful how it would go. The boat stood nearly up and down in the water, and the sea, rolling from under her, let her fall on the water with a force which seemed almost to stave her bottom in. By quietly sliding two oars forward along the thwarts, without impeding the rowers, we shipped two bow oars, and thus, by the help of four oars and the captain's strong arm, we got safely off, though we shipped several seas which left us half-full of water. We pulled alongside of the *Loriotte,* put her skipper on board, and found her making

preparations for slipping, and then pulled aboard our own ship.
Here Mr. Brown, always "on hand," had got everything ready,
so that we had only to hook on the gig and hoist it up when the
order was given to loose the sails. While we were on the yards,
we saw the *Loriotte* under way, and before our yards were mast-
headed the *Ayacucho* had spread her wings and, with yards
braced sharp up, was standing athwart our hawse. There is no
prettier sight in the world than a full-rigged, clipper-built brig
sailing sharp on the wind. In a moment our slip rope was gone,
the head yards filled away, and we were off. Next came the
whaler, and in a half an hour from the time when four vessels
were lying quietly at anchor without a rag out or a sign of motion, the bay was deserted, and four white clouds were standing
off to sea. Being sure of clearing the point, we stood off with our
yards a little braced in, while the *Ayacucho* went off with a taut
bowline, which brought her to windward of us. During all this
day, and the greater part of the night, we had the usual southeaster entertainment—a gale of wind, variegated and finally
topped off with a drenching rain of three or four hours. At daybreak the clouds thinned off and rolled away, and the sun came
up clear. The wind, instead of coming out from the northward,
as is usual, blew steadily and freshly from the anchoring ground.
This was bad for us, for being "flying light," with little more than
ballast trim, we were in no condition for showing off on a taut
bowline, and had depended upon a fair wind, with which, by
the help of our light sails and studding sails, we meant to have
been the first at the anchoring ground; but the *Ayacucho* was a
good league to windward of us, and was standing in in fine style.
By hauling every brace and bowline, and clapping watch tackles
on all the sheets and halyards, we managed to hold our own, and
drop the leeward vessels a little in every tack. When we reached
the anchoring ground, the *Ayacucho* had got her anchor, furled
her sails, squared her yards, and was lying as quietly as if nothing had happened for the last twenty-four hours.

We had our usual good luck in getting our anchor without
letting go another, and were all snug, with our boats at the boom
ends, in half an hour. In about two hours more the whaler came
in, and made a clumsy piece of work in getting her anchor, being obliged to let go her best bower, and finally to get out a

kedge and a hawser. They were heave-ho-ing, stopping and un-stopping, pawling, catting, and fishing, for three hours; and the sails hung from the yards all the afternoon, and were not furled until sundown. The *Loriotte* came in just after dark and let go her anchor, making no attempt to pick up the other until the next day.

SATURDAY, Nov. 14. This day we got under way, with the agent and several Spaniards of note as passengers, bound up to Monterey. We went ashore in the gig to bring them off with their baggage, and found them waiting on the beach, and a little afraid about going off, as the surf was running very high. This was nuts to us; for we liked to have a Spaniard wet with salt water, and then the agent was very much disliked by the crew, one and all; and we hoped, as there was no officer in the boat, to have a chance to duck them, for we knew that they were such "marines" that they would not know whether it was our fault or not. Accordingly we kept the boat so far from shore as to oblige them to wet their feet in getting into her, and then waited for a good high comber, and letting the head slue a little round, sent the whole force of the sea into the stern sheets, drenching them from head to feet. The Spaniards sprang out of the boat, swore, and shook themselves, and protested against trying it again, and it was with the greatest difficulty that the agent could prevail upon them to make another attempt. The next time we took care, and went off easily enough, and pulled aboard. The crew came to the side to hoist in their baggage, and we gave them the wink, and they heartily enjoyed the half-drowned looks of the company.

Everything being now ready, and the passengers aboard, we ran up the ensign and broad pennant (for there was no man-of-war, and we were the largest vessel on the coast), and the other vessels ran up their ensigns. Having hove short, cast off the gaskets, and made the bunt of each sail fast by the jigger, with a man on each yard, at the word the whole canvas of the ship was loosed, and with the greatest rapidity possible everything was sheeted home and hoisted up, the anchor tripped and catheaded, and the ship under headway. We were determined to show the "spouter" how things could be done in a smart ship, with a good crew, though not more than half their number. Before we doubled the point we were going at a dashing rate, and leaving the ship-

ping far astern. We had a fine breeze to take us through the
canal. The breeze died away at night, and we were becalmed
all day on Sunday, about halfway between Santa Barbara and
Point Conception. Sunday night we had a light, fair wind, which
set us up again; and having a fine sea breeze on the first part
of Monday, we had the prospect of passing without any trouble
Point Conception—the Cape Horn of California, where it begins
to blow the first of January and blows all the year round. Toward
the latter part of the afternoon, however, the regular northwest
wind, as usual, set in, which brought in our studding sails and
gave us the chance of beating round the point, which we were
now just abreast of, and which stretched off into the Pacific, high,
rocky, and barren, forming the central point of the coast for
hundreds of miles north and south. A capful of wind will be a
bagful here, and before night our royals were furled, and the
ship was laboring hard under her topgallant sails. At eight bells
our watch went below, leaving her with as much sail as she
could stagger under, the water flying over the forecastle at every
plunge. It was evidently blowing harder, but then there was not
a cloud in the sky, and the sun had gone down bright.

We had been below but a short time before we had the usual
premonitions of a coming gale: seas washing over the whole forward part of the vessel, and her bows beating against them with
a force and sound like the driving of piles. The watch, too,
seemed very busy trampling about decks, and singing out at the
ropes. A sailor can always tell by the sound what sail is coming
in, and in a short time we heard the topgallant sails come in, one
after another, and then the flying jib. This seemed to ease her a
good deal, and we were fast going off to the land of Nod when
—bang, bang, bang on the scuttle, and "All hands reef topsails
ahoy!" started us out of our berths. It not being very cold
weather, we had nothing extra to put on, and were soon on deck.
I shall never forget the fineness of the sight. It was a clear and
rather a chilly night; the stars were twinkling with an intense
brightness, and as far as the eye could reach there was not a
cloud to be seen. The horizon met the sea in a defined line. A
painter could not have painted so clear a sky. There was not a
speck on it. Yet it was blowing great guns from the northwest.
When you can see a cloud to windward, you feel that there is

a place for the wind to come from, but here it seemed to come from nowhere. No person could have told from the heavens, by their eyesight alone, that it was not a still summer's night. One reef after another we took in the topsails, and before we could get them hoisted up, we heard a sound like a short, quick rattling of thunder and the jib was blown to atoms out of the bolt-rope. We got the topsails set, and the fragments of the jib stowed away, and the fore-topmast staysail set in its place, when the great mainsail gaped open and the sail ripped from head to foot. "Lay up on that main yard and furl the sail, before it blows to tatters!" shouted the captain, and in a moment we were up, gathering the remains of it on the yard. We got it wrapped round the yard, and passed gaskets over it as snugly as possible, and were just on deck again when, with another loud rent, the fore-topsail, which had been double-reefed, split in two athwartships, just below the reef band, from earing to earing. Here again it was down yard, haul out reef tackles, and lay out on the yard for reefing. By hauling the reef tackles chockablock, we took the strain from the other earings, and passing the close-reef earing and knotting the points carefully, we succeeded in setting the sail, close-reefed.

We had but just got the rigging coiled up, and were waiting to hear "Go below, the watch!" when the main royal worked loose from the gaskets and blew directly out to leeward, flapping, and shaking the mast like a wand. Here was a job for somebody. The royal must come in or be cut adrift, or the mast would be snapped short off. All the light hands in the starboard watch were sent up, one after another, but they could do nothing with it. At length John, the tall Frenchman, the head of the starboard watch (and a better sailor never stepped on a deck), sprang aloft, and by the help of his long arms and legs, succeeded after a hard struggle—the sail blowing over the yardarm to leeward, and the skysail blowing directly over his head—in smothering it, and frapping it with long pieces of sennit. He came very near being blown or shaken from the yard several times, but he was a true sailor, every finger a fishhook. Having made the sail snug, he prepared to send the yard down, which was a long and difficult job; for frequently he was obliged to stop and hold on with all his might for several minutes, the ship pitching so as to make it

impossible to do anything else at that height. The yard at length
came down safe, and after it, the fore and mizzen-royal yards
were sent down. All hands were then sent aloft, and for an hour
or two we were hard at work making the booms well fast, unreeving the studding sail and royal and skysail gear, getting rolling ropes on the yards, setting up the weather-breast backstays,
and making other preparations for a storm. It was a fine night
for a gale, just cool and bracing enough for quick work without
being cold, and as bright as day. It was sport to have a gale in
such weather as this. Yet it blew like a hurricane. The wind
seemed to come with a spite, an edge to it, which threatened to
scrape us off the yards. The mere force of the wind was greater
than I had ever seen it before; but darkness, cold, and wet are
the worst parts of a storm to a sailor.

Having got on deck again, we looked round to see what time
of night it was, and whose watch. In a few minutes the man at
the wheel struck four bells, and we found that the other watch
was out, and our own half out. Accordingly, the starboard watch
went below and left the ship to us for a couple of hours, yet with
orders to stand by for a call.

Hardly had they got below before away went the fore-topmast
staysail, blown to ribbons. This was a small sail, which we could
manage in the watch, so that we were not obliged to call up the
other watch. We laid out on the bowsprit, where we were under
water half the time, and took in the fragments of the sail, and
as she must have some headsail on her, prepared to bend another
staysail. We got the new one out, into the nettings; seized on the
tack, sheets, and halyards, and the hanks; manned the halyards,
cut adrift the frapping lines, and hoisted away; but before it was
halfway up the stay it was blown all to pieces. When we belayed
the halyards, there was nothing left but the boltrope. Now large
eyes began to show themselves in the foresail, and knowing that
it must soon go, the mate ordered us on the yard to furl it. Being
unwilling to call up the watch who had been on deck all night,
he roused out the carpenter, sailmaker, cook, steward, and other
idlers, and with their help we manned the foreyard, and after
nearly half an hour's struggle mastered the sail, and got it well
furled round the yard. The force of the wind had never been
greater than at this moment. In going up the rigging, it seemed

absolutely to pin us down to the shrouds; and on the yard there was no such thing as turning a face to windward. Yet here was no driving sleet, and darkness, and wet, and cold, as off Cape Horn; and instead of a stiff oilcloth suit, southwester caps, and thick boots, we had on hats, round jackets, duck trousers, light shoes, and everything light and easy. All these things make a great difference to a sailor. When we got on deck, the man at the wheel struck eight bells (four o'clock in the morning) and "All starbowlines ahoy!" brought the other watch up. But there was no going below for us. The gale was now at its height, "blowing like scissors and thumbscrews"; the captain was on deck; the ship, which was light, rolling and pitching as though she would shake the long sticks out of her, and the sails gaping open and splitting in every direction. The mizzen topsail, which was a comparatively new sail, and close-reefed, split from head to foot in the bunt; the fore-topsail went in one rent from clew to earing, and was blowing to tatters; one of the chain bobstays parted; the spritsail yard sprang in the slings; the martingale had slued away off to leeward; and, owing to the long dry weather, the lee rigging hung in large bights at every lurch. One of the main-topgallant shrouds had parted; and, to crown all, the galley had got adrift and gone over to leeward, and the anchor on the lee bow had worked loose and was thumping the side. Here was work enough for all hands for half a day. Our gang laid out on the mizzen-topsail yard, and after more than half an hour's hard work, furled the sail, though it bellied out over our heads and again, by a slat of the wind, blew in under the yard with a fearful jerk, and almost threw us off from the footropes.

Double gaskets were passed round the yards, rolling tackles and other gear bowsed taut, and everything made as secure as could be. Coming down, we found the rest of the crew just laying down the fore rigging, having furled the tattered topsail, or rather swathed it round the yard, which looked like a broken limb, bandaged. There was no sail now on the ship but the spanker and the close-reefed main-topsail, which still held good. But this was too much after sail, and order was given to furl the spanker. The brails were hauled up, and all the light hands in the starboard watch sent out on the gaff to pass the gaskets; but they could do nothing with it. The second mate swore at them for a parcel of sogers, and sent up a couple of the best men; but they could do no better, and the gaff was lowered down. All hands were now employed in setting up the lee rigging, fishing the spritsail yard, lashing the galley, and getting tackles on the martingale, to bowse it to windward. Being in the larboard watch, my duty was forward, to assist in setting up the martingale. Three of us were out on the martingale guys and backropes for more than half an hour, carrying out, hooking, and unhooking the tackles, several times buried in the seas, until the mate ordered us in, from fear of our being washed off. The anchors were then to be taken up on the rail, which kept all hands on the forecastle for an hour, though every now and then the seas broke over it, washing the rigging off to leeward, filling the lee scuppers breast-high, and washing chock aft to the taffrail.

Having got everything secure again, we were promising ourselves some breakfast, for it was now nearly nine o'clock in the forenoon, when the main-topsail showed evident signs of giving way. Some sail must be kept on the ship, and the captain ordered the fore and main spencer gaffs to be lowered down, and the two spencers (which were storm sails, brand-new, small, and made of the strongest canvas) to be got up and bent, leaving the main-topsail to blow away, with a blessing on it if it would only last until we could set the spencers. These we bent on very carefully, with strong robands and seizings, and making tackles fast to the clews, bowsed them down to the waterways. By this time the main-topsail was among the things that have been, and we went aloft to stow away the remnant of the last sail of all those which were on the ship twenty-four hours before. The spencers were now the only whole sails on the ship and being strong and small, and near the deck, presenting but little surface to the wind above the rail, promised to hold out well. Hove to under these, and eased by having no sail above the tops, the ship rose and fell, and drifted off to leeward like a line-of-battle ship.

It was now eleven o'clock, and the watch was sent below to get breakfast, and at eight bells (noon), as everything was snug, although the gale had not in the least abated, the watch was set, and the other watch and idlers sent below. For three days and three nights the gale continued with unabated fury, and with singular regularity. There were no lulls, and very little variation in its fierceness. Our ship, being light, rolled so as almost to send the fore yardarm under water, and drifted off bodily to leeward. All this time there was not a cloud to be seen in the sky, day or night—no, not so large as a man's hand. Every morning the sun rose cloudless from the sea, and set again at night in the sea in a flood of light. The stars, too, came out of the blue one after another, night after night, unobscured, and twinkled as clear as on a still frosty night at home until the day came upon them. All this time the sea was rolling in immense surges, white with foam, as far as the eye could reach on every side, for we were now leagues and leagues from shore.

The between-decks being empty, several of us slept there in hammocks, which are the best things in the world to sleep in during a storm, it not being true of them, as it is of another kind of bed, "when the wind blows, the cradle will rock," for it is the ship that rocks, while they always hang vertically from the beams. During these seventy-two hours we had nothing to do but to turn in and out, four hours on deck and four below, eat, sleep, and keep watch. The watches were only varied by taking the helm in turn, and now and then by one of the sails, which were furled, blowing out of the gaskets and getting adrift, which sent us up on the yards; and by getting tackles on different parts of the rigging, which were slack. On the morning of the twentieth at daybreak, the gale had evidently done its worst, and had somewhat abated, so much so that all hands were called to bend new sails, although it was still blowing as hard as two common gales. One at a time, and with great difficulty and labor, the old sails were unbent and sent down by the buntlines, and three new topsails, made for the homeward passage round Cape Horn, and which had never been bent, were got up from the sail room, and under the care of the sailmaker were fitted for bending and sent up by the halyards into the tops, and, with stops and frapping lines, were bent to the yards, close-reefed, sheeted home, and hoisted. These were done one at a time, and with the greatest care and difficulty. Two spare courses were then got up and bent in the same manner and furled, and a storm jib, with the bonnet off, bent and furled to the boom. It was twelve o'clock before we got through, and five hours of more exhausting labor I never experienced; and no one of that ship's crew, I will venture to say, will ever desire again to unbend and bend five large sails in the teeth of a tremendous northwester. Toward night a few clouds appeared in the horizon, and as the gale moderated, the usual appearance of driving clouds relieved the face of the sky. The fifth day after the commencement of the storm we shook a reef out of each topsail, and set the reefed foresail, jib, and spanker; but it was not until after eight days of reefed topsails that we had a whole sail on the ship—and then it was quite soon enough, for the captain was anxious to make up for leeway, the gale having blown us half the distance to the Sandwich Islands.

Inch by inch, as fast as the gale would permit, we made sail on the ship, for the wind still continued ahead, and we had many days' sailing to get back to the longitude we were in when the storm took us. For eight days more we beat to windward under a stiff topgallant breeze, when the wind shifted and became variable. A light southeaster, to which we could carry a reefed topmast studding sail, did wonders for our dead reckoning.

FRIDAY, DECEMBER 4, after a passage of twenty days, we arrived at the mouth of the bay of San Francisco.

San Francisco · Monterey

OUR PLACE of destination had been Monterey, but as we were to the northward of it when the wind hauled ahead, we made a fair wind for San Francisco. This large bay, which lies in latitude 37° 58′, was discovered by Sir Francis Drake, and by him represented to be (as indeed it is) a magnificent bay, containing several good harbors, great depth of water, and surrounded by a fertile and finely wooded country. About thirty miles from the mouth of the bay, and on the southeast side, is a high point, upon which the presidio is built. Behind this, is the harbor in which trading vessels anchor, and near it, the mission of San Francisco, and a newly begun settlement, mostly of Yankee Californians, called Yerba Buena, which promises well. Here at anchor, and the only vessel, was a brig under Russian colors, from Asitka, in Russian America, which had come down to winter, and to take in a supply of tallow and grain, great quantities of which latter article are raised in the missions at the head of the bay. The second day after our arrival we went on board the brig, it being Sunday, as a matter of curiosity; and there was enough there to gratify it. Though no larger than the *Pilgrim,* she had five or six officers, and a crew of between twenty and thirty; and such a stupid and greasy-looking set I certainly never saw before. Although it was quite comfortable weather, and we had nothing on but straw hats, shirts, and duck trousers, and were barefooted, they had, every man of them, double-soled boots coming up to the knees, and well greased; thick woolen trousers, frocks, waistcoats, pea jackets, woolen caps, and everything in true Nova Zembla rig; and in the warmest days they made no change. The clothing of one of these men would weigh nearly as much as that of half our crew. They had brutish faces, looked like the antipodes of sailors, and apparently dealt in nothing but grease. They lived upon grease—ate it, drank it, slept in the midst of it,

and their clothes were covered with it. To a Russian, grease is
the greatest luxury. They looked with greedy eyes on the tallow
bags as they were taken into the vessel, and no doubt would have
eaten one up whole had not the officer kept watch over it. The
grease seemed actually coming through their pores, and out in
their hair, and on their faces. It seems as if it were this saturation
which makes them stand cold and rain so well. If they were to
go into a warm climate, they would all die of the scurvy.

The vessel was no better than the crew. Everything was in the
oldest and most inconvenient fashion possible: running trusses
on the yards, and large hawser cables coiled all over the decks,
and served and parceled in all directions. The topmasts, topgallant masts and studding-sail booms were nearly black for want
of scraping, and the decks would have turned the stomach of a
man-of-war'sman. The galley was down in the forecastle, and
there the crew lived in the midst of the steam and grease of the
cooking, in a place as hot as an oven and as dirty as a pigsty.
Five minutes in the forecastle was enough for us, and we were
glad to get into the open air. We made some trade with them,
buying Indian curiosities, of which they had a great number,
such as beadwork, feathers of birds, fur moccasins, etc. I purchased a large robe made of the skins of some animal dried and
sewed nicely together, and covered all over on the outside with
thick downy feathers taken from the breasts of various birds, and
arranged with their different colors so as to make a brilliant show.

A few days after our arrival the rainy season set in, and for
three weeks it rained almost every hour, without cessation. This
was bad for our trade, for the collecting of hides is managed dif-
ferently in this port from what it is in any other on the coast.
The mission of San Francisco, near the anchorage, has no trade
at all, but those of San José, Santa Clara, and others, situated on
large creeks or rivers which run into the bay, and distant between
fifteen and forty miles from the anchorage, do a greater business
in hides than any others in California. Large boats, manned by
Indians and capable of carrying nearly a thousand hides apiece,
are attached to the missions, and sent down to the vessels with
hides, to bring away goods in return. Some of the crews of the
vessels are obliged to go and come in the boats, to look out for
the hides and goods. These are favorite expeditions with the

sailors in fine weather; but now to be gone three or four days in
open boats in constant rain, without any shelter and with cold
food, was hard service. Two of our men went up to Santa Clara
in one of these boats, and were gone three days, during all which
time they had a constant rain, and did not sleep a wink, but
passed three long nights walking fore and aft the boat in the
open air. When they got on board, they were completely exhausted, and took a watch below of twelve hours. All the hides,
too, that came down in the boats were soaked with water, and
unfit to put below, so that we were obliged to trice them up to
dry, in the intervals of sunshine or wind, upon all parts of the
vessel. Our ship was nothing but a mass of hides, from the cat-
harpins to the water's edge, and from the jib-boom end to the
taffrail.

One cold, rainy evening about eight o'clock, I received orders
to get ready to start for San José at four the next morning in one
of these Indian boats, with four days' provisions. I got my oilcloth
clothes, southwester, and thick boots all ready, and turned into
my hammock early, determined to get some sleep in advance, as
the boat was to be alongside before daybreak. I slept on till all
hands were called in the morning; for, fortunately for me, the Indians, intentionally or from mistaking their orders, had gone off
alone in the night, and were far out of sight. Thus I escaped
three or four days of very uncomfortable service.

Four of our men, a few days afterward, went up in one of the
quarter-boats to Santa Clara, to carry the agent, and remained
out all night in a drenching rain in the small boat, where there
was not room for them to turn round; the agent having gone up
to the mission and left the men to their fate, making no provision
for their accommodation and not even sending them anything to
eat. After this, they had to pull thirty miles, and when they got
on board were so stiff that they could not come up the gangway
ladder. This filled up the measure of the agent's unpopularity,
and never after this could he get anything done by any of the
crew; and many a delay and vexation, and many a good ducking
in the surf, did he get to pay up old scores, or "square the yards
with the bloody quill-driver."

Having collected nearly all the hides that were to be procured,
we began our preparations for taking in a supply of wood and

water, for both of which San Francisco is the best place on the coast. A small island situated about two leagues from the anchorage, called by us "Wood Island," and by the Spaniards "Isla de los Angeles," was covered with trees to the water's edge; and to this two of our crew, who were Kennebec men and could handle an ax like a plaything, were sent every morning to cut wood, with two boys to pile it up for them. In about a week they had cut enough to last us a year, and the third mate, with myself and three others, was sent over in a large schooner-rigged open launch, which we had hired of the mission, to take in the wood and bring it to the ship. We left the ship about noon, but owing to a strong head wind, and a tide which here runs four or five knots, did not get into the harbor, formed by two points of the island, where the boats lie, until sundown. No sooner had we come to than a strong southeaster, which had been threatening us all day, set in, with heavy rain and a chilly atmosphere. We were in rather a bad situation: an open boat, a heavy rain, and a long night—for in winter in this latitude it was dark nearly fifteen hours. Taking a small skiff which we had brought with us, we went ashore, but found no shelter, for everything was open to the rain, and collecting a little wood, which we found by lifting up the leaves and brush, and a few mussels, we put aboard again, and made the best preparations in our power for passing the night. We unbent the mainsail, and formed an awning with it over the afterpart of the boat, made a bed of wet logs of wood, and, with our jackets on, lay down about six o'clock to sleep. Finding the rain running down upon us, and our jackets getting wet through, and the rough, knotty logs rather indifferent couches, we turned out, and taking an iron pan which we brought with us, we wiped it out dry, put some stones around it, cut the wet bark from some sticks, and striking a light, made a small fire in the pan. Keeping some sticks near to dry, and covering the whole over with a roof of boards, we kept up a small fire, by which we cooked our mussels, and ate them, rather for an occupation than from hunger. Still it was not ten o'clock, and the night was long before us, when one of the party produced an old pack of Spanish cards from his monkey-jacket pocket, which we hailed as a great windfall; and keeping a dim, flickering light by our fagots, we played game after game till one or two o'clock, when, becoming really tired, we went to our logs again, one sitting up at a time, in turn, to keep watch over the fire. Toward morning the rain ceased, and the air became sensibly colder, so that we found sleep impossible and sat up, watching for daybreak. No sooner was it light than we went ashore and began our preparations for loading our vessel. We were not mistaken in the coldness of the weather, for a white frost was on the ground, a thing we had never seen before in California, and one or two little puddles of fresh water were skimmed over with a thin coat of ice. In this state of the weather, and before sunrise, in the gray of the morning we had to wade off, nearly up to our hips in water, to load the skiff with the wood by armfuls. The third mate remained on board the launch, two more stayed in the skiff, to load and manage it, and all the water work, as usual, fell upon the two youngest of us; and there we were, with frost on the ground, wading forward and back from the beach to the boat with armfuls of wood, barefooted, and our trousers rolled up. When the skiff went off with her load, we could only keep our feet from freezing by racing up and down the beach on the hard sand as fast as we could go. We were all day at this work, and toward sundown, having loaded the vessel as deep as she would bear, we hove up our anchor, and made sail, beating out of the bay. No sooner had we got into the large bay than we found a strong tide setting us out to seaward, a thick fog which prevented our seeing the ship, and a breeze too light to set us against the tide; for we were as deep as a sand barge. By the utmost exertions, we saved ourselves from being carried out to sea, and were glad to reach the leewardmost point of the island, where we came to and prepared to pass another night more uncomfortable than the first, for we were loaded up to the gunwale, and had only a choice among logs and sticks for a resting place. The next morning we made sail at slack water with a fair wind, and got on board by eleven o'clock, when all hands were turned to to unload and stow away the wood, which took till night.

Having now taken in all our wood, the next morning a water party was ordered off with all the casks. From this we escaped, having had a pretty good siege with the wooding. The water party were gone three days, during which time they narrowly escaped being carried out to sea, and passed one day on an island, where one of them shot a deer, great numbers of which overrun the islands and hills of San Francisco Bay.

While not off on these wood and water parties, or up the rivers to the missions, we had very easy times on board the ship. We were moored stem and stern within a cable's length of the shore, safe from southeasters, and with very little boating to do; and as it rained nearly all the time, awnings were put over the hatchways, and all hands sent down between-decks, where we were at work day after day picking oakum until we got enough to calk the ship all over, and to last the whole voyage. Then we made a whole suit of gaskets for the voyage home, a pair of wheel ropes from strips of green hide, great quantities of spun yarn, and everything else that could be made between-decks. It being now midwinter and in high latitude, the nights were very long, so that we were not turned to until seven in the morning, and were obliged to knock off at five in the evening, when we got supper; which gave us nearly three hours before eight bells, at which time the watch was set.

As we had now been about a year on the coast, it was time to think of the voyage home; and knowing that the last two or three months of our stay would be very busy ones, and that we should never have so good an opportunity to work for ourselves as the present, we all employed our evenings in making clothes for the passage home, and more especially for Cape Horn. As soon as supper was over and the kids cleared away and each one had taken his smoke, we seated ourselves on our chests round the lamp, which swung from a beam, and each one went to work in his own way, some making hats, others trousers, others jackets, etc., etc., and no one was idle. The boys who could not sew well enough to make their own clothes laid up grass into sennit for the men who sewed for them in return. Several of us clubbed together and bought a large piece of twilled cotton, which we made into trousers and jackets, and giving them several coats of linseed oil, laid them by for Cape Horn. I also sewed and covered a tarpaulin hat, thick and strong enough to sit down on, and made myself a complete suit of flannel underclothing for bad weather. Those who had no southwester caps made them, and several of the crew made themselves tarpaulin jackets and trousers lined on the inside with flannel. Industry was the order

of the day, and everyone did something for himself; for we knew
that as the season advanced and we went farther south, we
should have no evenings to work in.

FRIDAY, DECEMBER 25. This day was Christmas, and as it
rained all day long, and there were no hides to take in and
nothing especial to do, the captain gave us a holiday (the first
we had had since leaving Boston), and plum duff for dinner.
The Russian brig, following the Old Style, had celebrated their
Christmas eleven days before, when they had a grand blowout
and (as our men said) drank in the forecastle a barrel of gin,
ate up a bag of tallow, and made a soup of the skin.

SUNDAY, DECEMBER 27. We had now finished all our business
at this port, and it being Sunday, we unmoored ship and got
under way, firing a salute to the Russian brig and another to the
presidio, which were both answered.

We sailed down this magnificent bay with a light wind, the
tide, which was running out, carrying us at the rate of four or
five knots. It was a fine day, the first of entire sunshine we had
had for more than a month. We passed directly under the high
cliff on which the presidio is built, and stood into the middle of
the bay, from whence we could see small bays making up into
the interior on every side, large and beautifully wooded islands,
and the mouths of several small rivers. If California ever becomes
a prosperous country, this bay will be the center of its prosperity.
The abundance of wood and water, the extreme fertility of its
shores, the excellence of its climate, which is as near to being
perfect as any in the world, and its facilities for navigation, af-
fording the best anchoring grounds in the whole western coast
of America, all fit it for a place of great importance; and indeed
it has attracted much attention, for the settlement of Yerba
Buena, where we lay at anchor, made chiefly by Americans and
English, and which bids fair to become the most important trading place on the coast, at this time began to supply traders, Russian ships, and whalers with their stores of wheat and frijoles.

The tide leaving us, we came to anchor near the mouth of the
bay under a high and beautifully sloping hill, on which herds of
hundreds and hundreds of red deer and the stag, with his high
branching antlers, were bounding about, looking at us for a moment and then starting off affrighted at the noises which we made

for the purpose of seeing the variety of their beautiful attitudes and motions.

At midnight, the tide having turned, we hove up our anchor and stood out of the bay, with a fine starry heaven above us—the first we had seen for weeks and weeks. Before the light northerly winds, which blow here with the regularity of trades, we worked slowly along, and made Point Año Nuevo, the northerly point of the Bay of Monterey, on Monday afternoon. It was ten o'clock on Tuesday morning when we came to anchor. The town looked just as it did when I saw it last, which was eleven months before, in the brig *Pilgrim*. The pretty lawn on which it stands, as green as sun and rain could make it; the pine wood on the south; the small river on the north side; the houses, with their white plastered sides and red-tiled roofs, dotted about on the green; the low, white presidio, with its soiled tricolored flag flying, and the discordant din of drums and trumpets for the noon parade—all brought up the scene we had witnessed here with so much pleasure nearly a year before, when coming from a long voyage and our unprepossessing reception at Santa Barbara. It seemed almost like coming to a home.

27

The Sunday Wash-up · On Shore · A Set-to · A Grandee · "Sail Ho!" · A Fandango

T HE ONLY other vessel in the port was a Russian government bark from Asitka, mounting eight guns (four of which we found to be Quakers), and having on board the ex-governor, who was going in her to Mazatlán, and thence overland to Vera Cruz. He offered to take letters and deliver them to the American consul at Vera Cruz, whence they could be easily forwarded to the United States. We accordingly made up a packet of letters, almost everyone writing, and dating them "January 1, 1836." The governor was true to his promise, and they all reached Boston before the middle of March—the shortest communication ever yet made across the country.

The brig *Pilgrim* had been lying in Monterey through the latter part of November, according to orders, waiting for us. Day after day Captain Faucon went up to the hill to look out for us, and at last gave us up, thinking we must have gone down in the gale which we experienced off Point Conception, and which had blown with great fury over the whole coast, driving ashore several vessels in the snuggest ports. An English brig which had put into San Francisco lost both her anchors; the *Rosa* was driven on a mudbank in San Diego; and the *Pilgrim*, with great difficulty, rode out the gale in Monterey, with three anchors ahead. She sailed early in December for San Diego and *intermedios*.

As we were to be here over Sunday, and Monterey was the best place to go ashore on the whole coast, and we had had no liberty day for nearly three months, everyone was for going ashore. On Sunday morning, as soon as the decks were washed and we had got breakfast, those who had obtained liberty began to clean themselves, as it is called, to go ashore. The usual outfit of pumps, white stockings, loose white duck trousers, blue jackets, clean checked shirts, black kerchiefs, hats well varnished, with a fathom of black ribbon over the left eye, a silk handkerchief flying from the outside jacket pocket, and four or five dollars tied up in the back of the neckerchief, and we were "all right." One of the quarter-boats pulled us ashore, and we steamed up to the town. I tried to find the church, in order to see the worship, but was told that there was no service except a Mass early in the morning; so we went about the town visiting the Americans and English and the natives whom we had known when we were here before. Toward noon we procured horses and rode out to the Carmel mission, which is about a league from the town, where we got something in the way of a dinner—beef, eggs, frijoles, tortillas, and some middling wine—from the *mayordomo*, who of course refused to make any charge, as it was the Lord's gift, yet received our present as a gratuity with a low bow, a touch of the hat, and *"Dios se lo pague!"*

After this repast we had a fine run, scouring the whole country on our fleet horses, and came into town soon after sundown. Here we found our companions who had refused to go to ride with us, thinking that a sailor has no more business with a horse than a fish has with a balloon. They were moored stem and stern in a grogshop, making a great noise, with a crowd of Indians and hungry half-breeds about them, and with a fair prospect of being stripped and dirked, or left to pass the night in the calabozo. With a great deal of trouble, we managed to get them down to the boats, though not without many angry looks and interferences from the Spaniards who had marked them out for their prey. Our forecastle, as usual after a liberty day, was a scene of tumult all night long, from the drunken ones. They had just got to sleep toward morning when they were turned up with the rest, and kept at work all day in the water carrying hides, their heads aching so that they could hardly stand. This is sailor's pleasure.

WEDNESDAY, JANUARY 6. Set sail from Monterey, with a number of Spaniards as passengers, and shaped our course for Santa Barbara. We had a smacking breeze for several hours, and went along at a great rate until night, when it died away, as usual, and the land breeze set in, which brought us on a taut bowline. Among our passengers was a young man who was the best representation of a decayed gentleman I had ever seen. He reminded me much of some of the characters in *Gil Blas*. He was of the aristocracy of the country, his family being of pure Spanish blood, and once of great importance in Mexico. His father had been governor of the province, and having amassed a large property, settled at San Diego, where he built a large house with a courtyard in front, kept a great retinue of Indians, and set up for the grandee of that part of the country. His son was sent to Mexico, where he received the best education and went into the first society of the capital. Misfortune, extravagance, and the want of funds, or any manner of getting interest on money, soon ate the estate up, and Don Juan Bandini returned from Mexico accomplished, poor, and proud, and without any office or occupation, to lead the life of most young men of the better families—dissolute and extravagant when the means are at hand; ambitious at heart and impotent in act; often pinched for bread; keeping up an appearance of style when their poverty is known to each half-naked Indian boy in the street, and they stand in dread of every small trader and shopkeeper in the place. He had a slight and elegant figure, moved gracefully, danced and waltzed beautifully, spoke the best of Castilian with a pleasant and refined voice and accent, and had throughout the bearing of a man of high birth and figure. Yet here he was, with his passage given him (as I afterward learned), for he had not the means of paying for it, and living upon the charity of our agent. He was polite to everyone, spoke to the sailors, and gave four reals—I dare say the last he had in his pocket—to the steward who waited on him.

Don Juan had with him a retainer who was as much like many of the characters in *Gil Blas* as his master. He called himself a private secretary, though there was no writing for him to do, and he lived in the steerage with the carpenter and sailmaker. He was certainly a character—could read and write extremely well, spoke good Spanish, had been all over Spanish America, and lived in every possible situation and served in every conceivable capacity, though generally in that of confidential servant to some man of figure. I cultivated this man's acquaintance, and during the five weeks that he was with us—for he remained on board

until we arrived at San Diego—I gained a greater knowledge of
the state of political parties in Mexico, and the habits and affairs of the different classes of society, than I could have learned
from almost anyone else. He took great pains in correcting my
Spanish, and supplying me with colloquial phrases and common
terms and exclamations in speaking. He lent me a file of late
newspapers from the City of Mexico, which were full of the tri-
umphal reception of Santa Anna, who had just returned from
Tampico after a victory, and with the preparations for his expe-
dition against the Texans. *"Viva Santa Anna!"* was the byword
everywhere, and it had even reached California, though there
were still many here, among whom was Don Juan Bandini, who
were opposed to his government, and intriguing to bring in
Bustamente. Santa Anna, they said, was for breaking down the
missions, or as they termed it—*"Santa Anna no quiere religion."*
Yet I had no doubt that the office of *administrador* of San Diego
would reconcile Don Juan to any dynasty, and any state of the
Church. In these papers, too, I found scraps of American and
English news, but which were so unconnected, and I was so ignorant of everything preceding them for eighteen months past,
that they only awakened a curiosity which they could not satisfy.
One article spoke of Taney as *Justicia Mayor de los Estados
Unidos* (what had become of Marshall? Was he dead, or banished?) and another made known, by news received from Vera
Cruz, that *El Vizconde Melbourne* had returned to the office of
"primer ministro," in place of *Sir Roberto Peel.* (Sir Robert Peel
had been minister, then? And where were Earl Grey and the
Duke of Wellington?) Here were the outlines of a grand parlia-
mentary overturn, the filling up of which I could imagine at my
leisure.

The second morning after leaving Monterey we were off Point
Conception. It was a bright, sunny day and the wind, though
strong, was fair, and everything was in striking contrast with our
experience in the same place two months before, when we were
drifting off from a northwester under a fore and main spencer.
"Sail ho!" cried a man who was rigging out a topgallant-studding-
sail boom.—"Where away?"—"Weather beam, sir!" and in a few
minutes a full-rigged brig was seen standing out from under
Point Conception. She rounded to, backed her main-topsail, and

showed her decks full of men, four guns on a side, hammock nettings, and everything man-of-war fashion, except that there was no boatswain's whistle, and no uniforms on the quarter-deck. A short, square-built man in a rough gray jacket, with a speaking trumpet in hand, stood in the weather hammock nettings. "Ship ahoy!"—"Hallo!"—"What ship is that, pray?"—"*Alert*."—"Where are you from, pray?" etc., etc. She proved to be the brig *Convoy*, from the Sandwich Islands, engaged in otter-hunting among the islands which lie along the coast. Her armament was from her being an illegal trader. The otter are very numerous among these islands, and being of great value, the government requires a heavy sum for a license to hunt them, and lays a high duty on every one shot or carried out of the country. This vessel had no license, and paid no duty, besides being engaged in smuggling goods on board other vessels trading on the coast and belonging to the same owners in Oahu. This was without doubt the same vessel that showed herself off Santa Barbara a few months before. These vessels frequently remain on the coast for years without making port except at the islands for wood and water, and an occasional visit to Oahu for a new outfit.

SUNDAY, JANUARY 10. Arrived at Santa Barbara, and on the following Wednesday slipped our cable and went to sea, on account of a southeaster. Returned to our anchorage the next day. We were the only vessel in the port.

Great preparations were making on shore for the marriage of our agent, who was to marry Doña Anneta de G— de N—y C—, youngest daughter of Don Antonio N—, the grandee of the place, and the head of the first family in California. Our steward was ashore three days making pastry and cake, and some of the best of our stores were sent off with him. On the day appointed for the wedding, we took the captain ashore in the gig, and had orders to come for him at night, with leave to go up to the house and see the fandango. Returning on board, we found preparations making for a salute. Our guns were loaded and run out, men appointed to each, cartridges served out, matches lighted, and all the flags ready to be run up. I took my place at the starboard aftergun and we all waited for the signal from on shore. At ten o'clock the bride went up with her sister to the confessional, dressed in deep black. Nearly an hour intervened, when the great doors of the mission church opened, the bells rang out a loud, discordant peal, the private signal for us was run up by the captain ashore, the bride, dressed in complete white, came out of the church with the bridegroom, followed by a long procession. Just as she stepped from the church door, a small white cloud issued from the bows of our ship, which was full in sight, the loud report echoed among the surrounding hills and over the bay, and instantly the ship was dressed in flags and pennants from stem to stern. Twenty-three guns followed in regular succession, with an interval of fifteen seconds between each, when the cloud cleared away, and the ship lay dressed in her colors all day. At sundown another salute of the same number of guns was fired, and all the flags run down. This we thought was pretty well—a gun every fifteen seconds—for a merchantman with only four guns and a dozen or twenty men.

After supper the gig's crew were called and we rowed ashore dressed in our uniforms, beached the boat, and went up to the fandango. The bride's father's house was the principal one in the place, with a large court in front, on which a tent was built capable of containing several hundred people. As we drew near we heard the accustomed sound of violins and guitars, and saw a great motion of the people within. Going in, we found nearly all the people of the town—men, women, and children—collected and crowded together, leaving barely room for the dancers; for on these occasions no invitations are given, but everyone is expected to come, though there is always a private entertainment within the house for particular friends. The old women sat down in rows, clapping their hands to the music and applauding the young ones. The music was lively, and among the tunes we recognized several of our popular airs, which we without doubt have taken from the Spanish. In the dancing I was much disappointed. The women stood upright, with their hands down by their sides, their eyes fixed on the ground before them, and slid about without any perceptible means of motion; for their feet were invisible, the hem of their dresses forming a perfect circle about them, reaching to the ground. They looked as grave as though they were going through some religious ceremony, their faces as little excited as their limbs; and on the whole, instead of the spirited, fascinating Spanish dances which I had expected, I found the

Californian fandango, on the part of the women at least, a lifeless affair. The men did better. They danced with grace and spirit, moving in circles round their nearly stationary partners, and showing their figures to great advantage.

A great deal was said about our friend Don Juan Bandini, and when he did appear, which was toward the close of the evening, he certainly gave us the most graceful dancing that I had ever

seen. He was dressed in white pantaloons, neatly made, a short jacket of dark silk, gaily figured, white stockings and thin morocco slippers upon his very small feet. His slight and graceful figure was well calculated for dancing, and he moved about with the grace and daintiness of a young fawn. An occasional touch of the toe to the ground seemed all that was necessary to give him a long interval of motion in the air. At the same time he was not fantastic or flourishing, but appeared to be rather repressing a strong tendency to motion. He was loudly applauded, and danced frequently toward the close of the evening. After the supper, the waltzing began, which was confined to a very few of the *gente de razón,* and was considered a high accomplishment, and a mark of aristocracy. Here too Don Juan figured greatly, waltzing with the sister of the bride (Doña Angustía, a handsome woman and a general favorite) in a variety of beautiful but, to me, offensive figures, which lasted as much as half an hour, no one else taking the floor. They were repeatedly and loudly applauded, the old men and women jumping out of their seats in admiration and the young people waving their hats and handkerchiefs. Indeed among people of the character of these Mexicans, the waltz seemed to me to have found its right place. The great amusement of the evening—which I suppose was owing to its being carnival—was the breaking of eggs filled with cologne, or other essences, on the heads of the company. One end of the egg is broken and the inside taken out, then it is partly filled with cologne, and the whole sealed up. The women bring a great number of these secretly about them, and the amusement is to break one on the head of a gentleman when his back is turned. He is bound in gallantry to find out the lady and return the compliment, though it must not be done if the person sees you. A tall, stately Don with immense gray whiskers, and a look of great importance, was standing before me when I felt a light hand on my shoulder, and turning round, saw Doña Angustía (whom we all knew, as she had been up to Monterey, and down again, in the *Alert*) with her finger on her lip, motioning me gently aside. I stepped back a little, when she went up behind the Don and with one hand knocked off his huge sombrero, and at the same instant with the other broke the egg upon his head, and springing behind me, was out of sight in a moment. The Don turned slowly round, the cologne running down his face and over his clothes, and a loud laugh breaking out from every quarter. He looked round in vain for some time, until the direction of so many laughing eyes showed him the fair offender. She was his niece, and a great favorite with him, so old Don Domingo had to join in the laugh.

Another singular custom I was for some time at a loss about. A pretty young girl was dancing—named, after what would appear to us the sacrilegious custom of the country, Espiritú Santo —when a young man went behind her and placed his hat directly on her head, letting it fall down over her eyes, and sprang back among the crowd. She danced for some time with the hat on, when she threw it off, which called forth a general shout, and the young man was obliged to go out on the floor and pick it up. Some of the ladies on whose heads hats had been placed threw them off at once, and a few kept them on throughout the dance, and took them off at the end and held them out in their hands, when the owner stepped out, bowed, and took it from them. I soon began to suspect the meaning of the thing, and was afterward told that it was a compliment, and an offer to become the lady's gallant for the rest of the evening, and to wait upon her home. If the hat was thrown off, the offer was refused, and the gentleman was obliged to pick up his hat amid a general laugh. Much amusement was caused sometimes by gentlemen putting hats on the ladies' heads without permitting them to see whom it was done by. This obliged them to throw them off or keep them on at a venture, and when they came to discover the owner, the laugh was often turned upon them.

The captain sent for us about ten o'clock, and we went aboard in high spirits, having enjoyed the new scene much, and were of great importance among the crew, from having so much to tell and from the prospect of going every night until it was over; for these fandangos generally last three days. The next day two of us were sent up to the town, and took care to come back by way of Capitan Noriego's and take a look into the booth. The musicians were still there on their platform, scraping and twanging away, and a few people, apparently of the lower classes, were dancing. The dancing is kept up, at intervals, throughout the day, but the crowd, the spirit, and the elite come in at night. The next night, which was the last, we went ashore in the same manner, until we got almost tired of the monotonous twang of the instruments, the drawling sounds which the women kept up as an accompaniment, and the slapping of the hands in time with the music, in place of castanets. We found ourselves as great objects of attention as any persons or anything at the place. Our sailor dresses—and we took great pains to have them neat and shipshape—were much admired, and we were invited, from every quarter, to give them an American sailor's dance; but after the ridiculous figure some of our countrymen cut in dancing after the Spaniards, we thought it best to leave it to their imaginations. Our agent, with a tight, black, swallow-tailed coat just imported from Boston, a high stiff cravat looking as if he had been pinned and skewered, with only his feet and hands left free, took the floor just after Bandini, and we thought they had had enough of Yankee grace.

The last night they kept it up in great style, and were getting into a high-go when the captain called us off to go aboard, for, it being southeaster season, he was afraid to remain on shore long. And it was well he did not, for that very night we slipped our cables, as a crowner to our fun ashore, and stood off before a southeaster which lasted twelve hours, and returned to our anchorage the next day.

28

An Old Friend · A Victim · California Rangers · News from Home · Last Looks

MONDAY, FEB. 1. After having been in port twenty-one days, we sailed for San Pedro, where we arrived on the following day, having gone "all fluking," with the weather clew of the mainsail hauled up, the yards braced in a little, and the lower studding sail just drawing, the wind hardly shifting a point during the passage. Here we found the *Ayacucho* and the *Pilgrim,* which last we had not seen since the eleventh of September—nearly five months; and I really felt something like an affection for the old brig which had been my first home, and in which I had spent nearly a year, and got the first rough-and-tumble of a sea life. She, too, was associated in my mind with Boston, the wharf from which we sailed, anchorage in the stream, leave-taking, and all such matters, which were now to me like small links connecting me with another world which I had once been in and which, please God, I might yet see again. I went on board the first night, after supper; found the old cook in the galley playing on the fife which I had given him as a parting present; had a hearty shake of the hand from him; and dove down into the forecastle, where were my old shipmates, the same as ever, glad to see me; for they had nearly given us up as lost, especially when they did not find us in Santa Barbara. They had been at San Diego last, had been lying at San Pedro nearly a month, and had received three thousand hides from the Pueblo. These were taken from her the next day, which filled us up, and we both got under way on the fourth, she bound up to San Francisco again and we to San Diego, where we arrived on the sixth.

We were always glad to see San Diego, it being the depot, and a snug little place, and seeming quite like home, especially to me, who had spent a summer there. We discharged our hides, and in four days were ready to sail again for the windward, and, to our great joy—*for the last time!* Over thirty thousand hides had been already collected, cured, and stowed away in the house, which, together with what we should collect and the *Pilgrim* would bring down from San Francisco, would make out her cargo. The thought that we were actually going up for the last time, and that the next time we went round San Diego point it would be "homeward bound," brought things so near a close that we felt as though we were just there, though it must still be the greater part of a year before we could see Boston.

I spent one evening, as had been my custom, at the oven with the Sandwich Islanders; but it was far from being the usual noisy, laughing time. It has been said that the greatest curse to each of the South Sea islands was the first man who discovered it; and everyone who knows anything of the history of our commerce in those parts knows how much truth there is in this; and that the white men, with their vices, have brought in diseases before unknown to the islanders, and which are now sweeping off the native population of the Sandwich Islands at the rate of one-fortieth of the entire population annually. They seem to be a doomed people. The curse of a people calling themselves Christian seems to follow them everywhere; and even here, in this obscure place, lay two young islanders whom I had left strong, active young men in the vigor of health, wasting away under a disease which they would never have known but for their intercourse with Christianized Mexico and people from Christian America. One of them was not so ill, and was moving about, smoking his pipe, and talking, and trying to keep up his spirits; but the other, who was my friend and *aikane*, Hope was the most dreadful object I had ever seen in my life—his eyes sunken and dead, his cheeks fallen in against his teeth, his hands looking like claws; a dreadful cough, which seemed to rack his whole shattered system, a hollow, whispering voice, and an entire inability to move himself. There he lay on a mat on the ground, which was the only floor of the oven, with no medicine, no comforts, and no one to care for or help him but a few Kanakas, who

were willing enough but could do nothing. The sight of him
made me sick and faint. Poor fellow! During the four months
that I lived on the beach we were continually together, both in
work and in our excursions in the woods and on the water. I
really felt a strong affection for him and preferred him to any of
my own countrymen there, and I believe there was nothing which
he would not have done for me. When I came into the oven he
looked at me, held out his hand, and said, in a low voice but
with a delightful smile, "*Aloha, Aikane! Aloha nui!*" I comforted
him as well as I could, and promised to ask the captain to help
him from the medicine chest, and told him I had no doubt the
captain would do what he could for him, as he had worked in
our employ for several years. I went aboard and turned into my
hammock, but I could not sleep.

Thinking, from my education, that I must have some knowledge of medicine, the Kanakas had insisted upon my examining
him carefully, and it was not a sight to be forgotten. One of our
crew, an old man-of-war'sman of twenty years' standing who had
seen sin and suffering in every shape, and whom I afterward
took to see Hope, said it was dreadfully worse than anything he
had ever seen, or even dreamed of. He was horror-struck, as his
countenance showed; yet he had been among the worst cases in
our naval hospitals. I could not get the thought of the poor fellow out of my head all night—his horrible suffering, and his apparently inevitable horrible end.

The next day I told the captain of Hope's state, and asked him
if he would be so kind as to go and see him.

"What? A damned Kanaka?"

"Yes, sir," said I; "but he has worked four years for our vessels,
and has been in the employ of our owners, both on shore and
aboard."

"Oh! he be damned!" said the captain, and walked off.

This same man died afterward of a fever on the deadly coast
of Sumatra, and God grant he had better care taken of him in
his sufferings than he ever gave to anyone else! Finding nothing
was to be got from the captain, I consulted an old shipmate who
had much experience in these matters, and got from him a recipe
which he always kept by him. With this I went to the mate, and
told him the case. Mr. Brown had been entrusted with the gen-

eral care of the medicine chest, and although a driving fellow, and a taut hand in a watch, he had good feelings, and was always inclined to be kind to the sick. He said that Hope was not strictly one of the crew, but as he was in our employ when taken sick, he should have the medicines; and he got them and gave them to me, with leave to go ashore at night. Nothing could exceed the delight of the Kanakas when I came bringing the medicines. All their terms of affection and gratitude were spent upon me, and in a sense wasted (for I could not understand half of them), yet they made all known by their manner. Poor Hope was so much revived at the bare thought of anything's being done for him that he was already stronger and better. I knew he must die as he was, and he could but die under the medicines, and any chance was worth running. An oven exposed to every wind and change of weather is no place to take calomel; but nothing else would do, and strong remedies must be used, or he was gone. The applications, internal and external, were powerful, and I gave him strict directions to keep warm and sheltered, telling him it was his only chance for life. Twice after this I visited him, having only time to run up while waiting in the boat. He promised to take his medicines regularly until we returned, and insisted upon it that he was doing better.

We got under way on the tenth, bound up to San Pedro, and had three days of calm and head winds, making but little progress. Arrived at San Pedro on the fourth day, and came to in the old place, a league from shore, with no other vessel in port and the prospect of three weeks, or more, of dull life—rolling goods up a slippery hill, carrying hides on our heads over sharp stones, and perhaps slipping for a southeaster.

TUESDAY, FEB. 23. This afternoon a signal was made from the shore, and we went off in the gig and found the agent's clerk, who had been up to the Pueblo, waiting at the landing place, with a package under his arm covered with brown paper and tied carefully with twine. No sooner had we shoved off than he told us there was good news from Santa Barbara. "What's that?" said one of the crew. "Has the bloody agent slipped off the hooks? Has the old bundle of bones got him at last?"—"No, better than that. The *California* has arrived." Letters, papers, news—and perhaps friends—on board! Our hearts were all up in our mouths, and we pulled away like good fellows; for the precious packet could not be opened except by the captain. As we pulled under the stern, the clerk held up the package and called out to the mate, who was leaning over the taffrail, that the *California* had arrived.

"Hurrah!" said the mate, so as to be heard fore and aft. "*California* come, and news from Boston!"

Instantly there was a confusion on board which no one could account for who has not been in the same situation. All discipline seemed for a moment relaxed.

"What's that, Mr. Brown?" said the cook, putting his head out of the galley. "*California* come?"

"Aye, aye, you angel of darkness, and there's a letter for you from *Bullknop* 'treet, number two-two-five—green door and brass knocker!"

The packet was sent down into the cabin, and everyone waited to hear of the result. As nothing came up, the officers began to feel that they were acting rather a child's part, and turned the crew to again; and the same strict discipline was restored, which prohibits speech between man and man while at work on deck, so that when the steward came forward with letters for the crew, each man took his letters, carried them below to his chest, and came up again immediately, and not a letter was read until we had cleared up decks for the night.

An overstrained sense of manliness is the characteristic of sea-faring men, or rather of life on board ship. This often gives an appearance of want of feeling, and even of cruelty. From this, if a man comes within an ace of breaking his neck and escapes, it is made a joke of; and any expression of pity, or any show of attention, would look unbecoming a man who has to face the rough-and-tumble of such a life. From this, too, the sick are neglected at sea, and a sick man finds little sympathy or attention, forward or aft. A man, too, can have nothing peculiar or sacred on board ship; for all the nicer feelings they take pride in disregarding, both in themselves and others. A thin-skinned man could not live an hour on shipboard. One would be torn raw unless he had the hide of an ox. A moment of natural feeling for home and friends, and then the frigid routine of sea life returned. Jokes were made on those who showed any interest in the expected news, and everything near and dear was made common stock for rude jokes and unfeeling coarseness, to which no exception could be taken by anyone.

Supper, too, must be eaten before the letters were read; and when at last they were brought out, they all got round anyone who had a letter and expected to have it read aloud, and have it all in common. If anyone went by himself to read, it was "Fair play, there, and no skulking!" I took mine and went into the sailmaker's berth, where I could read it without interruption. It was dated August, just a year from the time I had sailed from home; and everyone was well, and no great change had taken place. Thus for one year my mind was set at ease, yet it was already six months from the date of the letter, and what another year would bring to pass, who could tell?

As much as my feelings were taken up by my own intelligence from home, I could not but be amused by a scene in the steerage. The carpenter had been married just before leaving Boston, and during the voyage had talked much about his wife, and had to bear and forbear, as every man known to be married must aboard ship; yet the certainty of hearing from his wife by the first ship seemed to keep up his spirits. The *California* came, the packet was brought on board, no one was in higher spirits than he; but when the letters came forward, there was none for him. The captain looked again, but there was no mistake. Poor "Chips" could eat no supper. He was completely down in the mouth. "Sails" (the sailmaker) tried to comfort him, and told him he was a bloody fool to give up his grub for any woman's daughter, and reminded him that he had told him a dozen times that he'd never see or hear from his wife again.

"Ah," said Chips, "you don't know what it is to have a wife, and—"

"Don't I?" said Sails, and then came, for the hundredth time, the story of his coming ashore at New York from the *Constellation* frigate after a cruise of four years round the Horn, being paid off with over five hundred dollars, marrying, and taking a couple of rooms in a four-story house, furnishing the rooms (with a particular account of the furniture, including a dozen flag-bottomed chairs, which he always dilated upon whenever the subject of furniture was alluded to), going off to sea again, leaving his wife half-pay, like a fool, coming home and finding her "off, like Bob's horse, with nobody to pay the reckoning"—furniture gone, flag-bottomed chairs and all, and with it, his "long togs," the half-pay, his beaver hat, white linen shirts, and everything else. His wife he never saw, or heard of, from that day to this, and never wished to. Then followed a sweeping assertion, not much to the credit of the sex, if true, though he has Pope to back him. "Come, Chips, cheer up like a man, and take some hot

grub! Don't be made a fool of by anything in petticoats! As for your wife, you'll never see her again; she was 'up kellick and off' before you were outside of Cape Cod. You've hove your money away like a fool; but every man must learn once, just as I did, so you'd better square the yards with her and make the best of it."

This was the best consolation Sails had to offer, but it did not seem to be just the thing the carpenter wanted; for during several days he was very much dejected, and bore with difficulty the jokes of the sailors, and with still more difficulty their attempts at advice and consolation, of most of which the sailmaker's was a good specimen.

THURSDAY, FEB. 25. Set sail for Santa Barbara, where we arrived on Sunday, the twenty-eighth. We just missed seeing the *California*, for she had sailed three days before, bound to Monterey, to enter her cargo and procure her license, and thence to San Francisco, etc. Captain Arthur left files of Boston papers for Captain T—, which, after they had been read and talked over in the cabin, I procured from my friend the third mate. One file was of all the *Boston Transcripts* for the month of August 1835, and the rest were about a dozen *Daily Advertisers* and *Couriers*, of different dates. After all, there is nothing in a strange land like a newspaper from home. Even a letter, in many respects, is nothing in comparison with it. It carries you back to the spot better than anything else. It is almost equal to "clairvoyance." The names of the streets, with the things advertised, is almost as good as seeing the signs; and while reading "Boy lost!" one can almost hear the bell and well-known voice of "Old Wilson" crying the boy as "strayed, stolen, or mislaid!" Then there was the Commencement at Cambridge, and the full account of the exercises at the graduating of my own class. A list of all those familiar names (beginning as usual with Abbot, and ending with W) which, as I read them over one by one, brought up their faces and characters as I had known them in the various scenes of college life. Then I imagined them upon the stage, speaking their orations, dissertations, colloquies, etc., with the gestures and tones of each, and tried to fancy the manner in which each would handle his subject. Then I could see them receiving their A.B.'s from the dignified, feudal-looking president, with his *"auctoritate mihi commissa,"* and walking off the stage with their diplomas in their hands while on the very same day their classmate was walking up and down California beach with a hide on his head.

Every watch below for a week I pored over these papers, until I was sure there could be nothing in them that had escaped my attention, and was ashamed to keep them any longer.

SATURDAY, MARCH 5. This was an important day in our almanac, for it was on this day that we were first assured that our voyage was really drawing to a close. The captain gave orders to have the ship ready for getting under way, and observed that there was a good breeze to take us down to San Pedro. Then we were not going up to windward. Thus much was certain, and was soon known, fore and aft; and when we went in the gig to take him off, he shook hands with the people on the beach, and said that he never expected to see Santa Barbara again. This settled the matter, and sent a thrill of pleasure through the heart of everyone in the boat. We pulled off with a will, saying to ourselves (I can speak for myself at least), "Good-by, Santa Barbara!—This is the last pull here.—No more duckings in your breakers, and slipping from your cursed southeasters!" The news was soon known aboard, and put life into everything when we were getting under way. Each one was taking his last look at the mission, the town, the breakers on the beach, and swearing that no money would make him ship to see them again; and when all hands tallied onto the catfall, the chorus of "Time for us to go!" was raised for the first time, and joined in with full swing by everybody. One would have thought we were on our voyage home, so near did it seem to us, though there were yet three months for us on the coast.

Two days brought us to San Pedro, and two days more (to our no small joy) gave us our last view of that place, which was universally called the hell of California, and seemed designed in every way for the wear and tear of sailors. Not even the last view could bring out one feeling of regret. No thanks, thought I as we left the sandy shores in the distance, for the hours I have walked over your stones barefooted, with hides on my head; for the burdens I have carried up your steep, muddy hill; for the duckings in your surf; and for the long days and longer nights passed on your desolate hill watching piles of hides, hearing the sharp bark of your eternal coatis, and the dismal hooting of your owls.

As I bade good-by to each successive place, I felt as though one link after another were struck from the chain of my servitude. Having kept close in shore, for the land breeze, we passed the mission of San Juan Campestrano the same night, and saw distinctly by the bright moonlight the hill which I had gone down by a pair of halyards in search of a few paltry hides. *"Forsitan et haec olim,"* thought I, and took my last look of that place too. And on the next morning we were under the high point of San

Diego. The floodtide took us swiftly in, and we came to opposite our hide house, and prepared to get everything in trim for a long stay. This was our last port. Here we were to discharge everything from the ship, clean her out, smoke her, take in our hides, wood, water, etc., and set sail for Boston. While all this was doing, we were to lie still in one place, and the port was a safe one, and there was no fear of southeasters. Accordingly, having picked out a good berth in the stream with a good smooth beach opposite for a landing place, and within two cables' length of our hide house, we moored ship, unbent all the sails, sent down the topgallant yards and all the studding-sail booms, and housed the topgallant masts. The boats were then hove out, and all the sails, the spare spars, the stores, the rigging not rove, and in fact everything which was not in daily use, sent ashore and stowed away in the house. Then went all our hides and horns, and we left hardly anything in the ship but her ballast, and this we made preparation to heave out the next day. At night after we had knocked off and were sitting round in the forecastle smoking and talking and taking sailor's pleasure, we congratulated ourselves upon being in that situation in which we had wished ourselves every time we had come into San Diego. "If we were only here for the last time," we had often said, "with our topgallant masts housed and our sails unbent!"—and now we had our wish. Six weeks, or two months, of the hardest work we had yet seen was before us, and then—"Good-by to California!"

29

Loading for Home · A Surprise ·
Last of an Old Friend ·
The Last Hide · A Hard Case ·
Up Anchor, for Home!

W<small>E TURNED IN</small> early, knowing that we might expect an early call and sure enough, before the stars had quite faded, "All hands ahoy!" and we were turned to heaving out ballast. A regulation of the port forbids any ballast to be thrown overboard; accordingly our longboat was lined inside with rough boards and brought alongside the gangway, but where one tubful went into the boat, twenty went overboard. This is done by every vessel, for the ballast can make but little difference in the channel, and it saves more than a week of labor which would be spent in loading the boats, rowing them to the point, and unloading them. When any people from the presidio were on board, the boat was hauled up and ballast thrown in; but when the coast was clear, she was dropped astern again, and the ballast fell overboard. This is one of those petty frauds which every vessel practices in ports of inferior foreign nations, and which are lost sight of among the countless deeds of greater weight which are hardly less common. Fortunately a sailor, not being a free agent in work aboard ship, is not accountable; yet the fact of being constantly employed, without thought, in such things begets an indifference to the rights of others.

Friday, and a part of Saturday, we were engaged in this work, until we had thrown out all but what we wanted under our cargo on the passage home; when, as the next day was Sunday, and a good day for smoking ship, we cleared everything out of the cabin and forecastle, made a slow fire of charcoal, birch bark, brimstone, and other matters on the ballast in the bottom of the hold, calked up the hatches and every open seam, and pasted over the cracks of the windows and the slides of the scuttles and companionway. Wherever smoke was seen coming out, we calked and pasted, and, so far as we could, made the ship smoke-tight. The captain and officers slept under the awning which was spread over the quarter-deck, and we stowed ourselves away under an old studding sail which we drew over one side of the forecastle. The next day, from fear that something might happen, orders were given for no one to leave the ship, and as the decks were lumbered up with everything, we could not wash them down, so we had nothing to do all day long. Unfortunately, our books were where we could not get at them, and we were turning about for something to do when one man recollected a book he had left in the galley. He went after it, and it proved to be *Woodstock*. This was a great windfall, and as all could not read it at once, I, being the scholar of the company, was appointed reader. I got a knot of six or eight about me, and no one could have had a more attentive audience. Some laughed at the "scholars," and went over the other side of the forecastle to work and spin their yarns; but I carried the day, and had the cream of the crew for my hearers. Many of the reflections, and the political parts, I omitted, but all the narrative they were delighted with, especially the descriptions of the Puritans, and the sermons and harangues of the Roundhead soldiers. The gallantry of Charles, Dr. Radcliffe's plots, the knavery of "trusty Tompkins"—in fact, every part—seemed to chain their attention. Many things which while I was reading I had a misgiving about, thinking them above their capacity, I was surprised to find them enter into completely.

I read nearly all day, until sundown, when as soon as supper was over, as I had nearly finished, they got a light from the galley, and by skipping what was less interesting, I carried them through to the marriage of Everard, and the restoration of Charles the Second, before eight o'clock.

The next morning we took the battens from the hatches and opened the ship. A few stifled rats were found and what bugs, cockroaches, fleas, and other vermin there might have been on board must have unrove their lifelines before the hatches were opened. The ship being now ready, we covered the bottom of the hold over, fore and aft, with dried brush for dunnage, and having leveled everything away, we were ready to take in our cargo. All the hides that had been collected since the *California* left the coast (a little more than two years), amounting to about forty thousand, were cured, dried, and stowed away in the house, waiting for our good ship to take them to Boston.

Now began the operation of taking in our cargo, which kept us hard at work from the gray of the morning till starlight for six weeks, with the exception of Sundays and of just time to swallow our meals. To carry the work on quicker, a division of labor was made. Two men threw the hides down from the piles in the house, two more picked them up and put them on a long horizontal pole, raised a few feet from the ground, where they were beaten by two more with flails somewhat like those used in threshing wheat. When beaten, they were taken from this pole by two more, and placed on a platform of boards; and ten or a dozen men, with their trousers rolled up, were constantly going back and forth from the platform to the boat, which was kept off where she would just float, with the hides on their heads. The throwing the hides on the pole was the most difficult work, and required a sleight of hand which was only to be got by long practice. As I was known for a hide-curer, this post was assigned to me, and I continued at it for six or eight days, tossing in that time from eight to ten thousand hides, until my wrists became so lame that I gave in, and was transferred to the gang that was employed in filling the boats, where I remained for the rest of the time. As we were obliged to carry the hides on our heads from fear of their getting wet, we each had a piece of sheepskin sewed into the inside of our hats, with the wool next our heads, and thus were able to bear the weight day after day which would otherwise have soon worn off our hair, and borne hard upon our skulls. Upon the whole, ours was the best berth; for though the water was nipping cold early in the morning and late at night, and being so continually wet was rather an exposure, yet we got rid of the constant dust and dirt from the beating of the hides, and being all of us young and hearty, did not mind the exposure. The older men of the crew, whom it would have been dangerous to have kept in the water, remained on board with the mate, to stow the hides away as fast as they were brought off by the boats.

We continued at work in this manner until the lower hold was filled to within four feet of the beams, when all hands were called aboard to commence "steeving." As this is a peculiar operation, it will require a minute description.

Before stowing the hides, as I have said, the ballast is leveled off just above the keelson, and then loose dunnage placed on it, on which the hides rest. The greatest care is used in stowing, to make the ship hold as many hides as possible. It is no mean art, and a man skilled in it is an important character in California. Many a dispute have I heard raging high between professed "beachcombers" as to whether the hides should be stowed "shingling," or "back-to-back, and flipper-to-flipper," upon which point there was an entire and bitter division of sentiment among the savants. We adopted each method at different periods of the stowing, and parties ran high in the forecastle, some siding with "Old Bill" in favor of the former, and others scouting him, and relying upon "English Bob" of the *Ayacucho*, who had been eight years in California, and was willing to risk his life and limb for the latter method. At length a compromise was effected, and a middle course of shifting the ends and backs at every lay was adopted, which worked well, and which, though they held it inferior to their own, each party granted was better than that of the other.

Having filled the ship up in this way to within four feet of her beams, the process of steeving commenced, by which a hundred hides are got into a place where one could not be forced by hand, and which presses the hides to the utmost, sometimes starting the beams of the ship, resembling in its effects the jackscrews which are used in stowing cotton. Each morning we went ashore, and beat and brought off as many hides as we could steeve in the course of the day, and after breakfast went down into the hold, where we remained at work until night. The whole length of the hold, from stem to stern, was floored off level, and we began with raising a pile in the afterpart, hard against the bulkhead of the run, and filling it up to the beams, crowding in as many as we could by hand and pushing in with oars, when a large "book" was made of from twenty-five to fifty hides, doubled at the backs and put into one another like the leaves of a book. An opening was then made between two hides in the pile, and the back of the outside hide of the book inserted. Two long, heavy spars, called steeves, made of the strongest wood and sharpened off like a wedge at one end, were placed with their wedge ends into the inside of the hide which was the center of the book, and to the other end of each straps were fitted into which large tackles were hooked, composed each of two huge purchase blocks, one hooked to the strap on the end of the steeve, and the other into a dog fastened into one of the beams, as far aft as it could be got. When this was arranged, and the ways greased upon which the book was to slide, the falls of the tackles were stretched forward, and all hands tallied on, and bowsed away until the book was well entered, when these tackles were nippered, straps and toggles clapped upon the falls, and two more luff tackles hooked on with dogs in the same manner; and thus, by luff upon luff, the power was multiplied until into a pile in which one hide more could not be crowded by hand a hundred or a hundred and fifty were often driven in by this complication of purchases. When the last luff was hooked on, all hands were called to the rope—cook, steward, and all—and ranging ourselves at the falls, one behind the other, sitting down on the hides with our heads just even with the beams, we set taut upon the tackles, and striking up a song, and all lying back at the chorus, we bowsed the tackles home and drove the large books chock in out of sight.

The sailor's songs for capstans and falls are of a peculiar kind, having a chorus at the end of each line. The burden is usually sung by one alone, and at the chorus all hands join in—and the louder the noise, the better. With us, the chorus seemed almost to raise the decks of the ship, and might be heard at a great distance ashore. A song is as necessary to sailors as the drum and fife to a soldier. They can't pull in time, or pull with a will, without it. Many a time when a thing goes heavy, with one fellow yo-ho-ing, a lively song like "Heave, to the girls!" "Nancy oh!" "Jack Crosstree," etc. has put life and strength into every arm. We often found a great difference in the effect of the different songs in driving in the hides. Two or three songs would be tried, one after the other, with no effect—not an inch could be got on the tackles—when a new song struck up seemed to hit the humor of the moment, and drove the tackles "two blocks" at once. "Heave round hearty!" "Captain gone ashore!" and the like might do for common pulls, but on an emergency, when we wanted a heavy, "raise-the-dead" pull, which should start the beams of the ship, there was nothing like "Time for us to go!" "Round the corner," or "Hurrah! hurrah! my hearty bullies!"

This was the most lively part of our work. A little boating and beachwork in the morning; then twenty or thirty men down in a close hold, where we were obliged to sit down and slide about passing hides and rowsing about the great steeves, tackles, and dogs, singing out at the falls, and seeing the ship filling up every day. The work was as hard as it could well be. There was not a moment's cessation from Monday morning till Saturday night, when we were generally beat-out, and glad to have a full night's rest, a wash and shift of clothes, and a quiet Sunday. During all this time—which would have startled Dr. Graham—we lived upon almost nothing but fresh beef: fried beefsteaks three times a day—morning, noon, and night. At morning and night we had a quart of tea to each man, and an allowance of about a pound of hard bread a day; but our chief article of food was the beef. A mess consisting of six men had a large wooden kid piled up with beefsteaks cut thick and fried in fat, with the grease poured over them. Round this we sat, attacking it with our jackknives and teeth, and with the appetite of young lions, and sent back an empty kid to the galley. This was done three times a day. How many pounds each man ate in a day I will not attempt to compute. A whole bullock (we ate liver and all) lasted us but four days. Such devouring of flesh, I will venture to say, was seldom known before. What one man ate in a day over a hearty man's allowance would make a Russian's heart leap into his mouth. Indeed, during all the time we were on the coast, our principal food was fresh beef, and every man had perfect health; but this was a time of especial devouring, and what we should have done without meat I cannot tell. Once or twice, when our bullocks failed and we were obliged to make a meal on dry bread and water, it seemed like feeding upon shavings. Light and dry, feeling unsatisfied, and at the same time full, we were glad to see four quarters of a bullock, just killed, swinging from the foretop. Whatever theories may be started by sedentary men, certainly no men could have gone through more hard work and exposure for sixteen months in more perfect health, and without ailings and failings, than our ship's crew, let them have lived upon Hygeia's own baking and dressing.

FRIDAY, APRIL 15. Arrived, brig *Pilgrim,* from the windward. It was a sad sight for her crew to see us getting ready to go off the coast while they, who had been longer on the coast than the *Alert,* were condemned to another year's hard service. I spent an evening on board, and found them making the best of the matter and determined to rough it out as they might; but my friend S— was determined to go home in the ship, if money or interest could bring it to pass. After considerable negotiating and working, he succeeded in persuading my English friend Tom Harris— my companion in the anchor watch—for thirty dollars, some clothes, and an intimation from Captain Faucon that he should want a second mate before the voyage was up, to take his place in the brig as soon as she was ready to go up to windward.

The first opportunity I could get to speak to Captain Faucon, I asked him to step up to the oven and look at Hope, whom he knew well, having had him on board his vessel. He went to see him, but said that he had so little medicine, and expected to be so long on the coast, that he could do nothing for him, but that Captain Arthur would take care of him when he came down in the *California,* which would be in a week or more. I had been to see Hope the first night after we got into San Diego this last time, and had frequently since spent the early part of a night in the oven. I hardly expected, when I left him to go to windward, to find him alive upon my return. He was certainly as low as he could well be when I left him, and what would be the effect of the medicines that I gave him I hardly then dared to conjecture. Yet I knew that he must die without them. I was not a little rejoiced, therefore, and relieved, upon our return, to see him decidedly better. The medicines were strong, and took hold and gave a check to the disorder which was destroying him; and, more than that, they had begun the work of exterminating it. I shall never forget the gratitude that he expressed. All the Kanakas attributed his escape solely to my knowledge, and

would not be persuaded that I had not all the secrets of the
physical system open to me and under my control. My medicines,
however, were gone, and no more could be got from the ship,
so that his life was left to hang upon the arrival of the
California.

SUNDAY, APRIL 24. We had now been nearly seven weeks in
San Diego, and had taken in the greater part of our cargo and
were looking out every day for the arrival of the *California*, which
had our agent on board, when this afternoon some Kanakas who
had been over the hill for rabbits and to fight rattlesnakes came
running down the path, singing out, "Kail ho!" with all their
might. Mr. H., our third mate, was ashore, and asking them
particularly about the size of the sail, etc., and learning that it
was *"moku—nui moku,"* hailed our ship, and said that the
California was on the other side of the point. Instantly all hands
were turned up, the bow guns run out and loaded, the ensign
and broad pennant set, the yards squared by lifts and braces,
and everything got ready to make a good appearance. The
instant she showed her nose round the point, we began our
salute. She came in under topgallant sails, clewed up and furled
her sails in good order, and came to within good swinging
distance of us. It being Sunday, and nothing to do, all hands
were on the forecastle, criticizing the newcomer. She was a good,
substantial ship, not quite so long as the *Alert*, and wall-sided
and kettle-bottomed, after the latest fashion of south-shore cotton
and sugar wagons; strong too, and tight, and a good average
sailor, but with no pretensions to beauty, and nothing in the
style of a "crack ship." Upon the whole, we were perfectly satisfied that the *Alert* might hold up her head with a ship twice as
smart as she.

At night some of us got a boat and went on board, and found
a large, roomy forecastle (for she was squarer forward than the
Alert) and a crew of a dozen or fifteen men and boys sitting
around on their chests smoking and talking, and ready to give
a welcome to any of our ship's company. It was just seven
months since they left Boston, which seemed but yesterday to
us. Accordingly we had much to ask, for though we had seen
the newspapers that she brought, yet these were the very men

who had been in Boston and seen everything with their own
eyes. One of the green hands was a Boston boy from one of the
public schools, and of course knew many things which we wished
to ask about, and on inquiring the names of our two Boston
boys, found that they had been schoolmates of his. Our men had
hundreds of questions to ask about Ann Street, the boarding-
houses, the ships in port, the rate of wages, and other matters.

Among her crew were two English man-of-war'smen, so that
of course we soon had music. They sang in the true sailor's
style, and the rest of the crew, which was a remarkably musical
one, joined in the choruses. They had many of the latest sailor
songs, which had not yet got about among our merchantmen,
and which they were very choice of. They began soon after we
came on board, and kept it up until after two bells, when the
second mate came forward and called, "The Alerts away!"
Battle songs, drinking songs, boat songs, love songs, and everything else they seemed to have a complete assortment of, and I
was glad to find that "All in the Downs," "Poor Tom Bowline,"
"The Bay of Biscay," "List, Ye Landsmen!" and all those classical
songs of the sea still held their places. In addition to these, they
had picked up at the theaters and other places a few songs of a
little more genteel cast, which they were very proud of; and I
shall never forget hearing an old salt who had broken his voice
by hard drinking on shore and bellowing from the masthead in
a hundred northwesters, with all manner of ungovernable trills
and quavers—in the high notes, breaking into a rough falsetto,
and in the low ones, growling along like the dying-away of the
boatswain's "All hands ahoy!" down the hatchway—singing, "Oh
no, we never mention him."

> *Perhaps, like me, he struggles with*
> *Each feeling of regret;*
> *But if he's loved as I have loved,*
> *He never can forget!*

The last line, being the conclusion, he roared out at the top
of his voice, breaking each word up into half a dozen syllables.
This was very popular, and Jack was called upon every night
to give them his "sentimental song." No one called for it more
loudly than I, for the complete absurdity of the execution, and

the sailors' perfect satisfaction in it, were ludicrous beyond measure.

The next day the *California* commenced unloading her cargo, and her boats' crews in coming and going sang their boat songs, keeping time with their oars. This they did all day long for several days, until their hides were all discharged, when a gang of them were sent on board the *Alert* to help us steeve our hides. This was a windfall for us, for they had a set of new songs for the capstan and fall, and ours had got nearly worn out by six weeks' constant use. I have no doubt that this timely reinforcement of songs hastened our work several days.

Our cargo was now nearly all taken in, and my old friend the *Pilgrim*, having completed her discharge, unmoored, to set sail the next morning on another long trip to windward. I was just thinking of her hard lot, and congratulating myself upon my escape from her, when I received a summons into the cabin. I went aft, and there found, seated round the cabin table, my own captain, Captain Faucon of the *Pilgrim*, and Mr. R—, the agent. Captain T— turned to me and asked abruptly:

"D—, do you want to go home in the ship?"

"Certainly, sir," said I, "I expect to go home in the ship."

"Then," said he, "you must get someone to go in your place on board the *Pilgrim*."

I was so completely "taken aback" by this sudden intimation that for a moment I could make no reply. I knew that it would be hopeless to attempt to prevail upon any of the ship's crew to take twelve months more on California in the brig. I knew, too, that Captain T— had received orders to bring me home in the *Alert*, and he had told me when I was at the hide house that I was to go home in her; and even if this had not been so, it was cruel to give me no notice of the step they were going to take until a few hours before the brig would sail. As soon as I had got my wits about me, I put on a bold front, and told him plainly that I had a letter in my chest informing me that he had been written to by the owners in Boston to bring me home in the ship, and moreover that he had told me that I was to go in the ship.

To have this told him, and to be opposed in such a manner, was more than my lord paramount had been used to. He turned

fiercely upon me, and tried to look me down and face me out
of my statement; but finding that that wouldn't do, and that I
was entering upon my defense in such a way as would show to
the other two that he was in the wrong, he changed his ground,
and pointed to the shipping papers of the *Pilgrim*, from which
my name had never been erased, and said that there was my
name, that I belonged to her, that he had an absolute discretion-
ary power—and, in short, that I must be on board the *Pilgrim*
by the next morning with my chest and hammock or have someone ready to go in my place, and that he would not hear another
word from me. No court of star chamber could proceed more
summarily with a poor devil than this trio was about to do with
me, condemning me to a punishment worse than a Botany Bay
exile, and to a fate which would alter the whole current of my
future life; for two years more in California would have made
me a sailor for the rest of my days. I felt all this, and saw the
necessity of being determined. I repeated what I had said, and
insisted upon my right to return in the ship. I

> *"raised my arm, and tauld my crack,*
> *Before them a'."*

But it would have all availed me nothing had I been "some
poor body" before this absolute, domineering tribunal. But they
saw that I would not go unless "*vi et armis*," and they knew that
I had friends and interest enough at home to make them suffer
for any injustice they might do me. It was probably this that
turned the matter; for the captain changed his tone entirely, and
asked me if in case anyone went in my place, I would give him
the same sum that S— gave Harris to exchange with him. I told
him that if anyone was sent on board the brig, I should pity him,
and be willing to help him to that or almost any amount, but
would not speak of it as an exchange.

"Very well," said he. "Go forward about your business, and
send English Ben here to me!"

I went forward with a light heart, but feeling as angry, and
as much contempt, as I could well contain between my teeth.
English Ben was sent aft, and in a few moments came forward
looking as though he had received his sentence to be hanged.
The captain had told him to get his things ready to go on board

the brig the next morning, and that I would give him thirty dollars and a suit of clothes. The hands had "knocked off" for dinner, and were standing about the forecastle when Ben came forward and told his story. I could see plainly that it made a great excitement, and that unless I explained the matter to them, the feeling would be turned against me. Ben was a poor English boy, a stranger in Boston, and without friends or money; and being an active, willing lad and a good sailor for his years, was a general favorite. "Oh yes!" said the crew. "The captain has let you off because you are a gentleman's son, and have got friends, and know the owners; and taken Ben because he is poor, and has got nobody to say a word for him!" I knew that this was too true to be answered, but I excused myself from any blame, and told them that I had a right to go home, at all events. This pacified them a little, but Jack had got a notion that a poor lad was to be imposed upon, and did not distinguish very clearly; and though I knew that I was in no fault, and in fact had barely escaped the grossest injustice, yet I felt that my berth was getting to be a disagreeable one. The notion that I was not "one of them," which by a participation in all their labor and hardships, and having no favor shown me, had been laid asleep, was beginning to revive. But far stronger than any feeling for myself was the pity I felt for the poor lad. He had depended upon going home in the ship, and from Boston was going immediately to Liverpool, to see his friends. Besides this, having begun the voyage with very few clothes, he had taken up the greater part of his wages in the slop chest, and it was every day a losing concern to him; and like all the rest of the crew, he had a hearty hatred of California, and the prospect of eighteen months or two years more of high-droghing seemed completely to break down his spirit. I had determined not to go myself, happen what would, and I knew that the captain would not dare to attempt to force me. I knew, too, that the two captains had agreed together to get someone, and that unless I could prevail upon somebody to go voluntarily there would be no help for Ben. From this consideration, though I had said that I would have nothing to do with an exchange, I did my best to get someone to go voluntarily. I offered to give an order on the owners in Boston for six months' wages, and also all the clothes, books, and other matters which I should not want upon the voyage home. When this offer was published in the ship, and the case of poor Ben was set forth in strong colors, several who would not have dreamed of going themselves were busy in talking it up to others who they thought might be tempted to accept it; and at length one fellow, a harum-scarum lad whom we called Harry Bluff, and who did not care what country or ship he was in if he had clothes enough and money enough—partly from pity for Ben, and partly from the thought he should have "cruising money" for the rest of his stay—came forward and offered to go and "sling his hammock in the bloody hooker." Lest his purpose should cool, I signed an order for the sum on the owners in Boston, gave him all the clothes I could spare, and sent him aft to the captain, to let him know what had been done. The skipper accepted the exchange, and was doubtless glad to have it pass off so easily. At the same time he cashed the order, which was endorsed to him,* and the next morning the lad went aboard the brig, apparently in good spirits, having shaken hands with each of us and wished us a pleasant passage home, jingling the money in his pockets and calling out, "Never say die while there's a shot in the locker." The same boat carried off Harris, my old watchmate, who had previously made an exchange with my friend S—.

I was sorry to part with Harris. Nearly two hundred hours (as we had calculated it) had we walked the ship's deck together at anchor watch when all hands were below, and talked over and over every subject which came within the ken of either of us. He gave me a strong grip with his hand and I told him if he came to Boston again, not to fail to find me out and let me see an old watchmate. The same boat brought on board S—, my friend who had begun the voyage with me from Boston and like me, was going back to his family and to the society which we had been born and brought up in. We congratulated one another upon finding what we had long talked over and wished for thus brought about; and none on board the ship were more glad than ourselves to see the old brig standing round the point under

* When the crew were paid off in Boston, the owners answered the order, but generously refused to deduct the amount from the payroll, saying that the exchange was made under compulsion. They also allowed S— his exchange money.

full sail. As she passed abreast of us, we all collected in the waist and gave her three loud, hearty cheers, waving our hats in the air. Her crew sprang into the rigging and chains, answered us with three as loud, to which we, after the nautical custom, gave one in return. I took my last look of their familiar faces as they got over the rail, and saw the old black cook put his head out of the galley and wave his cap over his head. The crew flew aloft to loose the topgallant sails and royals; the two captains waved their hands to one another; and in ten minutes we saw the last inch of her white canvas as she rounded the point.

Relieved as I was to see her well off (and I felt like one who had just sprung from an iron trap which was closing upon him), I had yet a feeling of regret at taking the last look at the old craft in which I had spent a year, and the first year, of my sailor's life, which had been my first home in the new world into which I had entered, and with which I had associated so many things— my first leaving home, my first crossing the equator, Cape Horn, Juan Fernández, death at sea, and other things, serious and common. Yet with all this, and the feeling I had for my old shipmates condemned to another term of California life, the thought that we were done with it, and that one week more would see us on our way to Boston, was a cure for everything.

FRIDAY, MAY 6, completed the taking of our cargo, and was a memorable day in our calendar. The time when we were to take in our last hide we had looked forward to for sixteen months as the first bright spot. When the last hide was stowed away, and the hatches calked down, the tarpaulins battened onto them, the longboat hoisted in and secured, and the decks swept down for the night, the chief mate sprang up on the top of the longboat, called all hands into the waist, and giving us a signal by swinging his cap over his head, we gave three long, loud cheers, which came from the bottom of our hearts and made the hills and valleys ring again. In a moment we heard three in answer from the *California's* crew, who had seen us taking in our longboat, and—"the cry they heard, its meaning knew."

The last week we had been occupied in taking in a supply of wood and water for the passage home, and bringing on board the spare spars, sails, etc. I was sent off with a party of Indians to fill the water casks at a spring about three miles from the shipping, and near the town, and was absent three days, living at the town and spending the daytime in filling the casks and transporting them on oxcarts to the landing place, whence they were taken on board by the crew with boats. This being all done with, we gave one day to bending our sails, and at night every sail, from the courses to the skysails, was bent, and every studding sail ready for setting.

Before our sailing, an unsuccessful attempt was made by one of the crew of the *California* to effect an exchange with one of our number. It was a lad between fifteen and sixteen years of age who went by the name of the "reefer," having been a midshipman in an East India Company's ship. His singular character and story had excited our interest ever since the ship came into the port. He was a delicate, slender little fellow, with a beautiful pearly complexion, regular features, forehead as white as marble, black hair curling beautifully round it, tapering, delicate fingers, small feet, soft voice, gentle manners, and in fact every sign of having been well born and bred. At the same time there was something in his expression which showed a slight deficiency of intellect. How great the deficiency was, or what it resulted from— whether he was born so, whether it was the result of disease or accident, or whether, as some said, it was brought on by his distress of mind during the voyage—I cannot say. From his own account of himself, and from many circumstances which were known in connection with his story, he must have been the son of a man of wealth. His mother was an Italian woman. He was probably a natural son, for in scarcely any other way could the incidents of his early life be accounted for. He said that his parents did not live together, and he seemed to have been illtreated by his father. Though he had been delicately brought up, and indulged in every way (and he had then with him trinkets which had been given him at home), yet his education had been sadly neglected, and when only twelve years old he was sent as midshipman in the Company's service. His own story was that he afterward ran away from home, upon a difficulty which he had with his father, and went to Liverpool, whence he sailed in the ship *Rialto*, Captain Holmes, for Boston. Captain Holmes endeavored to get him a passage back, but there being no vessel to sail for some time, the boy left him, and went to board at a common sailor's boardinghouse in Ann Street, where he supported himself for a few weeks by selling some of his valuables. At length, according to his own account, being desirous of returning home, he went to a shipping office, where the shipping articles of the *California* were open. Upon asking where the ship was going, he was told by the shipping master that she was bound to California. Not knowing where that was, he told him that he wanted to go to Europe, and asked if California was in Europe. The shipping master answered him in a way which the boy did not understand, and advised him to ship. The boy signed the articles, received his advance, laid out a little of it in clothes and spent the rest, and was ready to go on board when, on the morning of sailing, he heard that the ship was bound upon the Northwest coast on a two or three years' voyage, and was not going to Europe. Frightened at this prospect, he slipped away when the crew was going aboard, wandered up into another part of the town, and spent all the forenoon in straying about the common and the neighboring streets. Having no money, and all his clothes and other things being in his chest on board, and being a stranger, he became tired and hungry, and ventured down toward the shipping, to see if the vessel had sailed. He was just turning the corner of a street when the shipping master, who had been in search of him, popped upon him, seized him, and carried him on board. He cried and struggled, and said he did not wish to go in the ship, but the topsails were at the masthead, the fast just ready to be cast off, and everything in the hurry and confusion of departure, so that he was hardly noticed; and the few who did inquire about the matter were told that it was merely a boy who had spent his advance and tried to run away. Had the owners of the vessel known anything of the matter, they would have interfered at once; but they either knew nothing of it or heard, like the rest, that it was only an unruly boy who was sick of his bargain. As soon as the boy found himself actually at sea, and on a voyage of two or three years in length, his spirits failed him; he refused to work, and became so miserable that Captain Arthur took him into the cabin, where he assisted the steward, and occasionally pulled and hauled about decks. He was in this capacity when we saw him; and though it was much better for him than the life in a forecastle, and the hard work, watching, and exposure which his delicate frame could not have borne, yet to be joined with a black fellow in waiting on a man whom he probably looked upon as but little, in point of education and manners, above one of his father's servants was almost too much for his spirit to bear. Had he entered upon this situation of his own free will, he could have endured it; but to have been deceived, and in addition to that, forced into it, was intolerable. He made every effort to go home in our ship, but his captain refused to part with him except in the way of exchange, and that he could not effect. If this account of the whole matter, which we had from the boy, and which was confirmed by all the crew, be correct, I cannot understand why Captain Arthur should have refused to let him go, especially being a captain who had the name not only with that crew, but with all whom he had ever commanded, of an unusually kindhearted man. The truth is, the unlimited power which merchant captains have on long voyages on strange coasts takes away a sense of responsibility, and too often, even in men otherwise well disposed, substitutes a disregard for the rights and feelings of others. The lad was sent on shore to join the gang at the hide house; from whence, I was afterward rejoiced to hear, he effected his escape, and went down to Callao in a small Spanish schooner, and from Callao he probably returned to England.

Soon after the arrival of the *California*, I spoke to Captain Arthur about Hope; and as he had known him on the voyage before, and was very fond of him, he immediately went to see him and gave him proper medicines, and under such care he began rapidly to recover. The Saturday night before our sailing, I spent an hour in the oven, and took leave of my Kanaka friends; and really this was the only thing connected with leaving California which was in any way unpleasant. I felt an interest and affection for many of these simple, truehearted men such as I never felt before but for a near relation. Hope shook me by the hand; said he should soon be well again, and ready to work for me when I came upon the coast next voyage as officer of the ship and told me not to forget when I became captain how to be kind to the sick. Old "Mr. Bingham" and "King Mannini" went down to the boat with me, shook me heartily by the hand, wished us a good voyage, and went back to the oven chanting one of their deep monotonous songs, the burden of which I gathered to be about us and our voyage.

SUNDAY, MAY 8. This promised to be our last day in California. Our forty thousand hides, thirty thousand horns, besides several barrels of otter and beaver skins, were all stowed below, and the hatches calked down. All our spare spars were taken on board and lashed; our water casks secured; and our livestock, con‑ sisting of four bullocks, a dozen sheep, a dozen or more pigs, and three or four dozen of poultry, were all stowed away in their different quarters: the bullocks in the longboat, the sheep in a pen on the fore hatch, the pigs in a sty under the bows of the longboat, and the poultry in their proper coop; and the jolly boat was full of hay for the sheep and bullocks. Our unusually large cargo, together with the stores for a five months' voyage, brought the ship channels down into the water. In addition to this, she had been steeved so thoroughly, and was so bound by the com‑ pression of her cargo, forced into her by so powerful machinery, that she was like a man in a strait jacket, and would be but a dull sailer until she had worked herself loose.

The *California* had finished discharging her cargo, and was to get under way at the same time with us. We having washed down decks and got our breakfast; the two vessels lay side by side, in complete readiness for sea, our ensigns hanging from the peaks, and our tall spars reflected from the glassy surface of the river, which since sunrise had been unbroken by a ripple. At length a few whiffs came across the water, and by eleven o'clock the regular northwest wind set steadily in. There was no need of calling all hands, for we had all been hanging about the forecastle the whole forenoon, and were ready for a start upon the first sign of a breeze. All eyes were aft upon the captain, who was walking the deck with every now and then a look to wind‑ ward. He made a sign to the mate, who came forward, took his station deliberately between the knightheads, cast a glance aloft, and called out, "All hands lay aloft and loose the sails!" We were half in the rigging before the order came, and never since we left Boston were the gaskets off the yards, and the rigging over‑ hauled, in a shorter time. "All ready forward, sir!"—"All ready the main!"—"Crossjack yards all ready, sir!"—"Lay down, all hands but one on each yard!" The yardarm and bunt gaskets were cast off, and each sail hung by the jigger, with one man standing by the tye to let it go. At the same moment that we sprang aloft, a dozen hands sprang into the rigging of the *California,* and in an instant were all over her yards, and her sails too were ready to be dropped at the word. In the meantime our bowgun had been loaded and run out, and its discharge was to be the signal for dropping the sails. A cloud of smoke came out of our bows, the echoes of the gun rattled our farewell among the hills of California, and the two ships were covered from head to foot with their white canvas. For a few minutes, all was uproar and apparent confusion: men flying about like monkeys in the rigging; ropes and blocks flying; orders given and answered; and the confused noises of men singing out at the ropes. The topsails came to the mastheads with "Cheerily, men!" and in a few minutes every sail was set, for the wind was light. The headsails were backed, the windlass came round "slip-slap" to the cry of the sailors.—"Hove short, sir," said the mate. "Up with him!"—"Aye, aye, sir."—A few hearty and long heaves and the anchor showed its head. "Hook cat!" The fall was stretched along the decks; all hands laid hold.—"Hurrah, for the last time!" said the mate, and the anchor came to the cathead to the tune of "Time for us to go," with a loud chorus. Everything was done quick, as though it were for the last time. The head yards were filled away, and our ship began to move through the water on her homeward-bound course.

The *California* had got under way at the same moment; and we sailed down the narrow bay abreast and were just off the mouth, and finding ourselves gradually shooting ahead of her, were on the point of giving her three parting cheers when suddenly we found ourselves stopped short, and the *California* ranging fast ahead of us. A bar stretches across the mouth of the harbor, with water enough to float common vessels, but being low in the water, and having kept well to leeward, as we were bound to the southward, we had stuck fast, while the *California,* being light, had floated over.

We kept all sail on, in the hope of forcing over, but failing in this, we hove aback, and lay waiting for the tide, which was on the flood, to take us back into the channel. This was somewhat of a damper to us, and the captain looked not a little mortified and vexed. "This is the same place where the *Rosa* got ashore," observed our redheaded second mate, most malapropos. A malediction on the *Rosa*, and him too, was all the answer he got, and he slunk off to leeward. In a few minutes, the force of the wind and the rising of the tide backed us into the stream, and we were on our way to our old anchoring place, the tide setting swiftly up and the ship barely manageable in the light breeze. We came to in our old berth opposite the hide house, whose inmates were not a little surprised to see us return. We felt as though we were tied to California, and some of the crew swore that they never should get clear of the "bloody" coast.

In about half an hour, which was near high water, the order was given to man the windlass, and again the anchor was catted; but not a word was said about the last time. The *California* had come back on finding that we had returned, and was hove to, waiting for us, off the point. This time we passed the bar safely, and were soon up with the *California*, who filled away and kept us company. She seemed desirous of a trial of speed, and our captain accepted the challenge, although we were loaded down to the bolts of our chain plates, as deep as a sand barge, and bound so taut with our cargo that we were no more fit for a race than a man in fetters, while our antagonist was in her best trim. Being clear of the point, the breeze became stiff and the royal masts bent under our sails, but we would not take them in until we saw three boys spring aloft into the rigging of the *California*, when they were all furled at once, but with orders to stay aloft at the topgallant mastheads, and loose them again at the word. It was my duty to furl the fore royal, and while standing by to loose it again, I had a fine view of the scene. From where I stood, the two vessels seemed nothing but spars and sails, while their narrow decks, far below, slanting over by the force of the wind aloft, appeared hardly capable of supporting the great fabrics raised upon them. The *California* was to windward of us, and had every advantage; yet while the breeze was stiff we held our own. As soon as it began to slacken, she ranged a little ahead, and the order was given to loose the royals. In an instant the gaskets were off and the bunt dropped. "Sheet home the fore royal!"—"Weather sheet's home!"—"Lee sheet's home!"—"Hoist away, sir!" is bawled from aloft. "Overhaul your clew lines!" shouts the mate. "Aye, aye, sir! All clear!"—"Taut leech! Belay! Well the lee brace, haul taut to windward"—and the royals are set. These brought us up again; but the wind continuing light, the *California* set hers, and it was soon evident that she was walking away from us. Our captain then hailed, and said that he should keep off to his course, adding, "She isn't the *Alert* now. If I had her in your trim, she would have been out of sight by this time." This was good-naturedly answered from the *California,* and she braced sharp up and stood close upon the wind up the coast, while we squared away our yards and stood before the wind to the south-southwest. The *California's* crew manned her weather rigging, waved their hats in the air, and gave us three hearty cheers, which we answered as heartily, and the customary single cheer came back to us from over the water. She stood on her way, doomed to eighteen months' or two years' hard service on that hated coast, while we were making our way to our home, which every hour and every mile was bringing us nearer to.

As soon as we parted company with the *California,* all hands were sent aloft to set the studding sails. Booms were rigged out, tacks and halyards rove, sail after sail packed upon her, until every available inch of canvas was spread, that we might not lose a breath of the fair wind. We could now see how much she was cramped and deadened by her cargo; for with a good breeze on her quarter, and every stitch of canvas spread, we could not get more than six knots out of her. She had no more life in her than if she were waterlogged. The log was hove several times; but she was doing her best. We had hardly patience with her, but the older sailors said: "Stand by! You'll see her work herself loose in a week or two, and then she'll walk up to Cape Horn like a race horse."

When all sail had been set, and the decks cleared up, the *California* was a speck in the horizon and the coast lay like a low cloud along the northeast. At sunset they were both out of sight, and we were once more upon the ocean, where sky and water meet.

Beginning the Long Return Voyage · A Scare

AT EIGHT O'CLOCK all hands were called aft, and the watches set for the voyage. Some changes were made, but I was glad to find myself still in the larboard watch. Our crew was somewhat diminished; for a man and a boy had gone in the *Pilgrim*, another was second mate of the *Ayacucho*, and a third, the oldest man of the crew, had broken down under the hard work and constant exposure on the coast and, having had a stroke of the palsy, was left behind at the hide house. By these diminutions, we were shorthanded for a voyage round Cape Horn in the dead of winter. Besides S— and myself, there were only five in the forecastle, who, together with four boys in the steerage, the sailmaker, carpenter, etc., composed the whole crew. In addition to this, we were only three or four days out when the sailmaker, who was the oldest and best seaman on board, was taken with the palsy, and was useless for the rest of the voyage. The constant wading in the water in all weathers to take off hides, together with the other labors, is too much for old men, and for any who have not good constitutions. Besides these two men of ours, the second officer of the *California* and the carpenter of the *Pilgrim* broke down under the work, and the latter died at Santa Barbara. The young man, too, who came out with us from Boston in the *Pilgrim* had to be taken from his berth before the mast and made clerk, on account of a fit of rheumatism which attacked him soon after he came on the coast. By the loss of the sailmaker, our watch was reduced to five, of whom two were boys, who never steered but in fine weather, so that the other two and myself had to stand at the wheel four hours apiece out of every twenty-four; and the other watch had only four helmsmen. "Never mind—we're homeward bound!" was the answer to everything; and we should not have minded this were it not for the thought that we should be off Cape Horn in the very dead of winter. It was now the first part of May, and two months would bring us off the Cape in July, which is the worst month in the year there, when the sun rises at nine and sets at three, giving eighteen hours night, and there is snow and rain, gales and high seas, in abundance.

The prospect of meeting this in a ship half-manned, and loaded so deep that every heavy sea must wash her fore and aft, was by no means pleasant. The *Alert* in her passage out doubled the Cape in the month of February, which is midsummer; and we came round in the *Pilgrim* in the latter part of October, which we thought was bad enough. There was only one of our crew who had been off there in the winter, and that was in a whale-ship much lighter and higher than our ship; yet he said they had man-killing weather for twenty days without intermission, and their decks were swept twice, and they were all glad enough to see the last of it. Yet pass it we must, and all hands agreed to make the best of it.

During our watches below we overhauled our clothes, and made and mended everything for bad weather. Each of us had made for himself a suit of oilcloth or tarpaulin, and these we got out, and gave thorough coatings of oil or tar, and hung on the stays to dry. Our stout boots, too, we covered over with a thick mixture of melted grease and tar, and hung out to dry. Thus we took advantage of the warm sun and fine weather of the Pacific to prepare for its other face. In the forenoon watches below, our forecastle looked like the workshop of what a sailor is—a Jack-of-all-trades. Thick stockings and drawers were darned and patched; mittens dragged from the bottom of the chest and mended; comforters made for the neck and ears; old flannel shirts cut up to line monkey jackets; southwesters lined with flannel, and a pot of paint smuggled forward to give them a coat on the outside; and everything turned to hand; so that although two years had left us but a scanty wardrobe, yet the economy and invention which necessity teaches a sailor soon put each of us in pretty good trim for bad weather, even before we had seen the last of the fine. Even the cobbler's art was not out of place.

Several old shoes were very decently repaired, and with waxed ends, an awl, and the top of an old boot, I made me quite a respectable sheath for my knife.

There was one difficulty, however, which nothing that we could do would remedy, and that was the leaking of the forecastle, which made it very uncomfortable in bad weather and rendered half of the berths tenantless. The tightest ships, in a long voyage, from the constant strain which is upon the bowsprit, will leak, more or less, round the heel of the bowsprit and the bitts, which come down into the forecastle; but in addition to this we had an unaccountable leak on the starboard bow, near the cathead, which drove us from the forward berths on that side, and indeed when she was on the starboard tack from all the forward berths. One of the after berths, too, leaked in very bad weather, so that in a ship which was in other respects as tight as a bottle, and brought her cargo to Boston perfectly dry, we had, after every effort made to prevent it in the way of calking and leading, a forecastle with only three dry berths for seven of us. However, as there is never but one watch below at a time, by "turning in and out" we did pretty well. And there being in our watch but three of us who lived forward, we generally had a dry berth apiece in bad weather.*

All this, however, was but anticipation. We were still in fine weather in the North Pacific, running down the northeast trades, which we took on the second day after leaving San Diego.

SUNDAY, MAY 15, one week out, we were in latitude 14° 56′ N., long. 116° 14′ W., having gone, by reckoning, over thirteen hundred miles in seven days. In fact, ever since leaving San Diego we had had a fair wind, and as much as we wanted of it. For seven days our lower and topmast studding sails were set all the time, and our royals and topgallant studding sails whenever she could stagger under them. Indeed, the captain had shown, from the moment we got to sea, that he was to have no boy's play, but that the ship had got to carry all she could, and

---

* On removing the cathead, after the ship arrived at Boston, it was found that there were two holes under it which had been bored for the purpose of driving treenails, and which, accidentally, had not been plugged up when the cathead was placed over them. This was sufficient to account for the leak, and for our not having been able to discover and stop it.

that he was going to make up by "cracking onto" her what she
wanted in lightness. In this way, we frequently made three
degrees of latitude, besides something in longitude, in the course
of twenty-four hours. Our days were spent in the usual ship's
work. The rigging which had become slack from being long in
port was to be set up; breast backstays got up; studding-sail
booms rigged upon the main yard, and royal studding sails got
ready for the light trades; ringtail set; and new rigging fitted and
sails got ready for Cape Horn. For with a ship's gear, as well as
a sailor's wardrobe, fine weather must be improved to get ready
for the bad to come. Our forenoon watch below, as I have said,
was given to our own work, and our night watches were spent
in the usual manner—a trick at the wheel, a lookout on the forecastle, a nap on a coil of rigging under the lee of the rail; a yarn
round the windlass end; or, as was generally my way, a solitary
walk fore and aft in the weather waist, between the windlass
end and the main tack. Every wave that she threw aside brought
us nearer home, and every day's observation at noon showed a
progress which, if it continued, would in less than five months
take us into Boston Bay. This is the pleasure of life at sea—
fine weather, day after day, without interruption, fair wind, and
a plenty of it, and homeward bound. Everyone was in good
humor, things went right, and all was done with a will. At the
dog watch, all hands came on deck and stood round the weather
side of the forecastle, or sat on the windlass and sang sea songs,
and those ballads of pirates and highwaymen which sailors delight in. Home, too, and what we should do when we got there,
and when and how we should arrive, was no infrequent topic.
Every night after the kids and pots were put away and we had
lighted our pipes and cigars at the galley, and gathered about
the windlass, the first question was:

"Well, Tom, what was the latitude today?"

"Why, fourteen, North, and she has been going seven knots
ever since."

"Well, this will bring us up to the line in five days."

"Yes, but these trades won't last twenty-four hours longer,"
says an old salt, pointing with the sharp of his hand to leeward.
"I know that by the look of the clouds."

Then came all manner of calculations and conjectures as to

the continuance of the wind, the weather under the line, the southeast trades, etc., and rough guesses as to the time the ship would be up with the Horn; and some, more venturous, gave her so many days to Boston Light, and offered to bet that she would not exceed it.

"You'd better wait till you get round Cape Horn," says an old croaker.

"Yes," says another, "you may see Boston, but you've got to 'smell hell' before that good day."

Rumors also of what had been said in the cabin, as usual, found their way forward. The steward had heard the captain say something about the Straits of Magellan, and the man at the wheel fancied he had heard him tell the "passenger" that if he found the wind ahead and the weather very bad off the Cape, he should stick her off for New Holland, and come home round the Cape of Good Hope.

This passenger—the first and only one we had had, except to go from port to port on the coast—was no one else than a gentleman whom I had known in my better days, and the last person I should have expected to have seen on the coast of California—Professor N—, of Cambridge. I had left him quietly seated in the chair of Botany and Ornithology in Harvard University, and the next I saw of him, he was strolling about San Diego beach in a sailor's pea jacket, with a wide straw hat, and barefooted, with his trousers rolled up to his knees, picking up stones and shells. He had traveled overland to the Northwest coast, and come down in a small vessel to Monterey. There he learned that there was a ship at the leeward about to sail for Boston, and taking passage in the *Pilgrim*, which was then at Monterey, he came slowly down, visiting the intermediate ports, and examining the trees, plants, earths, birds, etc., and joined us at San Diego shortly before we sailed. The second mate of the *Pilgrim* told me that they had got an old gentleman on board who knew me, and came from the college that I had been in. He could not recollect his name, but said he was a "sort of an oldish man" with white hair, and spent all his time in the bush, and along the beach, picking up flowers and shells and such truck, and had a dozen boxes and barrels full of them. I thought over everybody who would be likely to be there, but could fix upon no one, when the next day, just as we were about to shove off from the beach, he came down to the boat in the rig I have described, with his shoes in his hand and his pockets full of specimens. I knew him at once, though I should not have been more surprised to have seen the Old South steeple shoot up from the hide house. He probably had no less difficulty in recognizing me. As we left home about the same time, we had nothing to tell one another, and, owing to our different situations on board, I saw but little of him on the passage home. Sometimes, when I was at the wheel of a calm night and the steering required no attention and the officer of the watch was forward, he would come aft and hold a short yarn with me; but this was against the rules of the ship, as is, in fact, all intercourse between passengers and the crew. I was often amused to see the sailors puzzled to know what to make of him, and to hear their conjectures about him and his business. They were as much puzzled as our old sailmaker was with the captain's instruments in the cabin. He said there were three: the *chro*-nometer, the *chre*-nometer, and the *the*-nometer (chronometer, barometer, and thermometer). The *Pilgrim's* crew christened Mr. N. "Old Curious," from his zeal for curiosities, and some of them said that he was crazy, and that his friends let him go about and amuse himself in this way. Why else a rich man (sailors call every man rich who does not work with his hands, and wears a long coat and cravat) should leave a Christian country, and come to such a place as California to pick up shells and stones, they could not understand. One of them, however, an old salt who had seen something more of the world ashore, set all to rights, as he thought: "Oh, 'vast there!—You don't know anything about them craft. I've seen them colleges, and know the ropes. They keep all such things for cur'osities, and study 'em, and have men a' purpose to go and get 'em. This old chap knows what he's about. He ain't the child you take him for. He'll carry all these things to the college, and if they are better than any that they have had before, he'll be head of the college. Then, by and by, somebody else will go after some more, and if they beat him, he'll have to go again, or else give up his berth. That's the way they do it. This old covey knows the ropes. He has worked a traverse over 'em, and come 'way out here, where nobody's ever been afore, and where they'll never think of coming." This explanation satisfied Jack; and as it raised Mr. N.'s credit for capacity, and was near enough to the truth for common purposes, I did not disturb it.

With the exception of Mr. N., we had no one on board but the regular ship's company, and the livestock. Upon this we had made a considerable inroad. We killed one of the bullocks every four days, so that they did not last us up to the line. We, or rather they, then began upon the sheep and the poultry, for these never come into Jack's mess.* The pigs were left for the latter

* The customs as to the allowance of "grub" are very nearly the same in all American merchantmen. Whenever a pig is killed, the sailors have one mess from it. The rest goes to the cabin. The smaller livestock, poultry, etc., they never taste. And indeed they do not complain of this, for it would take a great deal to supply them with a good meal, and without the accompaniments (which could hardly be furnished to them) it would not be much better than salt beef. But even as to the salt beef they are scarcely dealt fairly with; for whenever a barrel is opened, before any of the beef is put into the harness cask, the steward comes up and picks it all over, and takes out the best pieces (those that have any fat in them) for the cabin. This was done in both the vessels I was in, and the men said that it was usual in other vessels. Indeed, it is made no secret, but some of the crew are usually called to help in assorting and putting away the pieces. By this arrangement, the hard, dry pieces, which the sailors call 'old horse,' come to their share.

There is a singular piece of rhyme, traditional among sailors, which they say over such pieces of beef. I do not know that it ever appeared in print before. When seated round the kid, if a particularly bad piece is found one of them takes it up, and addressing it, repeats these lines:

> "Old horse! old horse! what brought you here?"
> —"From Sacarap to Portland pier
> I've carted stone this many a year,
> Till, killed by blows and sore abuse,
> They salted me down for sailors' use.
> The sailors they do me despise,
> They turn me over and damn my eyes,
> Cut off my meat, and pick my bones,
> And pitch the rest to Davy Jones."

There is a story current among seamen that a beef-dealer was convicted at Boston of having sold old horse for ship's stores instead of beef, and had been sentenced to be confined in jail until he should eat the whole of it, and that he is now lying in Boston jail. I have heard this story often, on board other vessels besides those of our own nation. It is very generally believed, and is always highly commended, as a fair instance of retaliatory justice.

part of the voyage, for they are sailors, and can stand all
weathers. We had an old sow on board, the mother of a numerous
progeny, who had been twice round the Cape of Good Hope,
and once round Cape Horn. The last time going round was very
nearly her death. We heard her squealing and moaning one dark
night after it had been snowing and hailing for several hours,
and getting into the sty, we found her nearly frozen to death.
We got some straw, an old sail, and other things, and wrapped
her up in a corner of the sty, where she stayed until we got into
fine weather again.

WEDNESDAY, MAY 18. Lat. 9° 54′ N., long. 113° 17′ W. The
northeast trades had now left us, and we had the usual variable
winds which prevail near the line, together with some rain. So
long as we were in these latitudes, we had but little rest in our
watch on deck at night, for as the winds were light and variable,
and we could not lose a breath, we were all the watch bracing
the yards, and taking in and making sail, and "humbugging"
with our flying kites. A little puff of wind on the larboard quarter and then—"Larboard forebraces!" and studding booms were
rigged out, studding sails set alow and aloft, the yards trimmed,
and jibs and spanker in—when it would come as calm as a duckpond, and the man at the wheel stand with the palm of his hand
up, feeling for the wind. "Keep her off a little!" "All aback forward, sir!" cries a man from the forecastle. Down go the braces
again, in come the studding sails, all in a mess which half an
hour won't set right; yards braced sharp up; and she's on the
starboard tack, close-hauled. The studding sails must now be
cleared away, and set up in the tops, and on the booms. By the
time this is done, and you are looking out for a soft plank for a
nap—"Lay aft here, and square in the head yards!" and the
studding sails are all set again on the starboard side. So it goes
until it is eight bells—call the watch, heave the log, relieve the
wheel, and go below, the larboard watch.

SUNDAY, MAY 22. Lat. 5° 14′ N., long. 116° 45′ W. We were
now a fortnight out, and within five degrees of the line, to which
two days of good breeze would take us; but we had, for the
most part, what the sailors call "an Irishman's hurricane—right
up and down." This day it rained nearly all day, and being
Sunday, and nothing to do, we stopped up the scuppers and

filled the decks with rain water, and bringing all our clothes on deck, had a grand wash, fore and aft. The next day, the sun rising clear, the ship was covered fore and aft with clothes of all sorts hanging out to dry.

As we approached the line the wind became more easterly, and the weather clearer, and in twenty days from San Diego,

SATURDAY, MAY 28, at about 3 P.M., with a fine breeze from the east-southeast, we crossed the equator. In twenty-four hours after crossing the line, which was very unusual, we took the regular southeast trades. These winds come a little from the eastward of southeast, and with us they blew directly from the east-southeast, which was fortunate for us, for our course was south by west, and we could thus go one point free. The yards were braced so that every sail drew, from the spanker to the flying jib; and the upper yards being squared in a little, the fore and main-topgallant studding sails were set, and just drew handsomely. For twelve days this breeze blew steadily, not varying a point, and just so fresh that we could carry our royals, and during the whole time we hardly started a brace. Such progress did we make that at the end of seven days from the time we took the breeze, on

SUNDAY, JUNE 5, we were in lat. 19° 29′ S., and long. 118° 01′ W., having made twelve hundred miles in seven days, very nearly on a taut bowline. Our good ship was getting to be herself again, had increased her rate of sailing more than one-third since leaving San Diego. The crew ceased complaining of her, and the officers hove the log every two hours with evident satisfaction. This was glorious sailing. A steady breeze; the light trade-wind clouds over our heads; the incomparable temperature of the Pacific—neither hot nor cold; a clear sun every day, and clear moon and stars each night; and new constellations rising in the south and the familiar ones sinking in the north as we went on our course, "stemming nightly toward the pole." Already we had sunk the North Star and the Great Bear in the northern horizon, and all hands looked out sharp to the southward for the Magellan Clouds, which each succeeding night we expected to make. "The next time we see the North Star," said one, "we shall be standing to the northward, the other side of the Horn." This was true enough, and no doubt it would be a welcome sight; for sailors say that in coming home from round Cape Horn and the Cape of Good Hope, the North Star is the first land you make.

These trades were the same that in the passage out in the *Pilgrim* lasted nearly all the way from Juan Fernández to the line, blowing steadily on our starboard quarter for three weeks without our starting a brace, or even brailing down the skysails. Though we had now the same wind, and were in the same latitude with the *Pilgrim* on her passage out, yet we were nearly twelve hundred miles to the westward of her course; for the captain, depending upon the strong southwest winds which prevail in high southern latitudes during the winter months, took the full advantage of the trades, and stood well to the westward, so far that we passed within about two hundred miles of Ducie's Island.

We were now close upon the southern tropical line, and with so fine a breeze were daily leaving the sun behind us, and drawing nearer to Cape Horn, for which it behooved us to make every preparation. Our rigging was all examined and overhauled, and mended or replaced with new where it was necessary; new and strong bobstays fitted in the place of the chain ones, which were worn out; the spritsail yard and martingale guys and backropes set well taut; brand new fore and main braces rove; topgallant sheets, and wheel ropes, made of green hide laid up in the form of rope, were stretched and fitted; and new topsail clew lines, etc., rove; new fore-topmast backstays fitted; and other preparations made in good season, that the ropes might have time to stretch and become limber before we got into cold weather.

Bad Prospects · First Touch of Cape Horn · Icebergs · Temperance Ships · Lying Up · Ice · Difficulty on Board · Change of Course · Straits of Magellan

THERE BEGAN now to be a decided change in the appearance of things. The days became shorter and shorter, the sun running lower in its course each day, and giving less and less heat, and the nights so cold as to prevent our sleeping on deck; the Magellan Clouds in sight of a clear night; the skies looking cold and angry; and at times a long, heavy, ugly sea, setting in from the southward, told us what we were coming to. Still, however, we had a fine, strong breeze, and kept on our way under as much sail as our ship would bear. Toward the middle of the week the wind hauled to the southward, which brought us on a taut bowline, made the ship meet nearly head on the heavy swell which rolled from that direction; and there was something not at all encouraging in the manner in which she met it. Being so deep and heavy, she wanted the buoyancy which should have carried her over the seas, and she dropped heavily into them, the water washing over the decks. And every now and then, when an unusually large sea met her fairly upon the bows, she struck it with a sound as dead and heavy as that with which a sledge hammer falls upon the pile, and took the whole of it in upon the forecastle, and rising, carried it aft in the scuppers, washing the rigging off the pins and carrying along with it everything which was loose on deck. She had been acting in this way all of our forenoon watch below, as we could tell by the washing of the water over our heads and the heavy breaking of the seas against her bows (with a sound as though she were striking against a rock) only the thickness of the plank from our heads as we lay in our berths, which are directly against the bows. At eight bells the watch was called and we came on deck, one hand going aft to take the wheel, and another going to the galley to get the "grub" for dinner. I stood on the forecastle looking at the seas, which were rolling high as far as the eye could reach, their tops white with foam, and the body of them of a deep indigo-blue, reflecting the bright rays of the sun. Our ship rose slowly over a few of the largest of them, until one immense fellow came rolling on, threatening to cover her, and which I was sailor enough to know, by "the feeling of her" under my feet, she would not rise over. I sprang up on the knightheads, and seizing hold of the forestay with my hands, drew myself up on it. My feet were just off the stanchion when she struck fairly into the middle of the sea, and it washed her fore and aft, burying her in the water. As soon as she rose out of it, I looked aft, and everything forward of the mainmast except the longboat, which was griped and double-lashed down to the ringbolts, was swept off clear. The galley, the pigsty, the hen coop, and a large sheep pen which had been built on the forehatch were all gone in the twinkling of an eye—leaving the deck as clean as a chin new-reaped, and not a stick left, to show where they had stood. In the scuppers lay the galley, bottom up, and a few boards floating about, the wreck of the sheep pen—and half a dozen miserable sheep floating among them, wet through, and not a little frightened at the sudden change that had come upon them. As soon as the sea had washed by, all hands sprang up out of the forecastle to see what had become of the ship; and in a few moments the cook and Old Bill crawled out from under the galley, where they had been lying in the water, nearly smothered, with the galley over them. Fortunately, it rested against the bulwarks, or it would have broken some of their bones. When the water ran off, we picked the sheep up and put them in the longboat, got the galley back in its place, and set things a little to rights; but had not our ship had uncommonly high bulwarks and rail, everything must have been washed overboard, not excepting Old Bill and the cook. Bill had been standing at the galley door with the kid of beef in his hand for the forecastle mess when away he went, kid, beef, and all. He held onto the kid till the last, like a good fellow, but the beef was gone, and when the water had run off, we saw it lying high and dry, like a rock at low tide—nothing could hurt *that.* We took the loss of our beef very easily, consoling ourselves with the recollection that the cabin had more to lose than we, and chuckled not a little at seeing the remains of the chicken pie and pancakes floating in the scuppers. "This will never do!" was what some said, and everyone felt. Here we were, not yet within a thousand miles of the latitude of Cape Horn, and our decks swept by a sea not one half so high as we must expect to find there. Some blamed the captain for loading his ship so deep when he knew what he must expect, while others said that the wind was always southwest off the Cape in the winter and that, running before it, we should not mind the seas so much. When we got down into the forecastle, Old Bill, who was somewhat of a croaker—having met with a great many accidents at sea—said that if that was the way she was going to act, we might as well make our wills and balance the books at once, and put on a clean shirt. "'Vast there, you bloody old owl! You're always hanging out blue lights! You're frightened by the ducking you got in the scuppers, and can't take a joke! What's the use in being always on the lookout for Davy Jones?" "Stand by," says another, "and we'll get an afternoon watch below by this scrape." But in this they were disappointed, for at two bells all hands were called and set to work getting lashings on everything on deck; and the captain talked of sending down the long topgallant masts; but as the sea went down toward night, and the wind hauled abeam, we left them standing, and set the studding sails.

The next day, all hands were turned to on unbending the old sails and getting up the new ones; for a ship, unlike people on shore, puts on her best suit in bad weather. The old sails were sent down, and three new topsails, and new fore and main courses, jib, and fore-topmast staysail, which were made on the coast and never had been used, were bent, with a complete set of new earings, robands, and reef points; and reef tackles were

rove to the courses, and spilling lines to the topsails. These, with
new braces and clew lines fore and aft, gave us a good suit of
running rigging.

The wind continued westerly, and the weather and sea less
rough since the day on which we shipped the heavy sea, and we
were making great progress under studding sails, with our light
sails all set, keeping a little to the eastward of south; for the
captain, depending upon westerly winds off the Cape, had kept
so far to the westward that though we were within about five
hundred miles of the latitude of Cape Horn, we were nearly
seventeen hundred miles to the westward of it. Through the rest
of the week we continued on with a fair wind, gradually, as we
got more to the southward, keeping a more easterly course, and
bringing the wind on our larboard quarter, until

SUNDAY, JUNE 26, when, having a fine, clear day, the captain
got a lunar observation, as well as his meridian altitude, which
made us in lat. 47° 50′ S., long. 113° 49′ W., Cape Horn bearing,
according to my calculation, E.S.E. ½ E., and distant eighteen
hundred miles.

MONDAY, JUNE 27. During the first part of this day, the wind
continued fair, and as we were going before it, it did not feel
very cold, so that we kept at work on deck in our common clothes
and round jackets. Our watch had an afternoon watch below,
for the first time since leaving San Diego, and having inquired
of the third mate what the latitude was at noon, and made our
usual guesses as to the time she would need to be up with the
Horn, we turned in for a nap. We were sleeping away "at the
rate of knots" when three knocks on the scuttle, and "All hands
ahoy!" started us from our berths. What could be the matter?
It did not appear to be blowing hard, and looking up through
the scuttle, we could see that it was a clear day overhead; yet
the watch were taking in sail. We thought there must be a sail
in sight, and that we were about to heave to and speak her, and
were just congratulating ourselves upon it—for we had seen
neither sail nor land since we had left port—when we heard
the mate's voice on deck (he turned in "all standing," and was
always on deck the moment he was called) singing out to the
men who were taking in the studding sails, and asking where his
watch were. We did not wait for a second call, but tumbled up

the ladder, and there on the starboard bow was a bank of mist,
covering sea and sky, and driving directly for us. I had seen the
same before in my passage round in the *Pilgrim*, and knew what
it meant, and that there was no time to be lost. We had nothing
on but thin clothes, yet there was not a moment to spare, and
at it we went.

The boys of the other watch were in the tops, taking in the
topgallant studding sails, and the lower and topmast studding
sails were coming down by the run. It was nothing but "haul
down and clew up" until we got all the studding sails in, and
the royals, flying jib, and mizzen-topgallant sail furled, and the
ship kept off a little, to take the squall. The fore and main topgallant sails were still on her, for the "old man" did not mean to
be frightened in broad daylight, and was determined to carry
sail till the last minute. We all stood waiting for its coming when
the first blast showed us that it was not to be trifled with. Rain,
sleet, snow, and wind enough to take our breath from us and
make the toughest turn his back to windward! The ship lay
nearly over on her beam ends, the spars and rigging snapped and
cracked, and her topgallant masts bent like whipsticks. "Clew
up the fore and main topgallant sails!" shouted the captain, and
all hands sprang to the clew lines. The decks were standing
nearly at an angle of forty-five degrees, and the ship going like
a mad steed through the water, the whole forward part of her
in a smother of foam. The halyards were let go and the yard
clewed down, and the sheets started, and in a few minutes the
sails smothered and kept in by clew lines and buntlines.—"Furl
'em, sir?" asked the mate.—"Let go the topsail halyards, fore and
aft!" shouted the captain in answer, at the top of his voice. Down
came the topsail yards, the reef tackles were manned and hauled
out, and we climbed up to windward and sprang into the
weather rigging. The violence of the wind, and the hail and sleet
driving nearly horizontally across the ocean, seemed actually to
pin us down to the rigging. It was hard work making head
against them. One after another we got out on the yards. And
here we had work to do; for our new sails, which had hardly
been bent long enough to get the starch out of them, were as stiff
as boards, and the new earings and reef points, stiffened with
the sleet, knotted like pieces of iron wire. Having only our

round jackets and straw hats on, we were soon wet through, and it was every moment growing colder. Our hands were soon stiffened and numbed, which, added to the stiffness of everything else, kept us a good while on the yard. After we had got the sail hauled on the yard, we had to wait a long time for the weather earing to be passed; but there was no fault to be found, for French John was at the earing, and a better sailor never laid out on a yard; so we leaned over the yard and beat our hands on the sail to keep them from freezing. At length the word came—"Haul out to leeward!"—and we seized the reef points and hauled the band taut for the lee earing. "Taut band. Knot away!" and we got the first reef fast, and were just going to lay down when—"Two reefs—two reefs!" shouted the mate, and we had a second reef to take, in the same way. When this was fast, we laid down on deck, manned the halyards to leeward—nearly up to our knees in water—set the topsail, and then laid aloft on the main-topsail yard, and reefed that sail in the same manner; for as I have before stated, we were a good deal reduced in numbers, and to make it worse, the carpenter, only two days before, cut his leg with an ax, so that he could not go aloft. This weakened us so that we could not well manage more than one topsail at a time in such weather as this, and of course our labor was doubled. From the main-topsail yard, we went on the main yard, and took a reef in the mainsail. No sooner had we got on deck, than "Lay aloft there, mizzentopmen, and close-reef the mizzen topsail!" This called me, and being nearest to the rigging, I got first aloft, and out to the weather earing. English Ben was on the yard just after me, and took the lee earing, and the rest of our gang were soon on the yard, and began to fist the sail, when the mate considerately sent up the cook and steward to help us. I could now account for the long time it took to pass the other earings, for, to do my best, with a strong hand to help me at the dog's ear, I could not get it passed until I heard them beginning to complain in the bunt. One reef after another we took in until the sail was close-reefed, when we went down and hoisted away at the halyards. In the meantime, the jib had been furled and the staysail set, and the ship, under her reduced sail, had got more upright and was under management; but the two topgallant sails were still hanging in the buntlines, and

slatting and jerking as though they would take the masts out of
her. We gave a look aloft, and knew that our work was not done
yet; and sure enough, no sooner did the mate see that we were
on deck, than—"Lay aloft there, four of you, and furl the topgallant sails!" This called me again, and two of us went aloft, up
the fore rigging, and two more up the main, on the topgallant
yards. The shrouds were now iced over, the sleet having formed
a crust or cake round all the standing rigging, and on the weather
side of the masts and yards. When we got on the yard, my hands
were so numb that I could not have cast off the knot of the
gasket to have saved my life. We both lay over the yard for a
few seconds, beating our hands on the sail until we started the
blood into our fingers' ends, and at the next moment our hands
were in a burning heat. My companion on the yard was a lad
who came out in the ship a weak, puny boy from one of the
Boston schools—"no larger than a spritsail sheet knot," nor
"heavier than a paper of lampblack," and "not strong enough to
haul a shad off a gridiron," but who was now "as long as a
spare topmast, strong enough to knock down an ox, and hearty
enough to eat him." We fisted the sail together, and after six
or eight minutes of hard hauling and pulling and beating down
the sail, which was as stiff as sheet iron, we managed to get it
furled; and snugly furled it must be, for we knew the mate well
enough to be certain that if it got adrift again, we should be
called up from our watch below, at any hour of the night, to
furl it.

I had been on the lookout for a moment to jump below and
clap on a thick jacket and southwester; but when we got on deck
we found that eight bells had been struck, and the other watch
gone below, so that there were two hours of dog watch for us,
and a plenty of work to do. It had now set in for a steady gale
from the southwest, but we were not yet far enough to the
southward to make a fair wind of it, for we must give Tierra del
Fuego a wide berth. The decks were covered with snow, and
there was a constant driving of sleet. In fact, Cape Horn had set
in with good earnest. In the midst of all this, and before it
became dark, we had all the studding sails to make up and stow
away, and then to lay aloft and rig in all the booms, fore and
aft, and coil away the tacks, sheets, and halyards. This was pretty

tough work for four or five hands in the face of a gale which almost took us off the yards, and with ropes so stiff with ice that it was almost impossible to bend them. I was nearly half an hour out on the end of the foreyard trying to coil away and stop down the topmast studding sail tack and lower halyards. It was after dark when we got through, and we were not a little pleased to hear four bells struck, which sent us below for two hours, and gave us each a pot of hot tea with our cold beef and bread and what was better yet, a suit of thick, dry clothing, fitted for the weather, in place of our thin clothes, which were wet through and now frozen stiff.

This sudden turn, for which we were so little prepared, was as unacceptable to me as to any of the rest, for I had been troubled for several days with a slight toothache, and this cold weather, and wetting and freezing, were not the best things in the world for it. I soon found that it was getting strong hold, and running over all parts of my face; and before the watch was out I went aft to the mate, who had charge of the medicine chest, to get something for it. But the chest showed like the end of a long voyage, for there was nothing that would answer but a few drops of laudanum, which must be saved for any emergency, so I had only to bear the pain as well as I could.

When we went on deck at eight bells, it had stopped snowing and there were a few stars out, but the clouds were still black and it was blowing a steady gale. Just before midnight, I went aloft and sent down the mizzen royal yard, and had the good luck to do it to the satisfaction of the mate, who said it was done "out of hand and shipshape." The next four hours below were but little relief to me, for I lay awake in my berth the whole time from the pain in my face, and heard every bell strike, and at four o'clock turned out with the watch feeling little spirit for the hard duties of the day. Bad weather and hard work at sea can be borne up against very well if one only has spirit and health; but there is nothing brings a man down at such a time like bodily pain and want of sleep. There was, however, too much to do to allow time to think; for the gale of yesterday, and the heavy seas we met with a few days before while we had yet ten degrees more southing to make, had convinced the captain that we had something before us which was not to be trifled with, and orders were given to send down the long topgallant masts. The topgallant and royal yards were accordingly struck, the fly-ing-jibboom rigged in, and the topgallant masts sent down on deck, and all lashed together by the side of the longboat. The rigging was then sent down and coiled away below, and every-thing made snug aloft. There was not a sailor in the ship who was not rejoiced to see these sticks come down; for so long as the yards were aloft, on the least sign of a lull the topgallant sails were loosed, and then we had to furl them again in a snow squall, and "shin" up and down single ropes caked with ice, and send royal yards down in the teeth of a gale coming right from the South Pole. It was an interesting sight, too, to see our noble ship dismantled of all her top hamper of long tapering masts and yards and boom pointed with spearhead which ornamented her in port; and all that canvas which a few days before had covered her like a cloud from the truck to the water's edge, spreading far out beyond her hull on either side, now gone; and she stripped like a wrestler for the fight. It corresponded, too, with the desolate character of her situation—alone as she was, battling with storms, wind, and ice at this extremity of the globe, and in almost constant night.

FRIDAY, JULY 1. We were now nearly up to the latitude of Cape Horn, and having over forty degrees of easting to make, we squared away the yards before a strong westerly gale, shook a reef out of the fore-topsail, and stood on our way, east by south, with the prospect of being up with the Cape in a week or ten days. As for myself, I had had no sleep for forty-eight hours; and the want of rest, together with constant wet and cold, had increased the swelling so that my face was nearly as large as two, and I found it impossible to get my mouth open wide enough to eat. In this state, the steward applied to the captain for some rice to boil for me, but he only got a "No, damn you! Tell him to eat salt junk and hard bread, like the rest of them." For this, of course, I was much obliged to him, and in truth it was just what I expected. However, I did not starve, for the mate, who was a man as well as a sailor, and had always been a good friend to me, smuggled a pan of rice into the galley and told the cook to boil it for me and not let the "old man" see it. Had it been fine weather, or in port, I should have gone below and lain by until my face got well; but in such weather as this, and shorthanded as we were, it was not for me to desert my post, so I kept on deck, and stood my watch and did my duty as well as I could.

SATURDAY, JULY 2. This day the sun rose fair, but it ran too low in the heavens to give any heat, or thaw out our sails and rigging; yet the sight of it was pleasant, and we had a steady "reef-topsail breeze" from the westward. The atmosphere, which had previously been clear and cold, for the last few hours grew damp, and had a disagreeable wet chilliness in it; and the man who came from the wheel said he heard the captain tell "the passenger" that the thermometer had fallen several degrees since morning, which he could not account for in any other way than by supposing that there must be ice near us, though such a thing had never been heard of in this latitude at this season of the year. At twelve o'clock we went below, and had just got through dinner when the cook put his head down the scuttle and told us to come on deck and see the finest sight that we had ever seen. "Where away, cook?" asked the first man who was up. "On the larboard bow." And there lay, floating in the ocean several miles off, an immense, irregular mass, its top and points covered with snow, and its center of a deep indigo-color. This was an iceberg, and of the largest size, as one of our men said who had been in the Northern Ocean. As far as the eye could reach, the sea in every direction was of a deep-blue color, the waves running high and fresh and sparkling in the light, and in the midst lay this immense mountain-island, its cavities and valleys thrown into deep shade, and its points and pinnacles glittering in the sun. All hands were soon on deck looking at it, and admiring in various ways its beauty and grandeur. But no description can give any idea of the strangeness, splendor, and really the sublimity of the sight. Its great size—for it must have been from two to three miles in circumference, and several hundred feet in height—its slow motion as its base rose and sank in the water and its high points nodded against the clouds; the dashing of the waves upon it, which, breaking high with foam, lined its base with a white crust; and the thundering sound of the cracking of the mass, and the breaking and tumbling-down of huge pieces; together with its nearness and approach, which added a slight

element of fear—all combined to give to it the character of true
sublimity. The main body of the mass was, as I have said, of an
indigo-color, its base crusted with frozen foam; and as it grew
thin and transparent toward the edges and top, its color shaded
off from a deep-blue to the whiteness of snow. It seemed to be
drifting slowly toward the north, so that we kept away and
avoided it. It was in sight all the afternoon; and when we got
to leeward of it, the wind died away, so that we lay to quite near
it for a greater part of the night. Unfortunately, there was no
moon, but it was a clear night, and we could plainly mark the
long, regular heaving of the stupendous mass as its edges moved
slowly against the stars. Several times in our watch loud cracks
were heard, which sounded as though they must have run
through the whole length of the iceberg, and several pieces fell
down with a thundering crash, plunging heavily into the sea.
Toward morning a strong breeze sprang up, and we filled away
and left it astern, and at daylight it was out of sight. The next
day, which was

SUNDAY, JULY 3, the breeze continued strong, the air exceedingly chilly, and the thermometer low. In the course of the day
we saw several icebergs, of different sizes, but none so near as
the one which we saw the day before. Some of them, as well as
we could judge at the distance at which we were, must have
been as large as that, if not larger. At noon we were in latitude
55° 12′ S., and supposed longitude 89° 5′ W. Toward night the
wind hauled to the southward, and headed us off our course a
little, and blew a tremendous gale; but this we did not mind,
as there was no rain nor snow, and we were already under close
sail.

MONDAY, JULY 4. This was "Independence Day" in Boston.
What firing of guns, and ringing of bells, and rejoicings of all
sorts, in every part of our country! The ladies (who have not
gone down to Nahant for a breath of cool air, and sight of the
ocean) walking the streets with parasols over their heads, and
the dandies in their white pantaloons and silk stockings! What
quantities of ice cream have been eaten, and what quantities of
ice brought into the city from a distance, and sold out by the
lump and the pound! The smallest of the islands which we saw
today would have made the fortune of poor Jack if he had had it

in Boston; and I dare say he would have had no objection to being there with it. This, to be sure, was no place to keep the Fourth of July. To keep ourselves warm, and the ship out of the ice, was as much as we could do. Yet no one forgot the day, and many were the wishes and conjectures and comparisons, both serious and ludicrous, which were made among all hands. The sun shone bright as long as it was up, only that a scud of black clouds was ever and anon driving across it. At noon we were in lat. 54° 27′ S., and long. 85° 5′ W., having made a good deal of easting, but having lost in our latitude by the heading of the wind. Between daylight and dark—that is, between nine o'clock and three—we saw thirty-four ice islands of various sizes, some no bigger than the hull of our vessel and others apparently nearly as large as the one that we first saw; though as we went on the islands became smaller and more numerous and at sundown of this day a man at the masthead saw large fields of floating ice, called "field ice," at the southeast. This kind of ice is much more dangerous than the large islands, for those can be seen at a distance, and kept away from; but the field ice, floating in great quantities and covering the ocean for miles and miles, in pieces of every size—large, flat, and broken cakes, with here and there an island rising twenty and thirty feet, and as large as the ship's hull—this it is very difficult to sheer clear of. A constant lookout was necessary, for any of these pieces, coming with the heave of the sea, were large enough to have knocked a hole in the ship, and that would have been the end of us; for no boat (even if we could have got one out) could have lived in such a sea, and no man could have lived in a boat in such weather. To make our condition still worse, the wind came out due east just after sundown, and it blew a gale dead ahead, with hail and sleet, and a thick fog, so that we could not see half the length of the ship. Our chief reliance, the prevailing westerly gales, was thus cut off; and here we were, nearly seven hundred miles to the westward of the Cape, with a gale dead from the eastward, and the weather so thick that we could not see the ice with which we were surrounded until it was directly under our bows. At 4 P.M. (it was then quite dark) all hands were called, and sent aloft in a violent squall of hail and rain to take in sail. We had now all got on our "Cape Horn rig"—thick boots, southwesters coming down over our neck and ears, thick trousers and jackets, and some with oilcloth suits over all. Mittens, too, we wore on deck, but it would not do to go aloft with them on, for it was impossible to work with them and, being wet and stiff, they might let a man slip overboard for all the hold he could get on a rope; so we were obliged to work with bare hands, which, as well as our faces, were often cut with the hailstones, which fell thick and large. Our ship was now all cased with ice—hull, spars, and standing rigging—and the running rigging so stiff that we could hardly bend it so as to belay it, or still worse, take a knot with it, and the sails nearly as stiff as sheet iron. One at a time (for it was a long piece of work and required many hands) we furled the courses, mizzen topsail, and fore-topmast staysail, and close-reefed the fore and main topsails, and hove the ship to under the fore, with the main hauled up by the clew lines and buntlines, and ready to be sheeted home if we found it necessary to make sail to get to windward of an island. A regular lookout was then set, and kept by each watch in turn until the morning. It was a tedious and anxious night. It blew hard the whole time, and there was an almost constant driving of either rain, hail, or snow. In addition to this, it was "as thick as muck," and the ice was all about us. The captain was on deck nearly the whole night, and kept the cook in the galley, with a roaring fire, to make coffee for him, which he took every few hours and once or twice gave a little to his officers; but not a drop of anything was there for the crew. The captain, who sleeps all the daytime and comes and goes at night as he chooses, can have his brandy and water in the cabin, and his hot coffee at the galley, while Jack, who has to stand through everything and work in wet and cold, can have nothing to wet his lips or warm his stomach. This was a "temperance ship" and, like too many such ships, the temperance was all in the forecastle. The sailor who only takes his one glass as it is dealt out to him is in danger of being drunk, while the captain who has all under his hand, and can drink as much as he chooses, and upon whose self-possession and cool judgment the lives of all depend, may be trusted with any amount, to drink at his will. Sailors will never be convinced that rum is a dangerous thing by taking it away from them and giving it to the officers; nor that that temperance is their friend which takes from them what they have always had, and gives them nothing in the place of it. By seeing it allowed to their officers, they will not be convinced that it is taken from them for their good; and by receiving nothing in its place, they will not believe that it is done in kindness. On the contrary, many of them look on the change as a new instrument of tyranny. Not that they prefer rum. I never knew a sailor in my life who would not prefer a pot of hot coffee or chocolate in a cold night to all the rum afloat. They all say that rum only warms them for a time; yet if they can get nothing better, they will miss what they have lost. The momentary warmth and glow from drinking it; the break and change which is made in a long, dreary watch by the mere calling all hands aft and serving of it out—and the simply having some event to look forward to, and to talk about— give it an importance and a use which no one can appreciate who has not stood his watch before the mast. On my passage round Cape Horn before, the vessel that I was in was not under temperance articles, and grog was served out every middle and morning watch, and after every reefing of topsails; and though I had never drank rum before, and never intend to again, I took my allowance then at the capstan, as the rest did, merely for the momentary warmth it gave the system and the change in our feelings and aspect of our duties on the watch. At the same time, as I have stated, there was not a man on board who would not have pitched the rum to the dogs (I have heard them say so a dozen times) for a pot of coffee or chocolate; or even for our common beverage—"water bewitched, and tea begrudged," as it was.* The temperance reform is the best thing that ever was undertaken for the sailor; but when the grog is taken from him, he ought to have something in its place. As it is now, in most vessels it is a mere saving to the owners; and this accounts for the sudden increase of temperance ships, which surprised even

---

* The proportions of the ingredients of the tea that was made for us (and ours, as I have before stated, was a favorable specimen of American merchantmen) were a pint of tea and a pint and a half of molasses to about three gallons of water. These are all boiled down together in the "coppers," and before serving it out, the mess is stirred up with a stick, so as to give each man his fair share of sweetening and tea leaves. The tea for the cabin is of course made in the usual way, in a teapot, and drunk with sugar.

the best friends of the cause. If every merchant when he struck grog from the list of the expenses of his ship had been obliged to substitute as much coffee, or chocolate, as would give each man a potful when he came off the topsail yard on a stormy night, I fear Jack might have gone to ruin on the old road.*

But this is not doubling Cape Horn. Eight hours of the night our watch was on deck, and during the whole of that time we kept a bright lookout: one man on each bow, another in the bunt of the foreyard, the third mate on the scuttle, one on each quarter, and a man always standing by the wheel. The chief mate was everywhere, and commanded the ship when the captain was below. When a large piece of ice was seen in our way, or drifting near us, the word was passed along, and the ship's head turned one way and another, and sometimes the yards squared or braced up. There was little else to do than to look out, and we had the sharpest eyes in the ship on the forecastle. The only variety was the monotonous voice of the lookout forward—"Another island!"—"Ice ahead!"—"Ice on the lee bow!"—"Hard up the helm!"—"Keep her off a little!"—"Stead-y!"

In the meantime, the wet and cold had brought my face into such a state that I could neither eat nor sleep; and though I stood it out all night, yet when it became light I was in such a state that all hands told me I must go below and lie by for a day or two, or I should be laid up for a long time, and perhaps have the lockjaw. When the watch was changed, I went into the steerage and took off my hat and comforter and showed my face to the mate, who told me to go below at once, and stay in my berth until the swelling went down, and gave the cook orders to make a poultice for me, and said he would speak to the captain.

* I do not wish these remarks, so far as they relate to the saving of expense in the outfit, to be applied to the owners of our ship, for she was supplied with an abundance of stores of the best kind that are given to seamen, though the dispensing of them is necessarily left to the captain. Indeed, so high was the reputation of "the employ" among men and officers, for the character and outfit of their vessels and for their liberality in conducting their voyages, that when it was known that they had a ship fitting out for a long voyage, and that hands were to be shipped at a certain time, a half-hour before the time, as one of the crew told me, numbers of sailors were steering down the wharf, hopping over the barrels like flocks of sheep.

I went below and turned in, covering myself over with blankets and jackets, and lay in my berth nearly twenty-four hours, half asleep and half awake, stupid from the dull pain. I heard the watch called, and the men going up and down, and sometimes a noise on deck, and a cry of "Ice!" but I gave little attention to anything. At the end of twenty-four hours the pain went down, and I had a long sleep, which brought me back to my proper state; yet my face was so swollen and tender that I was obliged to keep to my berth for two or three days longer. During the two days I had been below, the weather was much the same that it had been, head winds, and snow and rain; or if the wind came fair, too foggy, and the ice too thick, to run. At the end of the third day the ice was very thick; a complete fog bank covered the ship. It blew a tremendous gale from the eastward, with sleet and snow, and there was every promise of a dangerous and fatiguing night. At dark the captain called all hands aft, and told them that not a man was to leave the deck that night; that the ship was in the greatest danger—any cake of ice might knock a hole in her, or she might run on an island and go to pieces. No one could tell whether she would be a ship the next morning. The lookouts were then set, and every man was put in his station. When I heard what was the state of things, I began to put on my clothes to stand it out with the rest of them, when the mate came below, and looking at my face, ordered me back to my berth, saying that if we went down, we should all go down together, but if I went on deck I might lay myself up for life. This was the first word I had heard from aft, for the captain had done nothing, nor inquired how I was, since I went below.

In obedience to the mate's orders, I went back to my berth, but a more miserable night I never wish to spend. I never felt the curse of sickness so keenly in my life. If I could only have been on deck with the rest, where something was to be done, and seen, and heard; where there were fellow beings for companions in duty and danger—but to be cooped up alone in a black hole, in equal danger but without the power to do, was the hardest trial. Several times in the course of the night I got up, determined to go on deck; but the silence which showed that there was nothing doing, and the knowledge that I might maké myself seriously ill for nothing, kept me back. It was not easy to sleep lying as I did with my head directly against the bows, which might be dashed in by an island of ice brought down by the very next sea that struck her. This was the only time I had been ill since I left Boston, and it was the worst time it could have happened. I felt almost willing to bear the plagues of Egypt for the rest of the voyage if I could but be well and strong for that one night. Yet it was a dreadful night for those on deck. A watch of eighteen hours, with wet, and cold, and constant anxiety, nearly wore them out; and when they came below at nine o'clock for breakfast, they almost dropped asleep on their chests, and some of them were so stiff that they could with difficulty sit down. Not a drop of anything had been given them during the whole time (though the captain, as on the night that I was on deck, had his coffee every four hours) except that the mate stole a potful of coffee for two men to drink behind the galley while he kept a lookout for the captain. Every man had his station, and was not allowed to leave it; and nothing happened to break the monotony of the night except once setting the main-topsails to run clear of a large island to leeward, which they were drifting fast upon. Some of the boys got so sleepy and stupefied that they actually fell asleep at their posts; and the young third mate, whose station was the exposed one of standing on the fore scuttle, was so stiff when he was relieved that he could not bend his knees to get down. By a constant lookout, and a quick shifting of the helm as the islands and pieces came in sight, the ship went clear of everything but a few small pieces, though daylight showed the ocean covered for miles. At daybreak it fell a dead calm, and with the sun, the fog cleared a little and a breeze sprang up from the westward, which soon grew into a gale. We had now a fair wind, daylight, and comparatively clear weather; yet, to the surprise of everyone, the ship continued hove to. Why does not he run? What is the captain about? was asked by everyone; and from questions, it soon grew into complaints and murmurings. When the daylight was so short, it was too bad to lose it, and a fair wind, too, which everyone had been praying for. As hour followed hour and the captain showed no sign of making sail, the crew became impatient, and there was a good deal of talking and consultation together on the forecastle. They had been beat-out with the exposure and hardship, and impatient to get out of it, and this unaccountable delay was more than they could bear in quietness, in their excited and restless state. Some said that the captain was frightened—completely cowed—by the dangers and difficulties that surrounded us, and was afraid to make sail; while others said that in his anxiety and suspense he had made a free use of brandy and opium, and was unfit for his duty. The carpenter, who was an intelligent man and a thorough seaman, and had great influence with the crew, came down into the forecastle and tried to induce the crew to go aft and ask the captain why he did not run, or request him, in the name of all hands, to make sail. This appeared to be a very reasonable request, and the crew agreed that if he did not make sail before noon, they would go aft. Noon came and no sail was made. A consultation was held again, and it was proposed to take the ship from the captain and give the command of her to the mate, who had been heard to say that if he could have his way, the ship would have been half the distance to the Cape before night—ice or no ice. And so irritated and impatient had the crew become that even this proposition, which was open mutiny, punishable with state prison, was entertained, and the carpenter went to his berth leaving it tacitly understood that something serious would be done if things remained as they were many hours longer. When the carpenter left, we talked it all over, and I gave my advice strongly against it. Another of the men, too, who had known something of the kind attempted in another ship by a crew who were dissatisfied with their captain, and which was followed with serious consequences, was opposed to it. S—, who soon came down, joined us, and we determined to have nothing to do with it. By these means, they were soon induced to give it up for the present, though they said they would not lie where they were much longer without knowing the reason.

The affair remained in this state until four o'clock, when an order came forward for all hands to come aft on the quarterdeck. In about ten minutes they came forward again, and the whole affair had been blown. The carpenter, very prematurely and without any authority from the crew, had sounded the mate as to whether he would take command of the ship, and intimated an intention to displace the captain; and the mate, as in duty bound, had told the whole to the captain, who immediately sent for all hands aft. Instead of violent measures, or at least an outbreak of quarter-deck bravado, threats, and abuse, which they had every reason to expect, a sense of common danger and common suffering seemed to have tamed his spirit and begotten something like a humane fellow feeling, for he received the crew in a manner quiet, and even almost kind. He told them what he had heard, and said that he did not believe that they would try to do any such thing as was intimated; that they had always been good men—obedient, and knew their duty, and he had no fault to find with them; and asked them what they had to complain of, said that no one could say that he was slow to carry sail (which was true enough) and that as soon as he thought it was safe and proper, he should make sail. He added a few words about their duty in their present situation, and sent them forward, saying that he should take no further notice of the matter, but at the same time told the carpenter to recollect whose power he was in, and that if he heard another word from him he would have cause to remember him to the day of his death.

This language of the captain had a very good effect on the crew, and they returned quietly to their duty.

For two days more the wind blew from the southward and eastward, or in the short intervals when it was fair, the ice was too thick to run; yet the weather was not so dreadfully bad, and the crew had watch and watch. I still remained in my berth, fast recovering, yet still not well enough to go safely on deck. And I should have been perfectly useless, for from having eaten nothing for nearly a week except a little rice, which I forced into my mouth the last day or two, I was as weak as an infant. To be sick in a forecastle is miserable indeed. It is the worst part of a dog's life, especially in bad weather. The forecastle shut up tight to keep out the water and cold air; the watch either on deck or asleep in their berths; no one to speak to; the pale light of the single lamp swinging to and fro from the beam, so dim that one can scarcely see, much less read by it; the water dropping from the beams and carlings and running down the sides; and the forecastle so wet, and dark, and cheerless, and so lumbered-up with chests and wet clothes, that sitting up is worse than lying in the berth! These are some of the evils. Fortunately, I needed no help from anyone, and no medicine; and if I had needed help, I don't know where I should have found it. Sailors are willing enough, but it is true, as is often said: No one ships for nurse on board a vessel. Our merchant ships are always undermanned, and if one man is lost by sickness, they cannot spare another to take care of him. A sailor is always presumed to be well, and if he's sick, he's a poor dog. One has to stand his wheel, and another his lookout, and the sooner he gets on deck again, the better.

Accordingly, as soon as I could possibly go back to my duty, I put on my thick clothes and boots and southwester and made my appearance on deck. Though I had been but a few days below, yet everything looked strangely enough. The ship was cased in ice—decks, sides, masts, yards, and rigging. Two close-reefed topsails were all the sail she had on, and every sail and rope was frozen so stiff in its place that it seemed as though it would be impossible to start anything. Reduced, too, to her topmasts, she had altogether a most forlorn and crippled appearance. The sun had come up brightly, the snow was swept off the decks and ashes thrown upon them, so that we could walk, for they had been as slippery as glass. It was of course too cold to carry on any ship's work, and we had only to walk the deck and keep ourselves warm. The wind was still ahead, and the whole ocean to the eastward covered with islands and field ice. At four bells the order was given to square away the yards, and the man who came from the helm said that the captain had kept her off to N.N.E. What could this mean? Some said that he was going to put into Valparaiso and winter, and others that he was going to run out of the ice and cross the Pacific, and go home round the Cape of Good Hope. Soon, however, it leaked out, and we found that we were running for the Straits of Magellan. The news soon spread through the ship, and all tongues were at work talking about it. No one on board had been through the straits, but I had in my chest an account of the passage of the ship *A. J. Donelson*, of New York, through those straits a few years before. The account was given by the captain, and the representation was as favorable as possible. It was soon read by everyone on board, and various opinions pronounced. The determination

of our captain had at least this good effect: it gave everyone
something to think and talk about, made a break in our life,
and diverted our minds from the monotonous dreariness of the
prospect before us. Having made a fair wind of it, we were
going off at a good rate, and leaving the thickest of the ice behind
us. This at least was something.

Having been long enough below to get my hands well warmed
and softened, the first handling of the ropes was rather tough;
but a few days hardened them, and as soon as I got my mouth
open wide enough to take in a piece of salt beef and hard
bread, I was all right again.

SUNDAY, JULY 10. Lat. 54° 10′, long. 79° 07′. This was our
position at noon. The sun was out bright, the ice was all left
behind, and things had quite a cheering appearance. We brought
our wet pea jackets and trousers on deck and hung them up in
the rigging, that the breeze and the few hours of sun might dry
them a little; and by the permission of the cook the galley was
nearly filled with stockings and mittens hung round to be dried.
Boots, too, were brought up, and having got a little tar and slush
from below, we gave them a thick coat. After dinner, all hands
were turned to to get the anchors over the bows, bend on the
chains, etc. The fish tackle was got up, fish davit rigged out, and
after two or three hours of hard and cold work, both the anchors
were ready for instant use, a couple of kedges got up, a hawser
coiled away upon the fore hatch, and the deep-sea lead line
overhauled and got ready. Our spirits returned with having
something to do, and when the tackle was manned to bowse
the anchor home, notwithstanding the desolation of the scene
we struck up "Cheerily ho!" in full chorus. This pleased the mate,
who rubbed his hands and cried out: "That's right, my boys—
never say die! That sounds like the old crew!" And the captain
came up on hearing the song, and said to the passenger, within
hearing of the man at the wheel: "That sounds like a lively crew.
They'll have their song so long as there're enough left for a
chorus!"

This preparation of the cable and anchors was for the passage
of the straits; for, being very crooked and with a variety of
currents, it is necessary to come frequently to anchor. This was
not by any means a pleasant prospect, for of all the work that

a sailor is called upon to do in cold weather, there is none so bad
as working the ground tackle. The heavy chain cables to be
hauled and pulled about decks with bare hands; wet hawsers,
slip ropes, and buoy ropes to be hauled aboard dripping in
water, which is running up your sleeves and freezing; clearing
hawse under the bows; getting under way and coming to at all
hours of the night and day, and a constant lookout for rocks and
sands and turns of tides—these are some of the disagreeables
of such a navigation to a common sailor. Fair or foul, he wants
to have nothing to do with the ground tackle between port and
port. One of our hands, too, had unluckily fallen upon a half
of an old newspaper which contained an account of the passage
through the straits of a Boston brig, called, I think, *The Peruvian,*
in which she lost every cable and anchor she had, got aground
twice, and arrived at Valparaiso in distress. This was set off
against the account of the *A. J. Donelson,* and led us to look
forward with less confidence to the passage, especially as no
one on board had ever been through, and the captain had no
very perfect charts. However, we were spared any further experience on the point, for the next day, when we must have been
near the Cape of Pillars, which is the southwest point of the mouth
of the straits, a gale set in from the eastward with a heavy fog,
so that we could not see half of the ship's length ahead. This of
course put an end to the project for the present; for a thick fog
and a gale blowing dead ahead are not the most favorable circumstances for the passage of difficult and dangerous straits.
This weather, too, seemed likely to last for some time, and we
could not think of beating about the mouth of the straits for a
week or two waiting for a favorable opportunity; so we braced
up on the larboard tack, put the ship's head due south, and
struck her off for Cape Horn again.

Ice Again · A Beautiful Afternoon · Cape Horn · "Land Ho!" · Heading for Home

IN OUR FIRST attempt to double the Cape, when we came up to the latiitude of it we were nearly seventeen hundred miles to the westward, but in running for the Straits of Magellan we stood so far to the eastward that we made our second attempt at a distance of not more than four or five hundred miles; and we had great hopes, by this means, to run clear of the ice, thinking that the easterly gales, which had prevailed for a long time, would have driven it to the westward. With the wind about two points free, the yards braced in a little, and two close-reefed topsails and a reefed foresail on the ship, we made great way toward the southward; and almost every watch, when we came on deck, the air seemed to grow colder, and the sea to run higher. Still we saw no ice, and had great hopes of going clear of it altogether when one afternoon about three o'clock, while we were taking a siesta during our watch below, "All hands!" was called in a loud and fearful voice. "Tumble up here, men!— Tumble up—don't stop for your clothes—before we're upon it!" We sprang out of our berths and hurried upon deck. The loud, sharp voice of the captain was heard giving orders as though for life or death, and we ran aft to the braces, not waiting to look ahead, for not a moment was to be lost. The helm was hard up, the after yards shaking, and the ship in the act of wearing. Slowly, with the stiff ropes and iced rigging, we swung the yards round, everything coming hard, and with a creaking and rending sound, like pulling up a plank which has been frozen into the ice. The ship wore round fairly, the yards were steadied, and

we stood off on the other tack, leaving behind us, directly under
our larboard quarter, a large ice island peering out of the mist
and reaching high above our tops while astern; and on either
side of the island, large tracts of field ice were dimly seen
heaving and rolling in the sea. We were now safe, and standing
to the northward; but in a few minutes more, had it not been
for the sharp lookout of the watch, we should have been fairly
upon the ice, and left our ship's old bones adrift in the Southern
Ocean. After standing to the northward a few hours, we wore
ship and, the wind having hauled, we stood to the southward
and eastward. All night long a bright lookout was kept from
every part of the deck, and whenever ice was seen on the one
bow or the other, the helm was shifted and the yards braced,
and by quick working of the ship she was kept clear. The accustomed cry of "Ice ahead!"—"Ice on the lee bow!"—"Another
island!" in the same tones, and with the same orders following
them, seemed to bring us directly back to our old position of
the week before. During our watch on deck, which was from
twelve to four, the wind came out ahead, with a pelting storm
of hail and sleet and we lay hove to under a close-reefed main-
topsail the whole watch. During the next watch it fell calm,
with a drenching rain, until daybreak, when the wind came out
to the westward, and the weather cleared up and showed us the
whole ocean, in the course which we should have steered had it
not been for the head wind and calm, completely blocked up
with ice. Here then our progress was stopped, and we wore ship,
and once more stood to the northward and eastward, not for the
Straits of Magellan, but to make another attempt to double the
Cape still farther to the eastward; for the captain was determined
to get round if perseverance could do it, and the third time, he
said, never failed.

With a fair wind we soon ran clear of the field ice, and by noon
had only the stray islands floating far and near upon the ocean.
The sun was out bright, the sea of a deep blue, fringed with the
white foam of the waves which ran high before a strong southwester. Our solitary ship tore on through the water as though
glad to be out of her confinement; and the ice islands lay
scattered on the ocean here and there, of various sizes and
shapes, reflecting the bright rays of the sun, and drifting slowly

northward before the gale. It was a contrast to much that we had lately seen, and a spectacle not only of beauty, but of life; for it required but little fancy to imagine these islands to be animate masses which had broken loose from the "thrilling regions of thick-ribbed ice" and were working their way by wind and current, some alone and some in fleets, to milder climes. No pencil has ever yet given anything like the true effect of an iceberg. In a picture, they are huge, uncouth masses stuck in the sea, while their chief beauty and grandeur—their slow, stately motion, the whirling of the snow about their summits, and the fearful groaning and cracking of their parts—the picture cannot give. This is the large iceberg, while the small and distant islands, floating on the smooth sea in the light of a clear day, look like little floating fairy isles of sapphire.

From a northeast course we gradually hauled to the eastward, and after sailing about two hundred miles, which brought us as near to the western coast of Tierra del Fuego as was safe, and having lost sight of the ice altogether, for the third time we put the ship's head to the southward, to try the passage of the Cape. The weather continued clear and cold, with a strong gale from the westward, and we were fast getting up with the latitude of the Cape, with a prospect of soon being round. One fine afternoon, a man who had gone into the foretop to shift the rolling tackles sung out at the top of his voice, and with evident glee, "Sail ho!" Neither land nor sail had we seen since leaving San Diego, and anyone who has traversed the length of a whole ocean alone can imagine what an excitement such an announcement produced on board. "Sail ho!" shouted the cook, jumping out of his galley. "Sail ho!" shouted a man, throwing back the slide of the scuttle, to the watch below, who were soon out of their berths and on deck. And "Sail ho!" shouted the captain down the companionway to the passenger in the cabin. Besides the pleasure of seeing a ship and human beings in so desolate a place, it was important for us to speak a vessel, to learn whether there was ice to the eastward, and to ascertain the longitude; for we had no chronometer, and had been drifting about so long that we had nearly lost our reckoning, and opportunities for lunar observations are not frequent or sure in such a place as Cape Horn. For these various reasons, the excitement in our little community was running high, and conjectures were made and everything thought of for which the captain would hail, when the man aloft sung out, "Another sail, large on the weather bow!" This was a little odd, but so much the better, and did not shake our faith in their being sails. At length the man in the top hailed and said he believed it was land, after all. "Land in your eye!" said the mate, who was looking through the telescope. "They are ice islands, if I can see a hole through a ladder." And a few moments showed the mate to be right, and all our expectations fled and instead of what we most wished to see we had what we most dreaded, and what we hoped we had seen the last of. We soon, however, left these astern, having passed within about two miles of them; and at sundown the horizon was clear in all directions.

Having a fine wind, we were soon up with and passed the latitude of the Cape, and having stood far enough to the southward to give it a wide berth, we began to stand to the eastward, with a good prospect of being round and steering to the northward on the other side in a very few days. But ill luck seemed to have lighted upon us. Not four hours had we been standing on in this course before it fell dead calm; and in half an hour it clouded up. A few straggling blasts, with spits of snow and sleet, came from the eastward, and in an hour more we lay hove to under a close-reefed main-topsail, drifting bodily off to leeward before the fiercest storm that we had yet felt, blowing dead ahead from the eastward. It seemed as though the genius of the place had been roused at finding that we had nearly slipped through his fingers, and had come down upon us with tenfold fury. The sailors said that every blast, as it shook the shrouds and whistled through the rigging, said to the old ship, "No you don't—No you don't!"

For eight days we lay drifting about in this manner. Sometimes—generally towards noon—it fell calm; once or twice a round copper ball showed itself for a few moments in the place where the sun ought to have been, and a puff or two came from the westward, giving some hope that a fair wind had come at last. During the first two days we made sail for these puffs, shaking the reefs out of the topsails and boarding the tacks of the courses; but finding that it only made work for us when the gale set in again, it was soon given up, and we lay to under our close reefs. We had less snow and hail than when we were farther to the westward, but we had an abundance of what is worse to a sailor in cold weather—drenching rain. Snow is blinding, and very bad when coming on a coast, but for genuine discomfort give me rain with freezing weather. A snowstorm is exciting, and it does not wet through the clothes (which is important to a sailor), but a constant rain there is no escaping from. It wets to the skin, and makes all protection vain. We had long ago run through all our dry clothes, and as sailors have no other way of drying them than by the sun, we had nothing to do but to put on those which were the least wet. At the end of each watch, when we came below we took off our clothes and wrung them out, two taking hold of a pair of trousers—one at each end—and jackets in the same way. Stockings, mittens, and all were wrung out also and then hung up to drain and chafe dry against the bulkheads. Then, feeling of all our clothes, we picked out those which were the least wet and put them on, so as to be ready for a call, and turned in, covered ourselves up with blankets, and slept until three knocks on the scuttle and the dismal sound of "All starbowlines ahoy! Eight bells, there below! Do you hear the news?" drawled out from on deck, and the sulky answer of "Aye, aye!" from below, sent us up again.

On deck, all was as dark as a pocket, and either a dead calm, with the rain pouring steadily down or, more generally, a violent gale dead ahead, with rain pelting horizontally, and occasional variations of hail and sleet—decks afloat with water swashing from side to side, and constantly wet feet, for boots could not be wrung out like drawers, and no composition could stand the constant soaking. In fact, wet and cold feet are inevitable in such weather, and are not the least of those little items which go to make up the grand total of the discomforts of a winter passage round the Cape. Few words were spoken between the watches as they shifted, the wheel was relieved, the mate took his place on the quarter-deck, the lookouts in the bows, and each man had his narrow space to walk fore and aft in, or rather to swing himself forward and back in, from one belaying pin to another—for the decks were too slippery with ice and water to allow of much walking. To make a walk, which is absolutely

necessary to pass away the time, one of us hit upon the expedient
of sanding the deck; and afterward, whenever the rain was not
so violent as to wash it off, the weather side of the quarter-deck,
and a part of the waist and forecastle, were sprinkled with the
sand which we had on board for holystoning; and thus we made
a good promenade, where we walked fore and aft, two and two,
hour after hour, in our long, dull, and comfortless watches. The
bells seemed to be an hour or two apart, instead of half an hour,
and an age to elapse before the welcome sound of eight bells.
The sole object was to make the time pass on. Any change was
sought for which would break the monotony of the time, and
even the two hours' trick at the wheel, which came round to
each of us in turn once in every other watch, was looked upon
as a relief. Even the never-failing resource of long yarns, which
eke out many a watch, seemed to have failed us now; for we
had been so long together that we had heard each other's stories
told over and over again till we had them by heart; each one
knew the whole history of each of the others, and we were fairly
and literally talked out. Singing and joking we were in no humor
for, and in fact any sound of mirth or laughter would have
struck strangely upon our ears, and would not have been tolerated, any more than whistling, or a wind instrument. The last
resort, that of speculating upon the future, seemed now to fail
us, for our discouraging situation, and the danger we were really
in (as we expected every day to find ourselves drifted back
among the ice) "clapped a stopper" upon all that. From saying,
"*When* we get home," we began insensibly to alter it to "*If* we
get home"—and at last the subject was dropped by a tacit
consent.

In this state of things, a new light was struck out, and a new
field opened, by a change in the watch. One of our watch was
laid up for two or three days by a bad hand (for in cold weather
the least cut or bruise ripens into a sore) and his place was supplied by the carpenter. This was a windfall, and there was quite
a contest who should have the carpenter to walk with him. As
Chips was a man of some little education, and he and I had had
a good deal of intercourse with each other, he fell in with me
in my walk. He was a Finn, but spoke English very well, and
gave me long accounts of his country—the customs, the trade,

the towns, what little he knew of the government (I found he was no friend of Russia), his voyages, his first arrival in America, his marriage and courtship—he had married a countrywoman of his, a dressmaker whom he met with in Boston. I had very little to tell him of my quiet, sedentary life at home; and in spite of our best efforts, which had protracted these yarns through five or six watches, we fairly talked one another out, and I turned him over to another man in the watch, and put myself upon my own resources.

I commenced a deliberate system of time-killing, which united some profit with a cheering-up of the heavy hours. As soon as I came on deck and took my place and regular walk, I began with repeating over to myself a string of matters which I had in my memory, in regular order. First, the multiplication table and the tables of weights and measures; then the states of the Union, with their capitals; the counties of England, with their shire towns; the kings of England in their order; and a large part of the peerage, which I committed from an almanac that we had on board; and then the Kanaka numerals. This carried me through my facts and, being repeated deliberately, with long intervals, often eked out the two first bells. Then came the Ten Commandments, the thirty-ninth chapter of Job, and a few other passages from Scripture. The next in the order that I never varied from came Cowper's "Castaway," which was a great favorite with me, the solemn measure and gloomy character of which, as well as the incident that it was founded upon, made it well suited to a lonely watch at sea. Then his lines to Mary, his address to the jackdaw, and a short extract from *Table Talk* (I abounded in Cowper, for I happened to have a volume of his poems in my chest), *"Ille et nefasto"* from Horace, and Goethe's "Erl King." After I had got through these, I allowed myself a more general range among everything that I could remember, in both prose and verse. In this way, with an occasional break by relieving the wheel, heaving the log, and going to the scuttle butt for a drink of water, the longest watch was passed away; and I was so regular in my silent recitations that if there was no interruption by ship's duty, I could tell very nearly the number of bells by my progress.

Our watches below were no more varied than the watch on

deck. All washing, sewing, and reading was given up, and we did nothing but eat, sleep, and stand our watch, leading what might be called a Cape Horn life. The forecastle was too uncomfortable to sit up in, and whenever we were below, we were in our berths. To prevent the rain and the sea water which broke over the bows from washing down, we were obliged to keep the scuttle closed, so that the forecastle was nearly airtight. In this little wet, leaky hole, we were all quartered, in an atmosphere so bad that our lamp, which swung in the middle from the beams, sometimes actually burned blue, with a large circle of foul air about it. Still, I was never in better health than after three weeks of this life. I gained a great deal of flesh, and we all ate like horses. At every watch, when we came below, before turning in the bread barge and beef kid were overhauled. Each man drank his quart of hot tea night and morning; and glad enough we were to get it, for no nectar and ambrosia were sweeter to the lazy immortals than was a pot of hot tea, a hard biscuit, and a slice of cold salt beef to us after a watch on deck. To be sure, we were mere animals, and had this life lasted a year instead of a month, we should have been little better than the ropes in the ship. Not a razor, nor a brush, nor a drop of water—except the rain and the spray—had come near us all the time; for we were on an allowance of fresh water, and who would strip and wash himself in salt water on deck in the snow and ice, with the thermometer at zero?

After about eight days of constant easterly gales, the wind hauled occasionally a little to the southward and blew hard, which, as we were well to the southward, allowed us to brace in a little and stand on, under all the sail we could carry. These turns lasted but a short while, and sooner or later it set in again from the old quarter; yet at each time we made something, and were gradually edging along to the eastward. One night after one of these shifts of the wind, and when all hands had been up a great part of the time, our watch was left on deck with the mainsail hanging in the buntlines, ready to be set if necessary. It came on to blow worse and worse, with hail and snow beating like so many furies upon the ship, it being as dark and thick as night could make it. The mainsail was blowing and slatting with a noise like thunder when the captain came on deck, and ordered it to be furled. The mate was about to call all hands when the captain stopped him, and said that the men would be beat-out if they were called up so often; that as our watch must stay on deck, it might as well be doing that as anything else. Accordingly we went upon the yard, and never shall I forget that piece of work. Our watch had been so reduced by sickness, and by some having been left in California, that with one man at the wheel we had only the third mate and three beside myself to go aloft; so that at most we could only attempt to furl one yardarm at a time. We manned the weather yardarm, and set to work to make a furl of it. Our lower masts being short, and our yards very square, the sail had a head of nearly fifty feet, and a short leech, made still shorter by the deep reef which was in it, which brought the clew away out on the quarters of the yard, and made a bunt nearly as square as the mizzen royal yard. Besides this difficulty, the yard over which we lay was cased with ice, the gaskets and rope of the foot and leech of the sail as stiff and hard as a piece of suction hose, and the sail itself about as pliable as though it had been made of sheets of sheathing copper. It blew a perfect hurricane, with alternate blasts of snow, hail, and rain. We had to "fist" the sail with bare hands. No one could trust himself to mittens, for if he slipped, he was a gone man. All the boats were hoisted in on deck, and there was nothing to be lowered for him. We had need of every finger God had given us. Several times we got the sail on the yard, but it blew away again before we could secure it. It required men to lie over the yard to pass each turn of the gaskets, and when they were passed, it was almost impossible to knot them so that they would hold. Frequently we were obliged to leave off altogether and take to beating our hands on the sail to keep them from freezing. After some time—which seemed forever—we got the weather side stowed after a fashion, and went over to leeward for another trial. This was still worse, for the body of the sail had been blown over to leeward, and as the yard was acockbill by the lying-over of the vessel, we had to light it all up to windward. When the yardarms were furled, the bunt was all adrift again, which made more work for us. We got all secure at last, but we had been nearly an hour and a half on the yard, and it seemed an age. It had just struck five bells when we went up, and eight were

struck soon after we came down. This may seem slow work, but
considering the state of everything, and that we had only five
men to a sail with just half as many square yards of canvas in it
as the mainsail of the *Independence*, sixty-gun ship, which
musters seven hundred men at her quarters, it is not wonderful
that we were no quicker about it. We were glad enough to get
on deck, and still more, to go below. The oldest sailor in the
watch said as he went down: "I shall never forget that main
yard—it beats all my going a-fishing. Fun is fun, but furling one
yardarm of a course at a time off Cape Horn is no better than
man-killing."

During the greater part of the next two days the wind was
pretty steady from the southward. We had evidently made
great progress, and had good hope of being soon up with the
Cape, if we were not there already. We could put but little confidence in our reckoning, as there had been no opportunities for
an observation, and we had drifted too much to allow of our
dead reckoning being anywhere near the mark. If it would clear
off enough to give a chance for an observation, or if we could
make land, we should know where we were; and upon these,
and the chances of falling in with a sail from the eastward, we
depended almost entirely.

FRIDAY, JULY 22. This day we had a steady gale from the
southward, and stood on under close sail, with the yards eased
a little by the weather braces, the clouds lifting a little, and showing signs of breaking away. In the afternoon I was below with
Mr. H—, the third mate, and two others, filling the bread locker
in the steerage from the casks, when a bright gleam of sunshine
broke out and shone down the companionway and through the
skylight, lighting up everything below, and sending a warm glow
through the heart of everyone. It was a sight we had not seen
for weeks—an omen, a godsend. Even the roughest and hardest
face acknowledged its influence. Just at that moment we heard
a loud shout from all parts of the deck, and the mate called out
down the companionway to the captain, who was sitting in the
cabin. What he said we could not distinguish, but the captain
kicked over his chair and was on deck at one jump. We could
not tell what it was, and anxious as we were to know, the discipline of the ship would not allow of our leaving our places.

Yet as we were not called, we knew there was no danger. We hurried to get through with our job, when, seeing the steward's black face peering out of the pantry, Mr. H— hailed him, to know what was the matter. "Lan' o, to be sure, sir! No you hear 'em sing out, 'Lan' o?' De cap'em say 'im Cape Horn!"

This gave us a new start, and we were soon through our work and on deck—and there lay the land, fair upon the larboard beam, and slowly edging away upon the quarter. All hands were busy looking at it—the captain and mates from the quarter-deck, the cook from his galley, and the sailors from the forecastle; and even Mr. N., the passenger, who had kept in his shell for nearly a month and hardly been seen by anybody, and who we had almost forgotten was on board, came out like a butterfly, and was hopping round as bright as a bird.

The land was the island of Staten Land, just to the eastward of Cape Horn, and a more desolate-looking spot I never wish to set eyes upon—bare, broken, and girt with rocks and ice, with here and there, between the rocks and broken hillocks, a little stunted vegetation of shrubs. It was a place well suited to stand at the junction of the two oceans, beyond the reach of human cultivation, and encounter the blasts and snows of a perpetual winter. Yet, dismal as it was, it was a pleasant sight to us, not only as being the first land we had seen, but because it told us that we had passed the Cape—were in the Atlantic—and that with twenty-four hours of this breeze might bid defiance to the Southern Ocean. It told us, too, our latitude and longitude better than any observation; and the captain now knew where we were as well as if we were off the end of Long Wharf.

In the general joy, Mr. N. said he should like to go ashore on the island and examine a spot which probably no human being had ever set foot upon; but the captain intimated that he would see the island, specimens and all, in—another place before he would get out a boat or delay the ship one moment for him.

We left the land gradually astern, and at sundown had the Atlantic Ocean clear before us.

Cracking On · Progress Home- ward · A Pleasant Sunday · A Fine Sight · By-play

IT IS USUAL in voyages round the Cape from the Pacific to keep to the eastward of the Falkland Islands; but as it had now set in a strong, steady, and clear southwester, with every prospect of its lasting, and we had had enough of high latitudes, the captain determined to stand immediately to the northward, running inside the Falkland Islands. Accordingly, when the wheel was relieved at eight o'clock, the order was given to keep her due north, and all hands were turned up to square away the yards and make sail. In a moment the news ran through the ship that the captain was keeping her off, with her nose straight for Boston and Cape Horn over her taffrail. It was a moment of enthusiasm. Everyone was on the alert, and even the two sick men turned out to lend a hand at the halyards. The wind was now due southwest, and blowing a gale to which a vessel close-hauled could have shown no more than a single close-reefed sail; but as we were going before it, we could carry on. Accordingly, hands were sent aloft, and a reef shaken out of the topsails, and the reefed foresail set. When we came to masthead the topsail yards, with all hands at the halyards, we struck up "Cheerily, men," with a chorus which might have been heard halfway to Staten Land. Under her increased sail, the ship drove on through the water. Yet she could bear it well; and the captain sang out from the quarter-deck, "Another reef out of that fore-topsail, and give it to her!" Two hands sprang aloft; the frozen reef points and earings were cast adrift, the halyards manned, and the sail gave out her increased canvas to the gale. All hands were kept on deck to watch the effect of the change. It was as much as she could well carry, and with a heavy sea astern, it took two men at the wheel to steer her. She flung the foam from her bows, the spray breaking aft as far as the gangway. She was going at a prodigious rate. Still, everything held. Preventer braces were reeved and hauled taut, tackles got upon the backstays, and each thing done to keep all snug and strong. The captain walked the deck at a rapid stride, looked aloft at the sails and then to windward; the mate stood in the gangway rubbing his hands and talking aloud to the ship: "Hurrah, old bucket! The Boston girls have got hold of the towrope!" and the like; and we were on the forecastle, looking to see how the spars stood it and guessing the rate at which she was going when the captain called out: "Mr. Brown, get up the topmast studding sail! What she can't carry she may drag!" The mate looked a moment but he would let no one be before him in daring. He sprang forward. "Hurrah, men! Rig out the topmast studding-sail boom! Lay aloft, and I'll send the rigging up to you!" We sprang aloft into the top; lowered a girtline down, by which we hauled up the rigging; rove the tacks and halyards; ran out the boom and lashed it fast, and sent down the lower halyards, as a preventer. It was a clear starlight night, cold and blowing; but everybody worked with a will. Some, indeed, looked as though they thought the "old man" was mad, but no one said a word. We had had a new topmast studding sail made with a reef in it—a thing hardly ever heard of, and which the sailors had ridiculed a good deal, saying that when it was time to reef a studding sail, it was time to take it in. But we found a use for it now; for there being a reef in the topsail, the studding sail could not be set without one in it also. To be sure, a studding sail with reefed topsails was rather a new thing; yet there was some reason in it, for if we carried that away, we should lose only a sail and a boom, but a whole topsail might have carried away the mast and all.

While we were aloft, the sail had been got out, bent to the yard, reefed, and ready for hoisting. Waiting for a good opportunity, the halyards were manned and the yard hoisted fairly up to the block; but when the mate came to shake the catspaw out of the downhaul and we began to boom-end the sail, it shook the ship to her center. The boom buckled up and bent like a whipstick, and we looked every moment to see something go; but being of the short, tough upland spruce, it bent like whale-bone, and nothing could break it. The carpenter said it was the best stick he had ever seen. The strength of all hands soon brought the tack to the boom end, and the sheet was trimmed down, and the preventer and the weather brace hauled taut to take off the strain. Every rope yarn seemed stretched to the utmost, and every thread of canvas, and with this sail added to her, the ship sprang through the water like a thing possessed. The sail being nearly all forward, it lifted her out of the water, and she seemed actually to jump from sea to sea. From the time her keel was laid she had never been so driven; and had it been life or death with every one of us, she could not have borne another stitch of canvas.

Finding that she would bear the sail, the hands were sent below, and our watch remained on deck. Two men at the wheel had as much as they could do to keep her within three points of her course, for she steered as wild as a young colt. The mate walked the deck looking at the sails and then over the side to see the foam fly by her, slapping his hands on his thighs and talking to the ship: "Hurrah, you jade, you've got the scent!— You know where you're going!" And when she leaped over the seas, and almost out of the water, and trembled to her very keel, the spars and masts snapping and creaking: "There she goes!—There she goes—handsomely!—As long as she cracks she holds!" while we stood with the rigging laid down fair for letting go, and ready to take in sail and clear away if anything went. At four bells we hove the log, and she was going eleven knots fairly; and had it not been for the sea from aft which sent the chip home, and threw her continually off her course, the log would have shown her to have been going much faster. I went to the wheel with a young fellow from the Kennebec who was a good helmsman, and for two hours we had our hands full. A few minutes showed us that our monkey jackets must come off; and, cold as it was, we stood in our shirt sleeves, in a perspira-tion, and were glad enough to have it eight bells, and the wheel relieved. We turned in and slept as well as we could, though the sea made a constant roar under her bows, and washed over the forecastle like a small cataract.

At four o'clock we were called again. The same sail was still on the vessel, and the gale, if there was any change, had increased a little. No attempt was made to take the studding sail in, and indeed it was too late now. If we had started anything toward taking it in, either tack or halyards, it would have blown to pieces, and carried something away with it. The only way now was to let everything stand, and if the gale went down, well and good; if not, something must go—the weakest stick or rope first —and then we could get it in. For more than an hour she was driven on at such a rate that she seemed actually to crowd the sea into a heap before her; and the water poured over the spritsail yard as it would over a dam. Toward daybreak the gale abated a little, and she was just beginning to go more easily along, relieved of the pressure, when Mr. Brown, determined to give her no respite, and depending upon the wind's subsiding as the sun rose, told us to get along the lower studding sail. This was an immense sail, and held wind enough to last a Dutchman a week —hove to. It was soon ready, the boom topped up, preventer guys rove, and the idlers called up to man the halyards; yet such was still the force of the gale that we were nearly an hour setting the sail, carried away the outhaul in doing it, and came very near snapping off the swinging boom. No sooner was it set than the ship tore on again like one that was mad, and began to steer as wild as a hawk. The men at the wheel were puffing and blowing at their work, and the helm was going hard up and hard down constantly. Add to this, the gale did not lessen as the day came on, but the sun rose in clouds. A sudden lurch threw the man from the weather wheel across the deck and against the side. The mate sprang to the wheel, and the man, regaining his feet, seized the spokes, and they hove the wheel up just in time to save her from broaching to, though nearly half the studding sail went under water, and as she came to the boom stood up at an angle of forty-five degrees. She had evidently more on her than she could bear; yet it was in vain to try to take it in—the clew line was not strong enough; and they were thinking of cutting away when another wide yaw and a come-to snapped the guys, and the swinging boom came in with a crash against the lower rigging. The outhaul block gave way, and the topmast studding-sail boom bent in a manner which I never before supposed a stick could bend. I had my eye on it when the guys parted, and it made one spring and buckled up so as to form nearly a half-circle, and sprang out again to its shape. The clew line gave way at the first pull, the cleat to which the halyards were belayed was wrenched off, and the sail blew round the spritsail yard and head guys, which gave us a bad job to get it in. A half-hour served to clear all away, and she was suffered to drive on with her topmast studding sail set, it being as much as she could stagger under.

During all this day and the next night we went on under the same sail, the gale blowing with undiminished force, two men at the wheel all the time; watch and watch, and nothing to do but to steer and look out for the ship, and be blown along—until the noon of the next day,

SUNDAY, JULY 24, when we were in lat. 50° 27′ S., long. 62° 13′ W., having made four degrees of latitude in the last twenty-four hours. Being now to the northward of the Falkland Islands, the ship was kept off, northeast, for the equator; and with her head for the equator and Cape Horn over her taffrail, she went gloriously on, every heave of the sea leaving the Cape astern, and every hour bringing us nearer to home, and to warm weather. Many a time, when blocked up in the ice, with everything dismal and discouraging about us, had we said if we were only fairly round, and standing north on the other side, we should ask for no more—and now we had it all, with a clear sea, and as much wind as a sailor could pray for. If the best part of the voyage is the last part, surely we had all now that we could wish. Everyone was in the highest spirits, and the ship seemed as glad as any of us at getting out of her confinement. At each change of the watch those coming on deck asked those going below, "How does she go along?" and got for answer the rate, and the customary addition: "Aye! And the Boston girls have had hold of the towrope all the watch, and can't haul half the slack in!" Each day the sun rose higher in the horizon, and the nights grew shorter, and at coming on deck each morning there was a sensible change in the temperature. The ice, too, began to melt from off the rigging and spars, and, except a little which remained in the tops and round the hounds of the lower masts, was soon gone. As we left the gale behind us the reefs were shaken out of the topsails, and sail made as fast as she could bear it; and every time all hands were sent to the halyards, a song was called for, and we hoisted away with a will.

Sail after sail was added as we drew into fine weather, and in one week after leaving Cape Horn the long topgallant masts were got up, topgallant and royal yards crossed, and the ship restored to her fair proportions.

The Southern Cross we saw no more after the first night, the Magellan Clouds settled lower and lower in the horizon, and so great was our change of latitude each succeeding night that we sank some constellation in the south, and raised another in the northern horizon.

SUNDAY, JULY 31. At noon we were in lat. 36° 41′ S., long. 38° 08′ W., having traversed the distance of two thousand miles, allowing for changes of course, in nine days. A thousand miles in four days and a half!—This is equal to steam.

Soon after eight o'clock the appearance of the ship gave evidence that this was the first Sunday we had yet had in fine weather. As the sun came up clear, with the promise of a fair, warm day and, as usual on Sunday, there was no work going on, all hands turned to upon clearing out the forecastle. The wet and soiled clothes which had accumulated there during the past month were brought up on deck; the chests moved; brooms, buckets of water, swabs, scrubbing brushes, and scrapers carried down, and applied until the forecastle floor was as white as chalk, and everything neat and in order. The bedding from the berths was then spread on deck and dried and aired, the deck tub filled with water, and a grand washing begun of all the clothes which were brought up. Shirts, frocks, drawers, trousers, jackets, stockings of every shape and color, wet and dirty, many of them moldy from having been lying a long time wet in a foul corner—these were all washed and scrubbed out, and finally towed overboard for half an hour, and then made fast in the rigging to dry. Wet boots and shoes were spread out to dry in sunny places on deck, and the whole ship looked like a back yard on a washing day. After we had done with our clothes, we began upon our own persons. A little fresh water, which we had saved from our allowance, was put in buckets, and, with soap and towels, we had what sailors call a fresh-water wash. The same bucket, to be sure, had to go through several hands, and was spoken for by one after another, but as we rinsed off in salt water pure from the ocean, and the fresh was used only to start the accumulated grime and blackness of five weeks, it was held of little consequence. We soaped down and scrubbed one another with towels and pieces of canvas, stripping to it; and then, getting into the head, threw buckets of water on each other. After this came shaving, and combing, and brushing; and when, having spent the first part of the day in this way, we sat down on the forecastle in the afternoon, with clean duck trousers and shirts on, washed, shaved, and combed, and looking a dozen shades lighter for it, reading, sewing, and talking at our ease with a clear sky and warm sun over our heads, a steady breeze over the larboard quarter, studding sails out alow and aloft, and all the flying kites abroad—we felt that we had got back into the pleasantest part of a sailor's life. At sundown the clothes were all taken down from the rigging—clean and dry—and stowed neatly away in our chests; and our southwesters, thick boots, guernsey frocks, and other accompaniments of bad weather put out of the way, we hoped, for the rest of the voyage, as we expected to come on the coast early in the autumn.

Notwithstanding all that has been said about the beauty of a ship under full sail, there are very few who have ever seen a ship literally under all her sail. A ship coming in or going out of port, with her ordinary sails, and perhaps two or three studding sails, is commonly said to be under full sail; but a ship never has all her sail on her except when she has a light, steady breeze very nearly, but not quite, dead aft, and so regular that it can be trusted, and is likely to last for some time. Then, with all her sails, light and heavy, and studding sails on each side, alow and aloft, she is the most glorious moving object in the world. Such a sight very few, even some who have been at sea a good deal, have ever beheld; for from the deck of your own vessel you cannot see her as you would a separate object.

One night while we were in these tropics I went out to the end of the flying-jib boom on some duty, and having finished it, turned round, and lay over the boom for a long time, admiring the beauty of the sight before me. Being so far out from the deck, I could look at the ship as at a separate vessel and there rose up from the water, supported only by the small black hull, a pyramid of canvas, spreading out far beyond the hull, and towering up almost, as it seemed in the indistinct night air, to the clouds. The sea was as still as an inland lake; the light trade wind was gently and steadily breathing from astern; the dark-blue sky was studded with the tropical stars; there was no sound but the rippling of the water under the stem; and the sails were spread out, wide and high—the two lower studding sails stretching on each side far beyond the deck; the topmast studding sails like wings to the topsails; the topgallant studding sails spreading fearlessly out above them; still higher, the two royal studding sails, looking like two kites flying from the same string; and highest of all, the little skysail, the apex of the pyramid, seeming actually to touch the stars, and to be out of reach of human hand. So quiet, too, was the sea, and so steady the breeze, that if these sails had been sculptured marble they could not have been more motionless. Not a ripple on the surface of the canvas, not even a quivering of the extreme edges of the sail—so perfectly were they distended by the breeze. I was so lost in the sight that I forgot the presence of the man who came out with me until he said (for he too, rough old man-of-war'sman as he was, had been gazing at the show), half to himself, still looking at the marble sails, "How quietly they do their work!"

The fine weather brought work with it, as the ship was to be put in order for coming into port. This may gave a landsman some notion of what is done on board ship.—All the first part of a passage is spent in getting a ship ready for sea, and the last part in getting her ready for port. She is, as sailors say, like a lady's watch, always out of repair. The new, strong sails which we had up off Cape Horn were to be sent down, and the old set, which were still serviceable in fine weather, to be bent in their place; all the rigging to be set up, fore and aft; the masts stayed; the standing rigging to be tarred down; lower and topmast rigging rattled down, fore and aft; the ship scraped, inside and out, and painted; decks varnished; new and neat knots, seizings, and coverings to be fitted; and every part put in order, to look well to the owner's eye on coming into Boston. This, of course, was a long matter and all hands were kept on deck at work for the whole of each day during the rest of the voyage.

Sailors call this hard usage; but the ship must be in crack order, and "We're homeward bound" was the answer to everything.

We went on for several days employed in this way, nothing remarkable occurring, and at the latter part of the week fell in with the southeast trades, blowing about east southeast, which brought them nearly two points abaft our beam. These blew strong and steady, so that we hardly started a rope until we were beyond their latitude. The first day of "all hands," one of those little incidents occurred which are nothing in themselves, but are great matters in the eyes of a ship's company, as they serve to break the monotony of a voyage, and afford conversation to the crew for days afterward. These small matters, too, are often interesting, as they show the customs and state of feeling on shipboard.

In merchant vessels, the captain gives his orders as to the ship's work to the mate in a general way, and leaves the execution of them, with the particular ordering, to him. This has become so fixed a custom that it is like a law, and is never infringed upon by a wise master, unless his mate is no seaman, in which case the captain must often oversee things for himself. This, however, could not be said of our chief mate, and he was very jealous of any encroachment on the borders of his authority.

On Monday morning the captain told him to stay the fore-topmast plumb. He accordingly came forward, turned all hands to, with tackles on the stays and backstays, coming up with the seizings, hauling here, belaying there, and full of business, standing between the knightheads to sight the mast—when the captain came forward, and also began to give orders. This made confusion, and the mate, finding that he was all aback, left his place and went aft, saying to the captain:

"If you come forward, sir, I'll go aft. One is enough on the forecastle."

This produced a reply, and another fierce answer, and the words flew, fists were doubled up, and things looked threatening.

"I'm master of this ship."

"Yes, sir, and I'm mate of her, and know my place! My place is forward, and yours is aft!"

"My place is where I choose! I command the *whole* ship; and you are mate only so long as I choose!"

"Say the word, Captain T., and I'm done! I can do a man's work aboard! I didn't come through the cabin windows! If I'm not mate, I can be man," etc., etc.

This was all fun for us, who stood by winking at each other and enjoying the contest between the higher powers. The captain took the mate aft, and they had a long talk, which ended in the mate's returning to his duty. The captain had broken through a custom which is a part of the common law of a ship, and without reason, for he knew that his mate was a sailor, and needed no help from him; and the mate was excusable for being angry. Yet he was wrong, and the captain right. Whatever the captain does is right, ipso facto, and any opposition to it is wrong, on board ship; and every officer and man knows this when he signs the ship's articles. It is a part of the contract. Yet there has grown up in merchant vessels a series of customs which have become a well-understood system, and have almost the force of prescriptive law. To be sure, all power is in the captain, and the officers hold their authority only during his will, and the men are liable to be called upon for any service; yet by breaking in upon these usages many difficulties have occurred on board ship, and even come into courts of justice, which are perfectly unintelligible to anyone not acquainted with the universal nature and force of these customs. Many a provocation has been offered, and a system of petty oppression pursued toward men, the force and meaning of which would appear as nothing to strangers, and doubtless do appear so to many "longshore" juries and judges.

Narrow Escapes · The Equator · Tropical Squalls · A Thunderstorm

THE SAME DAY, I met with one of those narrow escapes which are so often happening in a sailor's life. I had been aloft nearly all the afternoon at work, standing for as much as an hour on the fore topgallant yard, which was hoisted up, and hung only by the tye when, having got through my work, I balled up my yarns, took my serving board in my hand, laid hold deliberately of the topgallant rigging, took one foot from the yard, and was just lifting the other when the tye parted, and down the yard fell. I was safe, by my hold upon the rigging, but it made my heart beat quick. Had the tye parted one instant sooner, or had I stood an instant longer on the yard, I should inevitably have been thrown violently from the height of ninety or a hundred feet, overboard, or what is worse, upon the deck. However, "a miss is as good as a mile" a saying which sailors very often have occasion to use. An escape is always a joke on board ship. A man would be ridiculed who should make a serious matter of it. A sailor knows too well that his life hangs upon a thread to wish to be always reminded of it; so if a man has an escape, he keeps it to himself, or makes a joke of it. I have often known a man's life to be saved by an instant of time, or by the merest chance—the swinging of a rope—and no notice taken of it. One of our boys, when off Cape Horn reefing topsails of a dark night, and when there were no boats to be lowered away— and where if a man fell overboard, he must be left behind— lost his hold of the reef point, slipped from the footrope, and would have been in the water in a moment, when the man who was next to him on the yard caught him by the collar of his jacket and hauled him up upon the yard, with "Hold on another time, you young monkey, and be damned to you!" And that was all that was heard about it.

SUNDAY, AUGUST 7. Lat. 25° 59′ S., long. 27° 0′ W. Spoke the English bark *Mary-Catherine,* from Bahia, bound to Calcutta. This was the first sail we had fallen in with, and the first time we had seen a human form or heard the human voice, except of our own number, for nearly a hundred days. The very yo-ho-ing of the sailors at the ropes sounded sociably upon the ear. She was an old, damaged-looking craft, with a high poop and topgallant forecastle, and sawed off square stem and stern like a true English "tea wagon," and with a run like a sugar box.

The next day about 3 P.M. passed a large corvette-built ship, close upon the wind, with royals and skysails set fore and aft, under English colors. She was standing south by east, probably bound round Cape Horn. She had men in her tops, and black mastheads, heavily sparred, with sails cut to a *t,* and other marks of a man-of-war. She sailed well, and presented a fine appearance, the proud, aristocratic-looking banner of St. George, the cross in a blood-red field, waving from the mizzen. We probably were as fine a sight, with our studding sails spread far out beyond the ship on either side, and rising in a pyramid to royal studding sails and skysails, burying the hull in canvas, and looking like what the whalemen on the Banks, under their stump topgallant masts, call "a Cape Horner under a cloud of sail."

FRIDAY, AUGUST 12. At daylight made the island of Trinidad, situated in lat. 20° 28′ S., long. 29° 08′ W. At 12 M., it bore N.W. ½ N., distant twenty-seven miles. It was a beautiful day, the sea hardly ruffled by the light trades, and the island looking like a small blue mound rising from a field of glass. Such a fair and peaceful-looking spot is said to have been for a long time the resort of a band of pirates who ravaged the tropical seas.

THURSDAY, AUGUST 18. At 3 P.M. made the island of Fernando de Naronha, lying in lat. 3° 55′ S., long. 32° 35′ W.; and between twelve o'clock Friday night and one o'clock Saturday morning crossed the equator, for the fourth time since leaving Boston, in long. 35° W., having been twenty-seven days from Staten

Land—a distance, by the courses we had made, of more than four thousand miles.

We were now to the northward of the line, and every day added to our latitude. The Magellan Clouds, the last sign of South latitude, were sunk in the horizon, and the North Star, the Great Bear, and the familiar signs of Northern latitudes, were rising in the heavens. Next to seeing land, there is no sight which makes one realize more that he is drawing near home than to see the same heavens under which he was born shining at night over his head. The weather was extremely hot, with the usual tropical alternations of a scorching sun and squalls of rain; yet not a word was said in complaint of the heat, for we all remembered that only three or four weeks before we would have given nearly our all to have been where we now were. We had a plenty of water, too, which we caught by spreading an awning, with shot thrown in to make hollows. These rain squalls came up in the manner usual between the tropics.—A clear sky; burning, vertical sun; work going lazily on, and men about decks with nothing but duck trousers, checked shirts, and straw hats; the ship moving as lazily through the water; the man at the helm resting against the wheel, with his hat drawn over his eyes; the captain below, taking an afternoon nap; the passenger leaning over the taffrail watching a dolphin following slowly in our wake; the sailmaker mending an old topsail on the lee side of the quarter-deck; the carpenter working at his bench in the waist; the boys making sennit; the spun-yarn winch whizzing round and round, and the men walking slowly fore and aft with their yarns. A cloud rises to windward, looking a little black; the skysails are brailed down; the captain puts his head out of the companionway, looks at the cloud, comes up, and begins to walk the deck. The cloud spreads and comes on, the tub of yarns, the sail, and other matters are thrown below, and the skylight and booby hatch put on, and the slide drawn over the forecastle. "Stand by the royal halyards!" The man at the wheel keeps a good weather helm, so as not to be taken aback. The squall strikes her. If it is light, the royal yards are clewed down and the ship keeps on her way; but if the squall takes strong hold, the royals are clewed up, fore and aft; light hands lay aloft and furl them; topgallant yards clewed down, flying jib hauled down, and the ship kept off before it, the man at the helm laying out his strength to heave the wheel up to windward. At the same time a drenching rain, which soaks one through in an instant. Yet no one puts on a jacket or cap, for if it is only warm, a sailor does not mind a ducking, and the sun will soon be out again. As soon as the force of the squall has passed, though to a common eye the ship would seem to be in the midst of it: "Keep her up to her course again!"—"Keep her up, sir" (answer).—"Hoist away the topgallant yards!"—"Run up the flying jib!"—"Lay aloft, you boys, and loose the royals!"—and all sail is on her again before she is fairly out of the squall, and she is going on in her course. The sun comes out once more, hotter than ever, dries up the decks and the sailors' clothes; the hatches are taken off; the sail got up and spread on the quarter-deck; spun-yarn winch set a-whirling again; rigging coiled up; captain goes below; and every sign of an interruption is removed.

These scenes, with occasional dead calms lasting for hours, and sometimes for days, are fair specimens of the Atlantic tropics. The nights were fine, and as we had all hands all day, the watch were allowed to sleep on deck at night, except the man at the wheel and one lookout on the forecastle. This was not so much expressly allowed as winked at. We could do it if we did not ask leave. If the lookout was caught napping, the whole watch was kept awake. We made the most of this permission, and stowed ourselves away on the rigging, under the weather rail, on the spars, under the windlass, and in all the snug corners, and frequently slept out the watch, unless we had a wheel or a lookout. And we were glad enough to get this rest, for under the "all-hands" system, out of every other thirty-six hours we had only four below, and even an hour's sleep was a gain not to be neglected. One would have thought so to have seen our watch some night sleeping through a heavy rain. And often have we come on deck and finding a dead calm and a light, steady rain, and determined not to lose our sleep, have laid a coil of rigging down so as to keep us out of the water which was washing about decks, and stowed ourselves away on it, covering a jacket over us, and slept as soundly as a Dutchman between two feather beds.

For a week or ten days after crossing the line we had the usual variety of calms, squalls, head winds, and fair winds—at one time braced sharp upon the wind, with a taut bowline, and in an hour after slipping quietly along with a light breeze over the taffrail, and studding sails out on both sides—until we fell in with the northeast trade winds, which we did on the afternoon of

SUNDAY, AUGUST 28, in lat. 12° N. The trade-wind clouds had been in sight for a day or two previously, and we expected to take them every hour. The light southerly breeze, which had been blowing languidly during the first part of the day, died away toward noon, and in its place came puffs from the northeast, which caused us to take our studding sails in and brace up; and in a couple of hours more we were bowling gloriously along, dashing the spray far ahead and to leeward, with the cool, steady northeast trades freshening up the sea, and giving us as much as we could carry our royals to. These winds blew strong and steady, keeping us generally on a bowline, as our course was about north-northwest, until

SUNDAY, SEPT. 4, when they left us, in lat. 22° N., long. 51° W., directly under the Tropic of Cancer.

For several days we lay "humbugging about" in the horse latitudes, with all sorts of winds and weather, and occasionally, as we were in the latitude of the West Indies, a thunderstorm. It was hurricane month, too, and we were just in the track of the tremendous hurricane of 1830, which swept the North Atlantic destroying almost everything before it. The first night after the trade winds left us, while we were in the latitude of the island of Cuba, we had a specimen of a true tropical thunderstorm. A light breeze had been blowing directly from aft during the first part of the night, which gradually died away, and before midnight it was dead calm, and a heavy black cloud had shrouded the whole sky. When our watch came on deck at twelve o'clock, it was as black as Erebus. The studding sails were all taken in, and the royals furled; not a breath was stirring; the sails hung heavy and motionless from the yards; and the perfect stillness, and the darkness, which was almost palpable, were truly appalling. Not a word was spoken, but everyone stood as though waiting for something to happen. In a few minutes the mate came forward, and in a low tone which was almost a whisper told us to haul down the jib. The fore and mizzen topgallant sails were taken in in the same silent manner, and we lay motionless upon the water, with an uneasy expectation which, from the long suspense, became actually painful. We could hear the captain walking the deck, but it was too dark to see anything more than one's hand before the face. Soon the mate came forward again and gave an order, in a low tone, to clew up the main topgallant sail; and so infectious was the awe and silence that the clew lines and buntlines were hauled up without any of the customary singing out at the ropes. An English lad and myself went up to furl it; and we had just got the bunt up when the mate called out to us something—we did not hear what, but supposing it to be an order to bear a hand, we hurried and made all fast, and came down, feeling our way among the rigging. When we got down we found all hands looking aloft, and there, directly over where we had been standing, on the main topgallant masthead, was a ball of light which the sailors name a corposant (corpus sancti), and which the mate had called out to us to look at. They were all watching it carefully, for sailors have a notion that if the corposant rises in the rigging, it is a sign of fair weather, but if it comes lower down, there will be a storm. Unfortunately as an omen it came down, and showed itself on the topgallant yardarm. We were off the yard in good season, for it is held a fatal sign to have the pale light of the corposant thrown upon one's face. As it was, the English lad did not feel comfortable at having had it so near him, and directly over his head. In a few minutes it disappeared, and showed itself again on the fore topgallant yard, and after playing about for some time, disappeared again, when the man on the forecastle pointed to it on the flying-jib boom end. But our attention was drawn from watching this by the falling of some drops of rain, and by a perceptible increase of the darkness, which seemed suddenly to add a new shade of blackness to the night. In a few minutes low, grumbling thunder was heard, and some random flashes of lightning came from the southwest. Every sail was taken in but the topsails, still no squall appeared to be coming. A few puffs lifted the topsails, but they fell again to the mast, and all was as still as ever. A moment more and a terrific flash

and peal broke simultaneously upon us, and a cloud appeared
to open directly over our heads and let down the water in one
body, like a falling ocean. We stood motionless, and almost
stupefied; yet nothing had been struck. Peal after peal rattled
over our heads, with a sound which seemed actually to stop the
breath in the body, and the "speedy gleams" kept the whole
ocean in a glare of light. The violent fall of rain lasted but a
few minutes, and was succeeded by occasional drops and
showers; but the lightning continued incessant for several hours,
breaking the midnight darkness with irregular and blinding
flashes.

During all which time there was not a breath stirring, and
we lay motionless, like a mark to be shot at, probably the only
object on the surface of the ocean for miles and miles. We stood
hour after hour until our watch was out and we were relieved
at four o'clock. During all this time hardly a word was spoken,
no bells were struck, and the wheel was silently relieved. The
rain fell at intervals in heavy showers, and we stood drenched
through and blinded by the flashes, which broke the Egyptian
darkness with a brightness which seemed almost malignant,
while the thunder rolled in peals the concussion of which appeared to shake the very ocean. A ship is not often injured by
lightning, for the electricity is separated by the great number of
points she presents, and the quantity of iron which she has
scattered in various parts. The electric fluid ran over our anchors,
topsail sheets, and tyes; yet no harm was done to us. We went
below at four o'clock, leaving things in the same state. It is not
easy to sleep when the very next flash may tear the ship in two,
or set her on fire, or where the deathlike calm may be broken by
the blast of a hurricane taking the masts out of the ship. But a
man is no sailor if he cannot sleep when he turns in, and turn
out when he's called. And when, at seven bells, the customary
"All the larboard watch ahoy!" brought us on deck, it was a fine,
clear, sunny morning, the ship going leisurely along with a good
breeze and all sail set.

A Double-Reef-Topsail Breeze·
Scurvy· A Friend in Need·
Preparing for Port·
The Gulf Stream

FROM THE LATITUDE of the West Indies until we got inside the Bermudas, where we took the westerly and south-westerly winds which blow steadily off the coast of the United States early in the autumn, we had every variety of weather, and two or three moderate gales, or as sailors call them, double-reef-topsail breezes, which came on in the usual manner, and of which one is a specimen of all.—A fine afternoon; all hands at work, some in the rigging and others on deck; a stiff breeze, and ship close upon the wind, and skysails brailed down. —Latter part of the afternoon, breeze increases, ship lies over to it, and clouds look windy. Spray begins to fly over the fore-castle, and wets the yarns the boys are knotting—ball them up and put them below.—Mate knocks off work and clears up decks earlier than usual, and orders a man who has been employed aloft to send the royal halyards over to windward as he comes down. Breast backstays hauled taut, and tackle got upon the martingale backrope.—One of the boys furls the mizzen royal.— Cook thinks there is going to be "nasty work," and has supper ready early.—Mate gives orders to get supper by the watch, instead of all hands, as usual.—While eating supper, hear the watch on deck taking in the royals.—Coming on deck, find it is blowing harder, and an ugly head sea is running.—Instead of having all hands on the forecastle in the dog watch, smoking, singing, and telling yarns, one watch goes below and turns in, saying that it's going to be an ugly night, and two hours' sleep is not to be lost. Clouds look black and wild; wind rising, and ship working hard against a heavy head sea, which breaks over the forecastle and washes aft through the scuppers. Still, no more sail is taken in, for the captain is a driver and, like all drivers, very partial to his topgallant sails. A topgallant sail, too, makes the difference between a breeze and a gale. When a topgallant sail is on a ship, it is only a breeze, though I have seen ours set over a reefed topsail when half the bowsprit was under water and it was up to a man's knees in the lee scuppers. At eight bells, nothing is said about reefing the topsails, and the watch go below, with orders to "stand by for a call." We turn in growling at the "old man" for not reefing the topsails when the watch was changed, but putting it off so as to call all hands and break up a whole watch below. Turn in "all standing," and keep ourselves awake, saying there is no use in going to sleep to be waked up again.—Wind whistles on deck, and ship works hard, groaning and creaking and pitching into a heavy head sea, which strikes against the bows with a noise like knocking upon a rock.— The dim lamp in the forecastle swings to and fro, and things "fetch away" and go over to leeward.—"Doesn't that booby of a second mate ever mean to take in his topgallant sails?—He'll have the sticks out of her soon," says Old Bill, who was always growling and, like most old sailors, did not like to see a ship abused.—By and by an order is given.—"Aye, aye, sir!" from the forecastle; rigging is heaved down on deck; the noise of a sail is heard fluttering aloft, and the short, quick cry which sailors make when hauling upon clew lines.—"Here come his fore-topgallant sail in!"—We are wide-awake, and know all that's going on as well as if we were on deck.—A well-known voice is heard from the masthead singing out to the officer of the watch to haul taut the weather brace.—"Hallo! There's S— aloft to furl the sail!"—Next thing, rigging is heaved down directly over our heads, and a long-drawn cry and a rattling of hanks announce that the flying jib has come in.—The second mate holds onto the main topgallant sail until a heavy sea is shipped, and washes over the forecastle as though the whole ocean had come aboard; when a noise farther aft shows that that sail, too, is taking in. After this, the ship is more easy for a time; two bells are struck, and we try to get a little sleep. By and by—bang, bang, bang, on the scuttle—"All ha-a-ands a-ho-o-y!"—We spring out of our berths, clap on a monkey jacket and southwester, and tumble up the ladder.—Mate up before us, and on the forecastle singing out like a roaring bull, the captain singing out on the quarter-deck, and the second mate yelling like a hyena in the waist. The ship is lying over half on her beam ends, lee scuppers under water and forecastle all in a smother of foam.—Rigging all let go and washing about decks; topsail yards down on the caps, and sails flapping and beating against the masts; and starboard watch hauling out the reef tackles of the main topsail. Our watch haul out the fore, and lay aloft and put two reefs into it, and reef the foresail, and race with the starboard watch to see which will masthead its topsail first. All hands tally onto the main tack, and while some are furling the jib and hoisting the staysail, we mizzentopmen double-reef the mizzen topsail and hoist it up. All being made fast "Go below, the watch!" and we turn in to sleep out the rest of the time, which is perhaps an hour and a half. During all the middle and for the first part of the morning watch, it blows as hard as ever, but toward daybreak it moderates considerably, and we shake a reef out of each topsail, and set the topgallant sails over them; and when the watch comes up at seven bells for breakfast, shake the other reefs out, turn all hands to upon the halyards, get the watch tackle on the topgallant sheets and halyards, set the flying jib, and crack onto her again.

Our captain had been married only a few weeks before he left Boston, and after an absence of over two years, it may be supposed he was not slow in carrying sail. The mate, too, was not to be beaten by anybody; and the second mate, though he was afraid to press sail, was afraid as death of the captain, and being between two fears, sometimes carried on longer than any of them. We snapped off three flying-jib booms in twenty-four hours, as fast as they could be fitted and rigged out, sprung the spritsail yard, and made nothing of studding-sail booms. Besides the natural desire to get home, we had another reason for urging the ship on. The scurvy had begun to show itself on board. One man had it so badly as to be disabled and off duty, and the English lad, Ben, was in a dreadful state, and was daily growing worse. His legs swelled and pained him so that he could not walk; his flesh lost its elasticity, so that if it was pressed in it would not return to its shape; and his gums swelled until he could not open his mouth. His breath, too, became very offensive; he lost all strength and spirit, could eat nothing, grew worse every day, and in fact unless something was done for him, would be a dead man in a week at the rate at which he was sinking. The medicines were all, or nearly all, gone, and if we had had a chestful they would have been of no use; for nothing but fresh provisions and terra firma has any effect upon the scurvy. This disease is not so common now as formerly, and is attributed generally to salt provisions, want of cleanliness, the free use of grease and fat (which is the reason of its prevalence among whalemen), and last of all, to laziness. It never could have been from the latter cause on board our ship; nor from the second, for we were a very cleanly crew, kept our forecastle in neat order, and were more particular about washing and changing clothes than many better-dressed people on shore. It was probably from having none but salt provisions, and possibly from our having run very rapidly into hot weather after having been so long in the extremest cold.

Depending upon the westerly winds which prevail off the coast in the autumn, the captain stood well to the westward, to run inside of the Bermudas, and in the hope of falling in with some vessel bound to the West Indies or the Southern states. The scurvy had spread no farther among the crew, but there was danger that it might, and these cases were bad ones.

SUNDAY, SEPT. 11. Lat. 30° 04′ N., long. 63° 23′ W., the Bermudas bearing north northwest, distant one hundred and fifty miles. The next morning, about ten o'clock, "Sail ho!" was cried on deck, and all hands turned up to see the stranger. As she drew nearer, she proved to be an ordinary-looking hermaphrodite brig, standing south-southeast, and probably bound out from the Northern states to the West Indies, and was just the thing we wished to see. She hove to for us, seeing that we wished to speak her, and we ran down to her, boom-ended our studding sails, backed our main-topsail, and hailed her. "Brig ahoy!"—"Hallo!"—"Where are you from, pray?"—"From New York, bound to Curaçao."—"Have you any fresh provisions to spare?"—"Aye, aye, plenty of them!" We lowered away the quarter-boat instantly, and the captain and four hands sprang in and were soon dancing over the water, and alongside the brig. In about half an hour they returned with half a boatload of potatoes and onions, and each vessel filled away and kept on her course. She proved to be the brig *Solon,* of Plymouth, from the Connecticut River, and last from New York, bound to the Spanish Main with a cargo of fresh provisions, mules, tin bake pans, and other "notions." The onions were genuine and fresh, and the mate of the brig told the men in the boat as he passed the bunches over the side that the girls had strung them on purpose for us the day he sailed. We had supposed, on board, that a new President had been chosen the last winter, and just as we filled away, the captain hailed and asked who was President of the United States. They answered, "Andrew Jackson," but thinking that the old General could not have been elected for a third time, we hailed again, and they answered, "Jack Downing," and left us to correct the mistake at our leisure.

It was just dinnertime when we filled away, and the steward, taking a few bunches of onions for the cabin, gave the rest to us, with a bottle of vinegar. We carried them forward, stowed them away in the forecastle, refusing to have them cooked, and ate them raw with our beef and bread. And a glorious treat they were. The freshness and crispness of the raw onion, with the earthy taste, give it a great relish to one who has been a long time on salt provisions. We were perfectly ravenous after them. It was like a scent of blood to a hound. We ate them at every meal, by the dozen; and filled our pockets with them to eat in our watch on deck; and the bunches, rising in the form of a cone from the largest at the bottom to the smallest, no larger than a strawberry, at the top, soon disappeared. The chief use, however, of the fresh provisions was for the men with the scurvy. One of them was able to eat, and he soon brought himself to by gnawing on raw potatoes; but the other by this time was hardly able to open his mouth, and the cook took the potatoes raw, pounded them in a mortar, and gave him the juice to drink. This he swallowed by the teaspoonful at a time, and rinsed it about his gums and throat. The strong earthy taste and smell of this extract of the raw potato at first produced a shuddering

through his whole frame, and after drinking it, an acute pain
which ran through all parts of his body; but knowing by this
that it was taking strong hold, he persevered, drinking a spoonful
every hour or so, and holding it a long time in his mouth, until,
by the effect of this drink, and of his own restored hope (for he
had nearly given up in despair), he became so well as to be
able to move about, and open his mouth enough to eat the raw
potatoes and onions pounded into a soft pulp. This course soon
restored his appetite and strength, and in ten days after we
spoke the *Solon,* so rapid was his recovery that from lying helpless and almost hopeless in his berth, he was at the masthead
furling a royal.

With a fine southwest wind, we passed inside of the Bermudas, and notwithstanding the old couplet, which was quoted
again and again by those who thought we should have one more
touch of a storm before our voyage was up—

> *If the Bermudas let you pass,*
> *You must beware of Hatteras—*

we were to the northward of Hatteras, with good weather, and
beginning to count not the days, but the hours, to the time when
we should be at anchor in Boston Harbor.

Our ship was in fine order, all hands having been hard at work
upon her from daylight to dark every day but Sunday from the
time we got into warm weather on this side the Cape.

It is a common notion with landsmen that a ship is in her finest
condition when she leaves port to enter upon her voyage; and
that she comes home after a long absence

> *With overweathered ribs and ragged sails,*
> *Lean, rent, and beggared by the strumpet wind.*

But so far from that, unless a ship meets with some accident,
or comes on the coast in the dead of winter, when work cannot
be done on the rigging, she is in her finest order at the end of
the voyage. When she sails from port, her rigging is generally
slack; the masts need staying; the decks and sides are black and
dirty from taking in cargo; riggers' seizings and overhand knots
in place of nice seamanlike work; and everything, to a sailor's
eye, adrift. But on the passage home, the fine weather between

the tropics is spent in putting the ship into the neatest order. No merchant vessel looks better than an Indiaman, or a Cape Horner, after a long voyage, and many captains and mates will stake their reputation for seamanship upon the appearance of their ship when she hauls into the dock. All our standing rigging, fore and aft, was set up and tarred; the masts stayed; the lower and topmast rigging rattled down (or up, as the fashion now is); and so careful were our officers to keep the ratlines taut and straight that we were obliged to go aloft on the ropes and sheer poles with which the rigging was swifted in, and these were used as jury ratlines until we got close on the coast. After this, the ship was scraped, inside and out, decks, masts, booms, and all, a stage being rigged outside on which we scraped her down to the waterline, pounding the rust off the chains, bolts, and fastenings. Then, taking two days of calm under the line, we painted her on the outside, giving her open ports in her streak and finishing off the nice work on the stern, where sat Neptune in his car holding his trident—drawn by sea horses—and retouched the gilding and coloring of the cornucopia which ornamented her billethead. The inside was then painted, from the skysail truck to the waterways—the yards black, mastheads and tops white, monkey rail black, white, and yellow, bulwarks green, plank-sheer white, waterways lead-color, etc., etc. The anchors and ringbolts, and other ironwork, were blackened with coal tar; and the steward kept at work polishing the brass of the wheel, bell, capstan, etc. The cabin, too, was scraped, varnished, and painted; and the forecastle scraped and scrubbed, there being no need of paint and varnish for Jack's quarters. The decks were then scraped and varnished, and everything useless thrown overboard—among which the empty tar barrels were set on fire and thrown overboard of a dark night, and left blazing astern, lighting up the ocean for miles. Add to all this labor the neat work upon the rigging—the knots, Flemish eyes, splices, seizings, coverings, pointings, and graftings, which show a ship in crack order. The last preparation, and which looked still more like coming into port, was getting the anchors over the bows, bending the cables, rowsing the hawsers up from between-decks, and overhauling the deep-sea lead line.

THURSDAY, SEPTEMBER 15. This morning the temperature and

peculiar appearance of the water, the quantities of gulfweed floating about, and a bank of clouds lying directly before us, showed that we were on the border of the Gulf Stream. This remarkable current, running northeast nearly across the ocean, is almost constantly shrouded in clouds, and is the region of storms and heavy seas. Vessels often run from a clear sky and light wind, with all sail, at once into a heavy sea and cloudy sky, with double-reefed topsails. A sailor told me that on a passage from Gibraltar to Boston his vessel neared the Gulf Stream with a light breeze, clear sky, and studding sails out alow and aloft, while before it was a long line of heavy, black clouds lying like a bank on the water, and a vessel coming out of it under double-reefed topsails, and with royal yards sent down. As they drew near, they began to take in sail after sail, until they were reduced to the same condition; and after twelve or fourteen hours of rolling and pitching in a heavy sea before a smart gale, they ran out of the bank on the other side, and were in fine weather again, and under their royals and skysails. As we drew into it, the sky became cloudy, the sea high, and everything had the appearance of the going-off, or the coming-on, of a storm. It was blowing no more than a stiff breeze; yet the wind, being northeast, which is directly against the course of the current, made an ugly, chopping sea, which heaved and pitched the vessel about so that we were obliged to send down the royal yards, and to take in our light sails. At noon the thermometer, which had been repeatedly lowered into the water, showed the temperature to be seventy, which was considerably above that of the air—as is always the case in the center of the Stream. A lad who had been at work at the royal masthead came down on deck and took a turn round the longboat and looking very pale, said he was so sick that he could stay aloft no longer, but was ashamed to acknowledge it to the officer. He went up again, but soon gave out and came down, and leaned over the rail "as sick as a lady passenger." He had been to sea several years and had, he said, never been sick before. He was made so by the irregular, pitching motion of the vessel, increased by the height to which he had been above the hull, which is like the fulcrum of the lever. An old sailor who was at work on the topgallant yard said he felt disagreeably all the time, and was glad, when his job was done, to get down

into the top, or on deck. Another hand was sent up to the royal
masthead who stayed nearly an hour, but gave up. The work
must be done, and the mate sent me. I did very well for some
time, but began at length to feel very unpleasantly, though I
had never been sick since the first two days from Boston, and
had been in all sorts of weather and situations. Still, I kept my
place, and did not come down until I had got through my work,
which was more than two hours. The ship certainly never acted
so badly before. She was pitched and jerked about in all manner
of ways, the sails seeming to have no steadying power over her.
The tapering points of the masts made various curves and angles
against the sky overhead, and sometimes in one sweep of an
instant described an arc of more than forty-five degrees, bringing
up with a sudden jerk which made it necessary to hold on with
both hands, and then sweeping off in another long, irregular
curve. I was not positively sick, and came down with a look of
indifference, yet was not unwilling to get on the comparative
terra firma of the deck. A few hours more carried us through,
and when we saw the sun go down on our larboard beam in the
direction of the continent of North America, we had left the
bank of dark, stormy clouds astern, in the twilight.

Soundings · Sights from Home · Boston Harbor · Leaving the Ship

FRIDAY, SEPT. 16. Lat. 38° N., long. 69° 00′ W. A fine southwest wind, every hour carrying us nearer in toward the land. All hands on deck at the dog watch, and nothing talked about but our getting in—where we should make the land; whether we should arrive before Sunday; going to church; how Boston would look; friends; wages paid; and the like. Everyone was in the best spirits and, the voyage being nearly at an end, the strictness of discipline was relaxed; for it was not necessary to order in a cross tone what everyone was ready to do with a will. The little differences and quarrels which a long voyage breeds on board a ship were forgotten, and everyone was friendly, and two men who had been on the eve of a battle half the voyage were laying out a plan together for a cruise on shore. When the mate came forward, he talked to the men, and said we should be on George's Bank before tomorrow noon, and joked with the boys, promising to go and see them, and to take them down to Marblehead in a coach.

SATURDAY, 17. The wind was light all day, which kept us back somewhat; but a fine breeze springing up at nightfall, we were running fast in toward the land. At six o'clock we expected to have the ship hove to for soundings, as a thick fog coming up showed we were near them; but no order was given, and we kept on our way. Eight o'clock came, and the watch went below, and for the whole of the first hour the ship was tearing on with studding sails out alow and aloft, and the night as dark as a pocket. At two bells the captain came on deck and said a word to the mate, when the studding sails were hauled into the tops, or boom-ended, the after yards backed, the deep-sea end carried forward, and everything got ready for sounding. A man on the spritsail yard with the lead, another on the cathead with a handful of the line coiled up, another in the fore chains, another in the waist, and another in the main chains, each with a quantity of the line coiled away in his hand. "All ready there, forward?"— "Aye, aye, sir!"—"He-e-ave!"—"Watch ho! Watch!" sings out the man on the spritsail yard, and the heavy lead drops into the water. "Watch ho! Watch!" bawls the man on the cathead as the last fake of the coil drops from his hand, and "Watch ho! Watch!" is shouted by each one as the line falls from his hold, until it comes to the mate, who tends the lead, and has the line in coils on the quarter-deck. Eighty fathoms, and no bottom! A depth as great as the height of St. Peter's! The line is snatched in a block on the swifter, and three or four men haul it in and coil it away. The after yards are braced full, the studding sails hauled out again, and in a few minutes more the ship has her whole way on her. At four bells, backed again, hove the lead, and—soundings—at sixty fathoms! Hurrah for Yankeeland! Hand over hand we hauled the lead in, and the captain, taking it to the light, found black mud on the bottom. Studding sails taken in, after yards filled, and ship kept on under easy sail all night, the wind dying away.

The soundings on the American coast are so regular that a navigator knows as well where he has made land by the soundings as he would by seeing the land. Black mud is the soundings off Block Island. As you go toward Nantucket, it changes to a dark sand; then, sand and white shells; and on George's Banks, white sand; and so on. Being off Block Island, our course was due east, to Nantucket Shoals and the South Channel; but the wind died away and left us becalmed in a thick fog, in which we lay the whole of Sunday. At noon of

SUNDAY, SEPT. 18, Block Island bore, by calculation, N.W. ¼ W. fifteen miles; but the fog was so thick all day that we could see nothing.

Having got through the ship's duty, and washed and shaved, we went below, and had a fine time overhauling our chests, laying aside the clothes we meant to go ashore in and throwing overboard all that were worn-out and good for nothing. Away went the woolen caps in which we had carried hides on our heads for sixteen months on the coast of California; the duck frocks for tarring-down rigging; and the worn-out and darned mittens and patched woolen trousers which had stood the tug of Cape Horn. We hove them overboard with a good will, for there is nothing like being quit of the very last appendages and remnants of our evil fortune. We got our chests all ready for going ashore, ate the last duff we expected to have on board the ship *Alert,* and talked as confidently about matters on shore as though our anchor were on the bottom.

"Who'll go to church with me a week from today?"

"I will," says Jack, who said aye to everything.

"Go away, salt water!" says Tom. "As soon as I get both legs ashore I'm going to shoe my heels, and button my ears behind me, and start off into the bush, a straight course, and not stop till I'm out of the sight of salt water!"

"Oh, belay that! Spin that yarn where nobody knows your filling! If you get once moored stem and stern in old B—'s grogshop, with a coal fire ahead and the bar under your lee, you won't see daylight for three weeks!"

"No!" says Tom. "I'm going to knock off grog, and go and board at the Home, and see if they won't ship me for a deacon!"

"And I," says Bill, "am going to buy a quadrant and ship for navigator on a Hingham packet!"

These and the like jokes served to pass the time while we were lying waiting for a breeze to clear up the fog and send us on our way.

Toward night a moderate breeze sprang up, the fog however continuing as thick as before, and we kept on to the eastward. About the middle of the first watch a man on the forecastle sang out, in a tone which showed that there was not a moment to be lost, "Hard up the helm!" and a great ship loomed up out of the fog, coming directly down upon us. She luffed at the same moment, and we just passed one another, our spanker boom grazing over her quarter. The officer of the deck had only time to hail, and she answered, as she went into the fog again, something about Bristol—probably a whaleman from Bristol, Rhode Island, bound out. The fog continued through the night, with a very light breeze, before which we ran to the eastward, literally feeling our way along. The lead was heaved every two hours, and the gradual change from black mud to sand showed that we were approaching Nantucket South Shoals. On Monday morning the increased depth and deep-blue color of the water, and the mixture of shells and white sand which we brought up on sounding, showed that we were in the channel, and nearing George's. Accordingly the ship's head was put directly to the northward, and we stood on, with perfect confidence in the soundings, though we had not taken an observation for two days, nor seen land, and the difference of an eighth of a mile out of the way might put us ashore. Throughout the day a provokingly light wind prevailed, and at eight o'clock a small fishing schooner which we passed told us we were nearly abreast of Chatham Lights. Just before midnight a light land breeze sprang up, which carried us well along; and at four o'clock, thinking ourselves to the northward of Race Point, we hauled up on the wind and stood into the bay, north northwest, for Boston Light, and commenced firing guns for a pilot. Our watch went below at four o'clock, but could not sleep, for the watch on deck were banging away at the guns every few minutes. And indeed we cared very little about it, for we were in Boston Bay, and if fortune favored us, we could all "sleep in" the next night, with nobody to call the watch every four hours.

We turned out of our own will at daybreak, to get a sight of land. In the gray of the morning one or two small fishing smacks peered out of the mist; and when the broad day broke upon us, there lay the low sand hills of Cape Cod, over our larboard quarter, and before us, the wide waters of Massachusetts Bay, with here and there a sail gliding over its smooth surface. As we drew in toward the mouth of the harbor, as toward a focus, the vessels began to multiply, until the bay seemed actually alive with sails gliding about in every direction, some on the wind and others before it, as they were bound to or from the emporium of trade and center of the bay. It was a stirring sight for us, who had been months on the ocean without seeing anything but two solitary sails, and over two years without seeing more than the three or four traders on an almost desolate coast. There were the little coasters, bound to and from the various towns along the south shore, down in the bight of the bay, and to the eastward; here and there a square-rigged vessel standing out to seaward; and far in the distance, beyond Cape Ann, was the smoke of a steamer, stretching along in a narrow black cloud on the water. Every sight was full of beauty and interest. We were coming back to our homes, and the signs of civilization, and prosperity, and happiness from which we had been so long banished were

multiplying about us. The high land of Cape Ann and the rocks and shore of Cohasset were full in sight, the lighthouses standing like sentries in white before the harbors, and even the smoke from the chimneys on the plains of Hingham was seen rising slowly in the morning air. One of our boys was the son of a bucketmaker; and his face lighted up as he saw the tops of the well-known hills which surround his native place. About ten o'clock a little boat came bobbing over the water and put a pilot on board, and sheered off in pursuit of other vessels bound in. Being now within the scope of the telegraph stations, our signals were run up at the fore, and in half an hour afterward the owner on change, or in his counting room, knew that his ship was below; and the landlords, runners, and sharks in Ann Street learned that there was a rich prize for them down in the bay: a ship from round the Horn, with a crew to be paid off with two years' wages.

The wind continuing very light, all hands were sent aloft to strip off the chafing gear; and battens, parcelings, roundings, hoops, mats, and leathers came flying from aloft, and left the rigging neat and clean, stripped of all its sea bandaging. The last touch was put to the vessel by painting the skysail poles, and I was sent up to the fore with a bucket of white paint and a brush, and touched her off from the truck to the eyes of the royal rigging. At noon we lay becalmed off the lower lighthouse, and it being about slack water, we made little progress. A firing was heard in the direction of Hingham, and the pilot said there was a review there. The Hingham boy got wind of this, and said if the ship had been twelve hours sooner, he should have been down among the soldiers, and in the booths, and having a grand time. As it was, we had little prospect of getting in before night. About two o'clock a breeze sprang up ahead, from the westward, and we began beating up against it. A full-rigged brig was beating in at the same time, and we passed one another in our tacks, sometimes one and sometimes the other working to windward, as the wind and tide favored or opposed. It was my trick at the wheel from two till four, and I stood my last helm, making between nine hundred and a thousand hours which I had spent at the helms of our two vessels. The tide beginning to set against us, we made slow work, and the afternoon was nearly spent before we got abreast of the inner light. In the meantime, several vessels were coming down, outward bound; among which a fine, large ship, with yards squared, fair wind, and fair tide, passed us like a race horse, the men running out on her yards to rig out the studding-sail booms. Toward sundown the wind came off in flaws, sometimes blowing very stiff, so that the pilot took in the royals, and then it died away, when, in order to get us in before the tide became too strong, the royals were set again. As this kept us running up and down the rigging all the time, one hand was sent aloft at each masthead, to stand by to loose and furl the sails at the moment of the order. I took my place at the fore, and loosed and furled the royal five times between Rainsford Island and the Castle. At one tack we ran so near to Rainsford Island that, looking down from the royal yard, the island, with its hospital buildings, nice graveled walks, and green plats, seemed to lie directly under our yardarms. So close is the channel to some of these islands that we ran the end of our flying-jib boom over one of the outworks of the fortifications on George's Island and had an opportunity of seeing the advantages of that point as a fortified place; for in working up the channel we presented a fair stem and stern for raking from the batteries, three or four times. One gun might have knocked us to pieces.

We had all set our hearts on getting up to town before night and going ashore, but the tide beginning to run strong against us, and the wind, what there was of it, being ahead, we made but little by weather-bowing the tide, and the pilot gave orders to cockbill the anchor and overhaul the chain. Making two long stretches, which brought us into the roads, under the lee of the Castle, he clewed up the topsails and let go the anchor; and for the first time since leaving San Diego—one hundred and thirty-five days—our anchor was upon bottom. In half an hour more we were lying snugly, with all sails furled, safe in Boston Harbor—our long voyage ended; the well-known scene about us; the dome of the State House fading in the western sky; the lights of the city starting into sight as the darkness came on; and at nine o'clock the clangor of the bells ringing their accustomed peals, among which the Boston boys tried to distinguish the well-known tone of the Old South.

We had just done furling the sails when a beautiful little pleasure boat luffed up into the wind under our quarter, and the junior partner of the firm to which our ship belonged jumped on board. I saw him from the mizzen-topsail yard, and knew him well. He shook the captain by the hand, and went down into the cabin, and in a few moments came up and inquired of the mate for me. The last time I had seen him I was in the uniform of an undergraduate of Harvard College, and now, to his astonishment, there came down from aloft a "rough-alley"-looking fellow, with duck trousers and red shirt, long hair, and face burned as black as an Indian's. He shook me by the hand, congratulated me upon my return and my appearance of health and strength, and said my friends were all well. I thanked him for telling me what I should not have dared to ask; and if

> *the bringer of unwelcome news*
> *Hath but a losing office; and his tongue*
> *Sounds ever after like a sullen bell,*

certainly I shall ever remember this man and his words with pleasure.

The captain went up to town in the boat with Mr. H— and left us to pass another night on board ship, and to come up with the morning's tide under command of the pilot.

So much did we feel ourselves to be already at home, in anticipation, that our plain supper of hard bread and salt beef was barely touched, and many on board to whom this was the first voyage could scarcely sleep. As for myself, by one of those anomalous changes of feeling of which we are all the subjects, I found that I was in a state of indifference, for which I could by no means account. A year before, while carrying hides on the coast, the assurance that in a twelvemonth we should see Boston made me half-wild; but now that I was actually there, and in sight of home, the emotions which I had so long anticipated feeling I did not find, and in their place was a state of very nearly entire apathy. Something of the same experience was related to me by a sailor whose first voyage was one of five years on the Northwest coast. He had left home a lad, and after several years of very hard and trying experience, found himself homeward bound, and such was the excitement of his feelings that during the whole passage he could talk and think of nothing else but his arrival, and how and when he should jump from the vessel and take his way directly home. Yet when the vessel was made fast to the wharf and the crew dismissed, he seemed suddenly to lose all feeling about the matter. He told me that he went below and changed his dress; took some water from the scuttle butt and washed himself leisurely; overhauled his chest and put his clothes all in order; took his pipe from its place, filled it, and sitting down on his chest, smoked it slowly for the last time. Here he looked round upon the forecastle in which he had spent so many years, and being alone and his shipmates scattered, he began to feel actually unhappy. Home became almost a dream, and it was not until his brother (who had heard of the ship's arrival) came down into the forecastle and told him of things at home, and who were waiting there to see him, that he could realize where he was, and feel interest enough to put him in motion toward that place for which he had longed, and of which he had dreamed, for years. There is probably so much of excitement in prolonged expectation that the quiet realizing of it produces a momentary stagnation of feeling as well as of effort. It was a good deal so with me. The activity of preparation, the rapid progress of the ship, the first making land, the coming up the harbor, and old scenes breaking upon the view, produced a mental as well as bodily activity from which the change to a perfect stillness when both expectation and the necessity of labor failed left a calmness almost of indifference, from which I must be roused by some new excitement. And the next morning, when all hands were called and we were busily at work clearing the decks, and getting everything in readiness for going up to the wharves—loading the guns for a salute, loosing the sails, and manning the windlass—mind and body seemed to wake together.

About ten o'clock a sea breeze sprang up, and the pilot gave orders to get the ship under way. All hands manned the windlass, and the long-drawn "Yo heave ho!" which we had last heard dying away among the desolate hills of San Diego, soon brought the anchor to the bows; and with a fair wind and tide, a bright sunny morning, royals and skysails set, ensign, streamer, signals, and pennant flying, and with our guns firing, we came swiftly and handsomely up to the city. Off the end of the wharf, we rounded to and let go our anchor; and no sooner was it on the bottom than the decks were filled with people: customhouse officers; Topliff's agent, to inquire for news; others inquiring for friends on board, or left on the coast; dealers in grease besieging the galley to make a bargain with the cook for his slush; "loafers" in general; and last and chief, boardinghouse runners, to secure their men. Nothing can exceed the obliging disposition of these runners, and the interest they take in a sailor returned from a long voyage with plenty of money. Two or three of them, at different times, took me by the hand, remembered me perfectly, were quite sure I had boarded with them before I sailed, were delighted to see me back, gave me their cards, had a handcart waiting on the wharf on purpose to take my things up, would lend me a hand to get my chest ashore, bring a bottle of grog on board if we did not haul in immediately—and the like. In fact, we could hardly get clear of them to go aloft and furl the sails. Sail after sail, for the hundredth time—in fair weather and in foul—we furled now for the last time together, and came down and took the warp ashore, manned the capstan, and with a chorus which waked up half the North End and rang among the buildings in the docks, we hauled her in to the wharf. Here, too, the landlords and runners were active and ready, taking a bar to the capstan, lending a hand at the ropes, laughing and talking and telling the news. The city bells were just ringing one when the last turn was made fast and the crew dismissed; and in five minutes more not a soul was left on board the good ship *Alert* but the old shipkeeper who had come down from the counting-house to take charge of her.

Concluding Chapter

I TRUST that they who have followed me to the end of my narrative will not refuse to carry their attention a little farther, to the concluding remarks which I here present to them.

This chapter is written after the lapse of a considerable time since the end of my voyage, and after a return to my former pursuits; and in it I design to offer those views of what may be done for seamen, and of what is already doing, which I have deduced from my experiences and from the attention which I have since gladly given to the subject.

The romantic interest which many take in the sea, and in those who live on it, may be of use in exciting their attention to this subject, though I cannot but feel sure that all who have followed me in my narrative must be convinced that the sailor has no romance in his everyday life to sustain him, but that it is very much the same plain, matter-of-fact drudgery and hardship which would be experienced on shore. If I have not produced this conviction, I have failed in persuading others of what my own experience has most fully impressed upon myself.

There is a witchery in the sea, its songs and stories, and in the mere sight of a ship and the sailor's dress, especially to a young mind, which has done more to man navies and fill merchantmen than all the press gangs of Europe. I have known a young man with such a passion for the sea that the very creaking of a block stirred up his imagination so that he could hardly keep his feet on dry ground; and many are the boys in every seaport who are drawn away, as by an almost irresistible attraction, from their work and schools, and hang about the decks and yards of vessels with a fondness which it is plain will have its way. No sooner, however, has the young sailor begun his new life in earnest than all this fine drapery falls off, and he learns that it is but work and hardship, after all. This is the true light in which a sailor's life is to be viewed; and if in our books and anniversary speeches we would leave out much that is said about "blue water," "blue jackets," "open hearts," "seeing God's hand on the deep," and so forth, and take this up like any other practical subject, I am quite sure we should do full as much for those we wish to benefit. The question is: What can be done for sailors as they are—men to be fed, and clothed, and lodged, for whom laws must be made and executed, and who are to be instructed in useful knowledge, and above all, to be brought under religious influence and restraint? It is upon these topics that I wish to make a few observations.

In the first place, I have no fancies about equality on board ship. It is a thing out of the question, and certainly, in the present state of mankind, not to be desired. I never knew a sailor who found fault with the orders and ranks of the service; and if I expected to pass the rest of my life before the mast, I would not wish to have the power of the captain diminished an iota. It is absolutely necessary that there should be one head and one voice to control everything, and be responsible for everything. There are emergencies which require the instant exercise of extreme power. These emergencies do not allow of consultation, and they who would be the captain's constituted advisers might be the very men over whom he would be called upon to exert his authority. It has been found necessary to vest in every government, even the most democratic, some extraordinary, and at first sight alarming, powers, trusting in public opinion and subsequent accountability to modify the exercise of them. These are provided to meet exigencies which all hope may never occur, but which yet by possibility may occur, and if they should and there were no power to meet them instantly, there would be an end put to the government at once. So it is with the authority of the shipmaster. It will not answer to say that he shall never do this and that thing because it does not seem always necessary and advisable that it should be done. He has great cares and responsibilities; is answerable for everything; and is subject to emergencies which perhaps no other man exercising authority among civilized people is subject to. Let him, then, have powers commensurate with his utmost possible need; only let him be held strictly responsible for the exercise of them. Any other course would be injustice, as well as bad policy.

In the treatment of those under his authority, the captain is amenable to the common law, like any other person. He is liable at common law for murder, assault and battery, and other offenses; and in addition to this, there is a special statute of the United States which makes a captain or other officer liable to imprisonment for a term not exceeding five years, and to a fine not exceeding a thousand dollars, for inflicting any cruel punishment upon, withholding food from, or in any other way maltreating a seaman. This is the state of the law on the subject, while the relation in which the parties stand, and the peculiar necessities, excuses, and provocations arising from that relation, are merely circumstances to be considered in each case. As to the restraints on the master's exercise of power, the laws themselves seem, on the whole, to be sufficient. I do not see that we are in need at present of more legislation on the subject. The difficulty lies rather in the administration of the laws, and this is certainly a matter that deserves great consideration, and one of no little embarrassment.

In the first place, the courts have said that public policy requires that the power of the master and officers should be sustained. Many lives and a great amount of property are constantly in their hands, for which they are strictly responsible. To preserve these, and to deal justly by the captain, and not lay upon him a really fearful responsibility and then tie up his hands, it is essential that discipline should be supported. In the second place, there is always great allowance to be made for false swearing and exaggeration by seamen, and for combinations among them against their officers; and it is to be remembered that the latter have often no one to testify on their side. These are weighty and true statements, and should not be lost sight of by the friends of seamen. On the other hand, sailors make many complaints, some of which are well founded.

On the subject of testimony, seamen labor under a difficulty full as great as that of the captain. It is a well-known fact that they are usually much better treated when there are passengers on board. The presence of passengers is a restraint upon the captain, not only from his regard to their feelings and to the estimation in which they may hold him, but because he knows they will be influential witnesses against him if he is brought to trial. Though officers may sometimes be inclined to show themselves off before passengers by freaks of office and authority, yet cruelty they would hardly dare to be guilty of. It is on long and distant voyages, where there is no restraint upon the captain and none but the crew to testify against him, that sailors need most the protection of the law. On such voyages as these there are many cases of outrageous cruelty on record, enough to make one heartsick and almost disgusted with the sight of man; and many, many more which have never come to light, and never will be known until the sea shall give up its dead. Many of these have led to mutiny and piracy—stripe for stripe, and blood for blood. If on voyages of this description the testimony of seamen is not to be received in favor of one another, or too great a deduction is made on account of their being seamen, their case is without remedy; and the captain, knowing this, will be strengthened in that disposition to tyrannize which the possession of absolute power, without the restraints of friends and public opinion, is too apt to engender.

It is to be considered, also, that the sailor comes into court under very different circumstances from the master. He is thrown among landlords, and sharks of all descriptions; is often led to drink freely; and comes on the stand unaided, and under a certain cloud of suspicion as to his character and veracity. The captain, on the other hand, is backed by the owners and insurers, and has an air of greater respectability, though, after all, he may have but a little better education than the sailor, and sometimes (especially among those engaged in certain voyages that I could mention) a very hackneyed conscience.

These are the considerations most commonly brought up on the subject of seamen's evidence, and I think it cannot but be obvious to everyone that here positive legislation would be of no manner of use. There can be no rule of law regulating the weight to be given to seamen's evidence. It must rest in the mind of the judge and jury; and no enactment or positive rule of court could vary the result a hair in any one case. The effect of a sailor's testimony in deciding a case must depend altogether upon the reputation of the class to which he belongs, and upon the impression he himself produces in court by his deportment, and by those infallible marks of character which always tell upon a jury. In fine, after all the well-meant and specious projects that have been brought forward, we seem driven back to the belief that the best means of securing a fair administration of the laws made for the protection of seamen, and certainly the only means which can create any important change for the better, is the gradual one of raising the intellectual and religious character of the sailor, so that as an individual and as one of a class he may, in the first instance, command the respect of his officers, and if any difficulty should happen, may upon the stand carry that weight which an intelligent and respectable man of the lower class almost always does with a jury. I know there are many men who when a few cases of great hardship occur, and it is evident that there is an evil somewhere, think that some arrangement must be made, some law passed, or some society got up, to set all right at once. On this subject there can be no call for any such movement; on the contrary, I fully believe that any public and strong action would do harm, and that we must be satisfied to labor in the less easy and less exciting task of gradual improvement, and abide the issue of things working slowly together for good.

Equally injudicious would be any interference with the economy of the ship. The lodging, food, hours of sleep, etc., are all matters which, though capable of many changes for the better, must yet be left to regulate themselves. And I am confident that there will be, and that there is now, a gradual improvement in all such particulars. The forecastles of most of our ships are small, black, and wet holes which few landsmen would believe held a crew of ten or twelve men on a voyage of months or years; and often, indeed in most cases, the provisions are not good enough to make a meal anything more than a necessary part of a day's duty;* and on the score of sleep, I

---

* I am not sure that I have stated in the course of my narrative the manner in which sailors eat on board ship. There are neither tables, knives, forks, nor plates in a forecastle; but the kid (a wooden tub with iron hoops) is placed on the floor, and the crew sit round it, and each man cuts for himself with the common jackknife or sheath knife that he carries about him. They drink their tea out of tin pots holding little less than a quart each.

These particulars are not looked upon as hardships, and indeed may be

fully believe that the lives of merchant seamen are shortened by
the want of it. I do not refer to those occasions when it is
necessarily broken in upon; but, for months during fine weather,
in many merchantmen all hands are kept on deck throughout
the day, and then there are eight hours on deck for one watch
each night. Thus it is usually the case that at the end of a
voyage where there has been the finest weather, and no disaster,
the crew have a wearied and worn-out appearance. They never
sleep longer than four hours at a time, and are seldom called
without being really in need of more rest. There is no one thing
that a sailor thinks more of as a luxury of life on shore than a
whole night's sleep. Still, all these things must be left to be
gradually modified by circumstances. Whenever hard cases occur,
they should be made known, and masters and owners should be
held answerable, and will no doubt in time be influenced in their
arrangements and discipline by the increased consideration in
which sailors are held by the public. It is perfectly proper that
the men should live in a different part of the vessel from the
officers, and if the forecastle is made large and comfortable, there
is no reason why the crew should not live there as well as in
any other part. In fact, sailors prefer the forecastle. It is their
accustomed place, and in it they are out of the sight and hearing
of their officers.

As to their food and sleep, there are laws, with heavy penal-
ties, requiring a certain amount of stores to be on board, and
safely stowed; and for depriving the crew unnecessarily of food
or sleep, the captain is liable at common law, as well as under
the statute before referred to. Farther than this it would not be

---

considered matters of choice. Sailors in our merchantmen furnish their own
eating utensils, as they do many of the instruments which they use in the
ship's work, such as knives, palms and needles, marlinespikes, rubbers, etc.
And considering their mode of life in other respects, the little time they
would have for laying and clearing away a table with its apparatus, and
the room it would take up in a forecastle, as well as the simple character
of their meals—consisting generally of only one piece of meat—it is certainly
a convenient method, and as the kid and pans are usually kept perfectly
clean, a neat and simple one. I had supposed these things to be generally
known until I heard, a few months ago, a lawyer of repute who has had
a good deal to do with marine cases ask a sailor on the stand whether the
crew had "got up from table" when a certain thing happened.

safe to go. The captain must be the judge when it is necessary to keep his crew from their sleep; and sometimes a retrenching, not of the necessaries, but of some of the little niceties of their meals—as for instance *duff* on Sunday—may be a mode of punishment, though I think generally an injudicious one.

I could not do justice to this subject without noticing one part of the discipline of a ship which has been very much discussed of late, and has brought out strong expressions of indignation from many—I mean the infliction of corporal punishment. Those who have followed me in my narrative will remember that I was witness to an act of great cruelty inflicted upon my own shipmates; and indeed I can sincerely say that the simple mention of the word "flogging" brings up in me feelings which I can hardly control. Yet when the proposition is made to abolish it entirely and at once—to prohibit the captain from ever, under any circumstances, inflicting corporal punishment— I am obliged to pause, and I must say to doubt exceedingly the expediency of making any positive enactment which shall have that effect. If the design of those who are writing on this subject is merely to draw public attention to it, and to discourage the practice of flogging and bring it into disrepute, it is well; and indeed whatever may be the end they have in view, the mere agitation of the question will have that effect, and so far, must do good. Yet I should not wish to take the command of a ship tomorrow, running my chance of a crew, as most masters must, and know, and have my crew know, that I could not under any circumstances inflict even moderate chastisement. I should trust that I might never have to resort to it; and indeed I scarcely know what risk I would not run, and to what inconvenience I would not subject myself, rather than do so. Yet not to have the power of holding it up *in terrorem,* and indeed of protecting myself, and all under my charge, by it if some extreme case should arise, would be a situation I should not wish to be placed in myself, or to take the responsibility of placing another in.

Indeed, the difficulties into which masters and officers are liable to be thrown are not sufficiently considered by many whose sympathies are easily excited by stories, frequent enough and true enough, of outrageous abuse of this power. It is to be remembered that more than three-fourths of the seamen in our

merchant vessels are foreigners. They are from all parts of the world. A great many from the north of Europe, besides Frenchmen, Spaniards, Portuguese, Italians, men from all parts of the Mediterranean, together with Lascars, Negroes, and perhaps worst of all, the offcasts of British men-of-war and men from our own country who have gone to sea because they could not be permitted to live on land.

As things now are, many masters are obliged to sail without knowing anything of their crews until they get out at sea. There may be pirates or mutineers among them, and one bad man will often infect all the rest; and it is almost certain that some of them will be ignorant foreigners hardly understanding a word of our language, accustomed all their lives to no influence but force, and perhaps nearly as familiar with the use of the knife as with that of the marlinespike. No prudent master, however peaceably inclined, would go to sea without his pistol and handcuffs. Even with such a crew as I have supposed, kindness and moderation would be the best policy, and the duty of every conscientious man; and the administering of corporal punishment might be dangerous, and of doubtful use. But the question is not what a captain ought generally to do, but whether it shall be put out of the power of every captain, under any circumstances, to make use of even moderate chastisement. As the law now stands, a parent may correct moderately his child, and the master his apprentice, and the case of the shipmaster has been placed on the same principle. The statutes, and the common law as expounded in the decisions of courts and in the books of commentators, are express and unanimous to this point, that the captain may inflict moderate corporal chastisement for a reasonable cause. If the punishment is excessive, or the cause not sufficient to justify it, he is answerable; and the jury are to determine by their verdict in each case whether, under all the circumstances, the punishment was moderate, and for a justifiable cause.

This seems to me to be as good a position as the whole subject can be left in. I mean to say that no positive enactment going beyond this is needed, or would be a benefit to either masters or men, in the present state of things. This again would seem to be a case which should be left to the gradual working of its own cure. As seamen improve, punishment will become less necessary; and as the character of officers is raised, they will be less ready to inflict it; and still more, the infliction of it upon intelligent and respectable men will be an enormity which will not be tolerated by public opinion, and by juries, who are the pulse of the body politic. No one can have a greater abhorrence of the infliction of such punishment than I have, and a stronger conviction that severity is bad policy with a crew; yet I would ask every reasonable man whether he had not better trust to the practice becoming unnecessary and disreputable; to the measure of moderate chastisement and a justifiable cause being better understood, and thus the act becoming dangerous, and in course of time to be regarded as an unheard-of barbarity, than to take the responsibility of prohibiting it at once, in all cases, and in whatever degree, by positive enactment?

There is, however, one point connected with the administration of justice to seamen to which I wish seriously to call the attention of those interested in their behalf, and, if possible, also of some of those concerned in that administration. This is the practice which prevails of making strong appeals to the jury in mitigation of damages, or to the judge after a verdict has been rendered against a captain or officer for a lenient sentence, on the grounds of their previous good character, and of their being poor, and having friends and families depending upon them for support. These appeals have been allowed a weight which is almost incredible, and which I think works a greater hardship on seamen than any one other thing in the laws, or the execution of them. Notwithstanding every advantage the captain has over the seaman in point of evidence, friends, money, and able counsel, it becomes apparent that he must fail in his defense. An appeal is then made to the jury if it is a civil action, or to the judge for a mitigated sentence if it is a criminal prosecution, on the two grounds I have mentioned. The same form is usually gone through in every case. In the first place, as to the previous good character of the party. Witnesses are brought from the town in which he resides to testify to his good character and to his unexceptionable conduct when on shore. They say that he is a good father, or husband, or son, or neighbor, and that they never saw in him any signs of a cruel or tyrannical disposition.

I have even known evidence admitted to show the character he
bore when a boy at school. The owners of the vessel, and other
merchants, and perhaps the president of the insurance company
are then introduced; and they testify to his correct deportment,
express their confidence in his honesty, and say that they have
never seen anything in his conduct to justify a suspicion of his
being capable of cruelty or tyranny. This evidence is then put
together, and great stress is laid on the extreme respectability
of those who give it. They are the companions and neighbors of
the captain, it is said—men who know him in his business and
domestic relations, and who knew him in his early youth. They
are also men of the highest standing in the community and who,
as the captain's employers, must be supposed to know his
character. This testimony is then contrasted with that of some
half-dozen obscure sailors who, the counsel will not forget to
add, are exasperated against the captain because he has found
it necessary to punish them moderately, and who have combined
against him, and if they have not fabricated a story entirely, have
at least so exaggerated it that little confidence can be placed
in it.

The next thing to be done is to show to the court and jury
that the captain is a poor man, and has a wife and family, or
other friends, depending upon him for support; that if he is
fined, it will only be taking bread from the mouths of the
innocent and helpless, and laying a burden upon them which
their whole lives will not be able to work off; and that if he is
imprisoned, the confinement, to be sure, he will have to bear,
but the distress consequent upon the cutting him off from his
labor and means of earning his wages will fall upon a poor wife
and helpless children, or upon an infirm parent. These two topics,
well put, and urged home earnestly, seldom fail of their effect.

In deprecation of this mode of proceeding, and in behalf of
men who I believe are every day wronged by it, I would urge
a few considerations which seem to me to be conclusive.

First, as to the evidence of the good character the captain
sustains on shore. It is to be remembered that masters of vessels
have usually been brought up in a forecastle; and upon all men,
and especially upon those taken from lower situations, the con-
ferring of absolute power is too apt to work a great change.

There are many captains whom I know to be cruel and tyrannical men at sea who yet among their friends, and in their families, have never lost the reputation they bore in childhood. In fact, the sea captain is seldom at home, and when he is, his stay is short, and during the continuance of it he is surrounded by friends who treat him with kindness and consideration, and he has everything to please and at the same time to restrain him. He would be a brute indeed if after an absence of months or years, during his short stay—so short that the novelty and excitement of it has hardly time to wear off, and the attentions he receives as a visitor and stranger hardly time to slacken—if, under such circumstances, a townsman or neighbor would be justified in testifying against his correct and peaceable deportment. With the owners of the vessel, also, to which he is attached, and among merchants and insurers generally, he is a very different man from what he may be at sea when his own master, and the master of everybody and everything about him. He knows that upon such men, and their good opinion of him, he depends for his bread. So far from their testimony being of any value in determining what his conduct would be at sea, one would expect that the master who would abuse and impose upon a man under his power would be the most compliant and deferential to his employers at home.

As to the appeal made in the captain's behalf on the ground of his being poor and having persons depending upon his labor for support, the main and fatal objection to it is that it will cover every case of the kind, and exempt nearly the whole body of masters and officers from the punishment the law has provided for them. There are very few, if any, masters or other officers of merchantment in our country who are not poor men, and having either parents, wives, children, or other relatives depending mainly or wholly upon their exertions for support in life. Few others follow the sea for subsistence. Now if this appeal is to have weight with courts in diminishing the penalty the law would otherwise inflict, is not the whole class under a privilege which will, in a degree, protect it in wrongdoing? It is not a thing that happens now and then. It is the invariable appeal, the last resort, of counsel when everything else has failed. I have known cases of the most flagrant nature, where after every effort has been made for the captain, and yet a verdict rendered against him, and all other hope failed, this appeal has been urged, and with such success that the punishment has been reduced to something little more than nominal, the court not seeming to consider that it might be made in almost every such case that could come before them. It is a little singular, too, that it seems to be confined to cases of shipmasters and officers. No one ever heard of a sentence for an offense committed on shore being reduced by the court on the ground of the prisoner's poverty, and the relation in which he may stand to third persons. On the contrary, it had been thought that the certainty that disgrace and suffering will be brought upon others as well as himself is one of the chief restraints upon the criminally disposed. Besides, this course works a peculiar hardship in the case of the sailor. For if poverty is the point in question, the sailor is the poorer of the two; and if there is a man on earth who depends upon whole limbs and an unbroken spirit for support, it is the sailor. He too has friends to whom his hard earnings may be a relief, and whose hearts will bleed at any cruelty or indignity practiced upon him. Yet I never knew this side of the case to be once adverted to in these arguments addressed to the leniency of the court, which are now so much in vogue; and certainly they are never allowed a moment's consideration when a sailor is on trial for revolt, or for an injury done to an officer. Notwithstanding the many difficulties which lie in a seaman's way in a court of justice, presuming that they will be modified in time, there would be little to complain of were it not for these two appeals.

It is no cause of complaint that the testimony of seamen against their officers is viewed with suspicion, and that great allowance is made for combinations and exaggeration. On the contrary, it is the judge's duty to charge the jury on these points, strongly. But there is reason for objection when, after a strict cross-examination of witnesses, after the arguments of counsel, and the judge's charge, a verdict is found against the master, that the court should allow the practice of hearing appeals to its lenity supported solely by evidence of the captain's good conduct when on shore (especially where the case is one in which no evidence but that of sailors could have been brought against the accused) and then, on this ground, and on the invariable claims of the wife and family, be induced to cut down essentially the penalty imposed by a statute made expressly for masters and officers of merchantmen, and for no one else.

There are many particulars connected with the manning of vessels, the provisions given to crews, and the treatment of them while at sea upon which there might be a good deal said; but as I have, for the most part, remarked upon them as they came up in the course of my narrative, I will offer nothing further now except on the single point of the manner of shipping men. This, it is well known, is usually left entirely to shipping masters, and is a cause of a great deal of difficulty, which might be remedied by the captain, or owner, if he has any knowledge of seamen, attending to it personally. One of the members of the firm to which our ship belonged, Mr. S—, had been himself a master of a vessel, and generally selected the crew from a number sent down to him from the shipping office. In this way he almost always had healthy, serviceable, and respectable men; for anyone who has seen much of sailors can tell pretty well at first sight, by a man's dress, countenance, and deportment, what he would be on board ship. This same gentleman was also in the habit of seeing the crew together and speaking to them previously to their sailing. On the day before our ship sailed, while the crew were getting their chests and clothes on board, he went down into the forecastle and spoke to them about the voyage, the clothing they would need, the provision he had made for them, and saw that they had a lamp and a few other conveniences. If owners or masters would more generally take the same pains, they would often save their crews a good deal of inconvenience, besides creating a sense of satisfaction and gratitude which makes a voyage begin under good auspices, and goes far toward keeping up a better state of feeling throughout its continuance.

It only remains for me now to speak of the associated public efforts which have been making of late years for the good of seamen: a far more agreeable task than that of finding fault, even where fault there is. The exertions of the general association called the American Seamen's Friend Society, and of the other smaller societies throughout the Union, have been a true blessing to the seaman, and bid fair, in course of time, to change the whole nature of the circumstances in which he is placed, and give him a new name, as well as a new character. These associations have taken hold in the right way, and aimed both at making the sailor's life more comfortable and creditable, and at giving him spiritual instruction. Connected with these efforts, the spread of temperance among seamen, by means of societies called, in their own nautical language, Windward-Anchor Societies, and the distribution of books; the establishment of Sailors' Homes, where they can be comfortably and cheaply boarded, live quietly and decently, and be in the way of religious services, reading, and conversation; also the institution of Savings Banks for Seamen; the distribution of tracts and Bibles—are all means which are silently doing a great work for this class of men. These societies make the religious instruction of seamen their prominent object. If this is gained, there is no fear but that all other things necessary will be added unto them. A sailor never becomes interested in religion without immediately learning to read, if he did not know how before; and regular habits, forehandedness (if I may use the word) in worldly affairs, and hours reclaimed from indolence and vice, which follow in the wake of the converted man, make it sure that he will instruct himself in the knowledge necessary and suitable to his calling. The religious change is the great object. If this is secured, there is no fear but that knowledge of things of the world will come in fast enough. With the sailor, as with all other men in fact, the cultivation of the intellect and the spread of what is commonly called useful knowledge while religious instruction is neglected is little else than changing an ignorant sinner into an intelligent and powerful one. That sailor upon whom, of all others, the preaching of the Cross is least likely to have effect is the one whose understanding has been cultivated while his heart has been left to its own devices. I fully believe that those efforts which have their end in the intellectual cultivation of the sailor—in giving him scientific knowledge; putting it in his power to read everything without securing first of all a right heart which shall guide him in judgment; in giving him political information, and interesting him in newspapers, an end in the furtherance of which he is exhibited at ladies' fairs and public meetings, and complimented for his gallantry and generosity—are all doing a harm which the labors of many faithful men cannot undo.

The establishment of Bethels in most of our own seaports—and in many foreign ports frequented by our vessels—where the gospel is regularly preached, and the opening of "Sailors' Homes," which I have before mentioned, where there are usually religious services and other good influences, are doing a vast deal in this cause. But it is to be remembered that the sailor's home is on the deep. Nearly all his life must be spent on board ship, and to secure a religious influence there should be the great object. The distribution of Bibles and tracts into cabins and forecastles will do much toward this. There is nothing which will gain a sailor's attention sooner, and interest him more deeply, than a tract, especially one which contains a story. It is difficult to engage their attention in mere essays and arguments, but the simplest and shortest story in which home is spoken of, kind friends, a praying mother or sister, a sudden death, and the like, often touches the hearts of the roughest and most abandoned. The Bible is to the sailor a sacred book. It may lie in the bottom of his chest voyage after voyage, but he never treats it with positive disrespect. I never knew but one sailor who doubted its being the inspired word of God, and he was one who had received an uncommonly good education, except that he had been brought up without any early religious influence. The most abandoned man of our crew one Sunday morning asked one of the boys to lend him his Bible. The boy said he would, but was afraid he would make sport of it. "No!" said the man, "I don't make sport of God Almighty." This is a feeling general among sailors, and is a good foundation for religious influence.

A still greater gain is made whenever, by means of a captain who is interested in the eternal welfare of those under his command, there can be secured the performance of regular religious exercises, and the exertion on the side of religion of that mighty influence which a captain possesses for good, or for evil. There are occurrences at sea which he may turn to great account—a sudden death, the apprehension of danger or the escape from it, and the like, and all the calls for gratitude and faith. Besides, this state of things alters the whole current of feeling between the crew and their commander. His authority assumes more of the parental character, and kinder feelings exist. Godwin, though an infidel, in one of his novels, describing the relation in which a tutor stood to his pupil, says that the conviction the tutor was under that he and his ward were both alike awaiting a state of eternal happiness or misery, and that they must appear together before the same judgment seat, operated so upon his naturally morose disposition as to produce a feeling of kindness and tenderness toward his ward which nothing else could have caused. Such must be the effect on the relation of master and common seaman.

There are now many vessels sailing under such auspices in which great good is done. Yet I never happened to fall in with one of them. I did not hear a prayer made, a chapter read in public, nor see anything approaching to a religious service, for two years and a quarter. There were in the course of the voyage many incidents which made, for the time, serious impressions upon our minds, and which might have been turned to our good; but there being no one to use the opportunity, and no services the regular return of which might have kept something of the feeling alive in us, the advantage of them was lost, to some perhaps forever.

The good which a single religious captain may do can hardly be calculated. In the first place, as I have said, a kinder state of feeling exists on board the ship. There is no profanity allowed, and the men are not called by any opprobrious names, which is a great thing with sailors. The Sabbath is observed. This gives the men a day of rest, even if they pass it in no other way. Such a captain, too, will not allow a sailor on board his ship to remain unable to read his Bible and the books given to him; and will usually instruct those who need it in writing, arithmetic, and navigation, since he has a good deal of time on his hands, which he can easily employ in such a manner. He will also have regular religious services, and in fact by the power of his example and, where it can judiciously be done, by the exercise of his authority, will give a character to the ship and all on board. In foreign ports, a ship is known by her captain; for, there being no general rules in the merchant service, each master may adopt a plan of his own. It is to be remembered, too, that there are in most ships boys of a tender age whose characters for life are forming, as well as old men whose lives must be drawing toward a close. The greater part of sailors die at sea; and when they find their end approaching, if it does not, as is often the case, come without warning, they cannot, as on shore, send for a clergyman or some religious friend to speak to them of that hope in a Saviour which they have neglected, if not despised, through life; but if the little hull does not contain such a one within its compass, they must be left without human aid in their great extremity. When such commanders and such ships as I have just described shall become more numerous, the hope of the friends of seamen will be greatly strengthened, and it is encouraging to remember that the efforts among common sailors will soon raise up such a class; for those of them who are brought under these influences will inevitably be the ones to succeed to the places of trust and authority. If there is on earth an instance where a little leaven may leaven the whole lump, it is that of the religious shipmaster.

It is to the progress of this work among seamen that we must look with the greatest confidence for the remedying of those numerous minor evils and abuses that we so often hear of. It will raise the character of sailors, both as individuals and as a class. It will give weight to their testimony in courts of justice, secure better usage to them on board ship, and add comforts to their lives on shore and at sea. There are some laws that can be passed to remove temptation from their way and to help them in their progress; and some changes in the jurisdiction of the lower courts to prevent delays may, and probably will, be made. But, generally speaking, more especially in things which concern the discipline of ships, we had better labor in this great work, and view with caution the proposal of new laws and arbitrary regulations, remembering that most of those concerned in the making of them must necessarily be little qualified to judge of their operation.

Without any formal dedication of my narrative to that body of men of whose common life it is intended to be a picture, I have yet borne them constantly in mind during its preparation. I cannot but trust that those of them into whose hands it may chance to fall will find in it that which shall render any professions of sympathy and good wishes on my part unnecessary. And I will take the liberty, on parting with my reader, who has gone down with us to the ocean and "laid his hand upon its mane," to commend to his kind wishes, and to the benefit of his efforts, that class of men with whom for a time my lot was cast. I wish the rather to do this since I feel that whatever attention this book may gain, and whatever favor it may find, I shall owe almost entirely to that interest in the sea and those who follow it which is so easily excited in us all.